LIARS

Helen Daniel was born in Woodend, Victoria. After working as a secondary teacher for 10 years, she wrote a doctoral thesis on postwar Australian fiction. She works as a freelance critic and reviewer, and is a second-hand book dealer.

Her many articles and reviews on contemporary Australian fiction have been published in Australia and overseas. She has also published a study of the novels of David Ireland, *Double Agent* (Penguin, 1982).

by the same author

Double Agent

LIARS
Australian New Novelists

HELEN DANIEL

Penguin Books
assisted by the Literature Board
of the Australia Council

Penguin Books Australia Ltd,
487 Maroondah Highway, P.O. Box 257
Ringwood, Victoria 3134, Australia
Penguin Books Ltd,
Harmondsworth, Middlesex, England
Penguin Books,
40 West 23rd Street, New York, N.Y. 10010, U.S.A.
Penguin Books Canada Limited
2801 John Street, Markham, Ontario, Canada L3R 1B4
Penguin Books (N.Z.) Ltd,
182–190 Wairau Road, Auckland 10, New Zealand

First published by Penguin Books Australia, 1988

Typeset in Bem and Helios Light by Midland Typesetters, Maryborough, Victoria
Made and printed in Australia by Australian Print Group, Maryborough, Victoria

Daniel, Helen, 1946–
Liars, Australian New Novelsts

Bibliography.

ISBN 0 14 009788 0.

1. Novelists, Australian – 20th century. I. Title

A823'.309

Creative writing program assisted by the Literature Board of the Australia Council, the Federal Government's
arts funding and advisory body.

To Douglas Hofstadter, and all Liars

CONTENTS

ACKNOWLEDGEMENTS

I wish to thank Murray Bail, Peter Carey, David Foster, Nicholas Hasluck, David Ireland, Elizabeth Jolley, Peter Mathers and Gerald Murnane for permission to quote from their works as well as for providing access to manuscripts of their work in progress.

My thanks to all the publishers and authors who have given me permission to quote from the material to which they hold copyright and specifically the following: the editors of *Ariel, Westerly, Scripsi, The Age Monthly Review, Australian Literary Studies*; Angus and Robertson for extracts from *The Unknown Industrial Prisoner*; Cambridge University Press for an extract from Jean Franco's *An Introduction to Spanish American Literature*; Faber and Faber for extracts from *Bliss* and *Homesickness*; John Calder (Publishers) Ltd. for permission to quote from Alain Robbe-Grillet's *Snapshots and Towards a New Novel* (trans. Barbara Wright); Macmillan for extracts from *The Blue Guitar*; Norstrilia Press for extracts from *Landscape with Landscape*; Pan Books and Candida Baker for permission to quote from *Yacker*; University of Queensland Press for extracts from *Illywhacker, The Fat Man In History, War Crimes, Miss Peabody's Inheritance, Foxybaby* and *Contemporary Portraits*.

I also wish to thank Haags Gemeentemuseum and Cordon Art, Holland, for permission to reproduce the Escher lithographs and woodcut; Andrew Neophytou for his help in locating research material; and Douglas Hofstadter for his 'Eternal Golden Braid'.

ILLUSTRATIONS
Lithographs:
Drawing Hands (1948)
Waterfall (1961)
Ascending and Descending (1960)
Cube with Magic Ribbons (1957)
Convex and Concave (1955)
Print Gallery (1956)
Hand with Reflecting Sphere (1935)

Woodcut:
Still Life with Street (1937)

Lithographs and Woodcut reproduced by permission of Cordon Art, W. Pyrmontlaan 20, 3743 DE Baarn, Holland

Reproduction rights organised by courtesy of Haags Gemeentemuseum, The Hague.

All Cretans are liars.

Epimenides, a Cretan.

We have dreamt the world. We have dreamt it as firm, mysterious, visible, ubiquitous in space and durable in time; but in all its architecture we have allowed tenuous and eternal crevices of unreason which tell us it is false.

Borges

INTRODUCTION *THE LIAR'S PARADOX*

... like the most beautiful lies ... full of surprises, and adventures, and incongruities, and contradictions, and incredibilities ...

Ten years ago Brian Kiernan quoted these words of Mark Twain, at the start of *The Most Beautiful Lies*, his collection of short stories by Murray Bail, Peter Carey, Michael Wilding, Morris Lurie and Frank Moorhouse. At the start of *Illywhacker*, Peter Carey also quotes Twain on the lies of Australian history, 'all of a fresh new sort, no mouldy old stale ones', but Carey adds: 'but they are all true, they all happened'. In his novel about the liar Herbert Badgery, Carey plays not only with 'the most beautiful lies' but also with the assertion that 'they are all true, they all happened'. When Herbert Badgery announces on the first page of *Illywhacker* that he is a liar, it is a bold proposition of the Lie of fiction and the Liar's paradox.

The ancient paradox in philosophy, the so-called 'Epimenides paradox', is also known as the 'liar paradox'.[1] Epimenides' statement, 'All Cretans are liars', contains the same paradox as 'I am lying' or 'This statement is false', which rudely violates the accepted dichotomy of true/false. If you tentatively think it is true, it immediately backfires and makes you think it is false, and the same backfiring occurs once you've decided it is false. Like the Epimenides paradox, Herbert's statement rudely violates the accepted dichotomy of statements into true and false. Difficult enough with Epimenides — but what happens when it is a statement made by a character in a fiction? I am a liar. My story is a lie, inside the Lie of fiction, under the hand of Peter Carey.

The Epimenides paradox can be extended:

The following sentence is false.
The preceding sentence is true.

Separately these are 'innocent' statements, but together they have the same effect as the earlier paradox. The way they 'point' to each other forms an impossible loop. Much of the work of the Dutch graphic artist, M.C. Escher, originates in this loop, in paradox and double meaning. In his *Drawing Hands* (lithograph, 1948) each of two hands draws the other, conveying disorienting messages about subject and object. The left hand draws the right hand while the right hand draws the left hand. Levels which are ordinarily seen as hierarchical (that which draws and that which is drawn) turn back on each other. We seem to see a self-drawn picture and somehow fall for the illusion. Outside it all is Escher, his the undrawn but drawing hand outside the two-hand space—the hand of the Liar.

In Escher's implied chain of levels, often this chain is not linear, but forms a loop. For example, the 1961 lithograph *Waterfall* has an endless loop; in *Ascending and Descending* (lithograph, 1960) monks trudge forever in loops; and *Print Gallery* (lithograph 1956), is a picture of a picture which contains itself—or a picture of a gallery which contains itself or a town which contains itself or a young man who contains himself . . . In *Convex and Concave* and *Cube with Magic Ribbons*, there is a perpetual conflict between the different ways in which the elements can be read. There is a kind of flickering effect, flipping between two modes, so that it is difficult to distinguish clearly between figure and background, or between the concave and the convex. In some, mirror effects show how various spaces coincide and how, in the representation of this coincidence, the maker is invariably present.

Escher's work is a visual counterpart of the work of the Liars, the New novelists whose Lie is a literary *trompe l'oeil*, in which one level mirrors another: truth and illusion and reality and the Lie of fiction mirror each other. Like Escher's work, the Lie of fiction is built on paradoxes, always dialectic in nature, always two-faced, containing the doubleness of truth and falsity. All fiction is invention. Sometimes the realism persuades us of its truth. Sometimes we are duped by its untruth. Some writers play on our disbelief. These are the Liars, celebrating the artifice of fiction. The Liars are flaunting the Lie.

I find the work of the Liars intellectually exciting and satisfying in a way that more conventional fiction is not. Clearly this is a personal preference. Many important contemporary writers continue to use traditional modes. My aim is not to barrack, not to promote the Liars over more conventional novelists. The New fiction requires different kinds of responses from the reader and new ways of thinking about fiction. My aim is to explore the New ways of looking at reality. I also have a stubborn belief that somehow what is going on in the Liars' work is just closer to the truth of things, the way things are now. It is of course a paradox that my sense of this 'truth' comes from the work of Liars. For me, the paradox is that, in the end, the Liars are more truthful, because they tell things the way they really are, the way they are in reality.

And in the end the lies we tell define us.

So do the lies we believe.

A Liar needs a dupe, a writer needs a reader.

FIRST DIALOGUE

Liar in his office, with a Bach fugue playing softly in the background. The Escher print, *Drawing Hands*, is on the wall behind the Liar, who is drawing the Escher hands on his desk-pad, his image reflected in the mirrored wall opposite the Liar's desk. Distraught and haggard, the Reader enters and the consultation begins.

Liar It's a pleasure to meet you after all this time. I've been writing to you for years. How are you?

Reader I'm under terrible strain. I can't cope with all the demands on me. I just can't go on any more.

Liar I'm sorry to hear that. You seem to be in a bad way. Let me just have a look at your background . . . . Not unusual, I see. Your records show a conventional upbringing . . . realistic environment, stable and consistent characters . . . and I see you're used to logical narrative sequence. That's all pretty straightforward.

Reader That was before all this started. Now it's constant pressure and constant demands.

Liar I see. Before we go any further, just have a look at this inkblot, would you? Later we might do some word associations. For the moment, just tell me what you see. What's this?

Reader It looks like a smudge. No. Two smudges, as though the lines are drawn across the page, in a two-handed pattern. Two hands. Each one's drawing the other. And there's some shadow cast over it all. Someone watching. Plotting. Some menacing figure watching from a safe distance.

Liar Plotting, you think? This looks a promising case.

Reader It might look promising to you, but I get so tired—it's so hard being a reader these days. Writers can't be trusted any more. They're devious and unscrupulous, liars out to trap me. And don't tell me it's my imagination. I know it's true. I have to work with them. Work with liars, forced to collaborate.

Liar This is marvellous stuff. I'm beginning to feel better already. But you say writers 'can't be trusted any more'. Tell me, where did you get this idea of trust from?

Reader What do you mean? You've always been able to trust writers. They tell you everything, introduce you to characters and explain everything to you honestly. At least, once you could. Once it was all there ready for me—characters, plot, meanings, all worked out. Now I never know when I'm going to have to take on the responsibility myself. Sometimes I have to fill out the characters and supply some details about them, even a whole background for them. Even the plot—sometimes I have to put that all together at the end. Often the author pretends to help for a while, then, just when I'm beginning to relax, he suddenly jolts me and reminds me it's all lies . . . What kind of novel is that?

Liar It's such a relief to talk to you. You know I get so tired, coping with it all on my own. This is an exciting case. The whole phenomenon of trust is fascinating.

Reader It's not just some phenomenon for your entertainment. It's *real*. I used to be able to fantasize and identify with the characters. But now also they keep changing—playing different roles all the time. You're supposed to interpret the actions of characters coherently and plot the characters along continuities, find the irreducible individual psyche. Make character a coherent whole, consistent and intelligible. And behaviour . . . that's supposed to be continuously expressive of character.

Liar What a curious idea! You must have had some very traumatic experiences.

Reader Of course it's traumatic. All I get is inconsistencies of character: role-playing, guises and disguises of the self. Often it's a dispersal of character, a composite self, made up of marginal and partial selves—all scattered along the surfaces of its disguises. Instead of the permanence of a single self, all I get are the energies of a prospective self.

Liar That's right. So where's the problem?

Reader But it's worse than that—I even get more than one version of what happened, so that I have to try and decide which one is right. How am I supposed to know—when the author is making it up as he goes along? When he doesn't stick to the truth? He tells lies and, just when I'm starting to go along with them, he breaks it all up again. Where does that leave me?

Liar This is all very good for me. So reassuring.

Reader Look at it from my point of view. All I get is chaos and discontinuity. That's what I'm trying to get away from. The world's got enough problems, without you lot making up more. Look around us—everything is chaotic enough. Society's falling apart. And all you tell us is it's too complex to try and sort it out, that there isn't a set of principles that can fix it.

Liar You think a set of principles would fix it?

Reader Look, I've got my own problems. I can't even begin to think about the chaos out there. What about the chaos in here? I'm trying to make sense of myself and all you tell me is that self-knowledge and all knowledge is always contingent, blocked, tentative, never definitive. I thought I'd find out that modes of thought and action are coherent and explicable.

Liar That's nothing to be ashamed of. We all have these fantasies. It's quite normal to want coherence and quite natural to have secret fantasies about it. Nothing unnatural about it. Sometimes I'm tempted myself. I too have fantasies of order and continuity.

Reader I'm looking for connections between things, I mean, surely there has to be some sort of significance in the design, instead of shock and confusion? I expect coherence at least, but all I get is the unexpected, the bizarre, the contingent. I read one bit, and the next bit displaces it. I'm used to lines, chains of events, with one incident following on from another, so I feel I'm going somewhere. Here I'm just as likely to get running headings, as though you're deliberately trying to break it up. When things happen, they don't flow—they just sit side by side. There are no smooth transitions from one episode to another. They've lost their continuity and consequence. I don't get order. I get disorder.

Liar You mean that? You're not just being polite? Events really don't flow? You really do get disorder?

Reader Of course I do. What I get is designed to blur shapes and deceive me. Nothing is certain any more. It's like moving outward only to be checked and broken off by the complexity. Like coming

---

9

to an impasse of consciousness. It's almost as though you lot think there isn't any structure that can encompass all the chaos. I thought art was supposed to reflect reality, not dislocate our sense of reality.

Liar It really is dislocated? Honestly?

Reader Not honestly, no. By trickery and subterfuge and lies. But that's not all. The author keeps getting into the act and I end up an accomplice. That's the real issue. I have to work at it too, collaborate with plotters and counterplotters. I start reading and it all looks familiar, so I relax. Suddenly I get the bizarre and the absurd, just when I've got comfortable with it. Just when I've begun to suspend my disbelief.

Liar You certainly don't have to suspend your disbelief with me. No need for that here. Everything that goes on between us is in complete confidence.

Reader Confidence? Look, I'm being terrorized. What right do you have? I'm there quietly going about my business, just reading a novel, and suddenly a terrorist attack on my assumptions. I'm trapped there, an innocent victim, knowing someone's out to get me. What about Hasluck's *Truant State*? Do you know what happens to me at the end of that?

Liar Yes, it's beautiful. Superb ending. The murder of the reader. The writer looming up behind him. Murder. Fabulous stuff. I wish I'd thought of that.

Reader You try being the reader and see how it feels. I have to be constantly on the alert, suspicious. Nothing's as I expect—not even space and time. The time scales shift and space slips. I get this feeling of narrative having space—so it has borders, an underside, edges, gaps. I have terrible nightmares. Sometimes I wake up screaming.

Liar As bad as that? We'd better have a look at them. Try and interpret them. Sometimes nightmares reveal the deepest problems.

Reader You mean the basic problems? The underlying things?

Liar Yes ... the underlying things. I like that. Must note that one down. Under-lying.

Reader That's what it's all about, the under-lying. What's going on beneath the lying. Or behind it or something. In the spaces.

Liar Tell me about the nightmare you had last night.

Reader It's all blurred, dislocated. I am in a strange landscape. You're in it too, but everything is fragmented and you keep pushing me into a narrative gap, some kind of caesura, where you are lying in wait for me. I'm outside and inside at the same time, moving to and fro across the boundaries. A fugue of voices keeps rising and falling, changing all around me. I'm groping for solid ground, just beyond my reach.

Liar That's an easy one. That's just repressed fantasies of order and harmony. Visions of unity. Wish fulfilment stuff. I'm troubled by that myself.

Reader Well that's a recurring one. In another one, I'm searching through different levels and intersections. It's some kind of hierarchy but it's all tangled. I'm climbing up, but I seem to be ascending and descending at the same time. In the end I'm back where I started. Suddenly I realize I'm groping through words. They lie all around me, obscuring my vision, engulfing me.

Liar Words? I work with them. What sort of words? Good ones?

Reader Words that get more and more empty. Colder. Anti-novelist. Experimental. Irrealist. Nouveau nouveau roman. Post-realist. Post-contemporary. Then 'post anti-novel-novel'. New American Gothicist. The self-conscious mode. Post-modern. Then really murky ones. Surfiction and narcissistic narrative. And that's just the beginning. It gets worse, more bizarre. I stumble over covert and overt diegetic narratives, intramural and extramural textual levels and terms like linguistic heterocosm with its fictive referents, and autoreferentiality. I'm surrounded by texts, texts everywhere. By then all is dark and all meaning's lost. Suddenly through the gloom, I see some arcane ritual going on to which only those who know the signs are admitted. Then I see more words, structuralism, deconstruction, semiology and semiotics, and I wake up screaming.

Liar That's horrible. How awful. Nightmare words.

Reader At least that has an ending. Sometimes with a novel I can't even be sure when it's finished. It never settles into definitive, completed meaning. There seems to be a multitude of further episodes waiting to be told, so it seems always provisional, infinitely expandable. Surely novels have to have an end where everything is completed? Surely they have to have a beginning, a middle and an end?

Liar Yes, yes, but don't you see? Like Godard said about film—not necessarily in that order!

Reader I've got enough problems without bringing the film-Liars into it too. The mind reels: Fellini, Pasolini, Antonioni, Resnais and Godard.

Liar But it's all part of the same. When Robbe-Grillet was discussing *Last Year at Marienbad*, he talked about *larvatus prodeo*, 'I advance masked, but revealing my mask'. That's what it's all about, unmasking the components and techniques. The techniques of Godard and Resnais and the others are part of the same thing, unmasking the constituents and processes of our culture.

Reader Look I've got enough pressure on me as a reader, without tackling film. Let's stick to your job. You're supposed to work it all out beforehand, with beginnings and ends. And how about the endings? They're like a loop that takes you right back to the start. Where does it all end? The self becomes an elaborate fiction, a strategy and an artifice. And all I see is chaos. I think it's all a distortion. Reality's not like that.

Liar You mean reality's not chaotic?

Reader Of course, but it's not supposed to be like that in art. If we can't order our experience through art, where then?

Liar You want us to pretend? Tell lies?

Reader It's hard enough knowing we're being manoeuvred, but it's worse when it's all furtive and underhand.

Liar Underhand . . . I like that. Do you know Escher's work? There's a marvellous print of two hands drawing each other . . .

Reader I feel as though the centre of gravity has shifted.

PRELUDE *THE LOGIC OF THE LIAR*

The world consists of inter-reacting particles, the ever-changing pattern
a cause of much bafflement. Occasionally concern.

'The Partitions', Murray Bail

'Ah the Tlute the Tlute – who knows what the Tlute leally is my son?
Gotta hold two views at once. The Tlute is not this, is not that – is a
combination. . .'

Ar Wat, in *Moonlite*, David Foster

Behind the Liars' work is a sense that the centre of gravity has shifted, that the centre of gravity is no longer the self, and that the individual's determinations are no longer his. There is a pervasive sense that events in people's lives have only to a small degree originated in them, that man is deprived of the assurances the West has had for centuries. While we keep hoping the old moral and intellectual contrivances can still work, reality continually undermines our old computations. The New novel is working along new salients – which is not an isolated literary phenomenon, but part of the change in ideas about the relationship between man and the universe, related to general intellectual movements in science and metaphysics, as well as in art, film and theatre.

In the New novel, the centre of gravity is outside the self, in time and space and in the field-relations among things, in the laws of large numbers and in the incoherence of things. This shift in the centre of gravity represents a change of the old notion of man as a self-determining being at the centre of things, a notion which is premised on a logic of cause and effect. Our literary logic has tended to be linear. The mechanistic plots of the traditional novel are built on a causal logic in which events are decisive, bringing about direct consequences and leading to a conclusion. The logic of fiction has changed. Instead of the principles of integrity and unity, within which movement and dynamics take place, the New novel has a logic of contradiction and antagonism, of the dynamic contraries of experience that can cope with uncertainties, inconsistencies, double premises, paradoxes. Only by accepting the contradictions can we get outside the limits of our old imperialist *sic et non* logic, which tries to impose a specious consistency on reality. The new logic suggests the only way we can deal with contradictions is by accepting as true both terms of a contradiction, a logic of absurdity and paradox (like a Zen koan), accepting that contradictory principles do not exclude each other. It moves from the measurable along a scale of aggregates that extends composition beyond limits, from past harmonies to a contradictory universe. The New novel has a quantum logic of contradiction, the logic of Liars.

With startling metaphysical and epistemological implications, quantum physics has taught us that the world is a game of chance, in a gigantic multifoliate reality of parallel worlds, which overlap our perceived universe and jostle its atoms. Quantum theory is built on a new uncertainty principle, which shows that matter is allowed to roam more or less at random, although certain paths of behaviour are more probable than others. The world is ruled less by rigid laws than by chance and the uncertainties are an inherent property of matter, part of an absolute indeterminacy of the universe. Intruding into what seems to be a law-abiding cosmos is a randomness, a sort of microscopic anarchy, regulated only by the laws of probability. The inherent uncertainty of nature controls the structure of space and time, which are not merely the stage on which the cosmic drama is acted out, but part of the cast. Space and time can move about, change their shape and extension. Reality is not exclusively a property of the external world but is intimately bound up with our perception of the world, our presence as conscious observers. This is the famous problem of Schrodinger's Cat, the cat in the box experiment, and the question of quantum reality, whether quantum weirdness holds for everyday reality.[1] While we might retain the ordinary notion that the world exists objectively, we must adopt a quantum logic in thinking about it. Instead of the hypothesis of comprehensibility, quantum logic accepts that there are gaps, random factors, random behaviour, conditions not amenable to logic, which suggest that chance, randomness, is the actuality. The logic of cause and effect has been replaced by Heisenberg's Uncertainty Principle. Reality is random and literature now has to contend with the inherent uncertainty of matter, a randomness subject to the role of the observer – the indeterminacy of the universe.

In a zany, parodic way, David Foster examines this change in *Moonlite*, which, on one level, is a history of the links between scientific and metaphysical thought – a kind of picaresque along the lines of quantum logic. Foster traces changes in our concepts of the universe, starting on Hiphoray with the primitive notion that natural phenomena are manifestations of temperament in the cosmos, not causality. The universe is variously placid and benign, or subject to outbursts of petulance and anger, which might be appeased by sacrifice and ritual. When Donald proposes a causal explanation, the dazzling new concept of phenomena acting in accord with mechanistic Newtonian law, the MacEsaus marvel at the idea but see no conflict, happy to accommodate his view alongside their own. Later they manage to incorporate Christianity too, without any apparent discomfort or conflict. The MacEsaus are hospitable and amiable, willing to entertain all sorts of contradictory notions at the same time. The novel follows the development of quantum logic, through Finbar's mathematical research into optics and the quantum nature of light. The New novel is sometimes called the 'post-Christian novel',[2] which seems particularly apt in *Moonlite* when Finbar is sent down for mathematically disproving Christianity. He is then ready with his quantum logic for the next stage of his spiritual quest, which is Ar Wat's 'Tlute', the truth of contradiction.

Ar Wat's Tlute is the quantum logic of Niels Bohr's 'principle of complementarity', which accepts two mutually exclusive terms ('waves' and 'particles') as complementary, like two faces of an object which can never be seen at the same time but which must be visualized in turn to describe the object completely. Escher's *Cube with Magic Ribbons* is such a visual image, with the mind flipping between the two mutually exclusive modes, convex to concave. The corollary to Bohr's quantum principle is a new 'tolerance of ambiguity', breaking down the old antithesis of subject and object and closing the artificial gap between the knower and the known.

Instead of a linear movement running along a causal line to denouement and end-effect, much of the new literature is about new notions of the space-time complex. An entelechy, an end to which all things strive, becomes instead a set of correlations and connections within a time–space complex. Instead of linear progress, the new literature is more likely to be fragmented, discrete, discontinuous, with multistrands moving in and out of each other, in a world continually being reconstructed by the perceptions interacting with it. Playing with the geometry of things, the New novel is inside the mass of reality, searching for a perspective on a world of gigantic assemblage, full of contradictions, paradoxes and tautologies about time. In Calvino's *Cosmicomics*, there are paradoxes of space and time and change, marvellous bets on probabilities through eons of time, absurdist images of the observer in a cosmic geometry and haunting images of cosmic change. In the New fiction, events are contradictory possibilities we have to hold at the same time and the divisions of reality no longer appear to be precisely drawn, because space and time are in a sense elastic: they can stretch and shrink depending upon the observer.

Man is no longer the detached observer of a universe outside himself, who stands back surveying a natural order. Like the observer up the tree in Murray Bail's story, 'Life of the Party', the detached observer is a figment: there is no pure, uncontaminated reality, because the observer is a lens that changes the observed. The mind *is*, in part, the world and the sphere of consciousness is included in what is observed. The self is intruding into the world of time and space and influencing it. Time and space are not independent: the mind is part of the stage that it sets, where events take place, always within a zone of indeterminacy.

Much of the new literature is about changes in perspective, which John Berger discusses in *Ways of Seeing*.

The convention of perspective, which is unique to European art and which was first established in the early Renaissance, centres everything on the eye of the beholder. It is like a beam from a lighthouse – only instead of light travelling outwards, appearances travel in. The conventions called those appearances *reality*. Perspective makes the single eye the centre of the visible world. Everything converges on to the eye as to the vanishing point of infinity. The visible world is arranged for the spectator as the universe was once thought to be arranged for God.

According to the convention of perspective there is no visual reciprocity. There is no need for God to situate himself in relation to others: he is himself the situation. The inherent contradiction in perspective was that it structured all images of reality to address a single spectator who, unlike God, could only be in one place at a time.[3]

Instead of perspective proposing to the spectator that he was the unique centre of the world, the eye of the camera demonstrates that there is no centre. The visible, in continual flux, becomes fugitive.

The laws of perspective become a fiction, an artificial way of imposing the mind on things, to make the world look 'real'. Arguing that the eye of the camera exposes this contradiction, Berger quotes Soviet film director, Dziga Vertov, who wrote in 1923

I'm an eye. A mechanical eye. I, the machine, show you a world the way only I can see it. I free myself for today and forever from human immobility. I'm in constant movement. I approach and pull away from objects. I creep under them. I move alongside a running horse's mouth. I fall and rise with the falling and rising bodies. This is I, the machine, manoeuvring in the chaotic movements, recording one movement after another in the most complex combinations.

Freed from the boundaries of time and space, I co-ordinate any and all points of the universe, wherever I want them to be. My way leads towards the creation of a fresh perception of the world. Thus I explain in a new way the world unknown to you.[3]

Much of Murray Bail's work is about perspective and the space–time complex, often with an emphasis on the relation between photography and reality. In 'Cul-de-Sac (uncompleted)', Bail plays with the idea of cartographers mapping out the lines of reality and introduces a character who has made changes in the Laws of Perspective. Running throughout his collection, *Contemporary Portraits and Other Stories*, there is a continuing dialogue between Bail and the character from the opening story, on the theme of photography, the eye of the observer and the limits of realism. In *Holden's Performance*, Bail extends the theme of photography, the observing eye and the trajectories of event and contingency, surveying Australian history with a Liar's theodolite.

Inevitably notions of the self have also changed radically. Traditionally the self is constantly 'there', somehow behind conflicting moods and feelings, somehow a hidden constancy of which echoes periodically rise to consciousness. The old self exists within the flow of time, enduring behind or within change, a mobile self ever there underneath change. The self may be divided, baffled, fearful, confused, but it exists in some consistency. The New novel sees the self as a collection of conflicting selves, which form changing patterns. The self is often in a state of decomposition, a scattering of selves along different salients, partly due to the loss of any sustaining codes. Without the security of logic, we have to manage with probabilities, with uncertainties. How to identify the irreducible minimum of experience that is our own, authentically ours? How to seek integrity? Which role is the authentic one, which abstraction of the self, which posture, which artifact of the self, is authentic?

Samuel Beckett's characters reflect some of the changes in the sense of self. Baffling things happen to the Beckett figure, who is fixed in a condition, his consciousness shrinking back. By a logic of contradiction, he is alienated from the events that apparently happen to him, knows not his own identity. The reality of his existence doubtful, he feels he is leaning over an abyss, without any stable sense of self. He attends to those around him but has only dim intimations and recognitions. For Beckett, the self is vestigial, minimal, shadowy, stripped of all illusion and declining all consolation. His consciousness skeletal, man has become a residual being, smitten with silence, weighing up absence. Beckett's characters embody our consciousness that we have been dislodged from the centre of things, that under the surface there is only the incommunicable, the unsayable.

In the French *nouveau roman* of Butor, Sarraute, Robbe-Grillet and others, there is a new conception of self and time, its expansions and contractions, according to the movement of individual consciousness. There is also a preoccupation with *chosisme*, the surfaces of things, objects which are in the foreground, displacing traditional character – a topography of objects, manipulating and rearranging them, emphasizing their form and spatial relationships. Nathalie Sarraute's *Tropisms* are cinematic glimpses of banal situations in everyday life. The people *are* reactions to conditions they meet and their reactions are tropistic. There is only the surface, only the appearance. Sarraute plays with the mystery of the banal, the surface of the commonplace, listening to the hollow inside. Sarraute shows the contours of the modern self are tropisms, with nothing behind, only these figures approaching and evading each other, stricken with the banal.

Sarraute describes this as the 'Age of Suspicion', where reader and writer regard each other with distrust, confronting each other across empty ground, once the place of honour occupied by character. She suggests readers and writers have practically ceased to believe in character, with the result that characters, having lost the two-fold support that the novelist's and the reader's faith afforded them, and which permitted them to stand upright with the burden of the entire story resting on their broad shoulders, may now be seen to vacillate and fall apart.[4]

Once richly endowed with every asset and the recipient of every attention, character lacked for nothing. Since then, he has lost everything, has become a being devoid of outline, indefinable and intangible. His place of honour usurped by the author, he has become the converging point of the mutual distrust of writer and reader, each wary of the other's purposes. The writer plots

to dispossess the reader and entice him, at all costs, into the author's territory . . . Suddenly the reader is on the inside, exactly where the author is, at a depth where nothing remains of the convenient landmarks with which he constructs the characters. He is immersed and held under the surface until the end, in a substance as anonymous as blood, a magma without name or contours.[4]

The reader now must be constantly on the alert, suspicious, and the suspicion is the prelude to discovery.

While Australian readers too must be constantly on the alert and wary, the Australian New novel is different from the French *nouveau roman*. It too is exploring reality in new ways, through new literary forms and techniques, but along different salients from the French. Ours is not the way of the *nouveau roman*, with its pared down, stripped dispositions, which sometimes in Robbe-Grillet or others almost refine themselves off the page. The French Lie I find drab and often tedious. Our own Lies have more colour, vitality and absurdity. The Australian New novel is a prismatic play of mind, ludic and absurdist, a fabric of hazard, paradox, contradiction, instability – the instability that quantum physics shows us is at the core of things. In the Australian New novel, objects, things, are surfaces behind which there is an absurd or fantastic reality, sometimes surrealistic, shadows on the surface of the real. In the Australian New novel, character has not yet lost its place of honour, though the space it occupies is the subject of territorial dispute, its boundaries shifting. Behind character, underneath it, transgressing its rights, is the complicity of Liar and reader, interlocutors and collaborators.

The New novel in Australia is closer to South American fiction than to the *nouveau roman*. Because of the translation problem, much of the current Australian interest in South American literature seems curiously belated, with anachronistic cries of discovery uttered decades after the novels of Garcia Marquez, Borges, Carpentier, Fuentes, Asturias, Amado, Donoso and others were written. Part of the discovery is the affinity between the work of South American Liars and the work of Australian Liars. From the 1920s, quickening in the 1940s and 1950s, Spanish American writers such as Asturias, Carpentier, Rulfo, Sabato and Onetti began to experiment formally with new techniques, introducing stream of consciousness, unusual time sequences, *realismo magico* and complex structures. By the 1960s, the New writing was widespread and diverse, with circular narratives, discontinuity, fluid time sequences, self-conscious artifice, marvellous New fictions, in which chaos and continuity run in careless conspiracy through human affairs amid elaborate play between reality and illusion. The South American Liars were already flourishing in the 60s, spreading the Lie of fiction.

In *An Introduction to Spanish American Literature*, Jean Franco suggests that unlike European writers, Latin-American writers were

constantly faced with the odd, the extraordinary, the monstrous, seldom with anything that matched this European middle-class norm; and it was only by devising and inventing literary forms which could encompass these weird mutations that they could achieve a verisimilitude of their own. The linguistic virtuosity of a Cortazar, the fantasy of a Garcia Marquez, the superimposition of different strands of time and different geographical locations in Vargas Llosa, bring us nearer to the experience of Latin America than did the realist and naturalist novels of an earlier period.[5]

In Latin-American literature, there is a turning away from the realist mode to try and portray the nature of man in a vast disordered continent, because reality is too complex and bizarre, society too dispersed for the realist mode. But the 'weird mutations', the odd, the extraordinary and the monstrous, are not only South American but part of the topography of the vast disordered continent of twentieth century reality.

Rather than direct lines of influence, South American fiction, particularly the work of Borges and Marquez, offers a topography for the Australian Lie, the co-ordinates from which we might take our bearings. It offers a logic of contradiction and paradox, with magical realism, crossings to and fro between levels of reality, shifts of character and place, montage narrative, black absurdist comedy and self-conscious narratives inside the Lie of fiction. Amid all the sleight-of-hand narrative, the reader is the *lector–complice*, the accomplice of South American Liars. There are close affinities with the impulses and the strategies of Australian New novel, ranging from the work of the nineteenth-century Brazilian novelist David Ireland admires, Machado de Assis, and the 1920s work of Andrade and others, through to the work of contemporary South American Liars. Australian Liars too are mapping out a new way of seeing our own vast continent, crisscrossing its face with new lines of journey and exploration

The Liars have been at work in Australia for over 21 years and it is possible now, looking back, to identify the early appearances of the New novel, which at the time were sly, furtive inklings of change. The centre of gravity in the New writing began to shift in the late 60s and early 70s. The Australian New novel was born in 1966 in Melbourne, with the publication of Peter Mathers' *Trap*. This was followed quickly by Morris Lurie's *Rappaport* (1966), Barry Oakley's *A Wild Ass of A Man* (1967), and David Ireland's *The Chantic Bird* (1968). With his first collection, *Futility and Other Animals* (1969), then *The Americans, Baby* (1972), and *The Electrical Experience* (1974), Frank Moorhouse began his discontinuous narratives, with fields of fragments, disparate urban experience and ideological tensions in contemporary urban life. In the 1970s, Michael Wilding's literary gamesmanship and pastiche began with *The Short Story Embassy* (1975). Some of the changes are reflected in the short fiction of the 1970s, notably in the work of Bail, Carey, Moorhouse, Lurie and Wilding (the writers Brian Kiernan linked in his collection, *The Most Beautiful Lies*) and writers who found an outlet in *Tabloid Story*, founded in 1972 by Wilding and Moorhouse, with 'host' newspapers carrying short stories – fables, self-conscious fictions, stories in the confessional mode often of inner city life – which marked the early years of the resurgence of the short story form. Although some critics, such as Don Anderson, believe there is still 'an unexamined realist orthodoxy in Australian short fiction', there are many short Lies, including the short fabulous fictions of Bail, Carey, Ireland, Jolley, Murnane, Lurie and, one of the best younger Liars, Richard Lunn, whose short stories sometimes have the same startling power as Carey's *The Fat Man in History*. Morris Lurie's many collections of stories rove across the world through places disparate and moments desperate, characters in transit, wandering, displaced characters who rise high on waves of foolish hope, then pitch towards absurdity, within the cycle of failed and resurrected hopes ever pitted against outlandish disasters.

The 1970s was a decade of swift and varied development, with a number of Liars coming to the fore. By the 1980s, the Lie was flourishing and each year important New novels were published. In 1980, Bail's *Homesickness* and Hasluck's *The Blue Guitar*. In 1981, Carey's *Bliss*, Foster's *Moonlite* and Ireland's *City of Women*. In 1982, Murnane's *The Plains* and Hasluck's *The Hand That Feeds You*. In 1983, Jolley's *Mr Scobie's Riddle* and *Miss Peabody's Inheritance*, and Foster's *Plumbum*. In 1984, Hasluck's *The Bellarmine Jug* and Jolley's *Milk and Honey*. In 1985, Carey's *Illywhacker*, Jolley's *Foxybaby*, Murnane's *Landscape with Landscape* and Foster's *Dog Rock*. In 1986, Foster's *The Adventures of Christian Rosy Cross* and Jolley's *The Well*. In 1987, Hasluck's *Truant State*, Foster's *Testostero*, Bail's *Holden's Performance* and Ireland's *Bloodfather*. In 1988, Murnane's *Inland*, Jolley's *The Sugar Mother* and Carey's *Oscar and Lucinda* are being published. Mathers, Ireland, Foster, Carey, Bail, Hasluck, Jolley, Murnane: eight Liars advancing masked, but revealing their masks.

In the late 60s and 70s, as the New novel began to emerge, the most radical changes were in concepts of space and time. Whereas the realist novel often deploys the notion that memory 'composes' the past, a preliminary to order, in the New novel the disorder of the past remains, stubborn and intransigent. At the same time, the concept of space has been changing, both in the purposeful movement of the hero through place, and in the ways of crossing and re-crossing the lines and boundaries between place and time. These changes were most apparent in the emergence of the New picaresque, which grew out of the traditional mode of the quest. It opened time and space to become one major form of the Lie, exploring attitudes towards time and history, sometimes futurist and prophetic, more often with the political substratum of a re-assessment of the past and, like Barth's parody in *The Sot-Weed Factor*, a comic anti-history, a disavowal of the past.

The journey in search of identity has long been a theme of Australian fiction: sometimes a spiritual quest in search of ultimate truths; sometimes a rollicking and adventurous wandering, with travellers' tales narrated with a lively and generally light-hearted gusto. In the earlier picaresque novel, the quest gives shape to what are otherwise disorienting experiences and, because we are privy to the hero's thoughts and feelings, probabilities of events and reactions can be calculated and predicted. In the New picaresque, by contrast, no such calculations and predictions can be safely made, because neither the world nor the hero are stable and ordered, nor is the telling stable and ordered. The narrative, like the world it depicts, is often fragmented, even chaotic, certainly unpredictable and incalculable.

The New picaro tends to be cynical and disillusioned, perceiving the world as absurd, chaotic and disordered, consonant with his own experience of being propelled through a series of events which are random, bizarre, sometimes surreal. Sometimes the New picaro becomes an emblem of the outer disorder, not simply a witness, becoming a metaphor for it. He is sometimes adrift and purposeless, recoiling from a world he finds chaotic and disordered, often catapulted from one absurd situation to another. Often he cannot make sense of the world and so cannot find a way of being in the world that makes sense. In Oakley's novels, he is generally an incompetent, a clown–buffoon moving restlessly through a protean world and himself reflecting the outer disorder. He is more likely to despair than to discover truths, unlikely to find any grounds for affirmation, likely to discover that there is no real place for him in the world. He tends to feel both pursued and persecuted, suspects plots and manipulations, a kind of conspiratorial lurch of the world in his direction.

Character itself is fluid, not fixed and stable, but changing with the flux of circumstance, and the picaro adopts guises and disguises, to protect the inner self, roles and masks to hide behind. Events and circumstances of the outer chaos conspire to perplex and confuse rather than explore and consolidate our knowledge of character. In the novels of Oakley and Mathers, there is a multiple sense of self, sliding in and out of identities, playing different roles and changing guises, to keep ahead of the pursuing chaos. Oakley's heroes bumble ineptly through rising chaos in tides of foolish hope. In disguise, on the run, they swashbuckle with the world before beating a foolish retreat.

Some picaresque novels are written as memoirs through which the mind fumbles back, searching for some shape and pattern in its own chaotic but determining past, the mind both observer and participant in events, watching itself in the past with varying degrees of comic horror. In *A Wild Ass of A Man*, Oakley parodies the notion that memory can compose the past: when Muldoon stares back into the past, he is aghast that the chaos is intractable, even under the eye of the present. Commonly the picaro writes the memoir-narrative while in hiding, struggling to comprehend what has happened from the relative safety of a sanatorium or a monastery or sometimes underground, as a subterranean writer warding off the chaos above. In hiding, the picaro ponders on problematical questions: Is it safe to come out? Is it safe to return to the world? These bare questions usually begin with more complicated questions, which enmesh and entangle until they have to be disentangled right back to basic questions or until they actually split open and become just fragments: Is it? Is the world? Is? The picaro struggles to devise new ways of making sense of the world, in the hope of constructing another form of reality or remoulding it into new and more pleasing shapes.

Other New picaresque novels work through a conventional narrator, who acts as intermediary, part interpreter, part witness to the 'truth', and part straight guy, comic fall guy. Thus, in David Malouf's *Johnno* for example, the conventional Dante records with muted envy and regret the fantastic doings of Johnno himself, as he pushes reality into new, more diverting shapes. Dante is always left spluttering, fumbling for explanations, and his book about Johnno is a larger but still spluttering explanation. In Oakley's *Let's Hear It for Prendergast*, Prendergast is too busy to look back, pitting himself against the world, hatching new schemes, skirmishing with the outraged, then being routed into ignominious flight. He is the eternal *naïf*, unaware that the world is intractable, sublimely confident that it will ultimately yield to his poetic touch. Once Prendergast erupts into his peaceful life as 'failed writer', Morley is cast as his accomplice and is driven to plotting fantastic ways of eradicating Prendergast from his life, with bouts of premature elation at his own success. All the time Prendergast is expanding into his role, Morley is contracting into his, Sancho to Don Prendergast. Morley tries to capture

Prendergast on paper, contain him in literary analogues – Ibn Saud Prendergast, the Fisher King, a Rue Morgue creature, Genghis Khan Prendergast, the mad Ahab, even King Kong on the shrine, atop the blazing ruins of 200 years of history. The hapless Morley is the nervous disciple and accomplice, aghast and spluttering explanations.

The New picaresque often shifts towards a comic extravaganza, a kind of gargantuan miscellany of wildly entertaining parody and fantastic inventions in the manner of Vonnegut or Barth's *Giles Goat Boy*, or Pynchon's *Gravity's Rainbow*. In the 1970s, Walter Adamson's absurdist novel, *The Institution*, set up rival worlds of inner and outer reality, with Schiller's inner world transformed into a surrealistic institution, last bastion against the outer apocalyptic chaos, where the inmates, in wonderfully zany concerts, play music without instruments. Bill Reed also works in the comic extravaganza mode, with an extraordinary imaginative energy and verbal inventiveness. Like Mathers, Reed wages words against the encircling chaos and the pain of human absurdity, teasing out a preposterous new perspective on the ways words define and confine our perceptions. In *Ihe*, the lycanthropic hero is on a roving quest across Australia in search of the mythical Iheland, sustained by the lunatic hope that perhaps extinction is not forever. *Ihe* is a mock-heroic picaresque, with an intrepid wolfman on a lonely lupine quest for the last Tasmanian Tigress/WolfLady. Uncovering plots and conspiracies at every turn, Ihe 'the Werewolf of Melbourne' lopes through his fantastic mission to bring fertility to the dead heart of Australia. Accidents dog him, chance ambushes him and he is ever pursued by outraged officials, but he conceals his true lycanthropic purposes beneath the picaro's usual guises and disguises. Bill Reed's *Crooks* (1984) is also an extravaganza of words and comic happenings, an absurdist crime thriller, a parody picaresque journey through the seamy side of Sydney, with Frank R. Stein aided by The Gang, his comic grotesque 'companions in yarns'. As it cuts between events in Sydney and in Timor during the war, *Crooks* becomes a novel about writing, spiralling inwards through Frank's plan to assassinate his father – and so brandish a defiant fiction at his own absurdity.

In the cyclical development of literature, existing forms are broken open and, through a kind of literary cannibalism, the new feeds on the old. In the new conundrum of time and space there are not only Liars' versions of history and family sagas, but also Lies written within the mystery/detective mode. Unlike the comic extravaganza and the picaresque, the detective mode is elaborately and closely plotted within strong literary conventions, but it has an unlikely kinship with parody, in that both forms work through a doubling of narrative. As parody draws on a prior knowledge of the subject matter which it then over-turns, so reading a detective story is a conscious process of construction, following clues, intrepreting them and constructing theòries. Often the detective mode offers a surrogate to the reader (the Dr. Watson figure), who follows the detective around doubt-fully, asking questions. The double narrative is both as given by the author and, through this, a retrospective reconstruction of actual events. Thus the reader has two constructions running throughout, each striving against the other. So, in Robbe-Grillet's 'Les Gommes', the reader is aware that Daniel Dupont is still alive, but Wallas, the detective investigating his death, is not. The reader learns that Wallas will be Dupont's murderer, in a doubling of narrative wherein the reader has a collaborative role.

The doubleness, ambiguity and contradiction characteristic of the detective mode have attracted other Liars as diverse as Jorge Luis Borges, John Fowles and the Mexican novelist, Ibarguengoitia, as well as Aus-tralian Liars such as Foster (in the parody murder mystery, *Dog Rock*) and Hasluck (in his contemporary political and epistemological thrillers). In John Fowles' novel, *A Maggot*, there is tight intrigue in a complex investigation into the disappearance of a group of travellers in eighteenth-century England. Contestant versions of events are unfolded in the testimonies of witnesses, as the investigating lawyer, Ayscough, uncovers the layers of truth beneath the subterfuge of the original jour-ney. In the layering of versions and contingent mysteries the reader, like Ayscough, tests out theories and hypotheses, pitting his construc-tions against the truth as it is gradually disclosed – until with splendid literary boldness, Fowles thrusts us suddenly outside questions of truth and logic and reason into a new perception of notions of faith, of dis-sent and change. The mystery unclenches into a critique of the modern sense of self and an extraordinary celebration of dissent. As well as raising philosophical, political, chimerical and, surprisingly, feminist notions, Fowles suggests the 'far-fetched faith' of fiction, and it is this act of faith that is both the content and the mode of *A Maggot*. Fowles' 'far-fetched faith' demands the tolerance of ambiguity and contradic-tion implicit in the logic of the Liar.

Jorge Ibarguengoitia's *The Dead Girls* (1983) is a Liar's mystery/thriller, a dossier on human conspiracy with chance and a casebook of man's collaboration with random events to bring about his own bizarre fate. *The Dead Girls* is a black comedy based on fact, the discovery of the corpses of six prostitutes in the backyard of a small town brothel in Mexico. The novelist becomes the investigator, collecting testimonies and documentary evidence, and uncovering geometries of cause and chance, with the dispassionate tones of a police report doggedly maintained in the face of every bizarre twist and turn. The novel becomes a kind of existential thriller, the suspense vested as much in the machinations of chance as in the actions of its human accomplices. Through this emerges a portrait of contemporary Mexican society, its politics, law, its commerce and corruption, its poverty, prostitution and pay-offs. Within the black comedy of the whole, there are numerous quick scenes of grim humour and terrible irony, moving towards the girls' deaths as victims, not of some homicidal rampage, but of conspiracy between human agency and chance, the kind of casual conspiracy which, no chance pun, underlies the Lie.

One common theme in the work of the brilliant South American writer, Borges, is that of a man caught in a trap of his own construction. Borges often uses the detective mode, with the detective pitting reason, scheme and plan against existence. In 'Death and the Compass', Lonnrot, the detective investigating three murders, recognizes their determinate pattern and concludes a fourth is soon to occur. Believing he is acting freely, he calculates the time and the place geometrically, unwittingly constructing his own death-trap. In the work of the Liars, often the end loops back to the beginning, spiralling through the contrary workings of a 'secret plot' – the central notion of Borges' *ficciones*. In one of his essays, 'Narrative Art and Magic', Borges discusses the 'secret plot', the arcane element in narrative, and suggests the ideal novel should be 'a precise game of staying on the alert, of echoes and of affinities'. He argues that the infinitude of events, causal factors and influences which constitute a single human life are so complex that the writer who attempts to build a work of fiction on such material is pretentious and dishonest. He suggests writers abandon attempts at psychological realism (which is 'psychological fakery') and emphasize the narrative element by structuring detail to fit a pre-conceived, secret pattern. Borges insists that, however visible, solid and enduring our world, it nonetheless shows 'tenuous and eternal crevices of unreason', unexplainable paradoxes and inconceivable notions such as that of infinity – one god seeking another, a map of the world detailed enough to show the map itself which contains another map.

Borges' fantastic fables explore the chaos and futility of existence, the circularity of time, existence as a labyrinth without a centre. In 'The Circular Ruins', he suggests we are all projections of other people's dreams, like the protagonist who dreams a son only to find he has himself been dreamed by someone else. In 'Tlon, Uqbar, Orbis Tertius', objects from an imaginary planet appear in our world and subvert assumptions about the nature of reality. He considers there too the notion of a single plot arranged in all its possible permutations (a favourite device of Tlonian fiction). Many of Borges' fictions contain very precise details while the central situation is veiled in mystery, bringing a stubborn probability to the fantastic. In 'The Book of Sands', a bibliophile exchanges a black-letter Wycliffe Bible for a Book of Sands, so-named because the pages have no beginning or end. He acquires the book from a stranger with nondescript features, which are nevertheless described in detail. Alone with the infinite book, the narrator is overcome by the nightmarish, terrifying object. Among Borges' favourite motifs are the labyrinth and the library, the mirror and the double. In 'The Other', Borges himself plays the bemused speaker who meets a stranger of the same name, writing a book on the brotherhood of man. Through their meeting, the central character learns more about himself but the knowledge is illusory because it is a reflection of a person whose existence is doubtful.

Borges' work is so integral to the Lie that Borgesian is almost a synonym for Lying. His critical writings include a satire of a critic tackling Dante's *Divine Comedy*.

On 23 February 1931, it occurred to him that for it to be perfect, the description of the poem would have to coincide word for word with the poem . . . . On mature reflection he eliminated the preface, the footnotes, the index, and the name and address of the publisher, and handed Dante's poem to the printers.[7]

Unless he resorts to transcription, the critic's activity is paradoxically at odds with the literature of the fragmentary and indeterminate. Criticism works on the notion of continuity and unity, of coherent, persistent meaning, sorting out persistent themes or motifs or intentions, from the discrete, the fragmented, the contingent, the protean. Like the bubbles which seem to flip back and forth between concave and convex in Escher's *Cube with Magic Ribbons*, criticism and the New fiction seem mutually exclusive modes. The coherence and persistent meanings on the one hand and the fragments and the contingencies on the other are, like the waves and particles of quantum physics, complementary. Reading the Lie and critical responses to the Lie must therefore encompass this flickering, flipping from one to the other, taking in the processes and activities of reading within the patterns of narrative movement.

A central paradox of the New fiction is that the writer is constantly straining against the limits of a sequential form. The Liars tend to establish congruence and points of contiguity rather than consequence, sometimes a vast assemblage of events, which can even happen more or less independently of time, in a continuum. Sometimes the straining against the necessary form is through a fragmented narrative, a collage of voices; sometimes it loops through an inner spiral. In Elizabeth Jolley's Lie, characters move to and fro across the boundaries of fiction and reality and slide from one novel to another, in a play of 'voices' moving in and out in shifting configurations. In *Bliss*, Carey creates a double vision of Heaven and Hell, in layers of perception which culminate in the intersecting selves of Harry Joy and Alex Duval in the hospital. In *The Bellarmine Jug*, there is a fugal series of propositions and versions, each one supplanted by the disclosure of new material, with a crossing into another level of the whole. In Peter Mathers' novels, each successive voice supplants the previous one, in the manner of fugue.

The movement of the New novel is often contrapuntal and its form fugal. As Douglas Hofstadter describes in his monumental book, *Godel, Escher, Bach: An Eternal Golden Braid*,[8] the fugue is based on the disposition of individual components, the sense of the whole as a strange shimmering structure, delicate, intricate and self-involved, responding to components at various levels of its own configuration. In the fugue, there are two modes. We can either follow one individual voice at a time or listen to the total effect of all together, without trying to disentangle one from another. Each mode shuts out the other, and we flip back and forth from one to the other, involuntarily. But each independent voice fuses with the others to make a graceful totality, so that the whole is more than the sum of its parts and the choice is not simply between listening to the totality or following component voices. Within the fugue each new voice sets up complex consequences through several layers of structure. Sometimes the theme of the fugue is inverted and hidden among several other voices; sometimes the theme comes rushing up out of the depths. Each new voice sets up a shift in point of view which influences the others and changes our perspective on the strata of the whole. Gradually a volition emerges, a complicated internal configuration, and, as our expectations of what is ahead project back to the present, this becomes another component in our response to the whole. In this delicate distribution of patterns, the to and fro inner movement constantly changes the coherency and the whole becomes the agent slowly transforming itself, through an intricate configuration of both constant and varying parts. In the work of the Liars, often the reader follows the processes of assemblage, the gaps, the points of contiguity, the levels and strata, the level crossings, the reflections and refractions, that is, how the component 'voices' work together, in this fugal manner.

But the metaphor of the fugal form is not all that Hofstadter offers to readers of the New Novel. Beginning with the ancient 'liar's paradox', *Godel, Escher, Bach* is an exploration of the philosophy of mathematics, the nature of intelligence, hierarchical systems and self-reference. Although Hofstadter does not directly encompass literary questions in his book, his concept of the Strange Loop and the points of intersection in the Tangled Hierarchy is also at the core of the work of the Liars. The Strange Loop of the Lie.

Godel, Escher, Bach: An Eternal Golden Braid is sub-titled 'a metaphorical fugue on minds and machines in the spirit of Lewis Carroll'. It is structured as a counterpoint between Dialogues (which present new concepts metaphorically, creating a kind of intuitive background) and Chapters (which present the same concepts in more serious and abstract form). In the Dialogues, Hofstadter uses the characters of Achilles and the Tortoise, drawn from the work of Zeno of Elea (fifth century B.C.) and used too by Lewis Carroll in his 1895 work on the paradox of infinity. Each Dialogue is patterned on a different piece by Bach, through which Hofstadter explores the Incompleteness Theorem of Kurt Godel, which is the mathematical equivalent of the quantum Principle of Uncertainty. It is an extraordinary work, which is also playful, entertaining, exhilarating, full of exuberant games, acrostics, fugal tricks, paradoxes and Strange Loops – and is itself a beautiful example of the Strange Loop which is its central theme.

Hofstadter explores the phenomenon of the 'Strange Loop' or 'Tangled Hierarchy', in Bach's *A Musical Offering*, in the drawings of Escher and in the metamathematical work of Kurt Godel. The Strange Loop phenomenon occurs whenever, by moving up or down through levels of some hierarchical system, we unexpectedly find ourselves right back where we started. Implicit in the concept of Strange Loops is the concept of infinity since the Loop is a way of representing an endless process in a finite way. Hofstadter's book is built around the central notions of hierarchical systems and self-reference, in particular, the snarls which arise when systems turn back on themselves (science probing science, art violating the rules of art, humans thinking about their own minds). The book is a series of modulations leading from topic to topic and in the end, returning to its own beginning. The Dialogues examine an extraordinary range of related Godelian concepts: paradoxes of reasoning about reasoning about reasoning . . . ; 'Zentences' using Zen koans and Zen ideas in the philosophy of mathematics; concepts of 'figure' and 'ground' in Escher's art, of self-replication and self-reference, of knowledge in layers of contexts, and concepts of recursion in different structures, musical, geometric, mathematical and linguistic.

Hofstadter explores the Strange Loop in the fugues and canons of Bach's *A Musical Offering*, one large intellectual fugue in which many ideas and forms are woven together, with playful double meanings and subtle allusions, as well as a potentially infinite aspect, leading through successive modulations to remote provinces of tonality but returning us unexpectedly to the original key. The Loop is depicted visually in the paradoxes and illusions of Escher's drawings – and the viewer looking from outside is caught up in the endlessly rising loop in *Waterfall* or with the monks in *Ascending and Descending*. In the two step Strange Loop in *Drawing Hands*, hierarchical levels turn back on each other, creating a Tangled Hierarchy. The undrawn but drawing hand is outside the two-hand space, outside the Strange Loop. Godel's work is a mathematical counterpart, a translation into mathematical terms of the Liar paradox, using mathematical reasoning to explore mathematical reasoning. The Strange Loop is in the proof of Godel's Incompleteness Theorem, which hinges on writing a self-referential mathematical statement (in the same way as the liar paradox is a self-referential statement of language). Godel established that there are true statements of number theory which its methods of proof are too weak to demonstrate. Like the quantum revolution, Godel's Theorem brings philosophically disorienting messages about subject and object and the Strange Loops of human consciousness. The Godelian Theorem hinges on understanding not just one level at a time, but the way in which one level mirrors its metalevel and the consequences of this mirroring. The crucial point is in the level-crossing within Strange Loops, the point of crossing between different levels of the Tangled Hierarchy.

Escher's *Print Gallery* is a pictorial parable for Godel's Incompleteness Theorem. We can 'collapse' the whole into sections, perceiving levels within the Loop: the gallery is physically 'in' the town, the town is artistically 'in' the picture, the picture is mentally 'in' the person. At the centre of the whorl there is an apparent 'blemish', which shows Escher's signature, 'MCE'. Hofstadter shows that this centre is – and must be – incomplete. Escher could reduce its size, but not eliminate it. This is the eye of the Strange Loop, a Godel vortex where all levels cross.

Literature, in a sense, starts from the Godelian notion of the Loop – at least the elementary one-step loop of fiction. Magritte describes the one-step loop in his comments on his painting *The Human Condition 1*.

I placed in front of a window, seen from a room, a painting representing exactly that part of the landscape which was hidden from view by the painting. Therefore, the tree represented in the painting hid from view the tree situated behind it, outside the room. It existed for the spectator, as it were, simultaneously in his mind, as both inside the room in the painting, and outside in the real landscape. Which is how we see the world: we see it as being outside ourselves even though it is only a mental representation of it that we experience inside ourselves.[8]

34

This is the one-step Loop, when the tree exists for the spectator simultaneously inside the room in the painting and outside in the real landscape. In *Illywhacker*, Carey uses the image of a canvas to set up a more complex Loop, when Leah Goldstein insists she herself is not a liar and reproaches Herbert for stealing her writings.

And even then you have not done me the honour of thieving things whole but have taken a bit here, a bit there, snipped, altered and so on. You have stolen like a barbarian, slashing a bunch of grapes from the middle of a canvas.[9]

Through the notion of barbaric theft, slashing from the middle of the canvas, Carey sets up a more complex Godelian Loop, bringing more levels of the Lie into play. As in Borges' world of Tlon, where a book which does not contain its counterbook is considered incomplete, in the New fiction the Godelian Loop is complex and multiple, sometimes with three-step and four-step levels. What is crucial is understanding not just one level at a time, but the way each level points to its metalevel, the way truth and illusion and reality and the Lie of fiction mirror each other in a Tangled Hierarchy. Collaborators, Liar and reader in complicity together work their passage up and down this Tangled Hierarchy, crossing its intersections, catching glimpses of their own reflections and meeting each other inside the Strange Loop of reality and the Lie.

SECOND DIALOGUE

Reader is prowling round restlessly, the movement reflected in the mirrors. A cat lies coiled in front of the heater, a box beside him.

Reader Is that your cat? I didn't notice him last time.

Liar No, he's not mine. I'm just minding him for Schrodinger. He sleeps in here when he's not in the quantum box. Tell me, are you feeling better today?

Reader It's getting worse all the time. I feel dislocated, as though the centre of gravity has shifted. I just can't keep up with the demands on me. And every day there are more and more novels being published. Every day, new plots. Everywhere, not just here in Australia . . . . Have you ever been to South America?

Liar No, but I have close associates there. Marquez, Borges, Fuentes, Cortazar. Others. We correspond from time to time.

Reader I suspected that. I've been reading Cortazar's novel, *Hopscotch*. You'd like it. I'm the *lector-complice*, his accomplice. Except instead of taking me into his confidence, he sets out to disturb and confuse me. And what's more, I have to *write* it!

Liar That's right! Of course you do. Have you heard of Barthes' distinction between novels which are 'scriptible' and those which are 'lisible'? Some novels can be passively consumed and others demand some creative effort from the reader, so you're 'writing' the book as you read it.

Reader So what's wrong with passive consumption? It's much easier. I didn't get so tired. But *Hopscotch* – I've got to work it out for myself.

Liar I remember it. It works in different ways at the same time so you can read it either in numerical sequence or in an alternative numbered sequence suggested by the author.

Reader Or any sequence at all. The ordinary sequence is one story but if you follow the author's alternative sequence, then it's different, the action's simultaneous and contradictory. There's even a character, Morelli, whose writings are included in the second part of the novel, to mirror the whole lot. It's all directed at me – to displace and alienate me.

Liar It's like a maze, isn't it? It reminds me of the Richard Lunn story, 'Mirrors'.[1] Do you know it? The one with numbered fragments you read in a pattern of your own making, depending on the choices you yourself make at the end of each one. That's the one set in a mirror-maze, and the reader is inside a maze too, a narrative maze. At the end, it loops back to that start so it never really ends, but continues its inner spiral.

Reader What about the other Lunn story about mirrors? 'The Roger Mirror'.[2] I suppose you like that one too, where Roger sometimes sees his double who is tired of living in mirrors.

Liar Yes I do like that, with Roger feeling redundant, as though his presence is being supplanted by one with a greater claim. For a while, he dreams they're both balanced on a seesaw, but later, the balance shifts and he dreams of the double's death. When he tries to avert it, it becomes his own death, while the double watches from a train window.

Reader We're bound to look at stories about plots and victims from different angles. Depends who the victim is. It's usually me.

Liar Actually I prefer 'Marco the Molasses Man'.[2] That's a Lunn story too. Do you know it?

Reader Yes, I do. That's the one about Scarlatti, the evil impresario, who manipulates the one he's created, his poor innocent victim.

Liar: No, it's not. It's the one where Marco can contort himself into fascinating shapes because of his extraordinary bodily resilience, his elastic form. Sometimes Marco seems like a fat black spider asleep in a web of itself. He can twine his flesh into elaborate networks and lattices, even hang from the shreds of himself. Beautiful elasticity.

Reader Same story of course. Interesting the way you look at it. You're thinking about the strange beauty of the creation and I'm thinking about the evil creator and his manipulations.

Liar Don't forget the impresario is Lunn's creation. Where does that take us?

Reader Outside to Lunn the Liar . . . safely outside the frame.

Liar Have you ever heard of the paradox of the Authors' Triangle? By a man called Hofstadter who writes about Strange Loops in Bach and Escher, and in metamathematics. Godelian loops.

Reader I've heard of the Hofstadter book but he doesn't discuss literature, does he?

Liar No, apart from the Authors' Triangle he doesn't, but the Godelian Loop is very useful in literature. In the Triangle, there are three authors – Z, T, and E. Z exists only in a novel by T. T exists only in a novel by E. And strangely, E too exists only in a novel – by Z, of course. Is this possible?

Reader Yes, I know that one. It's possible if all three authors, Z, T, E, are themselves characters in another book, by H.

Liar That's right. The Z-T-E triangle is a Strange Loop, or Tangled Hierarchy, but the author H is outside the space in which that tangle takes place, in an inviolate space . . .

Reader . . . where Z, T, and E have no access to him.

Liar The Author's Triangle is also possible in *The Real Life of Sebastian Knight*.

Reader I read that recently. I'm still trying to decide whether the Nabokov novel I'd read was V's biography of Sebastian, or a fictionalized autobiography by Sebastian Knight or Knight's latest novel. It's like reading Flann O'Brien's *At Swim Two Birds*, writing about writing about writing, in an infinite regress.

Liar That's right, and outside the narrative frame is the Eschor-hand of the author. The same kind of Loop is in a lot of Australian novels, Carey's *Illywhacker*, Ireland's *The Chantic Bird*, Hasluck's *The Hand That Feeds You*. There's a lot. Jolley's *Miss Peabody's Inheritance* where Miss Peabody actually takes over from the writer. And *Foxybaby*, with Miss Porch running along the beach to meet her own characters. And Peter Mathers' novels, where he is outside the frame.

Reader Exactly. Safe. Inviolate. Where Z, T and E have no access to him. And nor do I. No come-back at all.

Liar What's the matter? You sound depressed.

Reader I am depressed. Tired. I'm tired of the strain, tired of play ing games. Games of Chinese boxes and infinite regress and novel-about-a-novel-about-a-novel.

Liar Games? You think these are games?

Reader Yes. Games and tricks. You're like the mythic Trickster.

Liar That's an unexpected compliment. Do you know what the Trickster symbolizes? The shaman, the medicine man. The Trickster's magical practices and his flights of intuition stamp him as a master of initiation.

Reader Master of initiation! Into what? Trendy games. It's very 'in' to write self-conscious fictions about writing a novel about a self-conscious fiction about writing a novel . . .

Liar Yes, I agree it's 'in', but why? It's not just trendy and they're not mere games. Of course there's a ludic component but underneath it's deadly serious. Underlying what you call games is an attempt to re-examine the processes and components of our whole culture. Not just in literature but in art, in epistemology, in mathematics, in information processing, in everything.

Reader It sounds to me as though we're back to mathematics and the Godelian Loop.

Liar Well, we are in a way. That's really metamathematics, metalogic. I'm very interested in it myself to tell the truth.

Reader To tell the truth? This *is* a new development.

Liar Just a slip of the tongue actually, only a rhetorical tail to the statement. Of course, metalogic is circular. It's what we were talking about last time in film. Unmasking the components and techniques of film. Part of the same thing, unmasking the constituents and processes of our culture. It's the same in literature. Part of a profound scrutiny of the processes behind our systems of thinking about reality, how they work. It's no game. It's the self-consciousness of our times.

Reader Let's just stick to literature. I can't cope with mathematics and art and all the rest as well. Besides, what is wrong with telling the truth?

Liar Actually it's the same thing . . . But let's not go too fast. Forget truth for the moment. We don't want to get tangled up in that at this stage. You still sound bitter.

Reader It's the strain. I told you, I'm under terrible pressure.

Liar I think it's time we tackled the beginnings of all this. The history of the case. Tell me, when did this trouble start?

Reader It's been going on for years. Since *Trap*. When was that? 1966. Twenty-two years ago. That was the start. Peter Mathers' noisome lies about the past. Pssst . . . You want to buy some feelthy pictures of Australian history? *Trap* is full of lies. Then *The Wort Papers*. And then it got worse in the seventies. Oakley, Ireland, then Foster. After ten years of it, there was no stopping them. All lies. More and more kept coming. Carey. Bail. Jolley. Hasluck. Adamson. Murnane. There seems to be no end to it. They won't stop. All those voices. And more keep coming. All telling me lies.

Liar: The seventies were good years for us. But look at the eighties. The Australian Lie coming of age.

Reader It's been going on a long time. I should have realized before that it was becoming critical.

Liar You shouldn't blame yourself for that. Critical conditions are not easy to face. Some people never recognize them.

Reader Yes, but it's not the first time. I've had a crisis before, in the fifties and sixties, when I was told the only good novels were metaphysical ones. I had terrible nightmares – of being imprisoned in a Fortress, at the mercy of the few trusties chosen by the governor. A captive in a critical condition. Recently John Docker wrote to me about it.

Liar Well, that's over now. Let's look at the present. Since Mathers was the first, let's start with him.

Reader Yes, but I can't even be sure who wrote his books. One is David David's diary and the other is a butterbox of papers collected by some other person called Matters.

Liar Don't forget Z, T, and E . . .

Reader I know, Peter H-Mathers and the hands, drawing Australian history.

Liar Yes, but it's more than that. Not just history but how we look at our history. Look at *Trap*. Voices and countervoices, each one supplanting the others, taking us through different levels and spirals of history – all recorded in David David's diary in the book written by Mathers. And it's all true.

Reader The outlying truth of Peter Escher–Mathers . . . Alarums and excursions.

ALARUMS AND EXCURSIONS *PETER MATHERS*

'They weren't sure what they'd got in Mathers and told others that I was a writer, mad and solitary, but bound to write something exceptional. They'd say, 'You wouldn't write anything nasty, would you?' and I'd look back with, No, I'm not like that.'

'Pittsburgh Identity: 0000000621'

AM SENDING YOU PERCY WORT PAPERS STOP YOU REMEMBER PERCY OF COURSE STOP THE WORTERIANA COMMA OF CELLULOSE COTTON GRAPHITE AND INK COMMA MAY AT FIRST SIGHT COMMA TOUCH AND SNIFF COMMA APPEAR INEDIBLE STOP EXAMINE CLOSELY HOWEVER AND NOTE ONCE APPETISING SPOTS OF HONEY MARMITE SARDINE STOP PAPERS COULD BE CONSIDERED OBJECTIONABLE SO I ADVISE THAT IF YOU ARE APPREHENDED EAT PAPERS STOP WEATHER HERE IS EXCELLENT AND AM LOOKING FORWARD TO EXCELLENT STORMS FOLLOWED BY EXCELLENT SUNSHINE AND WINDS STOP

Thomas went home. He did not want to see Matters' Worteriana. But it would come, as inevitably as night followed day, and as fearsome . . . He then sat down to read the letter...

Dear Thomas,

These are not Percy Wort's pp.; you're not getting out of it so easily. Percy disappeared on a new leaf/life fifteen years ago.

Well I've got what he left behind – to be exact, what he left BELOW – it's a box of story. Have read it. Here and there you'll find my comments. It's sure to be a goer and they're mad if they refuse it. You know them so butter them up. If they're crazy and you don't feel like bringing it out yourself get onto one of these yank cruise ships and flog it to some millionaire collector for the JFK Cornking Library. Ms is in a butterbox, a bit musty but the smellier the cheese the keener the epicure...

My room's lined with words, filled with them. In books, bundles and folders. On the light bulb, on pen, pencils, typewriter, enamel mug, collar, insteps. Do they move around at night? I should get the ladder and see if the right ones got back onto the light bulb . . .

In lines, thousands of them, black marks with white between ever flowing. Everything from: the shaving cut he stopped with lint from her navel, to: the rent lobe I staunched with eight hours sleep. Black marks on an orange . . . Groin's Trusses white on blue as though alphabet of heaven is falling. And all coming to an end they say. Farewell, Gutenberg, Caxton. Print interred. But not in a real one, no, not a real one, and do you know why it's not in a real turd? Because the communicating beast was com(m)a'd. I read yesterday that communication, through print, is finished. Words no longer *convey*. Film IS. Every frame tells a story. Twenty-odd of them a second. Grave wherein the words do sleep. Plastic grave clothes, coffin and marker, lens-decorated. However there's no keeping out graverobbers.

Peace,

MATTERS.

The Wort Papers[1]

•

MATHERS STARTS WITH A

sense that 'Nothing exists by itself . . . You've got to suggest all sorts of possible connections'.[2] This is no discreet formulation promising mild-mannered, quiet disclosure, but the starting point of frantic activity, more like ransacking a consciousness in search of the words to pit against chaos:

There are things, things behind and under things, things within and within that which is within. In motion, at rest. Changes within changes, exquisitely random . . . these things are protean . . . You watch things change. Or things change when watched.[3]

Change is 'exquisitely random', man an improbable agent in a contingent world, which he regards with suspicion and dismay, a spectator who discovers he is part of the spectacle. This is the dialogue running in exquisite dismay, through all Mathers' work. Do you watch things change? Or do things change when watched? Was I merely present, an innocent bypasser thrust ineluctably into a public scene? Am I an agent of change or changed? Am I tainted or do I taint? How to contain things in constant flux?

Mathers uses an elastic structure, the kind that can stretch and expand to contain a vast array of digressions, meanderings, vignettes, miscellanies, detours and tributaries – but the kind that snaps back when he lets go. Behind the narrative is constant tension, Mathers pulled taut. *Trap* and *The Wort Papers* contain numerous journeys within journeys and loose narrative manoeuvres which constantly disrupt the forward narrative line. Jack Trap and his abject diarist, David David, are starting points for seemingly endless digressions through the dark corners of Australian history, where sinister truths lurk. Mathers himself has suggested that he has much in common with Lawson, Collins, Clarke and the journals of explorers and visitors.[1] His novels do include journeys of discovery and exploration, even the odd obligatory bushfire, and have some of the conventions of personal memoirs, one a diary, the other a collection of family papers. But they contain, not decorous history celebrating pioneer courage and endurance, but a compendium of bizarre happenings, dastardly deeds in the ancestry of now worthy families, unseemly goings-on in our past going on into our present, a Liar's history which Mathers assures us is all true. The pioneering going on here is Mathers' own, pioneering the Australian Lie.

Mathers has pointed out that until Jack Trap, 'Aboriginals had been portrayed as noble downtrodden people who didn't snap back and didn't have a sense of humour'.[2] Not only Jack Trap but the novel *Trap* snaps back, an absurdist rejoinder in the argument Mathers is conducting with conventional views of time and space and Australian history. He has written of 'Old Evil, always inventing new aliases . . . tarted up, disguised, so as to appear only right and proper, inevitable manifestations of the absolutely contemporary'.[3] Pushing absurd and incongruous images across our pathway, he strips off the most seemly garments with which Australian history is tarted up and exposes the sordid and miserable flesh underneath. A natural subversive, Jack Trap is an outrage to cherished historical assumptions, notably those of the hapless David David. An absurdist stand-in for the reader, David David ponders on change, watching things change, or is it that things change when watched? Is it just that Trap was in the vicinity? Fearful deliberations and wry imaginings, frantic brushing down the mind to expunge the Trap taint. Behind David David, history breaks off its old liaisons and forms new and promiscuous dalliances, connections which are heathen, without regard for our most sacrosanct assumptions about our collective past.

Trap is also a Lie about writer and reader, with David David standing in for the reader, undergoing all the terrible crises and horrors of Trap's view of the world. His diary records the progress of Effect X, the insidious taint of Trap on a once worthy social worker, a rational and mature being, who contracts Trappism. *The Wort Papers* on the other hand is about words, about the writer and his words. Percy Wort, a latter-day William on the run, has been called 'an underdingo, larrikinetic, motorcycling visionary predicament hunter'.[4] Percy is also an agent of the Liar who, through the services of Matters, hounds and dements his brother Thomas, scapegoat for the reader. The novel is an extraordinary proliferation of papers, taxonomies, essays, fables, ponderings, medical bric-a-brac, pseudo-scientific speculations, tales, a wondrous collection of words in a butterbox. Some narrate journeys, past and present, some narrate verbal battles with the encroaching chaos, some are diversionary material to cover Percy Wort's retreat. Words are Percy Wort's way of contending with the encircling chaos, his ladder out of the Wortarium, by which he might make sense of the world at last and so climb to freedom.

In his article on Mathers' work, which I regard as one of the best critical articles ever written in this country, D.J.O'Hearn suggests that for Mathers history is not an orderly chronological assembly of material, but rather is fluid, protean, web-like. History is 'a composite of fact, fiction, myth, legend and accident', both personal and impersonal, interconnected and discontinuous. In *The Wort Papers*

It is as though the form of the novel creates a distinctive view of the human condition – at the core of things is both anarchy and inter-relatedness, chaos and continuity. No one perspective dominates its polar opposite more than momentarily, and there is no cause either for elation or despair.[5]

Mathers sees society as both anarchic and continuous, movement and counter-movement, never static, and this organic sense becomes the form and the content of his novels. Time and space are patterns of webs, enmeshed assemblages of lines of continuance, tenuous connections and delicate correspondences. Mathers uses a succession of narrative voices in a contrapuntal way each one supplanting its predecessor and dislocating our sense of order.

Some of the correspondences in *The Wort Papers* however are not so delicate. Mathers digs down into history and uncovers foul and noxious stuff which he leaves us holding while he wanders off down detours and sidetracks, concocting some disreputable connections. His is history on slimy trails, littered with its droppings and sloughed-off skins, the history behind the veneer, the kind of history that is always lurking, waiting to be told. Mathers' account of the past is labyrinthine, digressing with alacrity into minor figures, wandering off at tangents, then rejoining the main narrative line at unexpected intersections, uncovering sinister links with the present. It is a Liar's history, with Mathers outside the frame watching one Escher-hand drawing Australian time and space and history, while the other scrabbles for words to pitch at the chaos. It is history told by a Liar who insists it is true.

Mathers tells us that, plotted on a map of Australia, Percy Wort's childhood resembled a giraffe, but it is difficult to identify the creature mapped by joining up the points of Mathers' life. Born in England, in Fulham, in 1931, within a few months he was living with his family in Sydney. Brought up in Sydney at Rose Bay in the late 1930s, Mathers remembers vividly several journeys inland to uncles' farms and once spent a year on an uncle's farm near the Nullarbor in South Australia. At 19, Mathers worked in a steelworks at Port Kembla; around 1950, he studied agriculture for three years at Sydney Technical College and in the late 1950s, after a period in the wool industry, there was a period as an unsuccessful farmer. By the time *Trap* was published in 1966, Mathers was travelling in Europe with his wife and in the 1960s lived and worked in England, Europe and the United States. Recently he was for a time writer in residence at Darwin Institute. Now in his mid 50s Mathers lives in Melbourne, in inner-suburban Richmond.

On the literary map, among Australian writers he enjoys, Mathers points to other Liars (Moorhouse, Carey, Bail, Ireland, Wilding, Lurie, Foster) and, among writers outside Australia, he cites Barthelme, Gass, Camus, Marquez, Grass, Boll, Borges, Carpentier, Coover.[2] Mathers is naming his literary kin but his sheer inventiveness and comic energy, coupled with his extraordinary vision of history, mark him out from most of his Australian contemporaries. The comic inventiveness of Barry Oakley and Bill Reed sometimes pitches towards Mathers', more so David Foster's zany parodies. Mathers' work also has some broad affinity with David Ireland's, both writers representing constant change and disorder, yet ever watchful for the connections which break through the surface. The narrative fragments of Mathers' novels are longer and more labyrinthine than Ireland's, the connections running through time more webbed, and where Mathers' preoccupation is with the past and its sordid connections with the present, Ireland's work pushes towards the future. Yet, like Ireland, Mathers sees the writer as underminer, breaking up surfaces, causing chaos and then nicking off, disappearing into a hole until the next uprising.

Unfortunately Mathers has stayed in the hole for a long time and the next uprising has long been awaited. He has written several plays, and miscellaneous short stories some of which have been collected in *A Change for The Better* (1984), but no new novels have emerged since 1972. Rumours of hidden treasure troves of unpublished manuscripts cause grief and misery to his readers, some of whom make representations and deputations to Mathers to plead, cajole and keen. However, the legendary numbers of manuscripts may have dwindled: 'I have lost a few. Some are thumbed to extinction by editors. Some are bad, others incomprehensible. I've moved many times, some of the old ones get eaten.'[2] Murmurs of possible titles are heard: 'Chains', 'Flies', 'Fish', 'Sky', 'Hook', even 'Liver'. Mathers writes on, revealing in 1977, 'Every morning I sit at my desk. Too often I begin with a shapely piece and whittle away till it's a stump and a heap of shavings. When I glue it together, the laminations show.' In an interview in 1985,[6] Mathers insisted his manuscripts are not ready, although one, with the provisional title, 'Rabbits', about a city despatch manager who sends trucks throughout the continent and who inherits some bleak land, might be soon . . . In 1985, his play *The Mountain King* was staged at La Mama in Melbourne. Its hero a black skin-diver, it ranges from Melbourne to Western Australia and includes iron ore, company takeovers, eccentric potentates, nervous pawns, parking meters and pacemakers. Later in 1985, his second staged play, *Pelaco Bill, Adventures in the Shirt Trade*, was part of a series of plays from the Melbourne Writers' Theatre. Meanwhile importunate readers keep pounding on his Richmond door, literary beggars wailing for Lies.

Although leading critics such as Vincent Buckley and D.J. O'Hearn regard Mathers as part of the collection of important Australian writers with Lawson, Furphy, Richardson, Stead, White and Herbert, at the same time Mathers 'remains one of the great un-read'.[5] One of the reasons for that I think is the nature of literary time, in which writers can be swallowed up or mislaid. *Trap* was published in 1966, twenty-two years ago, *The Wort Papers* sixteen years ago, a long time in Australian readerly memory. Mathers is the pioneer of the Australian Lie and one of the world's great Liars. In our midst since 1966, perhaps he arrived early, premature, before the readers. Perhaps only now, by some time-warp, are readers ready to catch up with the Mathers Lie and join the clamouring throng at the Richmond door.

But readers have to move fast to catch up. Mathers is fleet of foot and word, the runway hazardous, particularly in *The Wort Papers* where he is motorized on the Norton. Teresa Dovey believes that the small readership of Mathers' novels is because of the risk he takes with narrative form:

the result is a loss of narrative interest, which depends to a large extent on a sense of meaningful continuity and a sense of the connectedness of parts. Not many readers are prepared to abandon themselves to the flux and flow and chance happenings of a high-speed trip on a Norton.[7]

The risk Mathers takes is the Lie. Dovey suggests 'Percy Wort is a kind of Sontagian hero, on the run from interpretation', with Mathers trying to subvert the illusion of meaningful continuity and to disrupt the false ordering of experience – and thereby to deny the possibility of interpretation. Yet both novels are about interpretation. Built on the diary form, *Trap* is about the gap in the diarist's understanding of what he is recording, his inability to interpret correctly the events going on around him, at the time they are taking place. Through the diary form, Mathers parodies the convention that memory *composes* the past. He suggests that, on the contrary, memory decomposes the artificial order which, in a makeshift way, it concocted hastily at the time. Interpretation is possible, but generally wrong, crooked. Getting hold of the right interpretation involves taking it all apart and starting again, which is what he does with Australian history, until he comes up with the Liar's history.

Behind the vast network of connections in *Trap* is a contest between the conventional David David, clinging to fixed entities, and Trap, who knows about chaos. But the extraordinary feature of *Trap* is that Jack Trap himself is essentially static within all the perturbation of the narrative present, while his diarist and biographer, the narrator who would track him down and contain him in words, becomes ever more frantic and disordered. In his excellent article, Vincent Buckley argues that *Trap*

is not about Trap as a single travelling consciousness experiencing a various world and moving from place to place in it. It is about Australian history as it reticulates into the present Australian society. Although Jack Trap does move around a lot, we are conscious less of his mobility than of a powerful fixity, settledness...a centre of significance and ambivalence who is encountered or sought by others.[8]

Buckley also argues the novel is about the present confronting its own determining past, and conducting 'a search for origins by showing with elaborate and unsettling care the hypocrisy inherent in current notions of how and why to conduct such a search'.[8] It is a search for interpretation, an interpretation elastic enough to hold, one which will not snap back.

Structurally, *Trap* seems to sprawl, but its framework is simple – a chronological sequence of diary entries over the period from April 1st to May 3rd, in which the diarist is in control of the entries and is recording faithfully with detachment and objectivity. The frame is complicated by the fact that on May 2nd, when Trap and his entourage are about to set out for the Naraki mission, there to stir up the residents in protest, the diarist re-reads his entries for the previous month and discovers in them the terrible taint of Trappism. So the diarist is forced to re-interpret, a two-step Loop inside the Lie, with Mathers and his reader outside watching from a further remove – extending it to a three-step Loop.

David David is the reader inside the novel, an absurd stand-in, our delegate, acting and reacting on our behalf, representing us. Trap is the fiction, the still point in a turning world, in which history, reality, appearances, all spin round David David faster and faster, throwing his carefully nurtured sense of himself and the world into chaos. At the start of the novel, Mathers, a Liar with a sense of fair play, gives fair warning of the dangers of exposure to the novel – a kind of all-encompassing literary caveat.

You go to him a reasonable conservative sort, a defender of established things and you leave fermenting with ideas of – wait for it – anarchism, nihilism, Buddhism, allisms and wild, general revolt.[9]

David David is duly warned, but he is assured, scoffing at Mrs Nathan's fear of Trap, proud of having emerged unscathed from his experience of Trap. At the end, when he has re-read the April entries in his diary, he is prey to consuming doubt and then, appalled, aghast, he realizes he is suffering from the Trap taint. Instead of his own salubrious influence on Jack Trap, as a purveyor of respectable attitudes, redeemer even, he becomes more apprentice than redeemer and contracts Effect X. Mathers' contract is on the reader but he is polite to the reader, at first. David David begins with worthy ambitions and a respectable sense of history, with no reason to doubt that things are as they seem. He sets out mature, stable, eminently respectable, proud of his rational and scientific approach, his moral earnestness. Detached, objective, but caring, a man of integrity. Politely, Mathers allows that this is his reader and presents his fiction – Effect X. It is an algebraic Lie, a thing of equations.

I must beware.
Adamov says that to know Trap is to be influenced by him. So – Trap produces Effect X. Therefore Adamov becomes X and I, David David Adamov X. (p.98)

David David contracts Effect X and, suffering from it, he searches for a cure, some healing image to cling to, some healthy, esteemed personage to model himself on, to ward off his feelings of impending doom: 'I could feel the rebellion clotting in my guts. How long would I have before the clot filled me?' (p.251). Not long. The prognosis is poor. Only a month, until the end of the novel when he joins Trap in beating up a sailor and is last seen giggling shamelessly at a newspaper report of his intrepid deed, the splendid exploit of tossing a brick through the ten-thousand-pound glass doors of the Megopolis Building.

But he began with confidence, sure of his own immunity, as complacent as his white ancestors.

At heart he is still the tribesman. Scratch him and the savage shows. He intends sneaking away because he knows I could dissuade him. How? Because, as Trap's biographer, I know most of his weaknesses. At first he used to mock me, but when he saw how my conclusions were based on scientific theory and experiment results he changed his tune. Chaos rules world affairs, I often told him. Man needs fixed entities. He needs a definite standard. What better standard is there than the Cosmos? (pp.9–10)

David David's battle for order accelerates to keep pace with the spread of the narrative, reaching back with it into the depths of the past and widening and deepening as it does. At the same time it is a parody re-enactment of the history Trap is disclosing, except that this time, white notions of order are broken up by the half-caste's notions of disorder. Before he re-reads his dairy entries for April, he explains to Trap, 'Chaos rules world affairs. Man needs fixed entities.'(p.9). Trap shows him that all is contingent, that there are no fixed entities.

As the structures of the present and of the past are steadily demolished, David David's quest for order becomes ever more frantic as he tries to find a refuge from the pursuing chaos. Seeking something snug and enclosed, he is drawn to the Circle. In the early part of the novel, when David David is first exposed to Trap's own past through Adamov's account of it, he is thrust closer to the Circle, seeing it as a saving enclave:

Having been tried by all and found wanting. Silly me, wet waif, wanderer, looking for something with a hole, a cave, a niche. For fool me, I have tried the lot – associations, clubs, churches, sects, unions, parties, families, all manner of bodies. Tried pictures and rock, oxygen and acetylene, paint and words, always words, words, words, but nothing there for me, no, not a thing.

Nothing, I mean, that could ease, would ease, things which would perhaps permit me to enter. But enter what? Ease and turmoil are all the same. But enter – so what? (p.68)

As David David searches for fixed entities he can enter, a hole, a niche, Trap breaks down the very structures David is trying to erect. Free-Rutt lures him with the notion that all is pre-ordained. 'We are puppets of uncontrollable powers. All we can do is understand, and anticipate them' (p.52). This is a moral haven, offering the fixed entities and the deterministic order of the Crabbed Circle, which David David finds more attractive than chaos and Trap. 'I experiment...I seek a way': perhaps the way is circular. When Trap widens the narrative and extends right back to his grandmother in Tierra del Fuego and then steadily examines all the connections from there through to the present, David David discovers the origins of the Circle and is plunged deeper and deeper into chaos. He, who imagined himself as 'the catalytic type' (p.56), finds himself undergoing radical change, while Trap remains a constant. Trap is the catalyst, the still figure, who wreaks changes and havoc in all around him.

The Circle is both the Consortium of power and money and also the Crabbed Circle, for which astrology provides the order of human existence. The Circle is an image of safety, safety in numbers, safety in containment. All the lines of history, connections and disconnections, cut across David David's circle, constantly breaching its circumference. This circle too, like the history beneath his feet, comes unstuck, unfixed. David David's faith in noble and heroic pioneers, custodians of culture warding off barbarians and riffraff, is dislodged by a different and shocking view of Australian history. He finds the Santymony wealth built on head-hunting, learns of savage and contemptuous exploitation, despoliation of the land, and worse, close links among Trap's forebears and those of the Consortium. The disease he has contracted continues its insidious growth. Although ever vigilant, he has become weighed down by the menace of Trap, walks with 'shoulders canted, bogey on a shoulder, no clear shape though, just a weighed presence' (p.281). The reader too, no clear shape, bogey on a shoulder, is infected with Effect X, reader-David David-Adamov-X, and is contagious.

David David clings to the role of observer, detached onlooker, imperturbably regarding the vagaries of Trap, and, in the midst of a tossing, sleepless night, decides 'This, I think, is my saving grace. My ability to see others as they really are. My honesty. My ability to stand off and observe them with complete detachment.' (p.99). Outside the frame, the reader too, no doubt, is confident of his honesty, his detachment and objectivity. Later David David discovers journal entries 'rotten with Trappisms. Trappissms.' (p.247). Too late. Prognosis grim - for the reader too.

While David David is examining himself for new X-symptoms, Mathers is behind the scenes, engaged in his own sinister purposes. He begins with the present, then opens the narrative out into Jack Trap's own past, building up the story of Trap's life through to the 1950s first, through Adamov, then through Trap's own narrative, when he takes over and brings the narrative through to the present. As it opens out, we hear more and more about the past, in narrative stretches which lengthen and complicate, more detail that accretes and proliferates. As this happens, we hear less about David David, who becomes, apart from occasional frantic murmurings and mutterings, a kind of spectre, a distant shadowy listener-diarist, hovering miserably over the narrative.

This kind of history is narrated by a succession of voices, each taking over from the other, so that David David's voice weakens and grows faint, plaintive, in the distance. The novel takes the form of a dark labyrinth, with dank interconnecting passages and tunnels, the light at the entrance dimming and disappearing as we are drawn further and further down through the subterranean layers of history where voices mutter and mute close by. The novel opens at the entrance and then plunges us down into the past, where all is connected. What Mathers exposes is this murky history, the seedy and disreputable, the noisome, Trap's kind. Trap's kind of history is constant change yet lines of continuance running ineradicably through to the present, to form shockingly new patterns of history.

In the first part of the novel, the unlovely Cruxtwist, Cyril the Steelcyl foreman, Maisie, and Nina (with her malicious tales about the Mayor's brothels) all narrate sequences which come together as a kind of composite image of Trap's world, sometimes embroidered by Nina. Digressions open up within digressions, encapsulated biographies inside others, subsections inside subsections. The story of Sodamjohn, the elderly gay cleaner, catches the Mathers' eye as he passes and he stops to tell it, before picking up the Cruxtwist threads again. David David is found gurgling foolishly, already. Mrs. Nathan phones again, with news of the campaign being built around Trap's journey to the Naraki mission: the theme is UMSA (Useful Members of Society Again). More gurgling. A few steps closer to the Crabbed Circle.

Then Adamov the schemer plays narrator, offering 'slabs' of narrative and subversive aphorisms. A life begins to take shape, from Trap's birth in 1916 through to the 1950s when he joined Steelcyl (Factory of All Nations), years of being cast as a habitual criminal and general subversive as well as infamous scaffoldwright. When Trap himself takes over the narrative, the shape of the life becomes plasticene and changes form. Trap hands the role of narrator around a circle of voices, each one supplanting its predecessor: first the Steelcyl works manager, then Cyril, the foreman soon to be encased in a cylinder, even Mrs. Paine, the landlady, with a few digressions along the way, into interesting stories like Sally's background, Trap's meeting her at the Black Cat. Lines of continuance run out of each section, into new branches, tributaries, new passages that veer off suddenly.

In the second part of the novel, these lines of continuance multiply and proliferate alarmingly. The narrative voices extend back suddenly to Trap's forebears in Tierra del Fuego in the early nineteenth century, Hobart in the 1830s, cedar-cutters in N.S.W. bush in the mid-nineteenth century, even traders in Maori shrunken heads: Armstrong Irish Trap (the first of the Trap line, 'in for a rough life, trapped, as it were, by himself'); Maria; old Meely; his employer, Skeets; Peters with extracts from his diary and the story of Feed; Flitch the Sydney merchant; Colonel Sancty-mony; Wilson and Sarah, Trap's parents; Oswald Potts. The narrative voices grow to a cacophony and David David records, 'I now understand, better than ever, the workings of minds near the ends of their tethers' (p.188). What Trap has shown him is history overturned and underlying, under the hand of the Liar.

People come to Trap clutching their own assumptions and attitudes, determined to make him fit into their patterns, to use and exploit him for their purposes, before fleeing like Colin Free. He arrives the intrepid parliamentary crusader, uplifter of the oppressed, champion of the rebel cause, eager to enlist Trap as a fellow rebel. He is first disarmed by Trap's dubious clothes, his 'tasteless' home, his petty bourgeois decor. He, a true and authentic anarchist, is peevish, puzzled by the delay of the small-time rebel, Trap, in hailing him as a big-time rebel. When he learns of Trap's false orchids and spurious stuffed birds, discomfiture shifts rapidly into alarm, then into horror at the nefarious deeds of Trap's dog. The sanctity of his career at stake, he finally flees down the back lane determined to raze the area and have Trap put away. This passage from posturing smugness to horror is characteristic of Trap's influence, Effect X at work, while Trap does nothing, just is – and by his very existence, he offends.

Effect X depends on expectations, lots of them: expectations of Trap, of history, of fiction. Mathers is pitting his own sordid Lie against the reader's expectations. Trap is an outrage because he is not what others expect of him. As an Aborigine, he is offensively ignorant of his place, lacking in respect for stereotypes. He ponders,

what on earth was expected of him? Should he burst into song or saddle a horse or spar or point 'a bone or throw a fleece or paint or dance? It seemed there was no escape. (p.116)

By failing others' expectations, Trap undermines and challenges their most cherished assumptions, disturbs their complacency and generates an anonymous fear. Often particular offences are manufactured in order to contain the general offensiveness of Trap, to give it names. Name it, tame it, disarm it. How to contain the unruly is the question running through the whole novel.

While David David plunges deeper into the chaos of existence, past and present, Jack Trap has been largely the still point in the turning narrative. Yet he too has times of despair and feels 'the dreadful weight of wasted time' (p.239). He is himself trapped and he ponders darkly on the possibilities, casting round for a way to break free. Brooding in his room on the possibilities of killing Mrs Paine, his landlady, Trap is self-mocking and finally he seeks refuge in the protective darkness of his wardrobe, as the room closes in on him. At Steelcyl, wearied by the hopelessness of ever being free of labels and categories, all the stereotypes by which people try to contain him, Trap contains Cyril, then calmly awaits arrest.

Throughout the novel, images of containment abound, constantly set against images of chaos and indeterminacy, of things amok. Mathers sets up notions of fixity and structure in a novel which ultimately parodies its own containment and is about its own effect. Effect X. So what is Effect X? Fiction. The Lie. Trap is the antithesis of order, a violation of all that is right-minded: stereotypes, categories, appearances, preconceptions, time-honoured principles, expectations, distinctions, the antithesis of all that makes the world predictable and calculable. Trap is an affront, a disorder in a categorical world, an outrage in a neatly ordered world. Trap is a defiance, resisting philanthropy, civilisation, tolerance, benevolence, patronage. Trap is history re-opened, interrogated, tortured until it breaks down and confesses its contradictions, its deviousness and double-dealings. Trap is the blur between distinctions, the smudge between categories. Trap is the uncontainable truth, which, like some dark, noisome creature, breaks out and stalks the streets with foul intent, leaving a trail across the mind. Effect X. Trap is fiction, the Lie.

The Wort Papers also is about history, about time and change and flux, with the writer burrowing down into it trying to see how it works or hiding from it in a cave or a wortarium, trying to contain and confine it in words. Like Trap, The Wort Papers has an extraordinary structure and a kind of eager elasticity, with numerous digressions into extravagant styles and forms which proliferate and accrete through the novel. But it is also about the Liar contemplating the word, wondering if he can entrust it with what he has to say. The memoir form in The Wort Papers loosely contains the narrative in a manner similar to the diary form and the presence of David David in Trap. But Percy Wort is both observer and participant, a mind groping through its own determining past in hope of making sense of experiences that at the time were perceived as chaotic. Percy reflects that, having decided to 'put it all down', he sounds like 'an herculean creature getting from under and depositing his burden – but with a crash or with infinite gentleness?' (p.19). And where to deposit it? Those questions run serpentine through the novel and, however tortuous the narrative digressions, however circuitous its route, Percy's struggle to make sense of himself in the midst of a disordered world is at its centre. Percy's memoirs are written from the wortarium, the underground cave to which he has retreated, there to grapple with the past in hope of discovering some way of being in the world that makes sense.

When the hapless Thomas receives the offensive butterbox with 'the worteriana', its equally offensive and ravaged contents of fifteen years, he is 'reminded of recent book made up of hodge-podge of diaries, papers, recollections, an anthology of rubbish and this'll be no improvement, no development' (p.18). At the start Mathers plays with the notion of the narrative as miscellany, like the 'recent book'. But Percy insists that, 'As befits a person with a somewhat scientific slant of mind, I am going to write this memoir in a plain straight-forward manner' (p.22). Percy is lying and behind him is the Liar, Mathers, who is plotting to subvert the reader's notions of direct, straightforward lines of narrative and sets up a Tangled Hierarchy of time and space and word. The Liar gives his word.

Percy writes from the uncertain shelter of the wortarium, an ever-changing locale according to the proximity of the besieging Thomas, Percy writing on the move, while shifting from cave to cave. In each locale, Percy is 'encaverned'.

Literally in a hole, and see no way out at present. What a situation. Die here unless I escape. Some say holes are essential for human existence, that holes generate the need to escape, that if holes did not exist it would be necessary to invent them . . .

This hole I'm in. Get out of it. To what? Another, perhaps. (p.257)

In his eight foot hole, Percy tries to 'Heap these words against the predicament and climb to safety' (p.259), clambering up the words to freedom. He is encaverned in the present, hiding from retribution for his last magnificent deed before he quitted the world (geligniting the bottle heap of the Uppersass Community Hall). He is also encaverned in the past, fumbling along the passages of memory towards the present. Caves recur in his experience in extraordinary ways, ranging from the Jenolan Caves to Thomas's entrepreneurial activities with caves, but he also inhabits 'Caves of recollection joined with one another by passages sometimes long and narrow' (p.105). Can words link them? Can words grope through caves and find a way out?

In *Trap*, Mathers leaves David David dodging Trappism in the foreground of the novel, while he himself nicks off into history. In *The Wort Papers*, the duo of Thomas and Matters are a marginal presence. Thomas, business executive, collector of the accoutrements of high social status, international traveller to unlikely places, life-long postulant to the world of business magnate and 'determined implementor of innovations' (p.2), as well as sometime aerial hunter of Percy, is also discontented, trapped by his position, dreaming of

a chance to be heroic in a cliché-ridden world and wearily despairing
('. . . if only I could become the old I Am' (p.13).) Through the
persecution of Matters, 'an unknown, racked writer' (p.10), Thomas
is compelled to submit to his past, driven back into the past there
to contemplate his origins. Apart from a general registering of shock
and disgust, Thomas' presence is limited, a shadowy figure like Matters himself. Matters' insistence that Thomas read the papers, his
involvement with Percy at the wortarium and his own literary activities, all suggest he is a kindred spirit to Percy. But like Thomas,
he is marginal, a go-between who presents the papers, rather than
a constant presence.

Constantly present in *The Wort Papers* is the tension within Percy's
own role, as both observer and participant, while Mathers plays with
the convention of the dispassionate spectator, faithfully recording
all for the reader. The papers reveal an extraordinary array of guises
and disguises adopted in defence against the outer chaos. At the same
time there are increasingly desperate sorties into literary fantasies as
a shield against the inner despair. The promised 'straightforward narrative' becomes a succession of roles and guises and fragments, which
cut into and across each other, with a rapidity and ingenuity that
keep pace with Percy's own mounting despair. This is Mathers on
the run, a fugitive like Percy, running on words, worrying that words
do not work any more, that words no longer *convey*.

Percy's childhood was spent 'on the run – or at least on the
move – for years' (p.123). William Wort's migratory instinct and
his 'lemming spirit' (p.125), require him to undertake numerous journeys across Australia, on such urgent missions as keeping the Camel
Corps out of Afghan hands, saving the Kimberleys from the Zionists
and 'getting in early' before the government makes the inland sea.
Further, William's pursuit of the ideal farm, as inculcated by the
ideal (English) farmer, requires more (but more modest) expeditions
near the coast. Throughout his travels, there is a sense of the innocent on the move, bearer of futile dreams and incongruous aspirations,
ever encountering those akin to himself. In the hilarious Orebul
Downs sequence, his dalliance with Mrs Tyme is punctuated by the
activities of Mr Tyme, who is warding off invaders and general,
unspecified menacers, forming a guerilla band and generally improving
the efficiency of his armoury. The climactic scene of the station burning and exploding from the ammunition, as well as William's

characteristic befuddled dismay, are the culmination of Mathers' parodies of journeys into the interior in search of riches, spiritual and other. Patrick White's Voss and Randolph Stow's Heriot (*To the Islands*) are spectres hovering over these splendidly satirical scenes of the intrepid seeker. But instead of seeking spiritual treasure, the Liar's seekers are on parodic quests, through black, zany absurdity. In part, *The Wort Papers* is a parody of the family saga; what Michael Wilding, in his review of the novel, calls the 'orderly hagiographical family chronicle of distinguished squattocracy or bourgeoisie'.[10] The parody abounds, particularly in relation to William, in the journeys of exploration and discovery, the myths of bush and mateship and the conventions of portraying the founder of the dynasty. Much of the parody proceeds from its structure, which summons up the convention at the same time as it subverts it through the digressions into essays, commentaries, observations on . . . , tales with a moral, all the miscellany of literary forms.

Like Percy, William is a role-player and adopter of disguises: he is sometime newspaperman, saviour of camels, 'Wandering Sharefarmer', bicyclist in the desert, seafarer in coffin tramp, soldier-wanderer after rainbows, quester in general. With Green, William Wort discusses sadly the Australian penchant for 'lots of airy-fairy schemes, dreams, Utopias, Utopia-NoWhere', as they dwell amid an arid broken land – and their eyes glaze over as they see it rich, fertile, teeming with lush growth. Ever out of kilter with the world, ever in pursuit of the mirage, William embodies the 'Great Australian Dream'. Part of Percy's later despair is that the world made no sense to William either.

Like *Trap*, *The Wort Papers* offers a new way of seeing the past, a new and subversive account of the way things were. As well as the old aliases and tarted-up disguises of truth, Mathers delights in exposing some contemporary absurdities. His targets are many and various, including the grazier mentality; small town rivalries like that between Peeny and Uppersass; urban attitudes to bushfolk (and the tourists Percy terrorizes); the quest for heroes; the kind of racist philanthropy which produced Taanish village; dwellers in communes like the Rushcutters Bay aquatic co-op; the fear of invasion by Zionists/Orientals/Communists or all of these in different combinations; the advertising and business world; the pastoralists who hold sway in government. Mathers' targets are all around him, as though the absurdity is almost overwhelming and he scarcely knows where to start or stop.

Percy ponders, 'I could not see much logic in my stand but then I could not see much logic anywhere' (p.24). The aliases and the tarted-up disguises are Percy's too. Caught up in events which have no pattern, no logic, and which drive him into hiding in the wortarium, like William, he dons disguises and plays roles in search of one which might fit. He is variously Uppersass rustic, and deadly foe of the Peenyites; fugitive from police, from Thomas, from retribution in general; one-time 'Mountain Correspondent' of the Peeny Gazette; essayist on cows, verandahs, et al., writer of tales for tots; deliverer of bon mots and therefore a subversive of workers; alias Percy Grudder, the notorious gangster; enthusiast for botanical bric-a-brac; hatcher of money-making schemes; wanderer of the Woomera, rider of the Norton; shame and scourge of the Wort family. Inside that multiplicity of guises lurks Percy Wort, although he is not sure about that. A mind now encaverned contemplates those guises and the possibility that he is only his disguises, some kind of perforation. He ponders again: 'I have plenty of spirit, the trouble is it lacks lumps, coagulations or clots, those bodies of agitation, drive, performance and belief' (p.119). He can find no 'coagulations', no centre for his existence, except perhaps 'I exist at this instant to write my impressions' (p.189). What to do without coagulations? Throughout the papers Matters delivers to the reluctant Thomas, he agonises over the question, 'What is the MATTER with me?' Percy seeks an answer first through William and, finding none, then shifts uncertainly to his own experience.

I brooded over invoices, statements, reports and cables. What was wrong with me? Every time I put foot to rung of the ladder of success, every time I tried to ascend the ladder of achievement, a rung broke. In fact I stood in a heap of broken rungs. Would it be my fate to turn the ladder upside down and climb from inverted success to a rungless void?

I had no faith. I was like a perforation in an invoice. My father and brother had faith – was it that there was only a limited amount in the family? (p.177)

Without a foothold, only broken rungs, he feels growing despair – which plays over even the most extravagantly comic sequences. The self-parodying word becomes the only word that conveys.

Uppersass tends to be invaded by voyeuristic tourists come to see the rustics in the hills, but it is sometimes a temporary refuge from the chaos beyond it. Journeys, often journeys within journeys, criss-cross the face of the narrative and Australia: the trip with Ann towards Alice Springs, the visit to the co-op at Rushcutters Bay (which yields a fiancee of the itinerant kind), the many trips to and from Sydney in pursuit of a job (most of these ignominiously terminated). The Norton carries Percy through a constantly changing world that leaves him at best incredulous, at worst despairing and yearning for a hideout. One of the best sequences is his journey towards Sydney on the Norton, his way strewn with puzzling encounters, strange adversities, incomprehensible circumstances, and an extraordinary diversity of people. He sets out with fresh and noble intentions, his faith renewed:

I INTEND MAKING THIS JOURNEY AS NEAR PERFECT AS POSSIBLE, I thought to myself. Would smile at everyone, succour the distressed and aid the needy. As I travelled south I would be the unfastener on the zip of the dashed centre line – behind me the line would open – its jaw unmesh – and radiance pour out! However . . . jaws? Letting the light out? Am I, there-fore, inside a mouth, at the back of teeth, in some vast cavern? And, if travelling south, am I driving down a gullet? THIS IS PESSIMISTIC THINK-ING, I told myself. Continue the journey . . . (p.209).

As usual, the gap between his plan and the actuality leaves him anguished and consumed with self-doubt. His plan is his plot, his fiction, tested against the chaos. He encounters variously Bill Jones, spouse of the soap-maker; inmates of Taanish Village, the targets of contempt in the guise of benevolence; Nance the hitchhiker and source of Percy's fears of exposure as a pot-runner; two horsemen who casually intimidate the police; Boot and his thuggish offsiders; Betty the working lady; the oyster stall lady and Rosie the gun-moll. An extraordinary gathering of people – characteristic of Percy's talent for the improbable and incomprehensible. His encounters leave him weakened, his supplies of hope running down. His resolve to be altruistic and ever a salubrious influence on all he meets dwin-dles, dries up amid his shifting fear of menaces and his various attempts at seduction and avoiding seduction. This journey, which concludes with appropriate absurdity at the Farmers' Plaza Hotel, reflects the picaresque mode at its most overt: the bewildering succession of events and persons in a mesh of tangled purposes, the befuddled consciousness marvelling at bizarre circumstances and the urge to move on in search of something comprehensible. Through all of it, the further and faster he goes, the thinner he becomes, a wispy thing of self-doubt, some evanescent presence spread thin across events.

Percy's childhood recollections draw much on the presence of Thomas – and his resolve to continue failing by Thomas' standards. While Thomas labours entrepreneurially (with caves, the shipwreck, guileless children bearing rabbit skins, bicycle tyres, even seeing commercial possibilities in William), Percy works on infiltrating the enemy.

We grew to be a pair of sturdy rustic youths. Tom affected the town manner, I the rural, but as my style was stronger our average rusticity was quite high. He walked as though to the pavement born, I tended to plod. He was the office boy, I the farmer. He could not avoid my rural effluvia. (p.94)

Whenever the untoward occurs, which is frequently, Percy suspects the machinations of Thomas, at least in the cheaper circumstances. Thomas tends to loom larger than life for Percy, as a spectre of all that is rigidly conventional and narrow, all that is inimical to those who do not conform. When Percy is hiding out in the wortarium, Thomas besieges him from plane, horseback, van (with loudspeaker cunningly announcing forgiveness), and, according to Matters, has contemplated bringing in the army or black trackers or an army of black trackers, and has even tried to have Percy certified or outlawed. Thomas poses as guardian of Percy, the partisan in the hills writing 'brother-on-the-run' memoirs, but schemes to extirpate Percy and all that is unspeakably Wort from his own nature.

The Wort is construed in Uppersass as a general menace, like termites or cancer insidiously undermining all that is decent – and it is this, the Wort, that Thomas would eradicate from his own respectable self. In the events leading up to the geligniting of the bottle heap (narrated through the device of the 'Uppersass Reporting Prize'), the disgust of the local notables at the noisome Wort in their community is apparent – and this Thomas must expunge (quite apart from the intrinsic pleasure of persecuting Percy). The conflict between Thomas and Percy becomes an image of the tight antagonism between the determinedly conventional and the wayward subversive, each trying to eradicate the other as if thereby to eradicate disorder from their own lives and so bring the world into shape with a private conception of it.

As the novel reaches more recent events, just before Percy's move to the underground, Percy speculates more and more on where he might live and under what circumstances it might be possible to tolerate a return to the world. In the present is growing despair and a growing sense of trapped futility, which he tries to confront, express and perhaps overcome. He examines the fact of being encaverned, aware that quitting this cave can only lead to another, then dodges away into fantasies of learning the flute, before his dilemma reasserts itself.

Percy, my friend, you should derail this train of thought. Such thoughts derange sleepers.

However, I am awake and aware. Which makes it a little less horrible. Correction, a lot less horrible for when I put them to paper I am calmed. A little. (I have just looked over my shoulder.)

When you are in a hole write yourself out of it. For example, think of all the long words beginning with A like Austral-ia, -asian, -orp, -oid, aluminium (etc.)...and add and add and assemble at any, at all cost...Heap these words against the predicament and climb to safety. (pp.258-9)

As he broods over the choice between emerging or remaining encaverned, Percy resorts increasingly to verbal springboards to leap out of his predicament, following through associative digressions and word-plays and wilful contemplation of obscure topics (like verandahs) to find temporary relief. Although it has been a characteristic of the papers generally, his recourse to such verbal escapes becomes more frequent. Earlier Percy has warned that, as a writer of memoirs, he is quite prepared to 'dodge, dummy, feint, or forget' (p.112) whenever appropriate – and this is the key to the novel's extraordinary structure. Many of the apparently random meanderings into essays, fables, pseudo-scientific dissertation and changes in narrative perspective, are attempts to gain distance from his predicament by dodging and feinting. The guises of essayist, teller of tales, purveyor of medical bric-a-brac, even muser on verandahs, allow some relief, like verbal panacea. Percy is experimenting, testing: are words antidotes?

Like Matters' room at the start of the novel, his cave is 'lined with words, filled with them . . . In lines, thousands of them, black marks with white between ever flowing.' Matters wonders if they move around at night and thinks 'I should get the ladder and see if the right ones got back onto the light bulb . . .'. This is Percy's predicament too, at the end of the novel, as he ponders on the death of the word as Matters has at the start.

And all coming to an end they say. Farewell, Gutenberg, Caxton. Print interred . . . I read yesterday that communication, through print, is finished. Words no longer *convey*. Film IS. Every frame tells a story. Twenty-odd of them a second. Grave wherein the words do sleep. Plastic grave clothes, coffin and marker, lens-decorated. However there's no keeping out graverobbers.

> Peace,
> MATTERS.

In the final section, 'Murmuring Off', Percy is torn between the urge to leave the wortarium and the knowledge that there is nowhere to go, no place for him. He concocts fantastic visitors and conversations (like William's climactic visions on the coffin tramp).

Resuscitation is possible. Subterranean resuscitation is, however, quite hopeless. Therefore, my ascension from this cavity is essential if I am to put my idea to the test. Leave everything behind. Rise naked . . . I do not think I'll do this.

I will get out though, because I am beginning to feel unsettled here.

My heart has just completed an inchoate monologue . . . It chatters still. To show who's master I intend going daubed and naked after all . . .

After a quick survey I have re-descended. It was marvellous up there. A visit to a new world, and like all discoveries, not without pain. Thistles. Damned heart twittering like a bat. Wants to stay down here. I am master. I intend going naked and daubed to collect suit. (pp.281-2)

His second egress, his second ascension to the world, is the death of a painted man, the body discovered three days later by Matters. Resuscitation takes place fifteen years later, when Matters mines the family archives, and sends Thomas a hitherto unknown manuscript recently unearthed near the village of Uppersass, the Worteriana. The butterbox containing the disinterred words of Percy Wort, infamography, is offered up by Matters, 'the mild-mannered acolyte to demon Percy' (p.18). Matters insists, 'I am beyond risk, and I have gone my own way, Thomas.' (p.282). Matters becomes the graverobber, pilfering a body of words to send to Thomas. Resuscitation of the word *is* possible.

In *The Wort Papers*, the satiric distortions, verbal slapstick and stylistic diversions are directed more to portraying the chaotic consciousness of the displaced Percy than the outer chaos. Words, wortiana, are the means of contending with chaos, dodging it, describing it, dodging it again. Words do convey. They survive, passed on from persona to persona, with a life of their own. The Lie lives. The Liar pitting his word against the chaos.

Gerard Windsor has suggested that Mathers is a hyperactive writer, who moves at an exhausting speed and that his stories in *A Change for the Better* have the same frantic pace as his novels.

The breakneck development of action, the verbal decathalon followed by the linguistic pentathlon, the mass migrations of characters on and off stage, the sheer impatience with leisurely scene setting, description, characterisation, the surrealistic slides flashing on in rapid succession, the snap of the one-liners closing off the story - these are what make for the exhilaration of Mathers' stories, but they can also make for indigestibility.[11]

The stories are zany, absurdist, dense, gathering momentum, then accelerating, and finally running amok, until Mathers stops suddenly, breathless. There is much verbal play and inventiveness, word-games and ponderings, a fabulous comic proliferation bursting out of a single starting notion. As the comedy accelerates, Mathers draws the reader right inside his world, imposing with a bizarre logic his bearings, vantage points and orientations.

The title story is deceptively simple and realistic. Mathers begins with a 'hills' story, with a sergeant complaining of generally nefarious goings-on in the hills, with a gently paced story of the joy of transition to healthy peeping-Tom sexuality. Then the pace quickens in 'The Henshaws', with a quickstep account of up-and-down vicissitudes of the couple's commercial activities, zany in its speed, and then more speed in the wondrous train journey of Arthur and Alwyn. In 'Immersion', Mathers takes a single notion, that of information 'in the pipeline' and creates out of it an image of a successful potentate, Malcolm in solemn conclave in his bathrooms, notably the last retreat, the master bathroom. His aide, Tom, admires Malcolm's battles with the vortex waters above 'the great sombre relay caverns where swirl eddies beyond number, the vast exchanges of pipedom.'[12] Tom, possessor of the secret, takes over.

Two stories in *A Change for the Better* relate to *Trap*, one an embellishment of Paine's Panacea still favoured by Trap's landlady, the other with an Aborigine accepted as a Maori prince. There are hills stories, one with echoes of the itinerant Worts, another with rustics infected by noxious urban notions. One of the best stories is 'Chains', with Mathers grappling with the problem of impostors and bikie-impersonators, who imitate the sacred utterances of motorbikery and infiltrate the Movement, the true keepers of the tradition and its archives. Mathers is moved to incorporate a literary, artistic and cultural miscellany of motorbikery, before narrating misadventures at the hands of Rustics, Churls and Arguers on their way to a picnic. There, in misery, humiliation and siege, the gang is lectured on sloth, greed, parisitism, upstartery and general grossness, until left ignominiously enchained. Another bikie story, 'Plaster, Culture, Rape and Deprivation', ponders on the decline and fall of The Slurch, their spirit of ruffianship lost, a club of professionals with only a few showpiece deviates.

In 'Minutes', a tightly packed story of barely contained inventive possibilities in a single situation, there is a knock at the door.

At 2.40 an urgent summons to the lane door. The mirrors showed two children on the step. The secretary was cautious. Neither of the children could have reached the knocker. They did not attempt to flee. Therefore:
Were they leaping tinies and not children
Were they doorstep bait set by hidden giants
Or waifs left by lurking charity collectors
Or epoxy spring-loaded sculptures left by a shy artist
Or window dressers' models loaded with gelignite Etc. (p.135)

Further hazardous investigations reveal that they are the Bitt children seeking sanctuary. 'Many names were uttered. The secretary issued the customary caution concerning the reckless use of names. Unpleasant experiences were alluded to. The young visitors nodded knowingly then searched the lobby for bugs.' (p.135). All the possibilities crowd and jostle each other, representing circumstances both fabulous and horrific, hinting at a world that might run amok at any moment and turn hostile, devious, menacing, even murderous. Such is the world Mathers creates that every knock at the door, every incident, contains multitudinous and milling possibilities which it is his task to examine, perhaps to contain, perhaps to fall back exhausted.

Ever accelerating, Mathers traces change, both change in his characters' circumstances and the kind of change which ensues when words are springboards. His characters make plans, flimsy fragile things which cannot withstand the battering of the world and which chance and chaos casually conspire to thwart and distort, while they look on with dismay. At the same time, words keep opening up to Mathers new possibilities, which he pursues energetically, until they too open up tangents and connections and subterranean notions, with more subterranean gurglings going on below. Mathers draws it all, with one hand at work on the other one, as though he is split and divided among his own warring selves, but outside the frame is the Escher hand of the Liar. Mathers' extraordinary verbal energy can be exhausting but out of it grows a comic extravagance which is bizarre and brilliant. His underdogs, bikies, hooligans, rustics, business executives, his families, his characters ever on the move, inhabit a world that seems sometimes dangerously inventive, as though about to run amok, but behind the alarums and excursions, the Liar scrabbles round for words and finds the words to contain the chaos. Words do convey and it is possible to survive.

The last word: Word *IS*.

THIRD DIALOGUE

Reader Listen to this. I've found some more words for Percy Wort to heap up down there in his hole . . . This is Robbe-Grillet, talking about the traditional role of the writer, the writer as speleologist.

The role of the writer traditionally consisted in burrowing down into Nature, in excavating it, in order to reach its most intimate strata and finally bring to light some minute part of a disturbing secret. The writer descended into the chasm of human passions and sent up to the apparently tranquil world (that of the surface) victorious messages describing the mysteries he had touched with his fingers. And the sacred vertigo which then overwhelmed the reader, far from causing him any distress or nausea, on the contrary reassured him about his powers of domination over the world. There were abysses, it was true, but thanks to these speleologists their depths could be sounded.[1]

Liar: So? What's the point? Mathers does that. He sends messages back up to the surface. He's a dedicated speleologist.
Reader Oh yes, Mathers is down there excavating, but look what he comes up with. Look at the messages *he* sends back up. Chaos and anarchy underneath us. And look at this bit about the reader: 'Far from causing him any distress or nausea . . .' And this part, 'reassured him of his powers of domination over the world'.
Liar You're only thinking about yourself. How do you think Percy Wort feels? And Mathers? How do you think he feels about the 'mysteries he touched with his fingers'? Groping about through all the murk down there? All the nasty murk of history.
Reader But that's not all. Robbe-Grillet added, 'The *word* thus func

tioned as an ambush into which the writer lured the universe and then delivered it into the hands of society." It's not the universe that's ambushed now. It's me. Mathers sets up the *word* as an ambush for the reader.

Liar The difference is that the surface is no longer tranquil.

Reader No, the difference is greater than that. I'm in the abyss now. Mathers is the subterranean writer breaking up the surfaces, causing chaos and then nicking off – disappearing into a hole until the next uprising. Leaving David David and me, aghast, giggling, spluttering. Seeing things differently. Vertigo.

Liar All right, it's vertigo but it's not sacred vertigo now. It's secular. Outside the sacred institutions of fiction.

Reader It's worse than secular. It's profane. Heathen.

Liar Mathers would love that. A heathen's history. Blasphemy. The end of all the old shibboleths. Sacred cows lying bloodied across our past, desecrated carcases.

Reader It's also contagious. He's passed it on to me. Who am I? Reader–David–David–Adamov–X–Mathers. How do I know where to draw the line between them? Or which way I'm seeing things? All of us are suffering from Effect X. We've all contracted it. If this is collaboration, what sort of a contract is it? Is it with me or *on* me? The line has to be drawn somewhere.

Liar Lines are tainted too, you know. The lines between things have changed. Objective and subjective, inner and outer, they're all tainted now. What about Heisenberg and the Uncertainty Principle in quantum physics? How do you think a scientist felt having to face this sort of thing? Listen to this:

. . . we can no longer consider 'in themselves' those buildingstones of matter which we originally held to be the last objective reality. This is so because they defy all forms of objective location in space and time, and since basically it is always our *knowledge* of those particles alone which we can make the object of science . . .

Hear that? All we can examine is our own knowledge. This is a *scientist* speaking. And that's not all. Heisenberg continues,

. . . the common division of the world into subject and object, inner world and outer world, body and soul, is no longer adequate, and leads us into difficulties. Thus even in science the object of research is no longer nature itself, but man's investigation of nature. Here, again, man confronts himself alone.[2]

Reader All right, so the old view of an objective reality 'out there' no longer holds. Nature is no longer an independent reality objectively apart from man. Does that justify heathen history and ambushes? Does it justify terrorizing me? Does it justify the Lie?

Liar I don't know about justifying but it's a reason. An explanation of the Lie. It's an important part of my logic. We can no longer objectively observe the world. At least, not without talking about the means of observation and the influence of the observer. So if man is both actor and spectator, participant and observer, then the emphasis shifts to observation as a form of interaction.

Reader Or transaction. Literature as a transaction, some kind of deal. Perhaps I could try negotiating a better deal. Better working conditions for readers. Maybe we could form a union. We could have strikes and picketers. Proper awards. Honest writers. No more lies and subterfuge.

Liar Depends what you're looking for. Just honesty? Or truth? Because the truth is uncertainty. And it's not just Heisenberg's Uncertainty Principle. It's more than the discovery of a residuum of chance in nature. It's recognizing an incorrigible ambiguity in the human act of observation. In the post-Heisenbergian world, all of us, even scientists, have had to learn to tolerate the ambiguity and accept the contradictions. What makes you think you should be immune?

Reader It was easier, more comfortable . . .

Liar Of course it was. Do you want comfort or truth? The truth is indeterminacy. Always the uncertainty holds, always there is a margin of indeterminacy . . . and ambiguity. There is also the quantum Principle of Complementarity. Not just waves and not just particles, but both. So you get 'wavicles'. Tolerating the ambiguity of both. That's the other aspect of this that really matters.

Reader All right, so you're saying that if the old opposites between inner and outer realities don't hold, I need a new tolerance of ambiguity. I suppose that means I need new versions of time and space too. No wonder I was feeling the strain.

Liar And new versions of history. If you reject a mechanistic view of time and space, you reject the old mechanistic view of history. If your sense of time and space changes, of course, your sense of history does too ... And it's not only an aesthetic change. It has a political substratum as well. It means an acute consciousness of time and it involves new stances towards the past. A disavowal of the past.

Reader Back to Mathers and Effect X.

Liar It's not only Mathers ... What about Carey? Bail? Hasluck? And Foster. Particularly Foster in this context, because of the quantum logic. *Moonlite* is a parody of a history of scientific and religious ideas, with a quantum perspective.

Reader What about *The Adventures of Christian Rosy Cross*? Alchemy in the fourteenth century.

Liar That's exactly what we've been talking about. The old divisions between spirit and matter, body and soul, inner and outer. Foster's on a quest for the secret of matter. Literary alchemy. If you want to show changes in the way we see things, wreak them! Transmutation.

Reader A Literary Alchemy. The writer as a Paracelsian adept, a demented hirsute figure, eyes aglow over the furnace, watching for the moment of conjunction when the fiction's cooked. So where does that leave me? As demented as the writer, transmuted too?

Liar It can't happen without you. So you're there too, collaborating. By quantum logic you influence what happens. You're not just a spectator. You're a participant now. No more standing back passively watching. A participant-observer.

Reader It was easier, just watching. It used to be a lot more comfortable when I could just follow through a logical sequence and see what happened.

Liar It was a lot more comfortable in the nineteenth century too, when the universe worked like clockwork. Everything ticking away to a logical end. Progress all around you. At least, that's how it seemed. The ticking we all hear now is different. Ticking away to the moment when a finger presses the button. Einstein said God doesn't play dice with the universe. He mightn't, but look at us.

Reader Do you think you can stop it with Lies?

Liar What if reality's a Lie? What if people look around them with a radical distrust and a profound disbelief? What if we feel we can't trust reality any more?

Reader Do you think Lying is going to change that?

Liar If you collaborate, we can change the way we see things. And the whole point of quantum logic is this – the way we see things actually changes the things we see.

Reader Literary alchemy. All you need is the Philosopher's Stone. The Liar's Stone . . .

Liar . . . which brings us to Foster. He's a literary alchemist. He takes matter and transmutes it through parody. Zany picaresques through space and time. Comic extravaganzas. Quests for the essence of things.

Reader Changing the way we see things.

Liar That's what parody is all about. Take the original, find its secret, then transmute it. There is always that double mode, the original's always there, underneath the parody. Two modes at once, and flipping from one to the other. Complementarity.

Reader Or convex and concave . . . Do you know the Escher print, *Cube with Magic Ribbons*?

Liar You beat me to it. I was going to ask you that. I have a feeling that my voice is going to be supplanted.

Reader We're collaborators, aren't we? In the laboratory together?

THE ALCHEMY OF THE LIE *DAVID FOSTER*

there *is*, a Seclet Art: there *is*, a way to blake through shadow. And when a man succeed in this art, he seear lainbow, and he hearer sound of thunder. And the sky is filled with dark cloud for him, and when he close his eye, he feela laindlop falling on his head. And this is the Tlute . . .

Moonlite, David Foster

We have made it, it is not
Real gold found naturally
But it is not counterfeit
Like gold made by Art
It excels that found in nature
In all but visibility
The impure and the blind may say
Fool's gold: but alchemists grew rich
Feeding the same invisible seed as we

The Fleeing Atalanta, David Foster

'Yes, anything that turns the mind towards chemistry is welcome in my laboratory; the problem is, deciding what to keep out.'

'How do you mean?'

'Well, after a few years at the bench, everything takes on chemical meaning. The mind, victim of an *idee fixe* and demented through overwork, starts to see everything in hermetic terms. It's not uncommon for a chemist to suffer delusions of mantic grandeur, in which he surveys the macrocosm as though from the right-hand side of God. Such a man eventually retires from the lab and moves into the study, where he sets about composing a lucubration that allows of as many interpretations as there are literates in the *oikoumene*. Such are the majority of chemical works, but the book M was written when practice kept pace with theory.'

'Then you don't think . . . '

'I never think, Christian. It's fatal to the bench chemist. I've seen it happen too many times. No, perseverance is the answer; speculation solves nothing. Any fool can speculate but making the Tincture demands Art. I don't deny the Resurrection, but see this retort in my hand? It is a retort. It is not the soul of man. It is not the womb of the Virgin Mother. It is not the belly of the Microprosopus. It's a retort, and nothing else. You see, when the ancient chemists decided to conceal their nomenclature, the favorite and natural butt for their spleen were their bitter antagonists, the mystics. Out of context, it's almost impossible for us to understand their satire. What was meant as parody is often taken for the Real Thing, and vice versa. That strike you as paradoxical?'

'Yes and no' says Christian.

'Why don't we make our own lead, Bernard?'

'We can't make base metals Christian; we don't know their composition. We can only make gold, which has no impure sulphur, by means of our Stone, which is pure quicksilver. Basically, that which is volatile and flees the fire, like a dove, is called soul; that which remains in the fire, like a salamander, is called body; and that which unites body and soul is called mercury, or spirit. Now if the soul remains with the body we have success. But what generally happens is the soul rises taking the body with it. To watch the furnace closely is the whole secret of the Art. Nature, alone, cannot effect the desired union of body and soul which is brought about by our Stone; there is no one to take the vessel from the heat.

'Basically speaking, the artist watches for the proper moment, and after the conjunction, fears nothing more from the fire: it's all in the books. When conjunction takes place, brought about by a well-tempered fire, the action of which is stopped by the watchful, many remarkable phenomena occur. Afterwards the artist rests . . . I cannot stress too strongly the secret is in the fire . . .

The Adventures of Christian Rosy Cross [1]

•

THE ART OF ALCHEMY IS the central dialectic of David Foster's work, in both form and content. Like fiction, alchemy is a dialectic between spirit and matter, between reality and vision, substance and reverie of mind. Alchemy is a language of unity and conjunction, of enlightenment and individuation, and a quest which drives the solitary alchemist through the mysteries of matter. 'The secret is in the fire': Foster's work becomes a dialectic of parody and celebration, of old and new forms, of spirit and matter, of reality and dream, of the self and the encompassing chaos. Two-faced, twin-edged, summoning up the original at the same time as it parodies it, parody proposes and deposes, inherits modes of thought and then disinherits them, denies them their legacy. It works along old salients of consciousness – of time and space and self – and shows them thinning, petering out until they fall back spent, unable to contend with contemporary existence. Summoning up the Tincture of his Art, Foster's is the alchemy of the Liar, forging fictions out of matter and transmuting reality into Lie.

The alchemical quest is the substance of the novel Foster regards as his *magnum opus*, *The Adventures of Christian Rosy Cross*. In the introduction to it, he discusses a kind of 'Sufic satire', that is, a work superficially satirical, yet incorporating at a structural level those very esoteric elements it purportedly ridicules. Such a work may be offered, with some equanimity, both to friend and foe, and indeed, in its very ambiguity, conforms to Hermetic tradition.

Foster's own work has a Hermetic ambiguity. It both satirizes and celebrates traditions and conventions of thought, and has some of the old antagonisms: between science and mysticism, reason and illogic; tyrannical mind and insurrectionary spirit; structures of thought reaching out to encompass the world and watching in profound dismay as the unencompassable stands defiant. The conflicts and tensions in his work spring from a constant awareness of the polarity of things. Parody – in its dialogue with celebration – becomes a language of conjunction.

Foster's characters are picaros on a grand scale, searching for the talismanic secret of things – the land of Purity, the Philosopher's Stone and the secret of the universe – the moment of conjunction and enlightenment, the fiery secret of truth. Behind it all is Foster's own quest for the secret of things, and his constant parody of his own Lie. In all the quests of his novels, Foster is the Liar groping through paradoxes and paradigms of twentieth century thought and mocking his own enterprise. In an interview in *Yacker*, Foster commented:

the sort of anger and cruelty that's obvious in most of my work is a source of consternation at an intellectual level, but I have to accept that, if I want to write, then hopefully these things will work themselves out.[2]

He once said, 'my despair is beyond political despair. It's almost theological despair'.[2] Yet his stance is the classic one of the satirist, a fundamental optimism. The satirist, like the alchemist, thinks he can change things, manipulate them into new shapes and substances, mould the world anew into more pleasing forms. Questioned about his work, Foster talks of

ambivalence, flippancy, obscurity, wit, gnosticism, guilt, schizophrenia, monomania, disgust, and the struggle to emerge from all this ratiocination grown tired towards something better . . .[3]

The struggle seems constant, the striving as relentless as the alchemist's, the Artist-adept bent over the furnace searching for the secret of matter, waiting for the moment of conjunction when base reality is transmuted into the Lie. Behind the parody, there is a radical innocence, a stubborn and ineradicable trust that the quest will pay off, that one day gold will appear in the fire.

Foster is kin to Barth, Pynchon, and Vonnegut, writing comic extravaganzas, absurdist quests for the essence of things and, with the Tincture of the Art, 'composing lucubrations that allow many interpretations'. Among Australian writers, with the exception of Furphy, he finds little in common with his own work. Foster's work has a driving energy which is comically inventive like Furphy's but which is also zanily extravagant, with a high voltage, both in language and in event. Like Mathers, an Australian writer he admires, Foster has a restless energy, a lunatic inventiveness, and can be exhausting. And like Mathers, Foster is drawn to the indeterminacy of the picaresque mode. Both have an acute consciousness of time and change, of history as the fast and furious passage of event across crowded place and space, with a horde of possibilities jostling for position. The energy behind Foster's and Mathers' work is similar, a tension between parody and celebration, high voltage energy and despair, an intensity of delight and disgust with the absurdity of things.

Foster takes conventions, of literature, of history and of ideas, and manipulates them to new ends. His base matter is the existing literary form: the family saga in *The Pure Land*, the picaresque mode in *Moonlite*, a stardom odyssey in *Plumbum*, the journey to the east in *The Adventures of Christian Rosy Cross*; the detective mode in *Dog Rock*. Because all his work is unmistakably parodic – of modes of thinking as well as literary form – he finds it depressing to have to make statements like: 'I'm essentially a farce writer' and 'I'm not a social-realist writer and I'm not trying to get down a portrait of life as it's lived but rather to describe the changes of thought . . .'.[2] It seems inconceivable that the parody form of his work could be missed, but Foster has found that some Australian critics do not

recognize the *form* of satire . . . . It appears quite beyond the average academic reviewer to treat a work in the genre to which it obviously belongs . . . . They're quite uncomfortable with modernism despite the fact that it's sixty years old, and they're *totally* at a loss with postmodernism. It's like an art critic getting up in front of a Picasso and saying: 'I can't really recognize any of the features in this landscape, so therefore it's bad art'.[2]

Foster's novels are comically extravagant and demanding, offering an abundance of propositions which are sometimes difficult to plumb and reluctant to yield up all their meanings. Drawing freely on an extraordinary range of ideas and philosophies, fleet of word and mind, he keeps up a flashing narrative pace which apparently outruns some critics.

Foster's work was first published about the time of *Trap* and *The Wort Papers* and the early Ireland novels. Born in 1944, he spent his early childhood in Katoomba in the Blue Mountains, where part of *The Pure Land* is set. He studied science at Sydney University and the A.N.U., and in 1970 spent a year in U.S.A on a post-doctoral fellowship. Like Danny in *The Pure Land*, he returned to Australia disaffected with science, and he began to write, working in different jobs, including a period as a removalist and, like D'Arcy D'Oliveres in *Dog Rock*, as a postman. Foster now lives with his wife Gerda and their children in Bundanoon, N.S.W.

His first book, *North South West*, a collection of three novellas, was published in 1973, and his second, *The Pure Land*, shared the 1974 *Age* Book of the Year Award. In 1977, there was a collection of short stories, *Escape to Reality*, a collection of poetry, *The Fleeing Atalanta*, which abounds with alchemical symbols, and, in collaboration with D. Lyall, a slight work of science fiction about dope and deviant scientists called *The Empathy Experiment*. In 1978 Foster won the Marten Bequest for prose, which enabled him to spend some time in the St.Kilda Islands in the Outer Hebrides off the west coast of Scotland. There he researched *Moonlite* (1981), which won the National Book Council Award and the N.S.W. Premier's Award. *Plumbum* followed in 1983, *Dog Rock* in 1985, in 1986 *The Adventures of Christian Rosy Cross* and in 1987 *Testostero*. His two most important novels I consider to be *Moonlite* and *Christian Rosy Cross*, but *Dog Rock* is a favourite too.

Foster's first significant work was *The Pure Land*, a novel about warring impulses, origins and dislocation, both private and national, which works through the convention of the family saga. The founder of the dynasty, Manwaring, leads his family to the promised land, United States, where they undergo trial and disillusion until his grandson, Danny, returns to Australia in search of an authentic past and the essence of a future. Through the three generations, Foster conducts a kind of family experiment, investigating the war of emotion and reason in the Manwaring bloodline, the first skirmish between the contestant forces in his work. In the mists of the Blue Mountains, clad in foolish hopes and innocent dreams, Manwaring is a creature of sentiment, seeker of euphoria, one with 'that familial surfeit of emotion'.[4] His life has a perilous uncertainty, a malaise of the spirit. In Katoomba, he gropes with his camera through 'his sere, beloved landscapes' (p.24) in search of vision, 'the familiar urge . . . a lust towards unity' (p.25). He is a seeker who regards his physical self as some excrescence, a scrotum dangling under his larger spiritual body. The turning point is his vision splendid in the bush when he stumbles onto a couple in a clearing and photographs them in pure wonderment. Then, a displaced person, he awaits the call to America – to the promised land. When he is offered a job as pornographic film-maker in the United States, his self-delusion is both poignant and comic: he is the perpetual innocent with soaring hopes, trusting the world will realize his dreams.

In the central sequence of the novel, both Manwaring and Janet are displaced persons, living in an America which is crude and garish, squalid and sullied. Her life a plinth for her son, Janet attempts to redeem the family line for the sake of Danny. She struggles to control the Manwaring impulses in herself, the urge to extremes and intensities, acting as 'some sort of half-way house, a *tertium quid* between her father and her son' (p.113). Behind Janet is the comic poignancy of Manwaring, now a religious fanatic in an ashram, a saffron-robed devotee of the Bhagavad Gita and a spectre hovering distantly over Danny's childhood and scientific studies. As Danny's discontent with science intensifies, he begins to conceive of the self not as an objective observer of one small corner of the universe, but as part of a continuum, where there is no observer and observed, no discontinuity. Mind and body are 'that old ignored nexus' (p.178). He insists that 'the alchemists have been misunderstood and their art perverted' (p.162) and, like Christian Rosy Cross, he becomes a seeker. Manwaring warns him intellect is the problem and suggests that, while few Australians experience the need for enlightenment, Australia may be 'the last place', the Land of Purity. Danny resolves to seek his Pure Land but the transition is painful. His journey back to the origins of things brings a profound inner numbness and self-mockery, a sense of being stripped down to a residual self.

Australia, Danny writes to Sylvia, is a very young country: 'why then does it seem so old? So worn out, so effete . . .' (p.206). Foster toys with notions of Australia as ten or twenty years behind the times, of an art which is derivative and a culture which is innocent. But Danny is teaching himself to regard time and space with a new set of co-ordinates, checking his academic habits of mind and eye. In the Blue Mountains, dislocated and purposeless, he seeks 'the head-waters of all this flowing, flowing'. The discovery of Manwaring's photographs authenticates his own origins and he lists them painstakingly, as if clues to his own identity. A discrepancy in dates confuses him, but he decides this is a final test, an illogic to test the apostate who has renounced his faith in fact and chosen a new faith in the continuum of existence. Danny is the Manwaring self transformed, come to conjunction. *The Pure Land* is finally a novel of wry celebration of the possibilities of private and national enlightenment. With inveterate optimism, Foster suggests an Australian self seduced by the sleazy appeal of America but wrenching itself back to examine its own origins and seek its own true substance.

Although Foster, like Danny, decided against a career in science, scientific thinking remains an important force in his novels, one of the warring parties in the dialectic of his work. His interest now is 'particularly the way many contemporary scientists see science as becoming mystical. The avant garde of scientists are now studying books like *The Tao of Physics*.'[5] The notion of a Taoist physics is the kind of paradox on which his work turns. His parody – whether religious, social, historical or philosophical – is directed at those modes of thought which try to reduce things to a single set of principles. His novels set up a comic rivalry between the encompassed and the encompassing, with the constant paradox of all that lies outside, unencompassable, recalcitrant, untouched. Foster's is a quantum logic of ambiguity and complementarity, the logic of Ar Wat's Tlute and Seclet Art in *Moonlite*. The driving force in all Foster's mythic and metaphysical quests is an intimation that, underneath the surface polarity, is the Seclet continuum of Tlute.

Moonlite, which I regard as Foster's best novel and one of the most important novels ever written in Australia, is an absurdist biography of Finbar ('Moonlite') MacDuffie and a parodic history of changes in our concepts of the universe, linking systems of scientific and religious thought. It starts on the island of Hiphoray with the notion that natural phenomena are manifestations not of causality but of cosmic spleen, temperamental outbursts which man can placate. When Donald suggests phenomena might act in accordance with reason and with laws of cause and effect, the MacEsaus marvel at the idea but see no conflict with their own animism. At Newbridge College Finbar's mathematical research into light and optics uncovers further cosmic data and principles of physical systems which undermine theology. He ponders on the statistical probability of Christianity and mathematically rejects it. He is sent down – which becomes Down Under in nineteenth century Gold Rush Australia. There Ar Wat explains the Tlute.

In Foster's work, every quest has many angles, every novel many levels and layers in a Tangled Hierarchy of reality and farce. *Christian Rosy Cross* is variously an alchemical quest for the essence of things, a journey to the east in search of Jungian unity, an analogue of the 1960s drug culture, and a mock-biography of the hoax-founder of Rosicrucianism. Set in an era of transition from late medieval religious thought to Renaissance scientific thought, it is also a parody of fledgling Protestantism. So too *Moonlite* has many faces and levels tangled together: Finbar is at once a prophet of Druidic and Christian lore in a comic picaresque, an inebriate Candide, a mathematical visionary, a larrikin quester and a quantum logician in a four-act farce. He is also an Albino Tiresias emigrating to the Colonies, in a parody of Australian Gold Rush history. In *Moonlite*, Foster plays with colonialism and political parody – from the mildewed society on the island of Mugg, ruled by The MacIshmael from his waterlogged fort, and dominated by his habit of trading island rights to pay off his creditors, to Hiphoray, where parliament worked smoothly in rotation between the two parties of the Gillies and the Murdos until Donald introduced talking and voting. Then on through the evolution of capitalist exploitation and notions of law on Hiphoray – and on again to the comic social and political reversals in Australia where Finbar stands as sole candidate for Premier in the land where everything is upside down.

On Hiphoray, 'going over' the cliffs is the central MacEsau rite – a rite of manhood and a sacred religious rite, designed to control the whims of Bel, the sun. Murdo and Gillie, the twin collective selves of the MacEsaus, listen carefully to Donald's rational, causal explanation of the sun's heavenly movements, but they are puzzled by his 'habit of letting one thing exclude another, equally likely'.[6] With a hospitable logic, the MacEsaus are happy to entertain contradictions, and a few more ritually reject causal logic and hurl themselves over the cliff, to bring back the sun and the light of vision. Here, amid images of light and dark, of vision and blindness, Finbar is born, an albino with thick white hair. The Son of the Dark Fairy, blinded by sunlight but with night vision, Finbar is ready for the numerous paradoxes of vision and optics running throughout *Moonlite*. When Finbar searches for a Sidhe fairy, he receives instead a blinding vision of the Spirit Host – the Holy Ghost, the only member of the Trinity worthy of attention in modern times. Against the Spirit, Finbar pits science and mathematics – logic.

On Hiphoray change is slow until the advent of Christian capitalism, the Reverend Campbell and tourism. Campbell, Finbar's mentor, inculcates fundamentalist theology in the respite between tourist ships. The tourist brochures promise 'Lost isle on the warl's edge, fust glimpses, savages frae the dawn o' time' (p.71), with MacEsaus running down the cliffs to fetch coins thrown by the visitors, a cottage industry making souvenir stuffed parrots and the island songs transcribed and transmogrified by the Friends of Hiphoray. After the first wave of wealthy, aristocratic tourists, come the nouveau riche, parvenu do-gooders, romantics and testy scholars, until eventually Hiphoray becomes a battleground between scientists and tourists, each seeking dominion over the islanders. The whole structure of Hiphoray society breaks down, but the tourists keep coming in hope of seeing a MacEsau 'go over'.

Moonlite is about angles of vision, and optics, as well as philosophical, political, scientific and social structures. Although existence, which is change and fluidity, is simplified with structures, Finbar tries out various structures and finds them wanting, unable to encompass the fluidity. He decides

the real problem – I see it in my lucid moments – is the incapacity of language to deal with the complexities of life, when categories become fluid.

We say a man is good or bad – but he's generally good in one respect, bad in another. And these respects are infinite . . . The beauty of the Catholic Church – and all such institutions – is that they simplify speech, by simplifying life . . . (p.207)

Finbar toys with this decided aesthetic advantage of Christianity but takes up reason instead. He becomes a mathematician at Newbridge College, a den of vice and hypocrisy, where assorted academics, politicians and lawyers strut and preen through the wondrous rituals and mores of academic life. Finbar encounters self-styled luminaries and penners of vapid poesy, and he becomes the scourge of theological debaters and of the depraved, the humourless prophet delivering a thunderous philippic, a pious creature and misfit mathematician.

Context is all and text nothing, and in the natural obfuscation, future adepts in politics and the law learn to flap their wings and fly, like gugas in a fog. No, thinks Finbar, thank God for maths, where elegance is possible, confusion never. (p.131)

With special glasses to correct his backscattering vision, he discovers the diurnal world and dedicates himself to optics and the geometric study of the optical phenomenon of the glory and the rainbow, pitting science and reason against the Light of God, trying to contain his visionary insights in elegant mathematial equations. The gnostic joker, Mungo, deplores Finbar's primitive causal approach and preaches the joys of alcohol, to enlarge his visionary powers. But, as Finbar begins the transition to new alcoholic visions, he uses logic to prove that nothing is certain, and insists that 'Life is a sequence of disparate events strung together by whim' (p.158). Tormented now by real and illusory problems of mathematics, truth and faith, he disproves Christianity and is sent down, with a new inebriate talent for grasping the ways of the world.

In Foster's work themes run up and down a Godelian Tangled Hierarchy and then loop around to their own beginnings, generally at breakneck speed in an extraordinary vortex of comic energy and interlocking layers and levels of narrative. *Moonlite* is a spiritual odyssey from primitive pantheism, pagan and Druidic faith, passing by some Biblical landmarks (Ishmael and Esau and Cain), on through fundamentalist Christianity to the dogmatics and exegetics of Newbridge, then on to Aboriginal spirituality. Through Finbar's life loop paradigms and paradoxes of religious thought, the whole a comic apocalyptic religious quest, with Finbar the spiritual quester, an eclectic picking through the metaphysical choices, including the Oriental offerings of Ar Wat's 'Seclet Art'.

'Ah the Tlute the Tlute – who know what the Tlute leally is my son? Gotta holda two views at once. The Tlute is not this, is not that is a combination.'

'Fair enough. But how do you know which view to select in a given predicament? You see, I'm a logical sort of cove hic.'

'Aha – *you* don't select. If *you* select you makar long choice! *You* don't leally exist! You justar – howyousay – leflection . . .'

'Yes, is clear now. Look alound you mate – you think is dead set?'

'I reckon!'

'No – is only shadow. Let me put it to you this way: there *is*, a Seclet Art: there *is*, a way to blake through shadow. And when a man succeed in this art, he seear lainbow, and he hearer sound of thunder. And the sky is filled with dark cloud for him, and when he close his eye, he feela laindlop falling on his head. And this is the Tlute . . .' (p.199)

The Tlute is contradiction, the self a reflection, reality only a shadow, but there is a Seclet Art to break through the shadow and see the rainbow.

Layers of complementary images of literary optics run through *Moonlite*: from Finbar's backscattering vision, his day and night vision, the theme of the glory and the rainbow at Newbridge, to Australia and 'the piebald pair' (p.205), Sunbeam and Finbar (now christened 'Moonlite'). Aboriginal and albino, black and white, night and day creatures, Moonlite and Sunbeam are soul mates, both primitives Christianized. They share spirits, The Host, Finbar's spirit–familiars, and the Wawa from Hiphoray, Sunbeam's home becoming the Land of the Dark Fairy (p.192). Both Moonlite and Sunbeam are linked with the Rainbow Fella and with Ar Wat's 'lainbow'. The novel has taken us far from the Newbridge theme of optics and rainbows, only to suddenly loop back to rainbows and the glory. Urged by Ar Wat to seek the Tlute in a mission camp at a garbage dump, Finbar is spreadeagled and staked by the wrists and ankles, there to undergo 'A sequence of vivid two-dimensional visions, beginning with a bird's eye view of Hiphoray' (p.212). The final test of whether Finbar is a spirit fella is to kill him, to see whether he comes back. After he undergoes ritual death and rebirth, an albino Christ-figure, he resolves to stand for Premier (unopposed) and rectify all the wrongs of the colony. But alas he dies and, in a portentous exit, Finbar, the Son of the Dark Fairy leaves Boomtown, while Foster delivers an apocalyptic oration to New West highlands as the Last Frontier, City of refuge, still clinging to the Old Way, worshipping the Travesty at two removes. Climb or Let Go, the patience of God is exhausted.

Moonlite is a parody of the convention of the gentleman-emigrant to the colonies, which intersects with the parody family saga which in turn cuts across the parody biography of the philosopher and visionary. In the layers of occult and religious speculation, of literary and historical parody, of zany and bizarre adventures, Finbar's course is full of unexpected twists and turns, and he becomes an absurd Candide, a larrikin Tiresias in a novel which delights in optic games and verbal paradoxes. *Moonlite* becomes also a 'Sufic' version of Australian history. Finbar travels to Australia in a succinct parody of convict transportation and arrives at the goldfields thirsting for an odyssey through the thirty-seven pubs of Boomtown. Punctuating his travels with outbursts of religious and mathematical lore, Finbar wanders through goldfields history, observing the Australian identity being forged out of a mixture of wayward European, Jewish, Shi'ite and Chinese traditions, particularly their several commercial lores. The Ockers are already filling the pubs of the burgeoning nation in the land where even the seasons are unnatural: 'No good this place . . . Never change'm *seasons* here! Leaves on trees all time same. No *nostalgia* possible this place. You deprived pella you!' (p.189–90). This is the land where everything is upside down and, in comic inversion, Foster plays with figures from Newbridge: Mungo has renounced drink and espoused a missionary piety, while Ducksbury from Haughty Manor has renounced his life as puffed-up stooge of the ruling class and become Comrade Ducksbury, champion of the oppressed workers. A comic reversal of alchemy, the Gold Rushes seem to promise an 'illicit alchemy' (p.108) whereby illicit wealth might turn to lead

if the new West Highlands becomes, as well as a penal colony, a treasure trove and cynosure for every rogue in the west, it's possible to envisage a total collapse of order and the eventual emergence of a culture that signs its name back to front and upside down, a veritable thieves' kitchen, where virtue is mocked, breeding reviled, discipline flouted and work eschewed. (p.106)

Foster plays inventively with the notion of a national alchemy in the Gold Rushes. Did transmutation take place? From the base matter of the Gold Rushes, what came forth? Spiritual gold? Or was the base matter intransigent, still base? Foster is the Artist-adept with Australian history in the furnace.

Michael Cotter suggests *Moonlite* is

'a quicksilver tale', a myth of the nature of colonialism: a stylistic interlocution of folklore, scientific and philosophic discourse, hilarious dialogue and situation, sermonic hellfire and a supremely irreverent narrative, whose cynical cheerfulness is sometimes almost overpowering.[7]

The quicksilver image of fluid mobility and alchemical change is also apt for the novel which in a sense is the very core of Foster's work, the 'magnum opus' he worked on for many years. *The Adventures of Christian Rosy Cross* is the key to all his work. Like *Moonlite*, it is mock-biography and a picaresque quest, at once ancestor and contemporary of the quests of Finbar and Danny, the rock band of *Plumbum* and the twins of *Testostero*. Like Danny and Finbar, Christian seeks unity of matter and psyche, mind and body, the alchemical 'spirit in matter'. Christian's adventures in search of the Philosopher's Stone in the fourteenth century are also, by comic analogue and anachronism, in the twentieth century.

In Hasluck's *The Bellarmine Jug*, the Rosicrucians are linked with the grim aftermath of the seventeenth century wreck of the *Batavia* and are part of a philosophical and historical thriller. Foster's interest is in the Rosicrucian link with alchemy, the duality of rose and cross. He draws on the Rosicrucian tradition as an expression of gnostic and hermetic traditions, using the arcane symbols of alchemy: sun and moon, leprosy, mercury, red tincture, Venus and Cupid, dew (Latin *ros*) and the Rosegarden, as well as geometric symbols. Foster also points to the links with Lutheranism and sees the Rosicrucian hoax as perhaps an attempt 'to insinuate the tenets of spiritual alchemy into the fledgling Protestant religion'. Through the period of transition in the history of ideas, from late medieval religious thought to Protestantism and Renaissance scientific thought, Foster continues his perennial quest for reconciliation of the two systems of thought and for the essence, the essential behind the contingent. Underneath the narrative is the constant paradox that the existence of Christian Rosenkreutz, the putative founder of the Rosicrucian Brotherhood, is historically a matter of hoax, counterfeit and conjecture. Foster takes historical hoax and celebrates it with his own mock version, on which he builds his own Lie. Underneath every step of Christian's journey are layers of narrative which mirror each other: below the historical hoax lies parody of the hoax 'facts', and below that are Foster's own counterfeit 'facts' of Christian's life. And underneath those layers in the Tangled Hierarchy is the Liar writing about the twentieth century, working his own alchemy.

Foster draws on the work of Michael Maier, a seventeenth century alchemist and apologist for the Rosicrucian movement, and on *The Chemical Marriage of Christian Rosencreutz*, a comic romance of travel through a hermetic wonderland – which purports to be his allegorical autobiography. Rich pickings here for the Liar. Foster's mock-biography uses the 'facts' of Christian's life: his birth into the noble family of the Comte de Rosencreutz in Germany in 1378; his early years in the cloister; at sixteen, his departure with a monk on a pilgrimage to the Holy Land; his time in Damascus and, in the city of Damcar, his meeting with wise men; his journey to Fez in Morocco and return to Europe via Spain, where the Spanish mocked his learning; and his return to Germany, where with four associates he started the secret Order of the Rosy Cross, with a secret language and ideals of perfecting the self and nature.

According to the 'legend', he remained in Germany until his death at the age of 106 in 1483 (the year of Luther's birth and ten years before the birth of Paracelsus). He was buried in a secret tomb, found 120 years later (with instructions for it to be opened at that time) – the period when the so-called Rosicrucian Manifestos began to appear, including a 1612 skit entitled *Universal Reformation of the Whole Wide World*. This becomes Christian's catchcry.

At the start, Foster is plotting the twin polarities of *ros* and cross.

Living is dangerous, but dying is most dangerous, as Heaven and Hell still exist. Life has meaning . . . They are good days, these early days, because the *ros*, the dew of reality, is still on earth, even the earth of Europe. (p.4)

In the cloister of his childhood, Christian is baptised in a mercury bath before Cornelius introduces him to the Art of the laboratory, the phials, furnaces and the philosophical egg seething in a vat of putrescent matter. Although the Thomist prior insists the Vas Philosophorum is man's soul, Christian is hooked and begins his alchemical quest for The One, the integration of matter and psyche. In this era of Papal Schism, of rivalry between Dominicans and Franciscans, Spanish Inquisition and heretics burning at the stake, Christian is at first a precocious and boorish anti-hero, suffering from a permanent erection and leprosy. When herbal nostra and ritual exorcism fail to cure him, he sets out with Brother Pal for the Holy Land, on an absurdist Pilgrim's Progress, in quest of his Grail.

The novel abounds in arcane and mythic symbols, with numerous comic twists and turns, such as the ritual mockery of Christian as a scapegoat in Venice or the ludic twist behind the ancient book he finds in Venice, which reveals the Art to the elect. Written in cipher, it is *The Light of Lights* by Rhases, but it is also the Book *M* of which Christian himself was the author – according to the hoax facts of Rosicrucian 'legend'. The novel abounds in twists and paradoxes like this, constantly compounding its own Lie. In Rhodes, which crawls with philosophers and chemists and rose-bushes, Christian learns from Bernard about the Red Tincture of the Philosophers, which transmutes metals into the purest gold. But all the Tincture was sold to a German Apothecary in a medicine called 'Leper's Mercury' – the medicine Christian was given. There are numerous instances of this kind of inner loop of narrative, so that as it runs forward it also spirals inwards, with a movement which is both progressive and looping back to its beginnings. Throughout *Christian Rosy Cross*, Foster plays with the Lie of fiction, the Tincture of the Artist–Alchemist, the Paracelsian writer. With ludic references to his own literary art, Foster suggests notions of composition, dissolution, lucubration and parody. Making the Tincture demands Art and 'Dissolution is the first part of our Art' (p.94). Start with dissolution and decomposition, make the Tincture of the Philosophers and the Tincture of the Lie.

In Part 2, 'Son of Christian Rosy Cross', Foster doubles the narrative into a two-faced movement between the drug culture of the twentieth century and the alchemical quest of the fourteenth century. Here, with his hookah of assass, Christian begins his 'trips' to and fro between hallucinatory Damcar and the 'real' Damascus, in and out of the two faces of the Lie. On his trips, Christian has Jungian encounters with The One, as well as undergoing ordeals real and mystical. The One is a lure, while the narrative doubles and redoubles into social, political and religious patterns. Christian escapes from horrific captivity as slave of Ismaili the sadistic emir, in accord with the hoax-facts of *The Chemical Wedding* and adopts the name Mohammed Ismaili. As a Muslim, he is initiated into the Brotherhood Lodge, undergoes the Ordeal of the Cross and receives the Rose. In the social and political double of gatekeepers and emirs, Christian plays pollmaster in an absurd election between the Grand Gatekeeper and his rival, the viceroy. On Christian's assass 'trips', he is warned by The One, who is also The Two, 'not to abandon Damascus for Damcar but to keep a foot in both'(p.102). With extraordinary narrative poise, Foster keeps a foot in both throughout the Damascus sequence: Christian and Muslim, Damcar and Damascus, Mineral and Vegetable Stone, fourteenth and twentieth century. Keeping 'a foot in both' is Foster's stance in all his work, the key to its turbulent energy and its search for The One.

In the midst of this double narrative, Christian gets a job with The Master, an ancestor of Ar Wat, who teaches chemical school by day and the fraud-squad by night. As comic contradictions and paradoxes keep swinging the narrative between the opposite poles of Damascus and Damcar, The Master explains the 'Method of the Sages', which is contradiction, the truth of opposites:

In the beginning we expect, as well as what we expect, the opposite. Later on we expect both, that is, we expect nothing. There are two worlds, Mohammad, the sun and its shadow, the sulphur and its mercury, and they can take up two orientations, like bipoles in a magnetic field. Consequently, there's always a bit of sun in the shadow, and always a bit of shadow in the sun. (p.91)

This is Ar Wat's Tlute, the logic of 'bipoles in a magnetic field' and the cyclic Foster logic of complementarity on which all his work is built. Sun in shadow, shadow in sun, it is the Liar's Tlute.

Christian sees the Chemical Truth: metals can be converted from one form to another, but there is no proof that the conversion proceeds towards gold nor that it stops at gold. He begins to conceive of a cyclic process, which is at once alchemical and a political cycle. In this era, conservatives and radicals speak as one, an era of the 'harmonic oscillator' (p.111). Damascus has the 'twilight' system of empires at their peak, poised to begin the decline, with ideas about to precipitate its downfall. The historical analogue holds, with Foster's intimation that now, in the twentieth century, we too stand poised, about to fall. Christian resolves to leave Damascus, with his barrel of assass. Forty days later, a traveller reports a pillar of salt (another alchemical symbol), the pillar of Christian himself, who has dissolved and recrystallized. ('Dissolution is the first part of our Art'). Etched on his cortex, Christian now has the whole Mystery of the Cosmos, the Crux of the Gnosis, the Essence of the Vegetable Wisdom. One of the magi, Christian has visited the dungeon which is the lowest point in the cosmos and, one of the 'Robbers of the Rosegarden', now has the Seclet in cipher – which he blurts out excitedly if unintelligibly. Now he is ready to commence the Reformation of the Whole Wide World, but his supplies of assass, essential to the enterprise, are dwindling. He has the Tincture, but never found the purest mercury in the world. What to do?

On his visit to the Grand Prognosticator in Fez, Morocco, he learns that in his next life he will be Martin Luther, (with chronic constipation from smoking Stone). Foster plays with documented links between Rosicrucians and Lutheranism (including the cross and rose of Luther's coat of arms) to anticipate the Protestant Reformation. In this era of Papal Schism (an extraordinary 'true' paradox), Christian is held for seven years in the dungeons of Avignon while the Papal Inquisitors debate the composition of his Stone. After the fall of Damascus, he decides to recant (although later Luther will not). With a bold historical artifice, Foster has the Rosicrucians waiting outside for their founder (who showed the Way and gave them the Book and the Stone). Appointed Papal Inquisitor, Christian sets out with his personal entourage, 'a crack unit, the flying squad' (p.140) including the radical, Adam Cadman, who believes in heretical things like justice and equality. Seeking out heretics, Christian continues his travels across France back to Germany, where he lives in the family castle until his death in 1483 – the year of Martin Luther's birth.

At the end, Christian dreams of an angel dressed as a rose, who warns him that as Luther he will fail the second path and that if he fails in his third and final attempt, 'the Mystery of That Which I Am, and That Which I Guard, will be lost to you always' (p.160). The third path,

This will fall to the Child of another Age, though strictly speaking, there are but two Ages, and two children; Christian the Cause, and Adam the Effect.

Cause is killed by Effect in this Work; thereafter the Two mingle, and become One. (p.161)

The third, which is given to few, is the haunting, elusive One, the talismanic image of unity and conjunction behind all Foster's novels, for which all his characters are searching. Throughout the novel the paradoxes shift and turn in a marvellous conundrum of reality, with changing dispositions of matter and mind, Christian and heretic, base metal and gold, East and West, body and soul, real and fabulous. In this extraordinary picaresque through the nature of matter and the substance of the self, Foster performs a literary alchemy, a transmutation of his own, bringing us to that final haunting image of The One with which he began.

Underneath the turning and twisting movement of Foster's work, the constancy is Foster's celebration of questing itself, the urge to search. He parodies the quest as it falters, breaks down and veers away in a new direction, becomes a new quest – or the old retraced. The energy of the novels is also the restlessness of constant quest, constant yearning for the Secret of the universe, with Foster parodying his own yearning. As paradoxes and contradictions double up the narrative, swinging it to and fro between opposite poles, underneath there is a poignant struggle to realize the truth of contradiction, the 'Method of the Sages', not just as an intellectual proposition but as a total reconciliation. Ar Wat's Tlute, the quantum logic of complementarity, the 'bipoles in a magnetic field' on which all Foster's work is built, is, like the Tao of Physics, an intimation of the existence of The One.

Foster once said, 'Alchemy is cyclic, logic is linear'.[8] The cyclic alchemy of *Christian Rosy Cross* is behind all Foster's novels, behind the warring impulses in the Manwaring bloodline in *The Pure Land* and behind the conflicting systems of religious and scientific thought in *Moonlite*. In *Testostero*, the 'bipoles in the magnetic field' become identical twins changing roles, twin poles of a single self, with Foster, beneath the farce, on a still poignant quest for The One. Behind *Plumbum* too is Foster's alchemical dream of conjunction and enlightenment, with his five questers the base elements being transmuted into the new unity of the band, until the conjunction will no longer hold. The quest for the transmutation of Plumbum (Latin for lead) starts with the five separate components of its members. The starting point recalls Bernard's words in Rhodes: 'we can't make base metals . . . we don't know their composition'. Foster plays with the notion of composition both through the music of the band and through the conjunction of their voices, in ways sometimes lunatic, sometimes surreal and absurdist – the exploits of the band ever more bizarre, the language ever more inventive and ludic. At the same time, he parodies rock journalism, the language of transmutation to rock band success. Behind this tissue of half-truths, distortion and bald lies, is Foster's own Lie, the deft, alchemical flick of his own fiction.

Out of the five improbable elements, with Foster watching for the moment of conjunction, the rock band is born. But the conjunction does not hold, must be constantly renewed against the inner and outer pressures which threaten to undo it. Like Christian Rosy Cross, the band goes on a journey to the east in search of enlightenment. In Bangkok success weakens because it undermines the band's concept of itself as a threatened entity. After the rise to success, then the plummet in Calcutta. Amid the endless phantasmagoria of India, the band disintegrates into five separate crazed worlds. The voices become disjunctive, as the band and the vision of conjunction fall apart. Then celebration takes over again with the lunatic success in Utrecht, the vision reincarnate and Foster still the defiant celebrant of the vision.

After the zany energy of *Moonlite* and *Christian Rosy Cross*, the first part of *Plumbum* seems curiously sober and subdued. In Canberra, which his characters generally regard as preposterous, we witness the birth of The Last Great Heavy Metal Rock Band of The

Western World. But its birth is protracted and the pace is languid, the reader lulled, although there is the faint, nervous suspicion that the narrative might suddenly accelerate and take off. And it does, at lunatic speed in the second half of the novel, where Foster is at his fabulous best, absurdist and zany comic. Much of the impact of the second half depends upon the slow and measured run-up in the first half. The vibrations of the novel, the rise and fall and the beat of chaos, pitch ever upward, ever faster. Foster delights in shattering the preconceptions he has carefully nurtured during the slow run-up to the second part of the novel. A gig at the Canberra R.S.L. today, tomorrow the world-stage and dizzying heights of fame and wealth. Five disparate ordinary beings today, tomorrow subsumed into one fabulous rock band identity, rocking to the rhythms of success. But his characters soar to pinnacles of comic chaos, playing the discords of chaos in the streets of Bangkok and the squalor of Calcutta. The band is ever ready to fall apart, ever on the verge of disintegration.

In Bangkok, they are saved by Nick, who arrives appropriately in a prime mover. Nick is an ambiguous figure, part incarnate deity and part manipulating agent, ready to launch the newly christened band, Plumbum. In Calcutta, where he leads and abandons them, the chaos catches up with the fugitives and all of them are engaged in a nightmarish struggle for survival in the bizarre Calcutta world. Felix (drums) works a rickshaw to finance his habit, running through the streets high on cobra venom. Rollo (keyboards) tries to negotiate with Calcutta – capitalistic enterprise, black-marketeer in postage-stamps, ivory, heart-starter tonics etc. With Jain haircut, Pete (bass) opens a medical clinic and ministers absurdly to the destitute of Calcutta. Sharon (vocals) enters a Kali trance and is lured into Ananda Marga. As Jason (lead guitar) searches for enlightenment, hailing Nick as an avatar of Vishnu, a deity incarnate, he loses not only his sight but his actual eyes. Like *Moonlite*, *Plumbum* plays with notions of enlightenment in Calcutta through images of vision and optics, with Jason becoming a blind visionary, a rock band Tiresias rapt in the squalor of Calcutta. All are adrift and destitute, periodically meeting to discuss the future of India, then wandering off again to listen for 'the click track', the fundamental rhythm that pervades reality.

Plumbum is episodic and disjunctive, with smatterings of random dialogue, muso journalism, random events, bizarre happenings. The Calcutta sequences are the most fragmented, Foster's comic energy darting from one scene to another – all the particles of the band's disintegration. When Nick saves them again, the band is catapulted up to fabulous wealth and fame in scenes of lunatic excess in Utrecht. *Plumbum* is a conjunction of the visionary and the heavy metal: the quest for enlightenment amid chaos, and lead the stubborn base metal that will not be transmuted to gold.

Trying to 'keep a foot in both' is not always a comfortable stance, the energies it generates sometimes too turbulent for balance. In his latest novel, *Testostero*, Foster keeps a foot in both poles of the magnetic field. The novel is a turbulent comedy of errors and mistaken identities, in the manner of a Feydeau farce. Like all his work, it too is multi-layered, at once an absurdist genealogical mystery, a parodic investigation of the nature $v.$ nurture theories of psychological development, as well as a parodic version of sliding identities. Separated identical twins, one reared in England and the other in Australia, are the subjects in an experiment conducted by their father, the father of modern psychology, Sir Cyril Surtout-Spoton. When they meet by chance in Venice, their quest for the truth of their origins propels them into fast-moving absurdity and tight convolutions of plot. The novel is as much a parody of form as content, a farce which is part narrative, part scripted theatrical scene, the whole a hybrid of play and novel, melodrama and narrative comedy of errors, spilling from Venice's masked Commedia dell' Arte.

Foster plays with the paradox that while there are no scientific laws governing individual behaviour there are regularities and calculable probabilities. He toys with the sinister effect of expectations which undermine our sense of the fearful complexity of the real world. Foster continues to expose more and more complications and unexpected twists in the plot, compounding the 'fearful complexity' of the world which becomes an image of the terrible tangles and conundra of circumstances behind an apparently simple reality. At the same time, he plays with literary probabilities, constantly undermining our expectations and calculations of what is around the next narrative corner, as well as challenging our grasp of what was around the previous one.

The central comic conception of the novel is derived from Sir Cyril's experiment, designed to slice the Gordian knot and separate nature from nurture. Separated at birth, one twin is given every advantage, the other sent to a culturally brutal place, Australia. The experiment suffered when a third triplet died at birth (planned as the control, consigned to a sensory deprivation tank!) and when Noel's surrogate mother failed to keep in touch. This is the scenario when Noel meets Leon in Venice and they are quickly tangled into a quest for explanations, as Foster plays with role-changes between the English aristocrat and the Ocker poet. After farcical plot twists in Scotland, one twin suffers brain damage and their identities become confused, out of which they concoct a deliberate scheme to switch roles and so explore another pole of the self, the opponent image of a twin identity.

After their role-change, narrated through the exchange of letters between England and Australia, both are in London in scenes with a huge cast of characters. The farcical complications almost run amok with sub-plots, intrigues and counter-plots, shootings and melodramatic deaths, secret motives and romances – and the absurdist Inspector Krisnamurthi trying to make sense of it all. The narrative seems to be spiralling inside itself at breakneck speed, with Leon and Noel stunned and confused like the reader, stumbling in and out, lurking under numerous beds, causing a chaotic confusion of identities in the midst of some very sharp parody of English aristocracy and Australian tourists on a package tour of London. Foster negotiates his way through a myriad permutations of cause and effect, 'the imprevisible plexus in which our destinies unfold'. When further complications take them to Venice, to discover the identity of the real father and the missing triplet who is alive after all, the entire cast is reassembled for the denouement. With more disguises and role-playing under cover of the Carnival in Venice, the plot thickens again with kidnapping, more stalking and lurking, some gangsters and henchmen, further sinister connections, smuggled artworks, and a dramatic rescue from the waters of Venice. All is finally revealed, and Leon becomes a famous art critic in Sydney and Noel a happy gondolier.

The complications of plot in *Testostero* I find overwhelming. The novel is about masks and sliding identities – the masks of nature and the masks of nurture. The whole is a parody of psychology and of the quest for the real self underneath the conundrum of circumstance. It is an absurdist picaresque and a pastiche of the literary convention of quest for identity – role-playing, sliding identities, putative and potential selves, a multiplicity of guises and disguises of individual existence. The whole novel is built on the paradox of bipolar identity, the twin components of a single Nature thrown into chaos by the absurdities of Nurture. Or is it the absurdities of Nature?

Amidst all the tumultuous passage across space and time in Foster's work, *Dog Rock* seems at first an eccentric novel because it is so contained, confined not only within the closed space of a small Australian country town, but within the postman's version of the town. It seems a highly improbable setting for a quest and this is the comic paradox on which the novel turns. Circumstances compound in *Dog Rock*, not through the free-wheeling movement of the picaresque mode but through the free-wheeling itinerant narrative of the postman. *Testostero*'s 'imprevisible plexus' of contingency and connection still holds, but the compounding of circumstances is involuted and subterranean, under the surface of a single place and a single observer. The postman becomes detective, the investigator on the trail of the mystery of Dog Rock, its secret lurking below the surface minutiae and conundra of banal, fugitive detail. The secret matter of Dog Rock is the Ripper. D'Arcy D'Oliveres is postman–quester, as dedicated to uncovering the secret of things as Christian and Finbar, but this time the secret is below the mundane, the trivial, the rustic, the comic secret horror of the Ripper. Foster's parody, with its companion celebration, is of the ambiguity of the town and of the grotesque lying beneath the mundane surface. Here Foster is not just keeping 'one foot in both': with superb comic poise one foot is lower than the other, one on top in the mundane surface, the other down below in the secret horror of Dog Rock.

Where *Plumbum* is a medley of disjunctive voices, *Dog Rock* is the voice of D'Arcy D'Oliveres. D'Arcy is the novel, deadpan and sardonic narrator of the comically vast and eccentric world of Dog Rock. Postman, Night Telephone Exchange Operator, bee-keeper, bird-watcher, English ex-baron, D'Arcy plays host to a silent, probably dumbstruck interlocutor and conducts him through the mysteries of the 'typically Aussie town' of Dog Rock, with its Antipodean shades of *Under Milk Wood*. Relentlessly digressive, rambling off at tangents but with an uncanny ability to find his way back to the main narrative line, D'Arcy potters through his monologue creating a comic collage that is a constant delight.

Sub-titled 'A Postal Pastoral', the novel opens up expectations of rustic idyll and charm, which, in true Foster style, are then confounded and comically exploited. Nothing ever happens in Dog Rock that is not essentially trivial – until 'something *quadrivial* happened'. Out of the quadrivial, all the proliferating detail, the digressions and asides, the gossip and the vignettes, the inhabitants emerge with all their sharp eccentricity and all the timeless rhythms of a small country town, wholly typical – except that one of the 776 residents is the Ripper who travels to the city to disembowel people. Out of this, with D'Arcy the absurdist detective, Foster creates an absurdist murder mystery, steadily exploiting the incongruity of the Ripper theme until the classic denouement, which has much to do with the prosthesis of a one-armed bee-keeper. A suspect himself, D'Arcy becomes detective, probing small and large mysteries, pondering on suspects: not farmers, not even the Dog Rock yobbos ('They might heckle but not, I think, disembowel . . .'⁹). The puzzle nags at D'Arcy: 'Now who among us would have reason to kill sufficient to make a trip to the city?' (p.55). In D'Arcy's search for the grotesque and the bizarre, the irrational and the inexplicable that lies beneath the stable and banal surface, he is the epistemologist-investigator searching for the secret of Dog Rock, for explanations which can encompass every clue.

Instead of the fast and furious action of the Foster picaresque, *Dog Rock* opens with 'A muffled sense of something happening but too slowly to be perceived' (p.22). Through the prism of D'Arcy's narrative, we see the nocturnal stirrings in Dog Rock, then its dawn movements, accelerating and complicating, minute by minute. A comic delight in itself, this orchestration of the voices and movements of the town in no way prepares the reader for the first casual reference to the Ripper. D'Arcy assembles the Ripper mystery unhurriedly, detouring into hen-keeping statistics, the problems of wombats on the roads, bee-keeping data, reminiscences of walking in the Cotswolds, gossipy anecdotes, and idle ponderings on the enigmas of time and change. To his silent companion, he comments on the host of minor characters who come and go, the nature of their mail, all the quintessential quirks of the town and its people. He is the omniscient narrator, the postman privy to all the secrets of Dog Rock, all the intimations of its past and its future strumming through the present.

Playing with nomenclature, Foster includes among the local notables Sergeant Cadwalloper, Simeon Fitzgibbon and Dullard McLollard; Terry Derry purveyor of honey who has not been seen by the townspeople for 40 years; and Dion Belvedere, the nocturnal Galahad on his motorbike. There are also Brahmin breeders (one a city oncologist with rustic ambitions) and no less than five Balthazars, all artist-malcontents and apparently interchangeable, a kind of undifferentiated plural-self. Local landmarks include the African Mission Opportunity Shop, Panorama Estate (a stealthy arm of the city), Miss Hathaway's Hospice for Homeless Horses, and Foggy Hollow, so named because of the terrain and the confused state of its inhabitants. All the quirks of the town are heightened by the imperturbably cool tone of D'Arcy and the bizarre fact that one of the townspeople disembowels selected city people.

Out of the mystery of the Ripper's identity grow attendant mysteries, plots and counterplots, and dark, rankling suspicions, many of which are directed at D'Arcy himself because he is English, an ex-Baron (and therefore enemy of the Aussie working man), owns a Jowett Javelin and, worse still, is a newcomer of only ten years' residence in Dog Rock. He ponders on communal attitudes to him and realizes that not only Sambo Fargo, his job-rival, Miss Hathaway and Sergeant Cadwalloper, but every Dog Rock resident has at least one reason for wanting him out. He becomes detective, the investigator of Dog Rock, vital mysteries including these imponderables: Whose bees killed Miss Hathaway's horses? Why was the wombat on the road? To whom was the Ripper's 'instrument' mailed? Why does Shutter 63 keep dropping on the telephone exchange? Who is running the international parrot-smuggling racket if there is one? All the clues are there, but hidden inside D'Arcy's freewheeling monologue. All is revealed finally in a clever parody of the conventional mystery thriller denouement. All the improbable and fugitive details are marshalled into an absurdist solution. *Dog Rock* is first and foremost a comic collage of the town, rich in eccentric characters and wildly improbable happenings, which are extended and complicated by the bizarre incongruity of the Ripper theme. This is an inside novel, with Foster charting the routes and landmarks of D'Arcy's world, conducting his peregrinations through D'Arcy. Skidding off at tangents, associative and loose, D'Arcy's narrative is the nexus of observer and observed, each spilling into the other, so that D'Arcy and Dog Rock are one. *Dog Rock* is alchemical too, an investigation into the secrets below the surface matter of the town, looking for a solution not only to a Jack-the-Ripper mystery, but to the mystery of the banal, the lead of life.

If alchemy is a dream, a reverie on possibility, it is also a creed with its own tenets of unity and conjunction and enlightenment. In the midst of all the contending opposites in the chaos of things, it postulates a secret which we will one day find. When we do, we will have found not just the secret of matter, but the 'spirit in matter', the unity of all things, The One. Alchemy is also an Art, with its own Tincture, its own furnace, its own arcane symbols, and its own adepts. In Foster's hands, it is a Liar's Art, the Liar–alchemist summoning up the base reality he will transmute, watching for the moment of conjunction, when the Lie becomes the truth. Alchemy is the Lie of Foster, with its language of conjunction, transmutation, its passionate quest, its lunatic intensity. Behind the dialectic of all his work, Foster is on his own quest for conjunction, essentially a poignant one, but through the Lie become zany, absurdist and self-parodying. The Lie is Foster's Tincture, the tale his gold. 'To watch the furnace closely is the whole secret of the art . . . it's all in the books.'

FOURTH DIALOGUE

Liar That's the Secret. That's how alchemy works. It's quantum logic, complementarity, half and half. Keeping a foot in both. One in reality, one in the Lie.

Reader Talking about keeping a foot in both and half and half . . . I'd like you to listen to this. This is Sterne, in *Tristram Shandy*:

Writing, when properly managed . . . is but a different name for conversation: As no one, who knows what he is about In good company, would venture to talk all; – so no author, who understands the just bounds of decorum and good-breeding, would presume to think all: The truest respect which you can pay to the reader's understanding, is to halve this matter amicably, and leave him something to imagine, in his turn, as well as yourself.[1]

I'm not sure about your sense of decorum and good-breeding. Nor your respect for my understanding.

Liar Interesting that you quote Sterne. Quite a few of my colleagues regard him as an ancestor. Still, I don't think you're being fair. I've treated you with every respect. But certain strategies and artifices are necessary if I'm going to change your perceptions.

Reader I know what you are trying to do. I understand Foster's Dissolution as the first part of the Art. You're trying to break up my perceptions and radically change my view of things. But I don't necessarily want to accept yours.

Liar Don't forget you came to me for help.

Reader That's true, but I think Sterne is right. We have to 'halve this matter' and halve it 'amicably'.

Liar You want half-truths? Is that what you're proposing? Half-truths?

Reader No. The point is I want a much greater say in this. You've had it your way so far. You say I'm the collaborator. All right, let's really collaborate on an equal footing. Equal opportunity. I want an equal opportunity to present my viewpoint.

Liar I would have thought this was a fair exchange. But if you feel I've been dominating, go ahead. It's all yours.

Reader Good. An amicable arrangement. We've been talking about principles of uncertainty and complementarity and so on. All the dualities and opposites, the 'Method of the Sages' in Foster's work. Complementarity is all very well but in my experience things are not so comfortable as opposites being complementary. Ambiguity is not easy to tolerate. It's not easy to accept contradictions. There's much more conflict than that for me and much more distrust. My problems are not solved by just accepting principles of uncertainty and ambiguity.

Liar Surely we have to get the general principles clear first?

Reader Do you think that while I'm reading, I should keep referring myself to quantum physics? Or epistemology? Or Godelian metamathematics? When I am reading, I'm not thinking about that. Nor do I want to. Let's talk about character and plot. That's much closer to my experience. My first points of reference. My entry to the Lie.

Liar It's mine too, of course.

Reader Is it? I'm not sure that's always true. I think your entry point is sometimes a central metaphor, like a machine, an institution, a landscape or some medium, like photography. Look at the Puroil refinery in *The Unknown Industrial Prisoner*, for example, or Merry-Lands in *The Flesheaters*, part mental hospital, part refuge . . .

Liar And landscape suggests Murnane's *The Plains*. Photography suggests Murray Bail . . . Sorry, I interrupted you.

Reader Sometimes I think your starting point is some disposition of time. By that I mean perhaps a sense of constant change, a consciousness of particles of time, whether past or present, or some intimation of the future.

Liar Or more simply, some historical period or mystery . . . Look at *Christian Rosy Cross* or *The Bellarmine Jug* and the whole mystery of the aftermath of the *Batavia* wreck.

Reader Yes that's true too, but before that the starting point comes from some kind of historicizing impulse, a kind of time-consciousness. Once like a marginal tic of consciousness, it has become what Susan Sontag calls 'an embrace of consciousness', the perspective that occupies the centre of our ability to understand everything. It's a perspective that constantly questions the value of human achievements and their claim to truth. We see everything in a stream of becoming. That seems to me to be a starting point for some of your colleagues.

Liar Like Mathers and Foster?

Reader Yes, among others. Hasluck has it too, and Carey and Bail. And David Ireland. But there's another starting point too, which seems to me a general delight in contest and challenge, a subversiveness, an iconoclastic impulse. I'm not suggesting that the whole thing's a game, but that it appeals to the gamester and trickster, the sense of play, the ludic sense. Who wrote that book *Homo Ludens*? Huizinga, that's right. Tracing the sense of play all through history. That seems to me a starting point sometimes, the 'homo ludens' in us all.

Liar Surely any literature is at base a strategy of play?

Reader Yes of course it is. In its deepest sense, that's almost a tautology. But the ludic component is not always an overt feature. Look at the differences in narrative strategies between *Tristram Shandy* and Jane Austen or, between Furphy's *Such is Life* and Christina Stead. Or Cervantes. Look at *Don Quixote* by comparison with Dostoyevsky. All I'm saying is that some fiction is more ludic, more conscious of its own artifice and strategies. You're not disputing that surely?

Liar I'm hardly in a position to ...

Reader But what I'm getting at is that whatever the starting point – and I'm sure it is not possible to generalise about that – it becomes character. That is the ground on which we meet. Wherever we both start from, that's where we meet.

Liar Not according to Nathalie Sarraute. Our ancestors might have, but she claims you and I now survey each other across empty ground, vacated by character.

Reader Fortunately that's not true in Australian fiction. Character has not been stripped of everything and dispossessed, disinherited. I agree with Sarraute that this is the Age of Suspicion, but the grounds of my suspicions are different from hers. I do have to be wary of you, as she suggests, but that also means being wary of your characters. Which brings me to my point . . . For me, character and plot are the starting point. That is my entry to the Lie of fiction. Wherever it goes, whatever Strange Loops or Tangled Hierarchies take me in and out of the Lie, I start with character and plot. That is my point of orientation. The way I get my bearings. And that is still true.

Liar But the way character and plot are presented has changed.

Reader Exactly. The moment I start relaxing into character and plot I know you're going to come up with something unexpected, bizarre, something disturbing that will shock me out of my complacency. You're going to undermine my sense of character and plot, break it up . . . That has now become the starting point for me.

Liar You say that calmly now. When we first met, it was making you very distraught.

Reader Of course it was. I remember when I first started reading *The Unknown Industrial Prisoner*, I read about sixty pages and stopped. No-one seemed to be in charge of it. The narrative was all in pieces. About thirty passing characters had already wandered in and out. I acquired a lot of detail about the workings of an oil refinery, most of it with a bizarre humour that was somehow grim. But no sign of the narrator or any one else willing to accompany me for more than a few pages at a time. When I continued reading it, the number of characters swelled to about two hundred, all of whom I knew only by nickname and all of whom continued to come and go, seemingly at random in quick fragments of incident. A few offered conflicting views of what was going on, then wandered off.

Liar It's a great novel. One of the most important novels ever written in this country.

Reader Of course it is. But at the time that's how it looked from my point of view . . . my half of this business. When I realised the main character *is* the Puroil refinery . . . and when I realised the machinery of plot *is* the machinery of Puroil, I began to see it differently. It took me a while to get to the stage where I start with suspicion of your intent.

Liar So you're more wary now.

Reader It's not just wariness across some genteel distance. I have to be more vigilant than that. It's all quite bloodthirsty. There is a lot of murder . . . Look at Sibley's fate in *The Glass Canoe*. He's there to observe, hoping to do some missionary work among the drinkers and he ends up a rotting carcase on the top of the pub.

Liar I wasn't very comfortable with that either, but for different reasons. You see him as an observer, I see him as a mock-writer. Sibley's there taking notes, writing it all down and suddenly he's dead. Talk about you and I meeting in the characters . . . I have to be vigilant too. What about the Carey short story, about the Pig Tyrant Homer?

Reader Oh yes. Poor Echion discovers Homer is planning to kill him and Odysseus is in cahoots with Homer and won't do anything to save him. The awful part is that, when he tries to escape, he dies in exactly the way Homer decided he would. The tragedy is he died for nothing. After all that, Homer left him out of the *Odyssey* completely. It's very sad.

Liar But he didn't die instantly. He was alive long enough to scrawl a message. KILL THE PIG TYRANT HOMER. How do you think I feel about that? Being seen as a Pig Tyrant?

Reader What about the ending of *Truant State*? The murder of the reader. We haven't got to Hasluck yet, but I have a lot to say about that later. And other murders.

Liar It's not always bloodthirsty. Sometimes there's natural death. I'm thinking of *Miss Peabody's Inheritance*. It's a much more dignified succession there, when Miss Peabody takes over after Diana's death from natural causes and quietly succeeds her as the writer.

Reader Nonetheless our version of the Age of Suspicion seems to involve a struggle to the death.

Liar And the more you are aware of that, the more ready I have to be to outwit you.

Reader Outwit? I thought we were collaborators?

Liar Well . . . yes. But it's competitive too. I mean, there is an element of rivalry. Rival viewpoints at least.

Reader At least you're being honest now. It *is* competitive. That's what I realized when I read *The Chantic Bird* . . .

Liar You wanted a guide and someone to point you in the right direction. You get a narrator in *The Chantic Bird*.

Reader Yes but look at him. An anonymous adolescent on the run, who rolls drunks, steals, taps a petrol line and derails a train . . . and then gives me instructions on how to do the same things myself! What sort of a narrator is that? He commits assault, arson, and murder . . .

Liar The murder of the 'watcher'. A case of mistaken identities. Some poor innocent he's invented as the 'watcher' because he thinks someone *ought* to be following him.

Reader It's not so much the watcher. What about the murder of Petersen, then dissecting the body, burning parts of it and throwing the rest to the lions at the zoo . . . How comfortable can I be with him as a character?

Liar But look at the identity of the victim: Petersen, the man who is writing his story, the writer. It's not particularly comfortable for me either.

Reader Come on . . . don't give me that. You're O.K. You're safely outside it, inviolate, beyond his reach. David Escher–Ireland. Watching the two Escher hands not just innocently drawing each other but competing for control of the book. Then one hand kills the other. But you're safe.

Liar Yes but the 'character' wins. The 'character' in Petersen's story kills him.

Reader That depends on how you look at it. The boy is also killing off a character in his narrative, who is trying to take over. A rival narrator. Not *dual* narration, but *duel* narration.. So we're both right. Double Agencies. Both propositions are true.

Liar That's my line. That's the Liar's Paradox.

DOUBLE AGENCIES *DAVID IRELAND*

It has been my aim to take a part, then build up piece by piece this mosaic of one kind of human life, this galaxy of painted slides, my bleak ratio of illuminations; to remind my present age of its industrial adolescence.

Well friend, I have not succeeded in putting back together those I have taken apart, for they are split, divided, fragmented, as I am split up and divided between page and character, speech and event, intention and performance.

The Unknown Industrial Prisoner

There were so many things in his head. Each sight or sound or feeling, each person, each word, was surrounded by constellations of others.

He had only to think the word to make others visible. Then they teemed round him, coruscating, tumbling pellmell like water released from a dam; teemed and multiplied for a great way into the distance, until they seemed infinite. So much, and all spun from a word.

He didn't have this feeling all day. Perhaps a little at a time was all he could cope with.

Everything, he reflected, must have a sort of infinity in it, and each thing linked up with each other thing.

Bloodfather

the world is indirect, there are no borders to reality; words, objects, thoughts, have only a diaphanous existence

City of Women

On a rising slope of prosperity, with widening horizons, the range of lives a man could lead becomes too great to ignore. Sudden and severe jolts to this prosperity: this was the Samurai's answer.

Sabotage, destruction, hardship, violence, blood. If there were enough men tramping the street, not all the barbed wire and police forces and national guards in the world could stop the blaze. Yes. He would go about the country, making panics . . .

Would there be others after him who would keep at this work of digging spurs into the softening flanks of the country? For they were needed. Nothing could last, no lessons remembered, but had to be repeated over and over in each generation. The social body had to be lashed and stung, wounded and bled regularly, before it sank back into laziness and ease, obesity and death.

THE GIFT OF LANGUAGE The Samurai arrived at his room. He fished out his latest notebook and tossed it into the small carton in which the others were neatly packed. He tipped them out on his bed and began to leaf through them. It was a crazy impulse, nevertheless he shuffled the notebooks as near as he could get to the order in which he had filled them, took a pad of notepaper from his little table and a Puroil ballpoint pen and started to write.

Catching sight of himself in the mirror on the opposite wall he smiled at his reflection, a thing he had never done before, but did not lay down his pen. Instead he went over to the old motto *Help, Care, Listen* that he had on the wall, crossed it out and wrote *Hate, Chaos, Leadership*. A more corrosive mixture.

Was he writing about the men he'd worked with? Did they exist? He had the feeling that now he had decided to leave them they had collapsed from inside like balloon faces when the air is gone. Were those men he knew or thought he knew, were they projections of himself? Only alive while he was with them? Extensions, reflections, enlargements of small characteristics of his own?

And the face in the mirror on that opposite wall: whose reflection was that?

113

What aimless forces had moulded him? A man born to change his world and until now denying himself the power . . .

He looked at his reflection again. A writer was a dangerous man, substituting words for crimes. He put his stolen biro to paper and words formed lightly in blue tracings. Were they original words, a private language? Or simply a re-arrangement of patterns he had become used to in his few years' exposure to the words that surrounded him. Patterns he was so familiar with they seemed to him his own voice

The Unknown Industrial Prisoner[1]

•

DAVID IRELAND HAS LONG admired the work of the nineteenth century Brazilian novelist, Machado de Assis, whose work includes 'The Psychiatrist',[2] a novella about a psychiatrist in the small town of Itaguai, who periodically changes the definitions of sanity and insanity. Starting with prominent citizens, his research gradually extends to the whole township, with the townspeople moving in and out of the institution, admitted and released according to whatever is the current definition. Like the psychiatrist, Ireland tests out new definitions of things, not only sanity and insanity, but also freedom and imprisonment, power and powerlessness, present and future, change and stasis, fiction and reality. At the same time, he examines the definition of being anywhere and the notion of the individual as a composite being, both inside and outside at the same time, both real and putative. Like the townspeople of Itaguai, who come and go from the Green House while the psychiatrist conducts his patient observations and research, Ireland's characters come and go too, crossing and recrossing the boundaries between reality and fantasy, while Ireland examines another definition of reality. In his Lie, a vast populace of characters come and go in quick splinters of incident, all under his scrutiny, in a constant passage of change. As he uncovers new contradictions, the definition of reality constantly changes and with it the definition of the Lie.

All Ireland's work is a literary *trompe l'oeil*, a literary Möbius strip, with two modes at once. Like Escher's *Cube with Magic Ribbons*, Ireland's novels have convex and concave modes, and perpetual rivalry between the two. Escher's paradoxes of object and observer, figure and background, have an equilibrium which produces a kind of flickering effect, so that it is difficult to distinguish clearly between the two. The double agencies of Ireland's work have the same flickering effect, shifting between subjective and objective, between inner and outer, between fiction and reality. In the flickering, paradoxes of the reader and the Liar keep surfacing.

In Ireland's first novel, *The Chantic Bird*, the definition of fiction keeps changing. The anonymous narrator is both character and writer, his words two fictions at once, within a novel that is two Lies at once. One is the Lie of fiction written by the Escher hand of Ireland. The other is the Lie of the narrator/character who is inside the frame, writing with his own Escher hand and competing with Petersen for control of the book – the book within the book. The narrative flips to and fro between two modes of the Lie. Ireland is the observer watching the two Escher hands, not quietly drawing each other, but competing, rival hands, until one murders the other. Like the psychiatrist in the Machado story, Ireland keeps changing the definitions of character, writer and fiction, and with it our definition of reality.

In *The Flesheaters*, the narrative is at once the objective reality of Merry Lands, and a subjective reality inside, in the perspex prism of Lee Mallory's consciousness. In *The Unknown Industrial Prisoner*, the Samurai is making his notes, splintering himself off into characters, while Ireland is doing the same, but the Puroil refinery exists outside them both. In *The Glass Canoe*, as Meat Man sits at his amber glass typewriter, touching its red keys, he is also in the Red Bar of the Southern Cross pub. In *City of Women*, there is a similar flipping from one mode to the other, between Billie Shockley's 'real' world inside her flat and the City where she moves around freely as Doc among the women who are her own component selves. The inner and outer images are ambivalent, with double agencies suggesting unity, although we remain conscious of the contradiction. Like the spatial paradox of Escher's *Print Gallery*, Lee is in Merry Lands in Lee, and Billie walks the City streets that run through her own flat.

In the geometry of Ireland's novels, the forward horizontal movement of narrative is constantly disrupted by crisscrossing vertical lines. In *The Unknown Industrial Prisoner*, vertical lines run up and down different levels of narrative, compounding perspectives on event and character – and at the same time enacting the imprisonment which is the novel's theme. *Prisoner* not only is about entrapment in the machinery of industrial society but also enacts that entrapment, through the motion of the narrative. As our angle of vision is complicated, our sense of the choices and freedoms of the characters is complicated too. Like the prisoners, we seek patterns and interpretations, try to preserve small freedoms. For the reader, the lines of choice include following a character we recognize as 'major', one like Great White Father or The Samurai or Glass Canoe. Or we might follow the narrative of the Home Beautiful underground resistance movement. Or we might pursue connections within the multitude of incident and circumstance which work towards the breakdown of Puroil – factors both accidental and contingent, as well as deliberate individual acts of sabotage. Those choices are there but Ireland constantly works against the reader's impulse to find and hold a single vantage point. Rather than consigning certain components to the 'background' as 'minor' characters or scenes, he insists on the multiple viewpoint. The novel is a vast collage of splinters of incident and shifting viewpoints, each one a component in the whole, each in contest with the others.

Deliberate disorder, deliberate randomising – these paradoxes become the Lie of Ireland. Without a clear distinction between foreground and background, between dominant and subordinate elements, we must position ourselves differently from moment to moment, fragment to fragment. Ireland works by deliberate ambushing, by using the intervening spaces between fragments, where we formulate expectations and contrive connections – which he then undermines. He deliberately breaks down the connections and leaves us with scattered bits and pieces of narrative, encouraging us to set up the connections ourselves, only to disturb and break them. He breaks up the narrative, exposing its edges, its levels, surprising us with combinations in a multi-layered narrative. It is a cut-up method, which fragments, takes apart, ever watchful for patterns and links, ready to break them up the moment they appear. The narrative is enacting the machinery of perception amid constant change, the rise and fall of random factors, chaos and contingency. The Ireland Lie is a plural perspective composed of essentially equivalent elements, a multitude of particles. Each particle shifts the perspectives slightly, within the broad movement of the whole. The novels become kaleidoscopic, with a myriad pieces of discordant images, splinters of narrative thrown into striking patterns and shapes, new compositions changing from moment to moment as the Liar shakes the kaleidoscope again.

In 1927, Ireland was born in the Sydney suburb of Lakemba, into a religious household, without newspapers or radios, where worldly things were forbidden. His father was one of the Plymouth Brethren and an insurance salesman, who lost his job during the Depression, so that the family moved around the Sydney suburbs many times during Ireland's childhood. Later Ireland worked at various jobs, including a period in the 1960s at the Shell oil refinery. After winning the 1966 *Adelaide Advertiser* prize, his first novel, *The Chantic Bird*, was published in 1968. In 1971, *The Unknown Industrial Prisoner* appeared (winner of the first of three Miles Franklin awards) and in 1972, *The Flesheaters*. Ireland was living with his wife and children in Winston Hills on the outskirts of Sydney until 1973 when he moved to the centre of Sydney to begin a solitary life as a full-time writer. His next novel, *Burn*, was published in 1974, based on a 1964 play, *Image in the Clay*. Ireland won the Miles Franklin award again in 1976, with *The Glass Canoe* and in 1979 for *A Woman of the Future*. He was the first novelist to receive the prestigious Miles Franklin award three times, but this third time caused some controversy when one of the judges, Professor Colin Roderick, dissented from the panel decision and declared the novel pornographic, 'literary sewage'.[3] Further controversy developed when the NSW Board of Senior School Studies removed *The Glass Canoe* from the recommended reading list for the NSW HSC course for 1983, on the grounds that it was 'pornographic'.[4] Another major novel, *City of Women*, was published in 1981 and in 1984, a minor one, *Archimedes and The Seagle*. Ireland has also written a few short stories, quick Lies with one central proposition, but these are minor aspects of his work.[5]

In 1987, *Bloodfather* was published, a major new novel and a *Künst-*

Ierroman with close connections with Ireland's own background as a child. The story of Davis Blood from birth to sixteen, it is the novel behind all Ireland's work, the novel of the encompassing consciousness, the Godelian eye of all his work. Ireland is now working on a sequel, crossing a hiatus of some fifty years to Davis at about seventy, with the further possibility of a trilogy. *Bloodfather* is a novel of origins, a founding vision celebrating the growth of an artistic consciousness, with the paradox of a sixteen year old with his own bloodfather vision. It is a crystalline novel of interior growth, in the deepest wellsprings of being, a locus of consciousness, measuring its own becoming and tracing the growth of vision from the eye to the word, from painter to writer. *Bloodfather* sings the vision behind all Ireland's work, an ancestry of the bloodlines from his first novel, a Godelian Loop which takes us back to the beginnings in *The Chantic Bird*, some twenty years before, a darker 'analogue of the writer as artist'.

The adolescent narrator of *The Chantic Bird* lives underground in Sydney, moving from hideout to hideout, making periodic raids on his society and writing his memoirs on the run. He is in recoil from a man-eat-man society of economic violence and savage materialism, where people are compressed into functions and trapped in servitude. Violent, predatory, cynical and offensive, the adolescent coolly documents his outrageous deeds, offering a manual of how to survive in a savagely competitive world: roll drunks, con, steal, tap a petrol line and derail a train. Worse, he commits arson, assault and murder, notably the murder of his biographer, Petersen, whose body is cut up, parts of it burnt and some parts thrown to the lions at the zoo. This is the writer as adolescent anarchist, emerging from dark places to attack at random, the writer as fugitive, on the run from captivity in society – and the writer as Liar, playing with the freedom of the Lie.

Freedom and mobility are all the adolescent narrator has: he lives on the run, moving from one hideout to another, from zoo to cave, from bush tent to cemetery, from boat to car, then to the ceiling of the house where Bee and the kids live. Dogged by the mysterious 'watcher', he himself becomes a watcher, observing the safe dulling routines of people's lives, despising the distrust and apathy, marvelling at the job-captives content with their imprisonment in collective life. In such a society he sets out to 'equalize', and at the start he enjoys the way he lives, 'coming out of a place that's dark and secret and leaving your mark on the people that hate the dark, then going back where they can't follow you'.[6] He rolls drunks, bashes kids, burns down buildings, extorts money, shoots another kid, derails a train. So he says. At times, the narrator takes a contrary delight in his own disruptive activities, often indulging his liking for playful gestures and outlandish jokes set to go off in the future. The Viking funeral is one of many comic scenes, where he plays the buffoon and celebrates his freedom. But *The Chantic Bird* is not a celebration of dissent, no free-wheeling novel of happy, rebellious energy. This is the edge of despair, a gauntlet narrative thrown at the reader. Unable to subscribe to any code of conduct and unable believe in any ideal, the narrator challenges us:

A lot of people are going to be upset when they read this. I can hear them asking why I do these things, even though I've just told them. They can tell me books full of things I shouldn't do, but who's going to tell me what I ought to do? Who? Besides the ratbags? (pp.86–7)

Freedom becomes circular and closes in on him, so that he is left pacing it out, searching for a breach in its walls. He insists that his way of life is only one remove from the moral order he sees all around him. 'You won't believe how much the same it seems to me and all the kids I know; getting a man's job by competition – or knocking him over the head.' (p.198) At ease in the world only when 'lawless as a meteor, burning what I touched' (p.15), he insists he is speaking for his generation. And he insists it all happens just as he says: it is all true.

In *The Chantic Bird* fictions are both horizontal and vertical. They run along the narrative line of murder, derailing trains and gratuitous violence, but at the same time they run up and down the levels of the Tangled Hierarchy of the novel. The novel purports to be autobiography, the memoirs of a boy who goes underground, but it is also written in collaboration with Petersen, and the narrator doubles as a character in Petersen's novel. This points to omissions, distortions and fabrications, as well as suggesting a composite work in which the boy and Petersen become absurdist rivals. Contradictory versions of his first meeting with Petersen and of Petersen's homosexual advances sit among contradictory versions of the boy's own relationship with Bee and the kids. The apparently simple line of the novel – the life of an adolescent living on the social fringes by criminal means – is complicated to take in the fictions woven by the narrator for Petersen and those woven by Petersen to enhance his own literary debut. The resentful character in Petersen's novel is also the author of his own competitive book and he begins to identify Petersen as dangerous. The character asserts his rights and resorts to the simple solution of killing Petersen and so wins control of the book. This is *his* story, his to concoct, his to fabricate.

As Petersen and the narrator become rivals, not only the rights of the character are at issue but the authenticity of the narrative. The murder of Petersen and disposal of his body, in gruesome detail, are the highlight of the novel's comic absurdity, but underneath that is another layer of fiction. The character kills off the writer – and the narrator kills off the notion of fiction in order to reassert its truth.

I've chopped out a few of his comments, where he went off the track a bit. You have to consider the readers, and you have to consider your own feelings, too. At least he didn't make my words come out differently; I checked through and they're as I told him. (p.185)

The style is simple, slangy, fluent, free-running and loose, skidding off at tangents like the boy's own chaotic passage through society. The narrator has checked the style to make sure Petersen has not distorted it, so now the reader can relax: all is authentic 'truth'. But one lie is withdrawn only in order to reinforce its central Lie. Just as he regards Petersen as a conventional person, one of the herd, intractably committed to the way things are, and sets out to shock Petersen out of his complacency, so the narrator spins fictions and lies for the reader – who also needs to be shocked out of his complacency with the way things are.

The real lie the narrator spins is the one in which he himself is entangled, the lie of freedom. As freedom becomes oppressive, the narrator realizes he is trapped inside its ambiguities. He begins to measure out his own existence, partly through Stevo.

I suppose I don't really want him to get like me. Some of the things I believe in wouldn't help him. Like idleness. You know, not doing the sort of things the authorities like . . . Besides, I can never stop hearing a sort of inside laughter that tells me beyond the next heartbeat there may be nothing. (p.67)

One measure of freedom is in the telling of the Chantic Bird tale. As Stevo's interest in the tale slows, so the narrator's quickens. He supposes Stevo is 'waking up that you get no magic in this life; getting the big rich beautiful song out of the little grey bird is fairy story stuff' (p.194). But, precocious, Stevo has known all along the ending of the tale, which is not magic but corruption – the price of freedom in a world of imprisonment and servitude. The narrator's own curiosity about the ending of the tale brings him to the real deceit – the deceit of 'magic', the deceit of uncorrupted freedom and beauty. Through the pattern of the narrator's dreams, Ireland has drawn images of the ambiguities of freedom, images like paintings which embody his revulsion against society, his deepest fears of confinement, isolation and death. The predicament configured in the dreams is finally resolved by his attack on the 'watcher', the shadowy counterpart he has created, a fiction designed to import purpose into the narrator's own free-wheeling emptiness. The body is a chance victim, tagged as the watcher in order to play out the ending of a fiction concocted not for us, not for Petersen, but for the narrator himself. Words are his last resort, the words of the book. Surely the reader will react to this 'tale told by a nobody. A mouth in the empty air' (p.201). The last fiction is the novel's ending, prefigured in the dream where he presides over a country town. Like the Samurai in *Prisoner* who decides to 'go about the country, making panics', he now determines to find a town of his own.

I knew I could survive anywhere, all I needed now was to get some practice working with other people. I had to forget my habit of going alone all the time. I'd need a stooge or two . . . A town of my own. Stolen cars, tow trucks, farm protection agent, local council, a town of my own. While the rest were looking upwards for bombs, I'd collapse them from the inside. (p.198)

The first of Ireland's characters who plans to head west, he might not make it. His chest pains are getting worse. Perhaps he stays in Sydney, starting on the task of collapsing the city from the inside.

The book the narrator has written is one way to collapse a town, dismantling it from the inside.

In Beckett's 'The Lost Ones', naked people are trapped for eternity inside an enormous mechanical cylinder: 200 naked bodies, in four categories based on the extent to which they actively search, use ladders, occupy niches, roam, or remain catatonically rooted to a spot. The bodies copulate occasionally, though joylessly. The people search for eternity, forever straining for a way out. The reader too is a searcher, looking for a way out of the cylinder, but there is never a way out, there is only the search. In *The Unknown Industrial Prisoner*, the cylinder is Puroil. The machine in fiction has long conjured up both awe and revulsion and has long signified determinism, but, in contemporary fiction, in the novels of Burroughs, Pynchon, Barth, and Vonnegut, the machine is also a metaphor for writing. David Porush identifies this kind of novel as a mode of its own, 'cybernetic fiction'.[7] Novels like *Gravity's Rainbow*, *Giles Goat-Boy*, *Sirens of Titan*, *The Crying of Lot 49*, are not only about technology and the implications of mechanization, but are also about the machinery of fiction, examining the techniques and strategies of the novel, the technology of fiction. *The Unknown Industrial Prisoner* is cybernetic fiction, in that its techniques, its literary technology, enact its industrial and social themes. The machine metaphor of Puroil is also the machinery of the narrative and the mechanism of industrial society, the Puroil refinery also a refinery for the reader's expectations.

Prisoner parodies the notion of society as a Newtonian clockwork mechanism: the perspective is post-Heisenbergian, with full play of indeterminacy and contingency, which is how Puroil works. The narrative moves by a kind of thrust and parry, action and counteraction, all the myriad fragments steadily coming together into a vast kaleidoscope of incidents, crossing over and running under each other, doubling back or darting ahead. A crowd of prisoners come and go in quick snatches of incident, their lives broken up into jagged edges of narrative, until Puroil explodes from its own contradictions. In a kind of spontaneous combustion, random event, accidents and isolated acts of sabotage all come together in the explosions. Australia is still a penal colony, still an outpost of foreign powers, the cities huge labour camps where the industrial prisoner is confined for the term of his working life, still bearing the residual ankle scars, still scratching off the days in cement walls. The prisoners of Puroil Australia live in dread of parole by retrenchment, until the pension grants a ticket-of-leave. Each man is set against his fellows, tightening his own chains in fear of freedom, which is an economic death. Unaware of his captivity, construing it as freedom to work, the industrial prisoner labours within the rigid ranks of Puroil. Its hierarchy soars up from the lower depths, the trusties and overseers, to the Termitary office workers and management, up to the heavenly heights of anonymous foreign shareholders. Flogged into submission by strike clauses, the unions play games with management. Every Puroil policy is a Catch 22 and clauses lie in wait across the Puroil wasteland.

Prisoner is an angry vision of dehumanizing collective life but it is also abrasively comic with a contrary delight in the very absurdities it exposes. Within the vast network of character and incident, Ireland traces the changing circumstances of numerous prisoners, comically exploiting the small freedom each one contrives for himself. Some characters emerge more prominently, notably the Great White Father, Samurai and Glass Canoe. The large Falstaffian figure, Great White Father, leads his groggy troops across the mangroves, to 'our little hole in the barbed wire' (p.29), to Home Beautiful, the purple and amber kingdom of girls and grog. There in the wilderness, he offers a 'vast underground movement of inertia', a kind of inner revolt inside the system, the Way of Eternal Oblivion.

They are prisoners of their own image of themselves . . . That's where I step in. I'll make them love this little taste of indulgence and oblivion so they'll think of nothing else, and treat everything else as so much illusion . . . Princes of the blood with me their king. That's what they miss: the colour, the natural subordination to a king whose authority is unquestioned and whose orders coincide with their desires . . . they need not equality because they can never be equal, but a purple and gold monarchy. The purple in their mind's eye, the gold in the amber of their beer. (pp.193–4)

The way of the Great White Father, later parodied as the Great White Feather, is contrasted with the deliberations of Samurai, a warrior transfixed, struggling to devise a way to translate his ideals into action. He becomes a troubled witness, making notes, until he decides on the tactics of guerilla warfare, waging words in a literary campaign, 'a programme of destruction to bring about a chaotic state of affairs' (p.362). Glass Canoe, wretchedly absurd, strives to surrender his whole identity to the company because, unable to believe in himself, he believes in Puroil. He becomes Puroil Man, a checklist of approved Puroil characteristics, but this leaves him adrift in the Puroil wasteland, the hollow man, who has lost even the last link of language. He dies a faceless, dehumanized man, stripped of himself.

Out of the vast canvas of characters in the novel, these three are more prominent, but the novel is the multitude of particles which make up the Puroil reality. The main character is Puroil itself. The monster slouching towards the future, its capricious machinery staggering fitfully into life, it lurches on through this machine age which is still the convict past. In the climactic explosions at the end, Puroil collapses from the inside, explodes from its own contradictions, but it will rise again, a grotesque machine phoenix carrying its prisoners inside it.

The Flesheaters is in part the surrealistic counterpart of *Prisoner*, the other face of industrial society, that of the unemployed, those suffering the dread disease of retrenchment, poverty, displacement. In the Merry Lands hospital of Australia, the outcasts of the Puroil prison become the inmates of another tyranny. Industrial labour becomes absurd therapy for those convalescing from bouts of half-pay, the contagion of redundancy or terminal cases of unemployability. Under the O'Grady government, the inmates play games of mindless obedience: the good are awarded the purple elephant stamp on the forehead; the rebellious are corrected with shock treatment. The Puroil hierarchy is extended into a universal hierarchy of flesheating predators, mouths ever opening on to devouring mouths.

Through all the layering of the novel, Ireland constantly undermines divisions between real and surreal, between sane and insane, between truth and fiction. Lee Mallory, narrator and writer, is a fugitive from the flesheating reality, purports to be a detached observer and voice of the inmates, but at the same time writes from his 'future' haven, a psychiatric hospital. The novel is Lee, the prism of his consciousness refracted backwards and forwards through time, refracted outwards into splinter characters. His Perspex prism with its five irregular surfaces is the stage of the novel. O'Grady, Clayton, Crystal, Scotty and Lee are refractions of his own inner conflict, contestant attitudes of himself in bizarre combinations, both sexual and intellectual. Through them, Lee can push a proposition about himself, a putative self, to its logical or illogical end. Appalled at the flesheating reality, Lee is determined to stand outside it as an observer, a man without belief, without guilt. Such a stance insists there are no connections, no continuities, that history is an illusion. His prism is an attempt to buttress that stance by projecting his own conflicts outside himself and disclaiming them. Like *City of Women*, *The Flesheaters* is both concave and convex, both inside Lee's Perspex prism and projected outside Lee into Merry Lands. Like Billie who founds a City in which to house the painful components of herself, Lee attempts to disclaim the disturbing components of himself – the flesheating that is a condition of existence.

The Flesheaters is a compressed and finely constructed novel, built out of fragments which explore the lives of the inmates as a group. Chained to her kennel is Granny, given injections by peashooter, barking at the next-door Granny who has a male pensioner to play with. The Bulk Buyers in their Ark room store up groceries against the future. Scotty the writer lives in tree-house isolation, gloriously above it all and feeding on a diet of exotic words. Lee's lover, Clayton, carries out experiments on animals, content with the flesheating world and eager to take his place in it. Amid all the shifting circumstances of the inmates, Lee's own intense, inner turmoil is a black comedy, until he confronts his own guilty complicity in events and, a flesheater too, flees to the psychiatric hospital. Manager, dictator, keeper of the inmates of Merry Lands, O'Grady is also Lee's father and a target for reprisal, listed in Lee's 'book of kills'. Their relationship stretches through the novel into a central ambiguity which reaches its climax in the crucifixion sequence. In a madhouse universe, the father crucifies the son in a wonderfully bizarre scene: father grumbling about the cost of the nails, son affixed to the boomerang murmuring forgiveness and proclaiming man as master of his own fate. Lee is more and more beleaguered, particularly after Crystal's death. Yet, unlike Scotty in his tree-house detachment, Lee does learn to live a little through words, refracting himself through the prism of words.

In *The Chantic Bird*, violence of word and deed, real or putative, is an act of revolt against the way things are. In *The Glass Canoe*, violence is a means of protecting and preserving the way things are, a means of resisting change. The drinkers at the Southern Cross pub, their tribal watering hole, are barricaded inside the present, worshipping their amber god and following faithfully the sacred laws passed down through generations of drinkers. Outside, the aged are scavengers, the middle class is barricaded in its safe houses, the job-captives are locked up, the police are paid off, the kids confuse TV and reality, big predators taunt little predators, the traffic and history flash by. Inside, the elders of the tribe dispense king-hit wisdom, Alky Jack discourses, the barmaids ferry the tribesmen in their glass canoes, sexual exploits are swapped, macabre and bawdy scenes flash by. Theirs is the language of the brawl and the king-hit, addressed to the preservation of a culture Ireland presents as comically tribal. Meat Man, the narrator, is the proud young tribesman recording and celebrating the mores and rituals of his people, but he is also the writer, trying to examine and contain the contradictions at his typewriter in Fortress Australia, with its glass keys, refracting the kaleidoscopic pieces of an absurdist tribal society. Comically opposed to Meat Man's version of the tribe is that of Sibley, outsider, Ph.D. thesis writer, a man who lets his beer go flat. Sibley is fired with missionary zeal, eager to investigate ways of assimilating the tribe into the civilized world. The novel is an abrasive parody of racial attitudes through this inverse view of Aboriginal society. The contest between Sibley's and Meat Man's versions of the tribe is rich in comic incongruity. But the intrepid Sibley becomes a harbinger of change and so he brings about his own death, a grisly comic horror in the novel. Sibley is the intruding writer, the parodic killjoy who is killed off. At the end of *The Glass Canoe*, the tribe renews the present with regenerative inter-tribal warfare.

In part, *The Glass Canoe* is a comic version of the will to preserve the present, a stubbornness of the present while time and history pass by. In *A Woman of the Future*, Ireland turns this will round to changing the present, the struggle to transmute it into the future. The present offers no place for Alethea's beauty, her reckless intelligence, her dreams of greatness and fertility. The drive of the novel is towards changing our intimation of the future through images of promise, fertility and freedom. The adolescent narrator of *The Chantic Bird*, rebellious and aggressive but caught in the ambiguities of freedom, becomes Alethea, the adolescent girl whose growth turns her away from the social imprisonments of the present to the savage fullpelt freedom of the future.

Her society is divided at the grading gate into two classes: the Frees are the failures, carrying out mock-work on the fringe of purposeful existence and undergoing aberrant bodily change; the Servers, the elite class, are permitted the luxury of work and so are confined to dulling routine. Ireland plays freely with definitions of freedom and servitude, in rivalry throughout the novel's social and moral paradoxes. The novel abounds in contestant images of time and change, of purpose and stasis, of growth and aberrant change, fertility and sterility, freedom and entrapment, present and future. Out of them, he fashions a new myth, a leopard image of the future, of the fertile centre, displacing the old myths of an inhospitable continent with an arid and lifeless centre. Like *Bloodfather*, *A Woman of the Future* explores the growth of a consciousness from infancy to eighteen, with Alethea both writer and character observing her own becoming. In both novels Ireland plays with the form of biography, proposing a linear, causal movement, only to disrupt this into an organic relationship of self and outer world, ripples of growth and change flowing out of the central consciousness. Ireland proposes this when Alethea is two and a half.

it seemed to me that everything was joined to everything else . . . all belonged to the whole picture, all together.

Later, as I grew, I never was without that feeling: that all things hang together, they connect by uncountable strings, good and bad together, the whole earth. It was as if I saw the particularity of all things, plus their necessary connection.

Later still, I extended that opinion, to cover all acts people were capable of, to all the odd things I saw.[8]

The movement of the novel is through this particularity of things 'plus their necessary connection'.

Like the butterbox of *The Wort Papers*, *A Woman of The Future* is a bundle of papers, tied up with string. The papers are the testaments and documents of Alethea's life, compiled when she is eighteen and vouched for by the editor as her own: diary entries, poems, schoolyard verse, anecdotes, essays, memories, all of them compositions

of herself, underneath which Ireland is composing a new image of
the future. It is a future stubbornly asserted against the old convention of the vast, infertile and inhospitable continent with emptiness
at its centre. On the contrary, the land is waiting:

It is a continent of dreams we inhabit, a waiting continent. All who have
set foot in its bush, its lonely places, know that silence. The continent
is dreaming. We have felt it and been afraid, and turned to trivial things,
and retired to the outer rim as if ready to depart. Everyday the quiet tides
of darkness roll over us from the menacing interior. (p.310)

Against the tameness of people and the timidity of the reality Australia has settled for, Ireland sets the image of the leopard's full pelt
power and the savage risk of freedom. Timidity is a trap, an industrial and social imprisonment, where powerlessness is more attractive
than the risks of freedom, where safe routine is less menacing than
change. This is also the paradox on which Puroil Australia turns,
the way it holds its prisoners.

Over the whole of *Woman of the Future* hangs the mystery of
Alethea's coming metamorphosis, but her leopard future is being
enacted throughout the novel. Amid the extraordinary proliferation
of detail, fugitive moments, thoughts, images and impulses, Alethea
is keeping track, hunting down her past, pursuing fugitive notions,
pouncing on connections as they break cover and appear briefly, then
holding her prey captive in words. The reader too must track down
the pattern and the shape of Alethea's growth, and hunt down the
future that lies static and in hiding in the present. While she grows
healthy and strong, she records in fragments the lives of the Frees
in her society and their bodily changes, as they grow appendages
and accessories. Surreal and absurdist images of aberrant growth
proliferate all around Alethea, paradoxes of change that is no change,
only stasis. A man grows a coffin from his side and is bereft when
it drops off. Two children take root, shooting out tendrils if stationary too long. A girl grows vulvae from her armpit, another grows
a map, or coins, or vines. The Inflatable Man runs across the horizon
until he wearies of it all and deflates himself out of existence. Huge
Wandering Crowds flow aimlessly through the streets, crossing the
paths of Wandering Oldies. Alethea's father dies each night on stage,
acting out changes in a play which runs throughout the novel, while

her mother recedes into the past, cocooned inside her Proust shed of remembrance. Only Alethea moves creatively through space and time, lured on by the risk and the promise of the future.

Alethea plays life as she played the Corner-game at school, with a fierce determination to win:

I could feel the joy of the full pelt run, the fierceness, the savage knowledge that some unwary kid was going to feel your weight suddenly and be borne to the ground underneath his conqueror.

And neither you nor he knew who it would be. It was a wild world of chance. Anything could happen. There may be someone there to hit or no one. You were no longer ruled by 'I should' but by 'I will'. And it was that part that fascinated my mind.

I'm the king of the castle.

And you're the dirty rascal. (p.39)

Later she plays the game of sex in the same way. As she plays Last in Lousy, Nipple-Napping, Tit Crunch, The Knee Crunch, Knuckles, so she plays all the games in the novel, each one a proposition about reality played out, pitting herself resolutely against chance, against the unknown contingency.

The sexual material is integral to the novel, not only because of the way she delights in mastering and winning, but also because of the male and female configurations of time and change which run throughout Ireland's work. The adolescent boy in *The Chantic Bird* attacking his society from the inside becomes the adolescent girl promising the future. Lee Mallory is of indeterminate sex, caught ambiguously between the guilty present and the inconceivable future. The Southern Cross Tribe of *The Glass Canoe* is unequivocally male and barricaded inside the present, violently resisting change. Alethea is female, freedom, fertility and, not the future, but the promise of the future. Like Machado de Assis' psychiatrist, Ireland is changing the definitions of things, in this case definitions of change, growth and the future.

Machado also wrote the novel *Epitaph for a Small Winner* which, like Ireland's minor novel, *Archimedes and the Seagle,* has a dog-narrator. Archimedes of Wolloomooloo is Ireland's narrator, a red setter who is literate and the author of this book. An innocent eye studying human society with grave and comic bewilderment, Archimedes is an Ireland creature, pondering on change, freedom and social order. The Book of Knowledge is Archimedes' fulcrum, his own book the lever to move the world. He begins with the political assertion that dogs are an oppressed proletariat with poor working conditions, disenfranchised under human tyranny, then extends this to questions of metaphysics, physics, the light and dark, the fluidity of existence, the shapes and varieties of truth. He marvels at constant change, delighting in the mystery of now, the contents of a single moment. The self is a composition of pieces, like his book.

Seagulls are petty, squabbling and selfish beings, but with the wondrous capacity to fly. Creatures of beauty and grace, creatures of selfish stupidity, they become a startling image of human society in suddenly surrealistic scenes. Glimpses of seagull tourists in buses, a gull magistrate, larrikin and derelict gulls, Mr Big and his gull heavies, a gull wedding, a parsonical gull and a sermon on the beach: all these break through the artifice of realism in Archimedes' world. The seagull scenes culminate in the haunting image of one solitary and idyllic 'seagle', with the majesty of an eagle, soaring above earthbound things, self-sustaining, disdaining the mundane world below where ordinary seagulls squabble and strut. Archimedes is drawn to the magical image of solitude, but settles for his own problematical and busy social activity below, content with the mystery and flow of ordinary existence. Although a minor novel, *Archimedes and the Seagle* is a work of celebration and optimism, light-hearted and fanciful, playing with serious notions of time and change, all within a sense of the sheer spectacle of existence, the wonder and mystery of it.

Ireland's best novels work on a dialectic of striving and contest, rivalries and double agencies, an impassioned struggle of contending forces. And the most impassioned of them all is in *City of Women*. *City of Women* is a major novel in Ireland's work, one that becomes a focus of the others. All his work is part of a continuum, sometimes like Jolley's work, where characters slide from one novel to another, reapppearing from different angles. Sometimes, it is through related images, like *The Flesheaters* and *Prisoner*, different faces of industrial servitude; or like *A Woman of the Future* and *The Chantic Bird*, different faces of adolescent revolt, the one trapped in a despairing role, the other turned to the future as an image of promise and fertility. Both novels are different faces of *Bloodfather*. *A Woman of the*

Future is also another face of *City of Women*, in that both have a female configuration, both propose images of the future. Of all Ireland's novels, *City of Women* is probably closest to *The Flesheaters*, because both novels present inner and outer worlds as one. In both the numerous characters are projections of the inner conflict of the one encompassing consciousness and both novels explore and enact the movement between the encompassed and the encompassing. *City of Women* is perhaps the most poignant of all Ireland's novels, which seems an odd comment on a novel which abounds with images of violence in a female future as tough and brutal as the old male order of *The Glass Canoe*. Yet it is the novel in which Ireland and his Lie are most vulnerable. It is a novel about the writer and fiction, the construction of the City of the Lie and the struggle to hold it against besieging reality.

By contrast with Alethea's growth in *A Woman of the Future*, the male and female images of *City of Women* seem a curious reversal. Billie Shockley, 62-year-old retired water engineer, is walled inside herself, grieving for her lost daughter, her only companion a leopard. Her plight is the inverse of Alethea's, but the very circumstances of her life become the means to freedom. Foreshadowing Aunt Mira from *Bloodfather*, Billie plays a game of illogic with words and asks

Q: When will I stop this mindless mockery and be at least serious about my own pain?
A: I can't. It's part of me. My weapons are my enemies. Fiddling about with words gets to be a habit of the lonely mind, as it clenches and unclenches, grasping nothing.[9]

Words are her allies. Out of words, clenching and unclenching, she creates the City of Women, each character a splinter of herself, each incident a fiction erected around her pain. At the start, Billie looks out across Sydney from the window of her flat and as she watches, it changes:

The outlines move and cross each other; it's not Corot quietness (I don't deserve that), it's Kandinsky, more like – a fantastic scribble, an Op art puzzle, a Bridget Riley, an eye-twister. (p.6)

The whole novel is a paradox, an eye-twister: *Prisoner* is Leger, *City of Women* is Kandinsky. The City is founded in the opening pages, as Billie remembers her father's words, which become her creed: 'In the beginning was the word. Hang on to words, words can arrange your life, words were invented to arrange our lives.'(p.3). With words, she founds her City. Behind the curious narrative stillness, the sense of events held still, are Billie's frantic strivings to maintain her City against the reality lying in wait outside the door of her flat – just as the old male order lies in wait at the Edge of the City. As Doc, she moves freely through the streets and pubs of the City, released from her lonely displacement by the strength of her fictions. She ministers to the women who suffer grotesque ailments and bizarre varieties of pain and loss – *her* pain, *her* loss, *her* intimations of decay and death.

Billie is 'Inventor, engineer, creator, exploiter, failed lover, failed friend, voyeur' (p.85), a voyeur observing the passages of love among her inventions, in the City she has engineered to contain her pain. The women she creates, all her characters are her allies, dangerous allies, who might at any moment betray her: first, the quick creation, then the narrow escape from recognizing herself in her creation; then the quick creation of a new one. We watch Billie fortifying her City against all onslaughts, watch her evasions and subterfuges, her dodging away into new characters when reality gets too close. We walk with Doc through the City streets, where she moves freely, generously, ministering to others. We are with her as she listens to the ailments of the women, sits in the Lover's Arms and the Conqueror's Arms, visits the women in their homes and watches some of them dying with their pets, some suffocating love with words and demands, some trapped in grief over past humiliations. We have heard tales of journeys beyond the Edge of the City and watched the dawn creep over its skyline, lighting up the parks and picking out the derelict women in the Domain. We have shared her horror at the attacks of Jack the Zipper, who also hovers over the City of her flat.

When reality starts pounding on the door of the City and threatens to break in, to force her to surrender her fictions and admit she is an old woman playing a harmless game, then Billie is caught on the Edge of her City, lost between two worlds. She stands pitiably exposed for a moment, until she puts out words as feelers: 'Light defines itself by what isn't light, doesn't it?' (p.167). The City defines itself by what is outside it, doesn't it? The Lie defines itself by truth, doesn't it? So she begins to grope her way back to the City, plugging up the breaches in the City walls. The men she saw with horror in the streets below disappear and the City is held. So Ireland gropes his way back to the Lie, until it is held.

City of Women is about the writer, both Billie and Ireland, splintering the self into characters. The novel is about writing and the meeting of fiction and reality, defining each other. Billie is the writer, the women her selves, each one a splinter of herself and an exorcism of her pain. The struggle to hold the City is both Billie's and Ireland's and the novel ends with triumph. The fiction contends with reality, the male with female, decay with growth, youth with old age, love with loss, displacement with belonging, word with object. And the City, like the reality beyond its Edge, holds. They survive together, each defining itself by the other.

Ireland is always the Escher-writer, but not without risks, because the hands also point back and the fall-out of defeat might spread its fatal contamination into the space outside the Lie, where the Liar sits. There is a dialectic which risks itself throughout his work. This is the dialectic Billie Shockley plays, the duel when she splits herself into contestant forces, clenching and unclenching in the duel of fiction and the Lie, a frantic activity in fear of grasping nothing. The Liar is out there urging us to take the risks of change, but it is risky for him too.

All Ireland's novels are built on a battle of structures, between the urge to order and the disorder of reality, which cannot be contained in the tidy structures we erect for it. Contestant forces define themselves through each other: freedom and servitude, chaos and order, growth and decay, connection and disconnection, reality and the Lie. These contestant forces are never still, never at peace. There is no defeat, no victory, only the constant striving. This constant transaction is the substance of Ireland's latest novel, *Bloodfather*.

Like *A Woman of the Future*, *Bloodfather* plays with the linear shape of biography, from birth to sixteen. Through Davis' growth, Ireland creates an extraordinary sense of an internal world, so that we lodge inside a vast and teeming consciousness which has its own geography and its own geometry. Davis Blood is a truly memorable figure one can see with extraordinary clarity, a consciousness which shimmers, translucent. Davis is present to the reader as if we could look up from the pages and find him standing watching, meditative, still, questing, fiercely independent, solitary, with a composure and stillness which enchant, a silence which changes. The narrative shifts to and fro easily, encompassingly, taking into itself fugitive impulses and imaginings, impinging contradictions, the burgeoning self reckoning out its own identity, as well as the strands of growth which become its axioms. At the same time, the narrative dances from Davis' innermost entanglements to the shifting creaking world outside him, the whole novel set on the perimeters of inner and outer reality, at the crossing point. The novel has a spaciousness which is in part structural, but much of the enlargement is a growing sense of possibility and of vision, with the novel pushing its boundaries out and back, extending its own space constantly. It is both intricate, made up of an elaborate sequence of splinters of incident like Ireland's earlier novels, and extraordinarily open, encompassing, enlarging. In its lattice structure, the whole construct of moving parts seems to take on its own volition.

Through Davis' meditations on the world around him, his intimation of the connectedness of things, the paradoxes of his drawings and, more generally, the continuing theme of transactions, Ireland reveals his world where all things are connected. All things, large and small, traffick together in an existence of constant transaction, constant change, with all things participating in one another. Against the dark vision of *The Flesheaters*, where all things prey and feed on each other, here all things share a luminous presence. Davis ponders on the fixtures others see in the world around him, the urge to order and fixity, words and language as impulses to order and containment. He marvels at humans straining to be more than human, 'as if we were gods'. His own intimations and measuring out of the world reveal a vast and shifting lattice of transactions in which he delights. Combined with the notion of liberation and the godhead in man which is enchained, hidden and denied, is Davis' sense of the constellations behind every moment:

He had only to think the word to make others visible. Then they teemed round him, coruscating, tumbling pellmell like water released from a dam;

teemed and multiplied for a great way into the distance, until they seemed infinite. So much, and all spun from a word.

He didn't have this feeling all day. Perhaps a little at a time was all he could cope with.

Everything, he reflected, must have a sort of infinity in it, and each thing linked up with each other thing.[10]

This is also the nature of the novel, a single consciousness that is a crevice into a vast and teeming universe. Davis becomes an eye, his transactions with the world around him opening up a new shimmering sense of existence.

In the early part of the novel, there is a growing sense of self and privacy, which is Davis' own and yet sometimes offers the pleasure of remembrance, as Ireland measures out sensibility and sensation, volition and value. There is a gentle meditative mood in the opening section and the child is a delight – his intuitions, his explorations and measuring out of the dimensions and shape of himself and his world, his tasting new words, his pride in his exploits, his sometime bafflement, his emerging sense of the interconnectedness of things, his groping in the crevices of his own experience, searching for a way to liberate innate possibilities. Closely linking the spiritual and the artistic in Davis' growth, Ireland explores the notion of the God in man and of releasing, liberating the inner potential – if only we knew the commands, like the vignette of the dog, Kellick, who waits in frustration and a peculiar pain for the commands that can release his hidden talents and possibilities. With her continuous inner song, Lillian bequeathes to Davis an intimation of the God in man which becomes the ground of his being and begins his attunement to his own 'inner song'. As Davis ponders on spiritual matters, one of the most striking features of the novel is Ireland's rendering of the numinous sense. This is often set against the orderliness and certainties of human existence which Davis sees as artificial, evasive, brittle, constructs of consciousness by which man barricades himself against change and thereby reduces his existence. Davis' own spontaneous delight in constant change, in things continuing in another form, is played out with a numinous sense of the world, which emerges in the contours of scene after scene. The prose in some passages is almost translucent, until the quick sharp twist back to day to day events. This kind of shift, from one mood and mode to another, generates much of the momentum as well as the spaciousness of the novel. It is one of those twists of vision by which Ireland can flip reality over and confront us suddenly with a new and disturbing way of seeing. Words are slipped off objects like gloves, until they take on their own unclad existence, a presence, and startlingly real.

The redoubtable Aunt Mira does her own kind of flipping. Aunt Ursula is a more serious and attentive presence, a figure of courage and dignity, with an intelligent cynicism, a devoted mentor gravely and lovingly offering a framework for Davis' own ideas. Aunt Mira on the other hand is magnificently oblivious to other people, yet her deliciously tangled and abrasive utterances are integral to the conflicts and tensions of the novel. Crazy, sarcastic, weirdly comic, often lewd, her fabulous images and utterances are a comic delight as well as a vital part of the intellectual substance of the novel. More than puns, hers is a game of verbal illogic and paradox twisting our expectations of sense, as images like these release marvellous possibilities: 'the sequins of events', 'just another member of the bland', 'being hit over the head with blunt concepts', 'a little collage is a dangerous thing', carving out 'a Nietzsche for yourself', 'feats of Klee' and 'uninhabited behaviour'. These are fun, but they also tease out verbal paradoxes which complement the visual paradoxes of Davis' drawings.

Many of Davis' drawings grow out of an Escher vision – the paradoxes of shape and line and perspective, which draw conflicting dimensions together, playing with time and space. Many of Davis' drawings seem to flip from one mode of vision to another or to contain a rival mode of vision. Some peel back layers of reality, like skins; some are prisms, windows into rival realities, past and present; some, like the Captive and Free series, are gently allusive images uncoiling out of Ireland's earlier novels. All bring together incongruent images, shapes and contours which undergo metamorphosis before us, opposites in unexpected conjunction, which push the boundaries of the novel out and back, until it dances with impinging images that take us into the depths of his consciousness. It is a consciousness which does not look for congruence but delights in the random contradictions of a myriad world. His drawings are an intimation of a world humming with a presence which permeates all things and conducts its transactions across all boundaries of time and space, of word and object and dream.

Through the questing consciousness of the novel, exploring, touching, pondering, peeling back surfaces and layers of possibility, Ireland generates Davis' sense of destiny, not only attunement to his own inner self, his own 'Internal God', but a sense of direction which, once grasped, will become his shape, the contour of his existence. Earlier, in the school scene of discovering axioms, Davis protested at the falsity of the axioms, the floating world of geometry inhabiting its own world of abstraction. Then this dissent shifted into a discovery of the enchantment of playing with forms and the beauty of speculative possibility, the quest for equalities and harmonies. This sequence is rendered gracefully, gradually building into a complex intellectual nexus in which Ireland explores the transactions between word and vision, writing and drawing. Davis realizes in time that his drawings grow out of words, ultimately that writing rather than painting will be his way in life. As Davis deliberates more on artistic matters, there is an increasing play between word and eye, word-Lie and visual-Lie. In the exhibition sequence in the Gallery, Davis realizes some paintings create their own laws, their own coherence, create their own axioms and become their own world. He recognises that art is a private geometry built on axioms the artist has created. But he is aware too that words are the essence of his vision, words are his truth.

When Davis starts planning a novel, designing a trellis, an expanding lattice, and decides on the title, the novel has reached a crystal Godelian moment, its gently self-reflecting point. By this point, Ireland has created his own private geometry built on his own axiom of an Internal God. Ireland explores art as transaction, both between artist and reality and between artist and audience. Beneath art, in its deepest springs, is a meditation on the transaction going on between the Liar and the reader. Like Escher's *Print Gallery*, Davis Blood is in the world which is in the gallery which is in Davis Blood. And, like the whorl at the centre with Escher's signature, Ireland's signature is here too, inside the Lie. It is in the end the novel of the Liar discovering the space between the Liar and the reader and celebrating the joy of the Lie.

FIFTH DIALOGUE

Reader What's that you're reading? *Slaughterhouse-Five*?
Liar Yes. I'm trying to work out a way to write a new kind of novel. There must be a way to write a Tralfamadorian novel.
Reader You mean like the novels on Vonnegut's planet?
Liar Yes. Listen to this, a Tralfamadorian talking about novels back home:

each clump of symbols is a brief, urgent message – describing a situation, a scene. We Tralfamadorians read them all at once, not one after the other. There isn't any particular relationship between all the messages, except that the author has chosen them carefully, so that, when seen all at once, they produce an image of life that is beautiful and surprising and deep. There is no beginning, no middle, no end, no suspense, no moral, no causes, no effects. What we love in our books are the depths of many marvellous moments seen all at one time.[1]

Imagine a reader like that . . . not worrying about beginnings and ends and causes. Just reading the whole thing at once, seeing the depths of all the marvellous moments at one time. What a reader!
Reader Tough isn't it? Having to make do with ordinary mortals. What a bind for you. Mere human readers. Anyway, do you really want to be a Tralfamadorian writer? No beginnings and ends? Everything happening at once?
Liar No, it's just a fantasy, but it would be more realistic, wouldn't it?
Reader Realistic? You want to write more realistically?
Liar No, not realistic, real. I want to *write real*. I'm wondering if Billy Pilgrim has the answer. He wants his countrymen to be able to see

---

139

as well as his little green friends on Tralfamadore. So he wants to prescribe 'corrective lens' for them. Maybe that would work. Special lens.

Reader I suppose Ireland's particles of narrative get close sometimes, so it seems to be all happening at once, a plural reality. But it's still one bit after the other. It's not the same as reading them all at once.

Liar Double vision works sometimes. Seeing two opposing views of things at once. Like Escher. Convex and concave. Or like *Bliss*. Harry Joy's heaven and hell, two in one . . .

Reader That sounds like Foster. What about Christian Rosy Cross? Damcar and Damascus and keeping a foot in both?

Liar Ar Wat's Tlute . . . the Seclet Art. 'A way to blake through shadow, seear lainbow . . . You justar – howyousay – leflection.'

Reader I'm afraid it's not so easy to see the rainbow . . .

Liar 'What you *flaid* of heh? You gotta fear in the two mind state, you got big tlouble! Gotta *lealise* that fear.'

Reader OK, Ar Wat, I remember, the Tlute's two-faced.

Liar Or four-eyed. Seeing double. Double vision. Or four-handed, like Escher. Two hands outside, two inside. You see, it's all there in Escher . . . convex and concave. See how we keep looping back to Escher?

Reader It's not only Escher. If you're dealing in doubles, we haven't really progressed at all. That takes us right back to Mathers as well as Foster.

Liar It takes us ahead too. What about Hasluck? Jolley? All the others? They're all in it . . . . You seem to think we should be moving in some linear fashion, crossing Liars off our list as we go. As if they were all lined up in sequence, demurely waiting their turn. They're not an orderly lot, you know. On the whole, they're more inclined to disorder. Chaos and contingency. Besides, I thought by now you realized the Lie is a Loop. A Tangled Hierarchy. Do you think you can just dispense with Mathers or Foster, once they've had their turn? Where's your Tralfamadorian eye? Elizabeth Jolley can't wait to get into all this double vision. She's having to restrain Miss Peabody.

Reader Look, Miss Peabody will just have to wait. She'll have to read some more letters from Diana or have a chat to Ar Wat.

Liar I'd love to hear that. What a marvellous idea! She could discuss literary optics with Finbar too. Imagine Finbar confronted by Miss Peabody! Or imagine her at Percy's wortarium, peering down the hole to where he's heaping up words . . . shortly to emerge naked and streak across the open! Miss Hailey in her pith helmet flagging down Percy as he zooms by on the Norton. Or rushing into the Southern Cross Hotel . . . 'Hoorool Meat Man, where are you? . . . Quickly, before the Muse strikes again!' The mind boggles at the possibilities.

Reader Look this is serious. You're getting carried away. I'm still at Merry Lands, with Lee's Perspex prism. Double vision and Billie Shockley's City. Reality knocking at the door of her flat.

Liar The City of fiction in battle with reality! Fiction wins! A triumph for the Lie! Mind you, fiction usually wins. Look at Murnane, the Liar on the Plains . . . the lone warrior defending the Plains. The Lie victorious again!

Reader Do you think there's always a winner? I would have thought it was a truce. Armistice.

Liar There's never a truce, only constant battle. Win a skirmish here, humiliated there, routed, ignominious defeat. One moment advancing in triumph, the next put to flight. It's relentless. One moment you glimpse the 'lainbow', the next moment murk.

Reader Some of your triumphs come from changing the rules. Which is cheating. Look at Machado de Assis changing the rules in 'The Psychiatrist'. Changing the definition of sanity. Look at the turmoil for the townspeople each time it's changed. If you can change the definitions, you're bound to triumph.

Liar Changing the definitions . . . Corrective lens. That's what it's all about. Look at *The Flesheaters*. New definitions of sanity and insanity at Merry Lands. Or look at Walter Adamson's novel, *The Institution*. Professor Longbeard's institution is part refuge and part psychiatric hospital. Look at the first consultation with Dr. Esau. Witty stuff. It's a marvellous place, where 'everybody can do what he can', a place outside time and space, where calendar, clock, paper, and mirrors are banned, pencils are only for newcomers, sharpened once a year. That's different layers of reality. Not cheating.

Reader It's a form of it. What about the double image of the Gemini with their secret cache of mirrors? Or the concert scene and music without instruments? All told with a dead-pan logic.

141

Liar Real and surreal at the same time. The boundaries between them blur.

Reader They blur outside too, where Chimpanzee and U are wandering towards the institution, all roads lead to Longbeard and its always 3.15. But suddenly there's chaos – the Generalissimo's mass extermination program and the imminent destruction of man. Suddenly Professor Longbeard and the Generalissimo become one.

Liar That's right. Longbeard is part saviour, offering the refuge in the rock fortress, part teacher, teaching the inmates the nature of freedom from time and space; and part dictator, who draws the institution closer to the outer world, until it becomes a microcosm of it. Then the Loop, a last crossing of the borders of fiction and reality.

Reader Right back where we started, with Schiller waiting for the attendants to take him to the institution. There is no institution. Adamson made it up out of Schiller's own life, his twin sisters, grandfather and father, his militaristic, strict mother. In his room there is the piano, a painting of a large house and a pile of closely written pages.

Liar So the institution and the Generalissimo are a surrealistic version of Schiller's real existence. That's not cheating. It is layers of meaning, jolting us from one level to another, revealing new ways of seeing earlier levels. All done with a mocking straight-faced manner, with delicate logic and paradox. The logic of the Liar. It is Marquez logic, magical realism.

Reader It's also a sleight of hand or of eye. Double vision. Seeing double, like Harry Joy. Heaven and hell in one.

Liar Or like *Pedro Paramo*, the Mexican novel by Juan Rulfo – which seems to be the story of a young landowner who inherits a farm loaded with debt, makes a good marriage and becomes the most powerful man in the country with a band of revolutionaries in his pay. But Pedro Paramo and the people involved with him are dead from the first pages of the novel . . . Life and death, reality and illusion, heaven and hell, life and death.

Reader That's not so new. That's been done before. Think of Flann O'Brien's *The Third Policeman*. The main character's dead and in hell for most of the novel. It's literary *trompe l'oeil*.

Liar It's not just literary optics, it's a dialogue. It's a form of Billy Pilgrim's corrective lens. Think of *The Death of Artemio Cruz* by Carlos Fuentes, narrated through the last thoughts of a dying man and the reflections of his family and business associates at his bed-side. Artemio's stream of consciousness is divided into two, the 'yo' which cannot relinquish the ego interest in business and public activities, and the deeper consciousness which addresses him as 'tu' and which recognizes that he has lived a false life of gesturing, without truth and authenticity. It's a dialogue between the real self and the lost possibilities of the self.

Reader Sounds like Harry Joy. What's the next chapter? It has to be Carey coming up next.

Liar Yes it is, but not only Harry Joy. Herbert Badgery too. Different layers and levels of reality. Crossing from one to the other. Douglas Hofstadter would like my friend Herbert Badgery. Godelian Loops and a Tangled Hierarchy.

Reader I thought you might have a special feeling for Herbert. I'm sure you get on well together. The smiling salesman. Would you buy a used car from this man?

Liar Herbert's O.K. He gives good value, and pays his way. He gives people what they want. Besides he warns you on the very first page. *Caveat emptor*. It's a Buyer Beware novel.

Reader But how valid is that? Is that all the law requires? A two-word warning at the start, then all sorts of shady practices and underhand deals.

Liar It's not a matter of laws. There are no laws governing this. It's an off-shore scheme, beyond the reach of the law.

Reader But look what Herbert's selling. Lies and inventions. It's a real con. Trafficking in Lies. There has to be more consumer protection than a two-word warning.

Liar Herbert's just the front man. There's much more to the business than that. You've got to see past him.

Reader If the front man's a self-confessed liar, what kind of business is it? He's not just selling used-cars. He's selling used-history. He's selling our own history to us.

Liar Of course. He's selling us back our own lies. The ones we've been buying for years. That's the point. The business of lies has been booming in Australia for two hundred years. Set a thief to catch a thief . . . Set a liar to catch the lies. Carey's been selling Lies for years. He's just admitting it. Or rather, Herbert's admitting it. You can't reveal everything about your business, particularly not to the consumer.

LIARS

Reader So you're asking me to buy from a liar, a con man, an illywhacker, a used-car dealer and a showman. What do I get out of the deal?

Liar Look, I'm a salesman myself. All Liars are salesmen. Selling a different way of seeing things. Selling corrective lens. You only buy if you want to see!

Reader Why should I buy from you? Or from Carey?

Liar It's free trade. You don't have to buy unless you want to be able to see. You have to try out different lens until you find the ones that suit your eyes. Try Carey's. Try Ireland's. Try Escher's. Keep trying until you find the ones that fit your vision. But buy . . .

LIES FOR SALE   *PETER CAREY*

The minute I think of an answer to something I can always think of ten different things that contradict it. So, as meanings become more layered, more complex, and even self-contradictory, I feel like I'm getting closer to the truth.[1]

Lies, dreams, visions – they were everywhere. We brushed them aside as carelessly as spider webs across a garden path. They clung to us, of course, adhered to our clothes and trailed behind us . . .

Illywhacker

My name is Herbert Badgery. I am a hundred and thirty-nine years old and something of a celebrity. They come and look at me and wonder how I do it. There are weeks when I wonder the same, whole stretches of terrible time. It is hard to believe you can feel so bad and still not die.

I am a terrible liar and I have always been a liar. I say that early to set things straight. *Caveat emptor*. My age is the one fact you can rely on, and not because I say so, but because it has been publicly authenticated. Independent experts have poked me and prodded me and scraped around my foul-smelling mouth. They have measured my ankles and looked at my legs. It is a relief to not worry about my legs any more. When they photographed me I did not care that my dick looked as scabby and scaly as a horse's, even though there was a time when I was a vain man and would not have permitted the type of photographs they chose to take. Apart from this (and it is all there, neatly printed on a chart not three feet from where I lie) I have also been written up in the papers. Don't imagine this is any novelty to me – being written up has been one of my weaknesses and I don't mention it now so that I may impress you, but rather to make the point that I am not lying about my age.

But for the rest of it, you may as well know, lying is my main subject, my specialty, my skill. It is a great relief to find a new use for it. It's taken me long enough, God knows, and I have not always been proud of my activities. But now I feel no more ashamed of my lies than my farts (I rip forth a beauty to underline the point). There will be complaints, of course. (There are complaints now, about the fart – my apologies, my fellow sufferers.) But my advice is to not waste your time with your red pen, to try to pull apart the strands of lies and truth, but to relax and enjoy the show.

I think I'm growing tits. They stuck their callipers into me and measured them. That'd be one for the books if I turned into a woman at this stage of life. It's only the curiosity that keeps me alive: to see what my dirty old body will do next.

I'm like some old squid decaying on the beach. They flinch when they look at me and they could not guess that there is anything inside my head but gruel, brain soup sloshing round in a basin. My voice has gone, so they could not know what changes have taken place in me: I may even, at last, have become almost kind.

Illywhacker[2]

·

ILLYWHACKER OPENS with the Liar's paradox: 'I am a terrible liar and I have always been a liar.' Herbert announces this early 'to set things straight'. He urges us not to waste time trying to 'pull apart the strands of lies and truth, but to relax and enjoy the show'. He is a liar and a showman, and he is also a salesman. He gives fair warning to the buyer, but he is a good salesman, his goods are glossy, and the *caveat* becomes a forgotten small-print clause. Herbert is a used-car salesman and, with his 'salesman's sense of history', he is also selling us used-history, second-hand history. So who is the previous owner of this history Herbert Badgery is selling? What kind of deal have they got going between them? Badgery is the go-between in the business of the Lie, the showman in the showroom, the previous owner, Peter Carey. As Herbert sells us second-hand history, Carey is outside the showroom, Carey–Escher watching Herbert Badgery's hands drawing each other. The Liar is Carey, the reader is the buyer, and the real business deal is the Lie of fiction. *Caveat emptor*.

Herbert Badgery is not only negotiating with the reader to sell us Carey's Lie. He is also the narrator, the *Spieler* go-between, the entrepreneur between the characters and the writer, and he is not an honourable intermediary: some of the history he is selling us has been stolen from Leah Goldstein. Outraged, Leah accuses Herbert of the theft:

A hundred things come to me, things that amused me at the time, touched me – and now I see they were only excuses to thieve things from me. And even then you have not done me the honour of thieving things whole but have taken a bit here, a bit there, snipped, altered and so on. You have stolen like a barbarian, slashing a bunch of grapes from the middle of a canvas. (p.549)

But who is the barbarian? Leah blames Herbert but she does not suspect the existence of the Pig Tyrant Carey.

At the start of *Illywhacker*, Herbert is beached, 'like some old squid decaying on the beach'. In Carey's story, 'Concerning the Greek Tyrant'[3], Homer's characters are beached too, waiting on the beach because Homer is tossing in a fever, afraid he cannot cope with the next episode, afraid Odysseus will accuse him of mismanagement, afraid of mutiny. Odysseus reminds him sharply that it is worse for the men waiting on the beach. Echion is a battle-scarred veteran, questioning the reason for his terrible sufferings, and so is a dangerous character who could start the mutiny Homer dreads. Suspicious of Odysseus, Echion reads his papers and finds they are not navigational but verse – and contain a plot to kill him. Angry, Echion resolves to escape but Homer, a man he did not know existed, intervenes and ties him up. Echion manages to free himself and escapes – only to die in exactly the way Homer had plotted. But Echion's death was for nothing. Homer scrubbed the episode. We are left with a strange pity for Echion – Echion who is only a possibility Carey sees in Homer's story, a possible character, not even a real character. Before he died, Echion scrawled in the dust, 'KILL THE PIG TYRANT HOMER WHO OPPRESSES US ALL' (p.205). What of Carey whose existence Echion never suspected? Echion dies ignorant of the existence of the real Pig Tyrant, Carey. Carey is Echion's killer – and gets off scot free, while Echion lies bleeding in the dust. Behind Homer is the Pig Tyrant Carey.

So who stole Leah Goldstein's story? Who is the barbarian who did the slashing? Herbert or Carey? Who killed Harry Joy and sent a Good Bloke to Hell? Who stole Herbert's daughter, broke up his marriage, sent him to prison, made him live for 139 years and left him beached like an old squid? The Pig Tyrant Carey. But then being written up is no novelty to Herbert, in fact it is one of his weaknesses. So he has some good business deal with the Liar, who is outside the showroom where Herbert is trying to sell us his used-history. So sit back, relax and buy. Lies for sale.

Bliss is a novel built on an Escher double vision of heaven and hell, life and death, bliss and despair. But it is not so simple as double vision: Carey writes of 'the infinite onion of the universe' and of peeling back layers and layers of reality. A Godelian layering runs throughout his work, up and down a Tangled Hierarchy. One of his best known stories is 'Peeling', where layer after layer is peeled away from the woman revealing first her marginal selves, and finally a white doll. Underneath the layers of reality, which Carey peels away one by one, is the white doll, an absurdist truth.

I like to write like a cartoonist – I look at things that exist and push them to their ludicrous or logical extension . . . When you push far enough, you can find yourself in some strange and original places. [4]

This is a Liar's push, 'ludicrous or logical' extensions of things, reminding us at every step of his own strategies and artifice. In 'The Fat Man in History', Carey comments on Alexander Finch.

He enjoys himself with these theories, he has a love of such constructions, building ideas like card houses, extending them until he gets dizzy and trembles at their heights. [5]

Thus does Carey build his fictions, like card houses, which leave the reader dizzy and trembling at their heights. Often Carey begins with the seemingly familiar, then suddenly jolts us into the surrealistic or the absurd. Often he works through a shift in our temporal or spatial bearings, disorienting the reader. His characters are sliding identities, who suddenly slip into a new marginal self or into a different time scale. Carey has a wonderful sense of play, enjoys playing with those incongruous aspects of reality that blur and trick, events that are no longer innocent but deceptive and devious. The Liar flaunting his Lie.

Born in 1943, Peter Carey grew up in Bacchus Marsh, Victoria, where his father ran the family car business. He attended Geelong Grammar for seven years, then studied science for one year at Monash

University, drawn to chemistry as a magical world, 'transmuting one element into another'.[6] In a way which recalls Foster, Carey found magic in

organic chemistry – which I never understood – but it was the alchemy of it that fascinated me, things changing into other things. So perhaps whatever it was I was looking for in organic chemistry I finally found in fiction.[7]

He then joined an advertising agency, where he worked with Barry Oakley, Morris Lurie and Bruce Petty. He lived in Melbourne until 1967, then he went to London and, in 1968, wrote a novel, 'this very maniacal and highly mandarin novel which out-Becketted Beckett and out-Robbe-Grilleted Robbe-Grillet'.[8] Now he mocks the obscurity of it and, believing firmly in 'the possibility of popular art that's good art in anybody's terms',[9] he prefers to write for as broad an audience as possible. He returned to Australia and advertising, which he wrote about in 'War Crimes'.

The story is actually just like real life, like working in an advertising agency. It pushes things to extremes a bit – people are shot rather than fired. But that's just the logic of business anyway . . . That's my business story.[9]

His first collection of short stories, *The Fat Man in History*, was published in 1974 and in 1980 the second, *War Crimes*, which won the New South Wales Premier's Award. A combined collection of his stories was published as *Exotic Pleasures* and his stories have been translated and published in Japanese, German, Dutch and Swedish.

Written while Carey lived in a Queensland commune and commuted to a Sydney advertising agency, his first novel, *Bliss*, won the New South Wales Premier's Award and the Miles Franklin and National Book Council Awards. Critics at the Cannes Film Festival were not enthusiastic about the film *Bliss*, but in 1985, it won the Australian Film Institute Awards – Best Film, Best Director, best Script (written by Carey and Ray Lawrence). His second novel, *Illywhacker* (1985) won *The Age* Book of the Year Award, The National Book Council Award, the Barbara Ramsden Award of the Victorian Fellowship of Australian Writers and was short-listed for the 1985 Booker Prize. First published in 1988, Carey's third novel,

Oscar and Lucinda, is a dazzling Lie set in the eighteen-sixties. Carey suggests,

A lot of it's to do – I think – with Christianity and Christian stories and their effect on our culture. I'm interested in that; I grew up with it around me, but the tales seem to have gone now, just the last echoes of them are around . . . [7]

Shades of the storytelling in *Bliss*, which is itself a 'post-Christian' novel. In a shimmering play of light and dark, *Oscar and Lucinda* is also about the molten mysteries in the manufacture of glass—and the manufacture of the Lie.

Carey's literary kin include Borges, Barthelme, Brautigan, Vonnegut, and in some ways Marquez whom Carey much admires for 'his ability to blend elements of fantasy and reality on a big scale, with some complexity'.[9] Other writers he enjoys include the French new wave writers (Sarraute, Robbe-Grillet, Butor), Kosinksi (especially *The Painted Bird*), Faulkner, Kerouac, Joyce and Nabokov 'who really loved setting little rabbit snares'.[9] Carey's stories bring to mind Borges' idea of the 'secret plot', the arcane element in narrative. Borges' theme of a man caught in a trap he has himself unwittingly constructed is Carey's theme in the story 'Kristu Du' as well as *Bliss*, but it runs throughout his work. Like Borges' stories, Carey's are often built on precise, substantiating detail which brings a weird air of probability to the fantastic and the bizarre, a disturbing vision of the unknown and the nightmarish emerging from inside the known.

In 'Crabs', Carey moves from the apparently familiar into the sudden futuristic or surrealistic world where the Karboys prowl and plunder, while Crabs himself, a nervous daredevil trying to escape from his own fears, finds himself plunged into the drive-in nightmare. The drive-in theatre is in part a refugee-camp, where he is stranded, being stripped of hope as his car is stripped first of two wheels, then of generator, carburettors, distributor, battery. He plots against his loss, struggling to reconstruct his hopes with the car, but under the bonnet are gaps, holes, emptinesses. Trucks arrive bringing other crippled cars, further distorting his hopes of escape. He decides that 'to be free, you must be a motor car or vehicle in good health' (*The Fat Man in History*, p.19), and so becomes one. When he moves freely outside the fence, he finds only a deserted world, and is left looking through the fence at the lights, the movement, the people inside the theatre boundaries. Carey himself has commented,

he spends all his time escaping from something which he finds unsatisfactory only to realise finally that what he's trying to escape from is the world, and there he is outside the fence.[8]

He is left trapped in the wasteland outside the fence.

In 'Peeling', the narrator is contemplating the prospect of unhurried exploration of the woman, Nile, preferring 'to know these things, the outside layers, before we come to the centre of things' (p.27). Their relationship, he insists, is 'beyond analysis', his sense of time is stilled – 'Normally it seems to be late afternoon'. He is content to contemplate change as a slow process, in slow motion, disappointed when she hastens it, and finds her behaviour promiscuous. His slowness is very deliberate, a practised discipline of eking out pleasures, for fear of emptiness, of nothing to do. In a world of white and her white dolls stripped of feature, where he would prefer more colour, 'more character about it', he contemplates 'moving layer after layer, until I discover her true colours' (p.24). He finds first the other marginal selves she contains, the young male, the woman beneath the male, but then as a stocking is unrolled, a limb disappears, until she is exposed as nothing, only the fragments of a small white doll without features. The more he tries to discover her true self, the more tightly he is embroiled in a surreal nightmare: the threads unravel and reveal nothing. 'Peeling' is a brilliant, surrealistic fiction of the fear that, if we peel back the layers of the infinite onion of the universe, there will be nothing, or only an image, without features.

Two stories hinge on absurd contradiction, an existential paradox. In 'Life and Death in the South Side Pavilion', Carey creates a Kafkaesque predicament, in which the narrator, Shepherd 3rd Class, is engaged in an absurd activity, employed by The Company to prevent the horses falling into the swimming pool and drowning. He feels bound to remain in his job until they all drown, which it is his job to prevent. When he deliberately allows them all to drown, so that he will be free and able to leave the Pavilion with Marie, replacement horses are delivered by The Company the next day. 'A

Windmill in the West' has a similar absurdity but is more elaborate. The American soldier stands at his post on the line of electrified fence, which shimmers away into the distance, dividing east and west, one side designated the United States, the other Australia. His duty, to prevent unauthorized people from crossing, is to be carried out in ignorance of the length, shape, status and function of the line. In isolation, ignorant of what the line divides, encircles or contains, he loses all orientation, confusing east and west, inside and outside. In the absence of categories, he tries to devise his own measurements and definitions, killing scorpions in order to calculate the area of desert now free of scorpions. The spatial dislocation extends to a dislocation of his sense of self, a loss of connection with his own reflected image.

He can see his face in the shaving mirror, like the surface of a planet, a photograph of the surface of the moon in 'Life' magazine. It is strange and unknown to him. He rubs his hands over it, more to cover the reflected image than to feel its texture. (p.63)

Unable to determine the significance of the aeroplane, he finally shoots it down. He acts distantly, as if observing his own actions and he has no categories by which to assess the significance of his action. Within a surrealistic structure, this is a marvellous Kafkaesque fiction of disorientation and loss of the categories by which we define and determine our actions.

'American Dreams' turns on the notion of the real and the artifice co-existing, the scale model the means of both realizing and destroying the dreams of the real country town. The idea of building, which runs through 'Kristu Du' and later *Illywhacker*, is part of Carey's transmutation of things as well as people. The story builds up the mystery of Gleason's actions, and speculates on his motives. The townspeople's dreams of the big city, wealth, modern houses and big motor cars, their American dreams, are realized through the model town. But the town is stilled too, stopped on the knife-edge of its self-consciousness, transfixed in the past. The narrator is left feeling guilty and, like the townspeople generally, bereft of his dreams. Unlike the slow, suspenseful building in 'American Dreams', 'Report on the Shadow Industry' immediately proclaims its central fiction of an industry, with factories, all the encumbrances of industrial technol-.

ogy and commercial marketing – of which the product is shadows. Shadows have different value, good and bad, beautiful and despairing, but, without shadows, there is 'the feeling of emptiness, that awful despair that comes when one has failed to grasp the shadow' (p.93). At the end, the narrator admits

My own feelings about the shadows are ambivalent, to say the least. For here I have manufactured one more: elusive, unsatisfactory, hinting at greater beauties and more profound mysteries that exist somewhere before the beginning and somewhere after the end. (p.94)

Carey turns the fiction round to comment on itself and the manufacture of shadows, without which there is only emptiness.

In 'The Fat Man in History', the revolution spawns a new notion of fat men as greedy oppressors and, somehow American, grotesque enemies of the people. Alexander Finch is the secretary of the clandestine 'Fat Men Against the Revolution', living communally with its leader Fantoni and four others in a slum ghetto, their only trusted link to the outside world, Nancy Bowlby. The story builds to the fantastic notion of eating her as a political protest, which in Finch's formal rationale becomes an act of consummation by which the Fat Men will purify the revolution. But it is Fantoni himself whom they devour, when the man-who-won't-give-his-name kills Fantoni and assumes his role. The unexpectedly chilling end is the discovery that the whole sequence is part of a continuing experiment, a study of revolution in a closed society in which Nancy always precipitates change and the heir-apparent, the-man-who-won't-give-his-name, always supplants the Fantoni.

These are unforgettable fictions, the kind which lodge in your mind ineradicably and open up new strange territories of the real. Reality smudges across into the fabulous and the fantastic, as these fictions construct their own points of reference and then suddenly offer us new bearings on an old reality. Out of this exploration of the dark myths comes a new perspective on the real. All the stories in *The Fat Man In History* have what Carey has called a 'cool, hard surface' [8], pared down, precise, with a finely tuned logic by which he elaborates the central absurdity or fabulous notion.

As a collection of short stories, *The Fat Man in History* I think is unsurpassed in Australian literature, even by *War Crimes* which is another brilliant collection. Carey has commented that, although his characters tend to be defeated, in *War Crimes* 'the characters are starting to win' because it is 'a more complex battle and a more complex defeat'.[9] In *War Crimes*, Carey explores collective fears and imaginings of the future. Vast and awful possibilities loom up out of the present, which the mind finds intolerable and shuns. Carey takes us into these possibilities, makes us examine them, recognize and work out our choices

In the title story, the narrator insists he is one of us.

And I am not mad, but rather I have opened the door you all keep locked with frightened bolts and little prayers. I am more like you than you know. You have not inspected the halls and attics. You haven't got yourself grubby in the cellars. Instead you sit in the front room in worn blue jeans, reading about atrocities in the Sunday papers.[10]

He knows he will, in the end, be judged, by people who 'have supported wars they have not fought in, and damned companies they have not had the courage to destroy' (p.241). He will be judged a tyrant, a psychopath, an aberrant accountant, but, in this war, he insists his conduct is no aberration, but a more deliberate version of the normal and accepted conduct of business in our world. This is the norm of commercial war, their methods of motivating salesmen 'historically necessary' (p.257). He and Bart have become 'the Andy Warhols of business' (p.268), and the story has, at moments, a macabre humour, with Bart strutting in his cowboy boots and waving his gun menacingly at top executives. The story has truly a black absurdist humour, full of menace and horror, which owes much to the cool, elaborating detail by which Carey relentlessly convinces us of its truth. It is set in the bitter disenchantment of the future, in a world in which there are roving gangs of vagabond unemployed and apocalyptic sects preach millennial doom, a future which is railing at its own disarray and 'surely, the Last Days'. The multitudinous unemployed camp around the boundaries of the food factories, executing the executive who appears outside its gates until they are themselves the victims of atrocities carried out by an army of workers under the orders of the accountant who watches from his window.

As I watched men run through the heat burning other men alive, I knew that thousands of men had stood on hills or roofs and watched such scenes of terrible destruction, the result of nothing more than their fears and their intelligence. (pp.281-2)

In the interests of business, Bart's hatred is diverted to the unemployed, by day obscure grey figures in a drab landscape, by night a menace licking at the face of darkness.

Some stories in *War Crimes* hinge on a central paradox, such as 'The Journey of a Lifetime', in which all the mystique and wonder of the train journey, so long anticipated, is sullied and corrupted by its purpose, a journey of execution and death. In 'The Uses of Williamson Wood', the grim, cruel reality of sexual assault smears across the girl's fantasy world, which becomes also the domain of her rebellion and revenge. Carey sustains the two worlds finely, as they blur into each other. Some longer stories are constructed out of a central absurdist notion, which Carey elaborates into an image of a futuristic society. In 'Do You Love Me?', he begins with the wondrous notion that parts of the country are becoming less real. Then he traces the beginnings of dematerialization, first of the neglected nether regions of the land, then of buildings and finally of people.

In 'The Chance', one of the best of Carey's stories, he sets up a futuristic world in a post-American era, where people undergo grotesque change in the Genetic Lottery. Social institutions are breaking down, abandoned ferries rust away, gangs of unemployed rove through the streets, people plunder and devastate isolated by fear and self-interest, religious sects are spawned – all through 'the total embrace of a cancerous philosophy of change' (p.76). The narrator begins to rediscover some of the moral values and categories of the remembered past but cannot avert the girl's grotesque change into an old hag so she can be part of the Hup revolutionary vanguard. In the Genetic Lottery, 'a new shrill current of desperate selfishness' (p.76) is carelessly fostered by the exploiting Fastalogians and the people are the blind accomplices to their own ruin. With each change, the self gains a new outer cladding and loses a little of the remembered past. The story grows from absurd notions of change and beauty, which twist around into ugly people in an ugly society. Underneath the blindness of the people is Carey's sense of an aesthetics of the real.

Throughout *War Crimes*, the notion of aesthetics recurs in fantastic ways. The narrator in the title story is horrified by factories which are for him monstrous yawning caverns in which terrible mutilations are carried out, but he is horrified too at the idea that factories might be less ugly, less brutal. In 'Exotic Pleasures', the superficial beauty of the silken blue Pleasure Bird blinds Lilly to its menace so that she becomes an accomplice to its ultimate 'complicated and elegant victory' (p.240) over Earth. In 'Kristu-Du', the aesthetics of an ideal blinds the architect to the ugliness and horror of the tyrant for whom he constructs his beautiful gleaming dome. Employed by a mass murderer but anaesthetized by his dream of Kristu-Du, the architect has an almost mystical faith in its saving power, 'an immense benevolent force capable of overthrowing tyrannies and welding tribes into nations' (p.187). He abrogates all moral values and categories in pursuit of his dream, but is left only with the twisting irony of an architectural error. Through all of these, as in 'The Chance', Carey suggests that an aesthetic which owes no allegiance to the real and the moral is a destructive force which threatens the future of our world.

In 'War Crimes', Carey says of Bart:

His mind was relentless in its logic, yet fanciful in style, so the most circuitous and fanciful plans would always, on examination, be found to have cold hard bones within their diaphanous folds. (p.256)

Carey's stories too have cold hard bones within their diaphanous folds. Carey has suggested,

The stories themselves ask questions. They say 'What if?' You look at the way people live their lives, and ask if they have to live like that; what happens if they organise themselves another way? [6]

Pushing the hypothetical through to horrifyingly logical limits, he speculates on what happens if the new shrill self-interest is unchecked, if unemployment is a matter of indifference, if the Americans stay, if the Americans go, if we pursue beauty according only to glossy phantoms of it and without regard for the beauty of the real world. He speculates on self-interest as the basis of ethical and political systems, watches the world begin to dematerialize, watches it taken

over by exotic birds and plants which destroy it, watches it submit
to an alien power in pursuit of an absurd notion of change and beauty.
His fictions shock and jolt the reader, startling him out of conventional attitudes and perhaps out of an apathy which is complicity
and assent to a grotesque future.

The caretaker who was the last to leave the I.C.I. building, just
as it was dematerializing in 'Do You Love Me?', looked almost translucent and claimed he had been able to see 'other worlds, layer upon
layer, through the fabric of the here and now' (p.22). In all Carey's
stories, there is a translucency, through which we glimpse the infinite
onion of the universe, with all its layers of reality. Carey sets up
extravagant worlds which reflect a fantastic mirror image of reality
and peels back layers in the Godelian hierarchy of existence. In *Bliss*,
Harry Joy also discovers 'that there were many different worlds, layer
upon layer, as thin as filo pastry'. His first death lasts for nine minutes,
during which time ecstasy touches him and he finds he can slide
between the spaces in the air. He recognizes 'the worlds of pleasure
and worlds of pain, bliss and punishment, Heaven and Hell'.[11] At
the very start of the novel, Carey sets up the double notions that
are our landmarks, the points from which we take our bearings as
we move through strange new territory. Life and death, pleasure
and pain, Heaven and Hell, bliss and punishment, embodiment and
disembodiment – these are the poles the novel offers at the start,
as Harry Joy slides between the spaces in the air above the earth peering
down at the body lying below. These familiar landmarks are complicated and blurred through the novel. Like Harry, Carey is a
cartographer, beginning with the known before exploring and mapping out a strange new territory, the double vision of the Lie.

Harry himself is a familiar figure at the outset: a Good Bloke,
a conventional family man, living in a conventional house and style,
in a conventional job. He is blind to the faults in others and to the
injustices of the world which is surely conventional too. He is 'not
particularly intelligent, not particularly successful, not particularly
handsome and not particularly rich'(p.10). His vision will be complicated, he will stumble into strange new territories of his own life.
He, who inhabits the middle ground of existence, will be thrust into
the extraordinary and the extreme.

He was like someone who has lain in bed too long eating rich food: within his soul there was suddenly a yearning for tougher, stronger things, for ecstasies, for the thrill of goodness perfectly achieved, to see butterflies in doorways in Belize, to be part of the lightning dance, to quiver in terror before the cyclone. (p.19)

Instead of being 'not particularly' anything, Harry Joy wants to feel the sharp edges of experience; he yearns for the bliss and the terror. In a Borgesian way, he finds both inside his own existence, when he peels back the surface layer with which he has been content and discovers new layers of his own existence, new perceptions of 'a universe made like an infinite onion'. (p.50)

Harry has been 'suckled on stories' in the innocent world of childhood, imbibing a world which was fresh and green:

Dew drops full of visions hung from morning grass and old Clydesdales stood silently in the paddock above the creek. Crickets sang songs and everything had meanings. The sky was full of Gods and Indians and people smiled at him, touched him, stroked him, and brought him extraordinary gifts from the world outside where there were, he knew, exotic bazaars filled with people in gowns, strange fruits piled high, the air redolent with spices, and Jesus Christ, and the Good Samaritan, always dressed in his dusty grey robe with its one red patch on the left sleeve, and the soldier offering the dripping red sponge of wine to Jesus, and there were small boiled sweets and white sheets and the smell of bread, and floor polish and, far away, New York, its glass towers trembling in an ecstasy of magic which was to become, his father said, one day, after the next flood, a splendid book read by all mankind with wonder. (p.15)

Bliss opens with a gathering of myths, myths of innocence and purity, myths that no longer hold. These myths, religious, moral, political and national, social and existential, are the myths of Harry Joy's time, which is our time. The opening of the novel is closely tied to narrative and storytelling, the inherited stories, the myths of Good and Evil and Clydesdales, of crickets and the smell of bread and floor polish, of moral landmarks lighting up the map of existence. In Harry's childhood, lit by the glow of the Vision Splendid, he received the myths. When Harry himself becomes the storyteller, passing on his heritage to his family, he transmits the stories imperfectly, without understanding them, and they take on different meanings. Vance Joy's stories have

drifted like groundsel seeds and taken root in the most unlikely places. They had rarely grown in the way he would have imagined, in that perfect green landscape of his imagination, intersected with streams and redolent of orange blossom.

In certain climates they became like weeds, uncontrollable, not always beautiful, a blaze of rage or desire from horizon to horizon. (p.20)

At the outset of the novel, Carey establishes the notion of a heritage received, transmitted without understanding and thereby changed, become weedlike, choking growth. It is a heritage of meaning, which in Harry Joy's time has been lost.

Vance's stories of New York contain apocalyptic visions and conflicts between Good and Evil, but like his other stories they have changed in Harry's telling. Amid the stories of Harry's childhood, always New York, New York, 'the most beautiful and terrible city on earth. All good, all evil exists there'. (p.18). Now, dreaming of New York, Bettina is marooned in one of the outposts of the American Empire. Subscribing to the articles of the American Faith, she believes in,

the benevolence of their companies, the triumph of the astronauts, the law of the market-place and the twin threats of Communism and the second-rate, although not necessarily in that order (p.94).

The townspeople are more ambivalent than Bettina, envying American power but 'wishing to reject it and embrace it all at once' (p.11), at once attracted and repelled. Set, according to the Liar, on the edge of the American Empire, *Bliss* plays with the talismanic myth of New York, the dream of its gleaming towers.

In a novel which is a post-Christian fable of our times, Harry tries to conceive a new eschatology, a new god, new myths for our time. He makes a list of all religions and, to the Reverend Desmond Pearce, announces his decision that they are all wrong. He ponders on the notion of a new god.

Maybe it's a god like none you've ever thought of. Maybe it's a 'they' and not a he. Maybe it's a great empty part of space charged with electricity. Maybe it's a whole lot of things in a space ship and flying saucers are really angels . . . I will tell you two things: the first is that there is an undiscovered religion, and the second is that there definitely is a Hell.' (p.42)

Harry begins an ontological quest for meaning, a post-Christian quest for salvation, in a post-Christian novel where salvation and damnation are not clear, untrammelled opposites but conjoined, twin modes like the concave and the convex of an Escher vision.

As Harry begins to move beyond the Christian landmarks, to map out the new territory he discovers in the universe, the god-like narrator becomes our guide and commentator. Like the disembodied Harry registering with sharp clarity the body lying down below, Carey's narrator watches from above, from outside, observing all that is played out in the narrative and commenting on it. He plays with time and sequence, anticipating future developments, retracing earlier events, disrupting the lines of his narrative and fracturing our sense of time. He watches Aldo in the restaurant, murmuring 'It would be another minute before he would know . . .' (p.11). He comments in collusive asides to the reader, nudging at us: 'It was not a question that would have occurred to Harry, who had never seen his family as you, dear reader, have now been privileged to.' (p.33). Like some literary deity, he knows all, sees and hears all, knows the past of all the characters, their dreams and delusions, can tell their stories in fragments, setting them in motion inside the story of Harry. He stands back, detached, grave, sometimes gently tolerant, sometimes wryly amused. Then he steps forward to comment, elaborate, dislocate and remind us of his artifice. He already knows where Harry is going, is already familiar with the territory, has already heard the story.

Harry Joy is trapped in a Hell which he has himself constructed. After his second death, Harry knows he is in Hell. He conducts periodic tests of his own sanity, making notes and observations on his own behaviour, and he amasses formidable evidence that this is Hell. On his white map of this 'unknown continent', he begins pencilling in marks, which are crude and inexact at first, 'but surely even Livingstone must have become lost occasionally and needed some high ground to see the lay of the land' (p.62). He is not only an explorer in the unknown territory of his life but also a zoologist devising keys and codes for classifying the creatures he finds in this new territory. It is an Orwellian classification and similar to Ireland's terms of freedom and captivity in *A Woman of the Future*. But in *Bliss* the captivity is another face of freedom, the double modes of sly actors. Harry learns how to identify the Actors employed by Those In Charge to persecute the Captives.

On his walks, he saw ugliness and despair where once he would have found an acceptable world: goitrous necks, phlegmy coughs, scabrous skin, lost legs, wall eyes, dropping hair, crooked spines, lost hope, and all of this he noted. (p.56)

But this dark vision of ugliness and deformity, an existential horror, is shifted suddenly, with Carey's usual incongruity, into Harry's unexpected boredom. He shrugs it off with a quick new optimism, only to have both the optimism and his car crushed by an elephant. This wonderfully parodic sequence culminates in Harry's testing out storytelling, preliminary lies, to save himself from the police, a comic anticipation of his own salvation at Bog Onion Road – and a quick glimpse of Herbert Badgery waiting in the wings, eager to start whacking the illy.

Released by the police, Harry Joy crosses the river Styx.

Barges carried their carcinogens up river and neon lights advertised their final formulations against a blackening sky.

Harry Joy, his face ghastly with hives, his suit filthy, his chest bleeding, his back sore, lounged sideways in the back seat, drugged with sweet success. The buildings of Hell, glossy, black-windowed, gleaming with reflected lights, did not seem to him unconquerable. It seemed that a person of imagination and resources might well begin to succeed here, to remain dry, warm, and free from punishment. (p.73)

He resolves to be Good, trying out self-abasement and humility, but that too shifts suddenly when, with residual doubt, he determines on One Last Test because the evidence so far he finds 'insufficient to justify this terrible, risky strategy of Goodness' (p.98). In the tree scene which is a fine parody of the Tree of Knowledge, Harry conducts the Final Test and at the windows of Hell, he discovers the full family horror – Bettina's infidelity with Joel, his children's incestuous commerce. Having discovering the infernal truth of his family, his friends and the products marketed by his agency, he recoils from it to the relative safety of the Hilton Hotel. As a diversion from 'the razor-blade tortures of Hell' (p.112), he fires his clients, Krappe Chemicals, and standing in the epicentre of Hell, he studies the cancer map. The whole sequence in the Hilton Hotel and the beginnings of Harry's education by his new mentor, Honey Barbara, 'pantheist, healer, whore' (p. 169), all culminate in David's financing his father's committal to the hospital. When, by the intervention of chance and contingency, Alex Duval is taken to the hospital in Harry's place, Harry enters the depths of his Hell and experiences a new horror, loss of identity, which is the climax of the novel and its double vision.

The hospital scenes have a splendid mixture of absurdity and horror as well as tightening the intellectual tensions of the novel. Until the outside intervention of the formidable wife of Alex Duval, Harry is steadily dispossessed of his own identity, stripped down to a residual self which is somehow not his own. The centre of his private gravity shifts and his determinations are no longer his own, but taken over by Alex. Harry contends not only with the institution but also with the constant presence of a rival claimant to the disputed commodity of Harry Joy's identity. The rival is actively resentful and reproachful at Harry's attempts to retrieve his own identity. It becomes wonderfully absurd, a kind of titanic struggle between them, each one tugging at the name and the identity of Harry Joy – the right to dress, walk, talk, behave, the right to be Harry Joy. It becomes a nightmare of dispossession, with Carey outside the frame delighting in the paradoxes, as the two Escher hands struggle for possession of Harry Joy's identity. This is classic Carey, with the companion figure of Nurse burying his memories in the garden for safe-keeping and periodically digging them up to see which ones have been stolen from him by shock treatment. Harry accompanies Nurse round the garden to check his store of memories, with the marvellous notion that one can lose one's whole identity by institutional theft or by the takeover bid of an old mate.

Through Alex, Carey exploits the notions of role-swapping and sliding identities, in which the self, whatever is left of it, is marginal, vestigial. Harry is upset in puzzling, contradictory ways by the changes in Alex as Alex grows into the role of Harry, and disconcerted by watching Alex/Harry's behaviour. It becomes a kind of split identity which they share, both marginal selves watching the shared self of Harry on which they both make claims. Harry begins to feel the pain of the people around him, developing a sympathy for the plights of others which is far removed from the figure at the start of the novel who was blind to other people and blind to the injustices of the world. But there is more to come: when Alex prevails upon Harry to accept that he should play Alex, not only does Harry quickly begin 'to embrace the pale, shuffling unhappiness of an Alex' (p.152), but as Harry/Alex his whole status in the community changes radically. He ponders on the folly of seeking 'salvation by giving away the trappings of power' (p.152), that is, the privilege of being Harry Joy, and realizes the consequences:

While he had still been the legitimate Harry Joy some power was attached to him . . . But once he was an Alex everyone knew he was a crumpled thing, a failure, defenceless. Three silk shirts were stolen from him and were worn, brazenly, in his presence . . .

They had authority over him. They made him sweep the concrete paths and he did it. They tried to feed him like an Alex. They did it for sport. For their amusement. They brought him big doughnuts and laughed at him when he pulled faces. (p.153)

At Nurse's insistence, he writes everything he learned from Honey Barbara, particularly about food, in the book for burial in the garden, for fear of losing that too. While the new Harry Joy confers with Alice in her office and orders the old men about, the new Alex hears him and is jealous, envying the loud happy laugh of Alex/Harry, envying his peace of mind. The masterly touch here is that after all Harry's deliberations on Actors playing out roles, the novel reaches this climactic sequence of role-playing and role-swapping, in which Alex and Harry become actors playing each other. They impersonate each other, identities sliding to and fro between them, the way Heaven and Hell have been impersonating one another, sliding to and fro throughout the novel. It is the climactic pitch of the double vision on which the entire novel is built, but unfortunately the novel now begins to falter and grow frail as Carey relaxes the doubleness.

It is ironic that happinesss is much more difficult to represent than misery and pain, that bliss is much more elusive than horror. In *Bliss*, this is a particularly pungent irony. Once the novel actually tackles bliss and salvation, it does not have the same impact or intensity as the earlier part. Honey Barbara and the idyllic existence in Bog Onion Road never manifest the same energy as the account of Harry's descent into Hell. The scenes of Honey Barbara as part of the household in Palm Avenue and the events leading to Bettina's death in the Mobil explosion, then the death of Joel, as well as the interpolated narrative of David's mock-heroic death, are all narrated briskly. But Harry himself is elusive at this stage, his motives enigmatic. Drawn to the feel of silk and money, his commercial energies are quickened again by Bettina's ability and her renewed vision of herself as a hot-shot on the way to New York. The notion of Hell recedes and Harry is content to regard himself as 'a prisoner with special privileges' (p.225).

The theme of cancer which has been sustained through the novel in moral, economic, health and political terms, develops into a futuristic vision of anarchy, against which Carey tries to set the Bog Onion Road version of salvation. It is an unequal battle and the supposedly idyllic existence of the community at Bog Onion Road does not stand up against the earlier black absurdity. In part Harry's salvation is story-telling, telling Vance's stories with new understanding.

And when he told stories about the trees and the spirits of the forest he was only dramatizing things that people already knew, shaping them just as you pick up rocks scattered on the ground to make a cairn. He was merely sewing together the bright patchworks of lives, legends, myths, beliefs, hearsay into a splendid cloak that gave a richer glow to all their lives . . . He insisted that the story was not his, and not theirs either. You must give something, he told the children, a sapphire or blue bread made from cedar ash. And what began as a game ended as a ritual. (p.277)

Through the ritual retelling of the myths, Harry Joy regains his lost heritage and retrieves the sustaining myths which he shares with the whole community of refugees hungry for ceremony and story. When he addresses the ritual words to the circle of trees where he will build his house, they are Vance's words, with Vance's pantheism. After his third death, he is a sigh in the trees and his heritage handed down to the children of Honey Barbara and Harry Joy.

Bliss examines the myths by which we live, the myths which have failed, the myths we have lost. With a splendid absurdity, it explores the existential horror lying just below the surface of the ordinary life of a Good Bloke. Yet just as it is built on double vision, flipping from heaven to hell, from freedom to captivity, from one Escher hand to the other, so it is a work of contrary energy and paradoxical affirmation, which insists that Harry Joy is not finally trapped in Hell but can discover and explore new territories of his own existence within the layers of the 'infinite onion' of the universe. *Bliss* is Carcy's storytelling, with Carey's narrator actually playing out the themes of the novel. It is also about storytelling with the storyteller quietly reminding us of the artifice and strategies of his own telling. It is a gentle strumming on the notion of lies and truth. In *Illywhacker*, no more quiet strumming, lies are the show, Herbert Badgery's subject, his specialty, his skill.

Let's relax and enjoy the show. We are in the hands of a Liar, and a showman, offering the best in entertainment, but a salesman too, working for a Liar and selling us Peter Carey's Lie, a conman.

'An illywhacker,' Leah Goldstein said loudly like someone fearful of burglars who descends the stairs, flashlight in hand, in the middle of the night.

'What's an illywhacker?' said Charles.

'Spieler,' explained Leah, who was not used to children. 'Eelerspee. It's like pig Latin. Spieler is ieler-spe and then iely-whacker. Illywhacker. See?'

'I think so,' Charles said.

'A spieler . . . A trickster. A quandong. A ripperty man. A con-man.' (pp.245-6)

Herbert is 139 years old, born in 1886, and so the novel opens in the year 2025 A.D., unless he is lying – which he is. He is like some ancient prophet, an androgynous seer, turning into a woman, growing tits and giving suck. Now beached by time 'like some old squid decaying on the beach' (p.12), he is also master of ceremonies, promising 'plenty of hanky-panky by and by relating to love of one sort or another' (p.12). His advice is 'to not waste your time with your red pen, to try to pull apart the strands of lies and truth, but to relax and enjoy the show' (p.12). From the opening proposition of the Liar's Paradox, *Illywhacker* is a play on truth, fiction, lies, spun by Herbert inside Carey's own web. The lies cling, adhere and trail behind us as Herbert spins his tales and whacks the illy, luring us deep inside his fictions, stopping only to remind us suddenly that he is a liar. And this he does with a true 'salesman's sense of history', exquisitely playing with time and fiction and the passage of the reader's credibility, and selling us not only lies which are his own and therefore his to sell, but also lies of our own, lies we already own. Spinner of tales and webs, illywhacker and deceiver, spieler, conman, distorter of truth and fabricator of fiction – this is the showman and narrator on whose word we, the readers, the believers and self-deceivers, the dupes, will always depend. Forget the finer points of truth, forget its boundaries and its lines of demarcation. Don't worry about who owns the Lies. The Lies are for sale. Just relax and enjoy the show.

Illywhacker is a constant delight, spinning splendid new fictions at every turn, lies which are beautiful and noble, some subsistence lies, some mean and ignoble, snivelling things, noisome, some simply bullshit. There are lies too which are political, some public and national, some historical. And there are lies which are personal, guises and disguises of the self. And some Lies which are literary, artifices of fiction. Adrian Mitchell calls it 'an aesthetics of the lie',[12] and certainly some are more beautiful than others, some ugly, some glossy, some tawdry, some makeshift put-up jobs, some made of sturdier stuff. But perhaps rather than aesthetics, *Illywhacker* is about the calibrations of the Lie and so about the calibrations of truth. What calibre suits our needs? How much truth do we really want? In the opening quotation from Mark Twain, Carey raises not only the notion of beauty and truth, but of novelty. Rich pickings for the Liar in the 'novelty' of history.

Australian history is almost always picturesque; indeed, it is so curious and strange, that it is itself the chiefest novelty the country has to offer and so it pushes the other novelties into second and third place. It does not read like history, but like the most beautiful lies; and all of a fresh new sort, no mouldy old stale ones. It is full of surprises and adventures, the incongruities, and contradictions, and incredibilities; but they are all true, they all happened.

How much novel truth do we want about our history? Behind the lies is not only Herbert's specialty, 'The role of lies in popular perceptions of the Australian political fabric' (p.488), but also a truth full of splendid incongruities and incredibilities, which we can buy if we want to from our own history. Herbert is selling us used-Australian history, second-hand history. It's a novelty but it's all true. *Caveat emptor.*

What is a 'salesman's sense of history'? It is timing, a quick sale before events run on or your buyers run off.

I do not mean about the course of it, or the import of it, but rather its scale of time, its pulse, its intervals, its peaks, troughs, crests, waves. I was not born in some Marxist planet out near Saturn where the days last a year and the inevitabilities of history take a century to show. I am from Venus, from Mars, and my days are short and busy and the intervals on my whirling clock are dictated by the time it takes to make a deal, and *that* is the basic unit of my time. And even if I have boasted about how I was a patient man when I sold Fords to cockies, shuffled cards, told a yarn, taught a spinster aunt to drive, I was not talking about anything more than a day or two of my life, and *then* off down the road with the order in my pocket. (p.343)

Carey's salesman's sense of Australian history is like that of the other great Australian salesman, Peter Mathers – it has the pulses and intervals and crests of history, a history which is chaotic and yet continuous, full of bizarre twists and turns, tenuous connections and absurd lines of continuance. The fantastic and the bizarre are embedded in the stubbornly substantial and convincing. Characters come and go apparently at random, slipping off the edge of the narrative, like Phoebe and the schemer Nathan Schick, only to re-appear later. The narrative slithers in complex traces across the page, inside skins likely to be sloughed off at any moment. Like the snakes slithering through *Illywhacker*, the narrative itself is serpentine and sinuous, uncoiling its snake lines as if never-ending, until it tapers and finally reveals the sub-caudal scales of the tail. The tip of the Liar's tale.

In contemporary Australian fiction, *Illywhacker* is closest to Mathers' novels and like them, it is a form of picaresque novel, a narrative that proliferates through time and space, in which the protagonist takes on a series of roles and guises, partly because reality palls and partly because it is the only way to deal with reality – then off down the road. Like Percy Wort, whose guises sprawl through the parody family saga, Herbert plays a series of roles, changing with his chaotic passage through history. Bow-legged, blue-eyed, head shaved bald for twenty-one years, Herbert is variously Aviator with Morris Farman Shorthorn; an illiterate who learns to read in his fifties, correspondence student and later graduate; manipulator, using frailty and decency as a prisoner; used car salesman selling T-models to cockies; child assistant cannon vendor; trickster; nationalist; herpetologist; thespian; walker who favours the Gentleman's Stroll; bigamist; purloiner of church hall; architect and builder of flimsy structures with improbable materials. He is also one-time resident of Mallee hole in ground; wanderer of Western District, nomad across the face of Victoria; paternal conman with son with snake trick; hatcher of schemes; master of his own visibility; urger and enthusiast in general. But there is more: he is also a dealer and trafficker in lies, forger swapping notions of himself for accommodation, lies his currency; a thief and plagiarist, filcher of Leah's writings; and finally 139-year-old androgynous patriarch and concocter of family saga of the 'fatally flawed Badgerys'; writer, with the callused writing finger, 'the liar's lump'; and above all, spieler, the storyteller addressing a spellbound audience

At the start of his tale, with the exquisite sense of timing of a dealer and an illywhacker, Herbert assures us there is little he looks forward to as much as the story of November 1919, when he was thirty-three (mythically speaking, just the right age). We are hooked, snared, thrust right into the middle of the show, as Herbert lands in Balliang East, in the middle of a lie about a snake, in the middle of the lives of the McGrath family, to whom he delivers value, swapping lies and fictions for free accommodation. As he counts the day of his revenge on his father on the Punt Road hill as the day of his birth, so he counts this day of landing in Balliang East as the start of his adult life. And with the true storyteller's timing, while he unfolds his tale, Herbert keeps interrupting his own narrative, to anticipate, darting head to hint at the exciting developments awaiting us there, or to retrace, darting back to an earlier episode to draw out the storyteller's connections, so that the narrative proliferates sideways and backwards as well as running ahead. Out of it grows a sense that behind every yarn, every vignette, every thread, lies another story and another and another. The forward movement of the narrative is constantly disrupted as though the narrative is conical or cuneiform and only the tip is showing: the further one delves, the more the story enlarges, deepening and complicating in a tangled hierarchy.

One of the extraordinary features of *Illywhacker* is the range of its settings and times. The snake narrative uncoils through the Western District, across Balliang, Geelong, Anakie, Terang, Bendigo, the Ballarat area, moving to Melbourne and the Maribyrnong house, Woodend, Jeparit and the Mallee, Bacchus Marsh and the Underhill family, then wends its way through Victoria, a few passages to Queensland, before coiling itself into Sydney – only to uncoil again for some overseas scenes in Rome and Japan. It slithers across the face of Australian history, from the Lambing Flat riots, the shearers' strike of the 1890s, the colonial era where Imaginary Englishmen strut across society, through the period of the Wobblies, the rise of aviation, the 1930s, the Depression, the Second World War and the influx of Americans, the 1950s and on into the 1970s, from there to the putative future. Herbert's 139 year life encompasses all this, either in truth or in the artifice of lie. His childhood was nomadic, his father a wandering cannon salesman, with rounds of ammunition for sale to squatters to ward off marauding shearers. He sloughs off that life with revenge on the Punt Road hill and enters the life with Goon Tse Ying, which offers him the gift of invisibility – a lie which underlies Sonia's disappearance and is later contested in the struggle over Goon's Book of Dragons. He wanders then, marries, nearly marries in Nambucca Heads until foiled by a corgi, sells cars, becomes an aviator, until his debut, when he drops down from the skies to Vogelnest's paddock.

From the moment he lands in Balliang East, Herbert is trapped inside his own snake-lie, driven to ingenious concoctions to substantiate it until the snake strikes and, killing Jack, kills off the future Herbert had devised. To Jack McGrath who is dreamer and visionary, Herbert delivers value by offering the 'gift' of the richly packaged lie of his aviator self.

I was an Aviator. That was my value to them. I set to work to reinforce this value. I propped it up and embellished it a little. God damn, I danced around it like a bloody bower-bird putting on a display. I added silver to it. I put small blue stones around it. (p.33)

When others contribute 'creamy coats of credibility' to his lie, then it becomes beautiful, the nasty speck of grit transformed into the lustrous pearl and the dream of an aircraft factory. Jack McGrath becomes Herbert's straight man, the willing dupe on the other side of Herbert's lie: 'There was nothing to protect us from each other. We were elements like phosphorus and air which should always be kept apart' (p.29). The liar and the self-deceiver, the salesman and his willing customer, in idyllic union until the snake strikes. There is a snake biding its time, waiting to strike the other dupe too, the one duped by the other Liar, Carey – the reader of *Illywhacker*.

But a lie, though a tenuous thing in constant need of support and embellishment, is also a version of the self, a cloak.

It was the trouble with the world that it would never permit me to be what I was. Everyone loved me when I appeared in a cloak, and swirled and laughed and told them lies. They applauded. They wanted my friendship. But when I took off my cloak they did not like me. They clucked their tongues and turned away. My friend Jack was my friend in all things but was repulsed by what I really was . . . could only like the bullshit version of me. (p.79)

Impatient with the confines of reality, Phoebe loves the liar: 'You have invented yourself, Mr Badgery, and that is why I like you. You are what they call a confidence man. You can be anything you want'. (p.91). Her vision of their lives together is simple: 'We will invent ourselves'. In Maribyrnong, Herbert's inventions are more architectural and domestic, a matter of scavenging for things timber. Phoebe takes a poetic turning, writing poems Herbert cannot read. Now he looks back:

But now I know a poem can take any form, can be a sleight of hand, a magician's trick, be built from string and paper, fish or animals, bricks and wire.

I never knew I was a hired hand in the construction of my wife's one true poem. I knew only, in the midst of its construction, that Horace would puzzle me with his sympathetic eyes which would not hold mine when I confronted him. (p.201)

On the edge of the novel, Horace is another marvellous Carey character: mid-wife, devotee of Phoebe, poet, housekeeper, epileptic, frequenter of strange literary rooming houses, faithful companion and itinerant Rawleigh's man, a man of many faces and roles, an incipient Herbert without the lies. Phoebe, self-indulgent and preening like a caged budgie, is in the mainstream of the first book of the narrative, until she slips over to the wings to wait for the third book, there to re-appear as a free spirit, combining her literary aspirations with her powers of sexual persuasion, playing the role of one of the great characters and hostesses of Sydney.

When Phoebe flies out of the cage she perceives as Herbert's life, he is comforted by Molly McGrath for a year, until he enters the itinerant phase again, this time complete with Charles, Sonia and the Dodge, roving Victoria in quest of survival, until he meets Leah Goldstein. Thespian now, for six or seven years, Herbert becomes part of Badgery and Goldstein (Theatricals) and Pet Suppliers, with detours into political acts which culminate in the glorious battle (and Pyrrhic victory) with John Oliver O'Dowd and his bully boys. Nathan Schick, schemer, entrepreneur, vanguard of the Americans, enters the narrative with his flashy show in Ballarat, until the departure of Leah to tend the injured Izzie and begin spinning her inventions, then the disappearance of Sonia. Herbert's encounter with Goon Tse Ying in Grafton and the bizarre severing of Goon's finger bring him to Rankin Downs Prison and, with his new literacy, to a B.A. by correspondence and new inklings of political lies.

By the third book, the centre of gravity has shifted to Charles, first amid the plague in the Mallee staring in comic bafflement and consternation at his dismantled bike, then, oblivious of all omens, launching into his marriage to Emma and the opening of his pet shop. From here the development of the pet shop itself holds the centre of the stage. As Carey weaves a vast pattern of time and place, with interpolations, crosscurrents of narrative, silvery trails of related tales that could have been told, its main forward thrust through the Badgery family and through a hundred years of history is to the Pet Emporium, into which the fortunes of all the main characters are finally subsumed. Herbert's role shifts with it, from itinerant and thespian, to prisoner living on the 'perfumed razor blades' of Leah's inventions, to patriarch and finally writer. As he writes and records, still spinning lies and fabrications, the narrative shifts forward again into the next generation, with Hissao taking charge of the family fortunes.

Herbert's role is apparently more passive in Book 3, perhaps the reason that some reviewers of *Illywhacker* found that part less successful than Books 1 and 2, feeling the narrative palls and the interest wanes.[13] I find, on the contrary, that the narrative begins to tighten and intensify here, because it is at this point that Carey's conception of his illywhacker is expanding: Herbert moves steadily out of the lies of his own existence into the political and national lies of Australia, without diminishing the artifice of his own role. His role changes throughout the novel, but the major change is revealed in the sudden disclosure of the lies of his version of events. In her 'book-keeping', which, amid the dullness of her life with Izzie, has become her sacred time, Leah's letters have offered Herbert the salvation of invention. He decides 'There was nothing left for me but to teach myself to be an author. It was the only scheme available'. (p.548). In a succinct and skilful sequence, Carey shifts our perspective on Leah and Herbert and the whole status of the narrative, when Leah complains that Herbert has stolen her material and stolen it like a barbarian. What follows is a contestant version of Herbert's narrative, not only alleging that his version is a concoction of stolen fragments of her writings but with specific disclaimers of details and challenges to his interpretation and representation of specific incidents. They share the same publisher, Doodles Casey, and, according to Leah, have already collaborated on other books, notably 'Gaol Bird', but Herbert regards the real subject of Leah's writings as 'not the people but the landscape and its roads . . . the raw optimistic tracks that cut the arteries of an ancient culture before a new one had been born' (p.553). Placed at a critical point in the novel, this whole sequence is crucial to our perception of Herbert's role in exposing the lies of Australia.

The lies of *Illywhacker* have such convincing substance that the issue of their truth fades and retreats, but the man with 'the liar's lump', the callused writing finger, keeps reminding us of the Lie. This is the content and the movement of the novel, and this final reminder through Leah is the culmination of the Lie of the novel. After Herbert's luminous discovery (through M.V.Anderson) that a liar might be a patriot, his last scheme is Carey's scheme, the big Lie, the all-encasing one of *Illywhacker*. Carey weaves the web of historical lies into his narrative, the lies of settlement and Aborigines, the lies of English colonization, the lies of whole eras, as in the 1930s.

Lies, dreams, visions – they were everywhere. We brushed them aside as carelessly as spider webs across a garden path. They clung to us, of course, adhered to our clothes and trailed behind us . . . (p.326)

As well as the lies that cling and entrap, Herbert knows all too well the allure of lies, their soft, warm comfort:

It is why we believed the British when they told us we were British too, and why we believed the Americans when they said they would protect us. In all these cases, of course, there is a part of us that knows the thing is not true, and we hold it closer to ourselves because of it, refusing to hold it out at arm's length or examine it against the light. (p.187)

The lies of Australia, its history, its society, its independence, its economy, its architecture, are finally exposed amid Sydney, the city of trickery and illusions. The lies include the lie of 'Australia's Own Car' which is 'one more element in an old-pattern of self-deception' (p.505), the lie of the Holden which is at the centre of Bail's *Holden's Performance*. All these are inside the vast Lie of Carey.

The Pet Emporium, which to Herbert and Hissao always is like stepping into a vision, every edge sharp, every colour intense, steadily becomes ever more bizarre and absurd: Mr Lo conducting ferocious arguments with an imaginary umpire, Emma practising courtesan arts in her cage with its pink venetian blinds, Herbert architecturally engaged in demolition work, then, after Charles' death, at his window amid the neon sign, enthroned high above Pitt Street while angels or parrots trill attendance. Through the schemes of Major Nathan Schick, the juggler with a myriad schemes arcing through the air, The Best Pet Shop in the World thrives in war-time and the 1940s, fed by Americans. In time it becomes dependent on smuggling of Australian animals, and bribery of customs officials, then a financial disaster, then a rusting slum until, following the absurdist death of the last recorded golden-shouldered parrot, it is reborn with Japanese investment. Like his grandfather and mentor, Hissao is an architect, building 'like a liar, like a spider – steel ladders and walkways, catwalks, cages in mid-air, in racks on walls, tumbling like waterfalls.' (p.597). His features inexplicably Japanese, Hissao is the putative future, given suck by Herbert as he waits for revolution.

Illywhacker abounds with pets, animals – snakes, parrots, goannas – generally caged and entrapped. From Herbert's first being entrapped in his own snake-lie, to the image of Phoebe as a trapped parrot, from Leah's snake-dance to Charles' instinctive skill with snakes and his peculiar impulse to tell the whole snake truth, down to the last sub-caudal scales, the pattern of snakes and snake images slithers through the narrative. When Herbert learns to read, he is transformed. 'I was an old python with his opaque skin now shed, his blindness gone, once again splendid and supple, seeing the world in all its terrifying colours.' (p.337). Amid the images of cages and entrapment, amid the lies coiling and uncoiling through the novel, the narrative sheds a succession of opaque skins, until we glimpse an image of the future, splendid and supple, with the world in all its terrifying colours. Australia, The Best Pet Shop in the World, becomes a human museum, its caged exhibits an endangered species, Australians: shearers, manufacturers, lifesavers, inventors, masons, Aborigines, bushmen, artists and writers, Leah a Melbourne Jew and Herbert the 139-year-old exhibit, who cannot die 'because this is my scheme. I must stay alive to see it out.' (p.600). In the vast human museum of Australia, 'the very success of the exhibit is their ability to move and talk naturally within the confines of space' (p.599), as though real, as though not just exhibits of a historical lie, displaying their own capacity for self-deception. Herbert and Hissao are left amid 'this splendid four storey mirage', in the land of the lie.

Illywhacker is an extraordinary blend of comic vignettes, absurdist notions, zany fictions and convincing images of time and place rich in corroborative detail, which have an ineradicable, stubborn substance constantly challenged by the artifice of the novel. It is a vast and generous novel in which wondrous scenes abound, some of them fugitive, fleeting scenes, sharp with Carey's quick sense of a single, telling detail; some more sustained with collusive character and circumstance: Leah's emu dance when Herbert first meets her; the car selling sequence in Woodend; the battle with John Oliver O'Dowd and his bully boys; Father Moran's tale of seeing a fairy; the sergeant's thrusting the bottled finger at Herbert; the dismantling of Charles' bike by Les Chaffey, where it occurs to Charles that he has fallen among mad people; Emma's retreat to the goanna cage and the nurturing of the goanna foetus; Herbert's period of imprisonment; Sonia's fascination with the insubstantiality of things. Ob-

sessed with truth in all its endless detail, Charles is 'a poor salesman
. . . because the truth told thus, is of no interest to the average pun-
ter' (p.387). With his 'salesman's sense of history', Herbert's telling
of it is in the true illywhacker style, playing on all its high points,
teasing out its tangles where major strands knot together, interrupting
the narrative to go back to some earlier episode or run ahead to anticipate some later development, telling yarns within yarns, running
off at tangents and detours when they promise richer tales, but never
losing the way back. Episodes spread tentacles which run on into
the future or, at the most climactic moments, take a sudden dramatic turning, are left open, hanging. We are left baffled, bewildered,
impatient to know, captive and waiting for explanations, which Carey
withholds with a true storyteller's timing.

Herbert's story is an Australian family saga, with the family legacy
of lies bequeathed to his children and to theirs. 'Spawned by lies,
suckled on dreams, infested with dragons' (p.359), their family history is the Australian history of lies, of self-deception, of dreams
and visions preferred to truth – the calibrations of self-deception which
leaves Australia a human museum, a pet shop. Throughout
Illywhacker, Carey bares and flaunts his own artifice, with a rich canvas
of fictions, within the marvellous strategies of the Liar and his character, liars together, partners spinning their webs of lies which cling
and adhere and trail around the reader.

Like *Illywhacker*, Carey's third novel, *Oscar and Lucinda*, is a vast
and teeming Lie which conjures up marvellous images at every flick of
the Liar's hand. Set in the 1860s, it is an absurdist novel about the
passage of Christian stories to Australia and about the stakes in the
Christian bet on God. But *Oscar and Lucinda* is more than the myriad
past behind the Gleniffer church in the present, more than the passage of dreams across the face of the 1860s. It is also a dazzling Lie
about the manufacture of glass—and the manufacture of the Lie.

Behind the Prince Rupert Glassworks in Sydney, there is another
factory, the 'fancy-factory' of the mind, where Lucinda and the
Reverend Oscar Hopkins manufacture their dreams. And behind this
is Carey's own 'fancy-factory', the Liar's workshop with its own
molten mysteries, where the Lie is manufactured. As the narrator
writes, he holds in his left hand a Prince Rupert's drop, 'not the
fabled glass stone of the alchemists, but something almost as magical' (Sec. 32).[14] Formed by dropping molten glass into water, a

Prince Rupert's drop seems unbreakable but, if the slender tail is nipped with pliers, it bursts into a myriad fragments, scattering grains of glass. A spectacular moment of 'fireworks made of glass. An explosion of dew. Crescendo. Diminuendo. Silence.' (Sec. 32). A Liar's moment. With his pliers, the Liar grips the tail of the past. In one dazzling movement, all the slivers of time and chance are spread out before us. An explosion of word and image. Crescendo. Diminuendo. Silence.

Oscar and Lucinda is a Liar's Prince Rupert's drop, one which shines and dances with a shimmering play of light and dark, the luminous, magical fireworks of the Lie.

Lucinda discovers the wonder of Prince Rupert's drops as a child and so learns

glass is a thing in disguise, an actor, is not solid at all, but a liquid . . . invisible, solid, in short, a joyous and contradictory thing, as good a material as any to build a life from. (Sec. 32)

Entranced by the molten mysteries of Prince Rupert's Glassworks and delighting in the construction of fancies, Lucinda dreams of building a structure of glass, a pyramid, a tower, an arcade of glass spun like a web, until she conceives the fabulous image of a glass church. When the lives of Oscar and Lucinda lock together, Oscar, like Lucinda, becomes entranced with the manufacture of glass. He too is captivated by the image of the glass church, dancing around it like a brolga, seeing 'light, ice, spectra'. He sees that glass is the gross material closest to the soul, free of imperfection, an avenue for glory. An actor, a contradiction, glass is a Liar's substance. *Oscar and Lucinda* is the Liar's brolga dance through the light and spectra of the Lie.

Oscar appears a praying mantis, a scarecrow, with wild red hair, a neat triangular face and a luminous innocence. He has a reedy, fluting voice and flapping hands, and knees which click when he runs, a nervous scuttling motion. He is a superb ungainly creature, angular, but also light, airy, 'made from the quills of a bird' (Sec. 4). A man of 'holy profligacy' (Sec. 42), who lacerates himself with his paradoxes, Oscar is a very moving figure, from the start in Hennacombe, where he is trapped in his own bewilderment and grief.

For Oscar the toss of the tor in the hopscotch game reveals the will of God, commanding him to emigrate to New South Wales, as the earlier toss commanded him to leave Theophilus and become Anglican. He receives Wardley-Fish into his life as a spiritual messenger, an agent of the Lord sent to reveal the wonders of the racetrack and the proper religious activity of backing horses. In the spiritual conundrum on which the novel turns, Oscar sees his passion for gambling as vile, but his notebooks of betting data as diaries of his communion with God.

The delightful Wardley-Fish, with his awkward kindness and enduring love for Oscar, recognizes that Oscar is 'one of those trick drawings in *Punch* which have the contradiction built in so that what seems to be a spire one moment is a deep shaft the next.' (Sec. 42). This is the *trompe l'oeil* of Oscar's Escher self, the spire soaring up into dazzling light, and the shaft reaching down into the darkness of hell. The whole novel is lit by this Escher vision of spire and shaft, light and dark, the shimmering light and mysteries of glass, yet the nightmarish images of darkness and hell.

For Oscar and Lucinda, existence is gloriously random, life the play of chance, the roll of the dice—and the dividend, 'We are *alive* . . . We are alive on the very brink of eternity'. (Sec. 88) Spurning all the structures of safe passage through their lives, Oscar and Lucinda choose the exquisite knife-edge of risk. Both reject the vouchsafed life inside accepted boundaries of religious, social and moral codes, and, for Lucinda, 'The Glass Lady', the life inside the conventional roles of women in colonial society.

In colonial New South Wales, Lucinda Leplastrier is a contained creature, with,

a clean, starched stillness. But the stillness was coiled and held flat. Like a rod of ebony rubbed with cat's fur, she was charged with static electricity. (Sec. 21)

Two gamblers on an arc towards each other, Lucinda and Oscar are partners, two players across hemispheres, looking for a game. Lucinda is alienated from colonial society by her dress, her spinsterhood, her aloofness, her gambling – and her dreams. She pits herself passionately against male voodoo, determined to manufacture her dreams at her Prince Rupert's Glassworks. Yet her life is split between the glass dream and the circle of card players at D'Abbs' house, the circle which is for her an abstraction of human endeavour, the electric edge of life. Forever in search of a game, she prowls across Sydney to the Chinese fan-tan room, as she later prowls through the *Leviathan*, in search of the electric ecstasy of the game.

The novel abounds in images of safety, vouchsafed lives, with edges dulled. Against this, Oscar and Lucinda choose the risk and place their bets.

Like working out the odds, Carey scatters chance circumstances over the face of the novel: the Christmas pudding which turns Oscar away from Theophilus; the chance death of Lucinda's father on Palm Sunday; the chance that Wardley-Fish took Oscar to Epsom the first time; the chance of the sermon on Christmas Day, which disposed Oscar and Lucinda to accept Jeffris' proposal of leading the expedition; the chance that Wardley-Fish, who might have saved Oscar, was robbed and forced to return to Sydney; Oscar's chance encounter with Miriam Chadwick, who becomes the narrator's great-grandmother. A vast array of marginal figures press forward into the novel, from the Reverend Dennis Hasset, entranced by Lucinda's coiled stillness, to the preening d'Abbs in his habitat, from the stern fundamentalist Theophilus with the trembling hymnal soul, to the thin brittle soul of Melody Clutterbuck. As contingent character and chance event flow around them, Oscar and Lucinda play out the gamble and wager everything.

Giddy with fear of the water, Oscar's journey on board the *Leviathan* is a nightmare the hopscotch will of God has demanded of him. While up above, there is phosphorescence, the sea studded with sparkles of light, a luminescent sea of globes of fire, Oscar is below, a creature of dark, caught in the web of his own phobia, 'a sad and ugly creature in a fairytale, one forever exiled from the light and compelled to skulk, pale, big-eyed, sweat-shiny in the dark steel nether regions.' (Sec. 53). Searching for a game, Lucinda journeys through the innards of the Gargantuan *Leviathan* to a nightmare of some monstrous creature pouring black effluent up from its stomach into the sky.

In a triumph of contingency, with the Liar waiting eagerly for the moment, the two lives come together, Oscar and Lucinda in a moment of joyous conjunction, discovering a partner. Oscar is in a cloud of electricity, Lucinda both enchanted and appalled by his innocence. When Lucinda confesses her gambling Oscar articulates the notion on which the novel turns, that gambling is noble, part of the divine design. Religious faith is a wager, a bet on the existence of God, in which we stake our lives on a structure of fancies.

'Our whole faith is a wager, Miss Leplastrier, We bet . . . we bet that there is a God. We bet our life on it. We calculate the odds, the return, that we shall sit with the Saints in paradise.'

'I cannot see,' he said, 'that such a God, whose fundamental requirement of us is that we gamble our mortal souls, every second of our temporal existence . . . It is true! We must gamble every *instant* of our allotted span. We must stake *everything* on the unproveable fact of His existence.' (Sec. 57)

In this splendidly Dostoyevksian proclamation, the Reverend Oscar Hopkins insists gambling is a part of the divine scheme of things. Later Lucinda proudly asserts 'We are gamblers, in the noble sense. We believe all eternity awaits us.' (Sec. 82) We bet on the spiritual dividends.

At the Glassworks, Oscar becomes Lucinda's tangle-legged usurper, until she reveals her precious dream of the glass church. Now the moment of conjunction – glass and gamble become one. Now the splendid leap of the Lie – the glass church becomes their bet, in which Oscar and Lucinda are one, the glass church their progeny.

Born of Christian thinking, the glass church and its delivery to the Reverend Hasset is 'a knife of an idea, a cruel instrument of sacrifice, but also one of great beauty, silvery curved, dancing with light'. (Sec. 82) Oscar bets on the benefits of sacrifice in hope of winning Lucinda's heart through the prism of the church. Both are betting their inheritance – Lucinda her fortune, Oscar his faith. The period they spend together in the cottage at Longnose Point is a coda period in the novel, a touching period of haven for them both, but quickened by the lure of the bet on the glass church. As the expedition leaves, Lucinda feels the absurdity of the whole venture, the packaged glass church not 'the crystal-pure, bat-winged structure of her dreams' (Sec. 93), but a heavy folly.

Like Lucinda's nightmarish drive through Sydney at night, on the way to the Chinese gambling den, Oscar's journey is a longer and more horrific nightmare, a hellish journey into the heart of darkness. The passage of the church across unmapped territory is a dark emblem of the cost of their fancy and the cost of the Christian fancy.

Adrift and besmirched inside a laudanum nightmare, Oscar is trapped under the tyranny of Jeffris, and, during the massacre of the Aborigines, tied to a tree, he becomes a horrified, wailing witness. At Bellingen, under the crushing weight of evil, Oscar is gaunt and scraped out, haunted by his complicity in the massacre, until, in the evil heart of the land, he is driven to the murder of Jeffris. A black and absurdist Christ figure, still bearing the rope burns from the time of the massacre, Oscar becomes a man afire, burning and dancing in his own firelight, as he constructs the glass church for its final passage on the water.

Out of all the patterning of light and dark, it is the hellish darkness with which the novel ends, culminating in Oscar's death, inside his own nightmare. He wins the bet with Lucinda on the glass church, and loses the bet on God. As the glass church slides down its tilting ramp, the fractured panes of glass open to admit his ancient enemy. The flying foxes close on the river seem 'like angels with bat wings. He saw it as a sign from God. He shook his head, panicking in the face of eternity'. (Sec. 112) He dies screaming, caught in the sheet-folds of a nightmare, realizing, Like Lucinda, the glass church is 'a product of the Deuce's insinuations into the fancy-factory of his mind' (Sec. 112), a terrible folly.

If the novel is Conradian in its journey into the heart of darkness, it is also Dosteyevskian in its reach of dark and light, its religious themes of risk and gamble. In a wry literary joke, Carey even posits a link with George Eliot through Lucinda's mother which Lucinda herself disclaims when she finds Eliot out of sympathy. There are other nineteenth-century literary shadows. The style is sometimes Dickensian, wonderfully comic, with quick sketches like Mrs Stratton's walking at an angle for carrying books, thus revealing her donnish nature, or Mrs Williams' hairbrushing; or Bishop Dancer's vision of Sydney as 'an orphan's party with a dressing-up box' (Sec. 69), with maids donning tiaras, piemen dressed up as gentlemen. Or the image of the d'Abbs house, like a ball of string, a grand expensive tangle in which the pristine d'Abbs dances. In spite of all the literary play which conjures up nineteenth-century literary kin, the flickering shadows of Dickens and Eliot, the darker presence of Conrad and Dostoyevsky, yet here is unmistakably a contemporary Australian Lie.

Oscar and Lucinda is a post-Christian novel, an absurdist black comedy of the life of Reverend Oscar Hopkins, a man of burning faith, playing the hopscotch game of God's will. There is a dark absurdity in the scene of Oscar's standing among the lettuces at the Stratton house and declaring himself a theological refugee, 'called' to the Anglican faith; or the scene of Oscar, blindfolded, caught inside his own fear, being loaded in a cage by crane on to the *Leviathan*, a man of faith obedient to his God. This is the man who brought the Christian stories up the river with him, the stories which have vanished now as the Gleniffer church has vanished, replaced by thistles. No sign now of what the church has meant to the narrator's family: Palm Sundays, resurrections, water into wine, loaves and fishes, 'all those cruel and lofty ideas'. The narrator hears the echoes, feels the brush of ghostly presence and wonders. The great-grandson searches for an explanation of the vanished stories, meditating on the shadowy presences.

Oscar is a creature manufactured out of slivers of gospel stories: Jonah and the Whale and the parting of the waters are transmuted into the massive ship, the *Leviathan* where Oscar huddles below in the dark. Jesus' walking on the water becomes translated into Oscar's terror of water and death in water. No Lazarus here either, only the death of Stratton, the murder of Jeffris and the massacre of Aborigines. No miracles of driving out demons here, only the voracious gambling monster which must be fed. God spoke from the Burning Bush but here there is a fiery light and burning fire of Oscar assembling the glass church. The river that turned to blood, the story of Jesus rising from the dead and ascending to heaven – these become in the hands of the Liar, Oscar pulled down into the river waters surrounded by bat-winged figures, a sacrifice offered up to the limits of his own dream. New stories start here, handed down to Kumbaingiri Billy by his aunt, Oscar's Aboriginal Mary Magdalen, on the day Jesus came to Bellingen to construct the glass church and reach Boat Harbour by Good Friday.

In this post-Christian novel, Australia is not a Christian landscape.

You could feel it in the still shadows along watercourses. She felt ghosts here, but not Christian ghosts, not John the Baptist or Jesus of Galilee. There were other spirits, other stories, slippery as shadows. (Sec. 37)

Oscar finds his Randwick flock 'creatures of their landscape',

Sydney was a blinding place. It made him squint. The stories of the gospel lay across the harsh landscapes like sheets of newspaper on a polished floor. They slid, slipped, did not connect to anything beneath them. It was a place without moss or lichen, and the people scrabbling to make a place like troops caught under fire on the hard soil.' (Sec. 66)

The narrator marvels that, in this ancient landscape, as his great-grandfather drifted up the Bellinger River, inside the glass church, Oscar saw nothing.

The country was thick with sacred stories more ancient than the ones he carried in his sweat-slippery leather Bible. He did not even imagine their presence. Some of these stories were as small as the transparent anthropods which lived in puddles beneath the river casuarinas. These stories were like fleas, thrip, so tiny that they might inhabit a place (inside the ears of the seeds of grass) he would later walk across without even seeing. In this landscape every rock had a name, and most names had spirits, ghosts, meanings. (Sec. 107)

The glass church, with ice-walls of light, drifting down the river through the ancient landscape, with the black-suited figure inside, is a superb image of the incongruity of Christian faith in this landscape. The church cracks and crazes, into ice-knives hanging over Oscar's head, with jigsaw edges refracting a spectrum of colours over his hands. Up above, the sky is blemished, or curdled, and the glass so splintered it is almost opaque. Christianity cracks like glass, breaking up in the face of the ancient landscape.

But what of the Liar's fancy-factory, with its molten mysteries? No folly this, no insinuations of a literary Deuce here. This is a splendid unforgettable Lie, which dances with light and dark, an Escher vision of spire and shaft, light and dark, the shimmering light and mysteries of glass and nightmarish images of darkness and hell. The reader has only to break the tail of this magical Prince's Rupert's drop, open *Oscar and Lucinda*, and the spectacular vision begins, an explosion of magical words.

SIXTH DIALOGUE

Reader Where are your pliers? You seem to have everything to hand. Surely you have pliers in your workshop?

Liar My fancy-factory. Yes, here they are. Ready?

Reader No, wait. Once you have broken it, it's finished. Perhaps it's better to keep it for a while.

Liar No, It's too tempting. Anyway, Carey's got lots more of these Prince Rupert's drops. You wait and see. Here we go . . . An explosion of dew. A dazzling display of firewords. Perhaps we need protective lens . . .

Reader Do you remember those 3–D lens people used to wear in picture theatres, so as soon as you put them on the film seemed to leap out at you. Take them off and it all becomes subdued again, back to 2–D. Except I think the lens in *Illywhacker* are about 4–D. Lies inside lies inside the novel by the Liar Carey. Historical lies and the Lie of fiction tangled together.

Liar Yes, and look at all the *true* lies in *Illywhacker* – all the lies of Australian history. Very Godelian. And how about Herbert selling them back to us! What a conman.

Reader Set a conman to catch the con. Set a liar to catch the lies. Except that they're all our own. Political lies. Private ones, snivelling little lies to get us out of a corner, the big sweeping lies that grow tangled and multi-layered like the Pet Emporium. Even Australia's Own Car is a lie.

Liar Of course, but wait till you see what Bail does with the Holden in *Holden's Performance*. From the used-car salesman to the car itself! Holden Shadbolt – Australia's Own Car complete with specifications, and Australia's own mechanical consciousness at the same time. Sees all, records it all, from every perspective but has no interior. Brilliant novel.

Reader What do you mean from every perspective?

Liar Just what I say. In the Lie, you can handle a whole lot of perspectives at once. You just start with one line.

Reader One line is not a perspective.

Liar Of course it is . . . I've been reading an article by Escher about lines and boundaries. It's here. Listen to this.

No one can draw a line that is not a boundary line; every line splits a singularity into a plurality. Every closed contour, no matter what its shape, whether a perfect circle or an irregular random form, evokes in addition the notions of 'inside' and 'outside' and the suggestion of 'near' and 'far away', of 'object' and 'background'.[1]

So every line is a boundary line and a perspective on plurality.

Reader Yes, but what I'm getting at is the perspective on reality. There are *laws* about it. That's what I'm getting at . . . the laws of Perspective. Remember in Bail's 'Cul de Sac (uncompleted)' the eminent citizen who discovered some of the Laws of Perspective?

Liar The statue stepped down from his plinth. So?

Reader The laws must be upheld somehow. Remember Roy Biv talking to the statue? If Perspective makes the single eye the centre of the visible world, so that everything converges on the single eye as the universe was once thought to be arranged for God . . .

Liar . . . but perspective structured all images of reality to address a single spectator who, unlike God, could only be in one place at a time. Don't forget Finbar disproved Christianity. These are post-Christian times.

Reader If that's traditional perspective, what kind of perspective holds now? What are the new Laws?

Liar New legislation to remedy anomalies in the Laws of Perspective! Wigged advocates, lawyers pleading for change to redress flaws in the Laws.

Reader Lawyer–Liars. We've got one of those. Hasluck. We could get him to prepare a draft of new guidelines, ready for new legislation to cover changes in perspective.

Liar Law reform. Severe penalties for breaking the Laws of perspective – merciless punishment, stiff fines and hard labour, harsh sentences. As a deterrent. A new tough police force equipped with modern communications systems ... computers and word processors. Enforcing the laws of perspective.

Reader You're getting carried away. You seem to have overlooked a few boundaries between reality and fantasy.

Liar Well what do you expect? I'm a Liar. I don't have to stay within any boundary lines. I don't accept them.

Reader Remember in that same story, Bail has the Chief talking to Biv about geometry and topography. He says that, if Truth is measurable, the work they do is untainted. Their lines never lie. Where a line stops there's an intersection.

Liar Intersections and hierarchical levels. Yes. Escher's boundary lines.

Reader I think it's a matter of geometry. If the inherent contradiction in perspective is that it's all addressed to a single spectator who could only be in one place at a time, then we need a new geometry.

Liar New shapes, new space – new lens.

Reader Yes but unlike the Chief, I believe it *is* tainted work. Of course it's tainted. It's like David David trying to protect himself from the Trap taint, but finding it insidious, infectious, contaminating everything. There's no uncontaminated truth. No untainted reality. Truth is not measurable.

Liar But not everyone knows that. Why shouldn't Bail do a bit of measuring. Liars like measuring truth.

Reader You remember Billie Shockley looking out the window of her flat, watching Sydney change, become Kandinsky? If Ireland's Kandinsky ...

Liar I'm not sure that's generally so. There's a lot of Leger in *Prisoner*, for example. The machine and the working man, the unexpected lines and shapes, static in the midst of dynamic.

Reader That's true, but I think Kandinsky holds for more of Ireland's work ... If Ireland's Kandinsky, Bail is surely Mondrian. Meditations on the horizontal and vertical, the geometry of space ...

Liar A new topography of time and space.

Reader I was also thinking of the dialogues Mondrian wrote, the ones published in *De Stijl*, dialogues on abstract and natural reality. I was thinking about them when I read Bail's stories.

Liar What's the connection? Are you thinking about our conversations? Is this the self-conscious mode, the loop back to our dialogues? You and I together in our own Godelian Loop?

Reader No, I was not thinking of that at all. There's enough Looping already, without you and I getting into the picture.

Liar But we are in the picture. We *are* inside the frame. Do you think it's more honest to leave *us* out? We're not just observers – we can't be. That's the whole point, the role of the observer has changed. Look at Bail's 'Life of the Party'. The man up the tree trying to watch what happens when he's not there. But when his guests are leaving, someone toots the horn to say goodbye to him. There's no such thing as an objective, detached observer.

Reader I'm not suggesting there is. Of course we are already inside the frame. But I'm thinking of how. Mondrian's dialogues reminded me of Heubler and Bail's dialogues with him.

Liar Poor Heubler. I bet he's sorry he spoke. He must have realized his proposition of photographing everyone alive in the world was rather ambitious, but I don't think he realized what he was getting into when he announced it to Murray Bail.

Reader And how about that exhibition in *Homesickness*? The one in London of X–ray photos of Renaissance paintings, showing the artists' 'real' intentions, ghost-like in the photos. The one that exposed all their appalling errors in composition and perspective. Bail uses photography to strip away illusion, but he doesn't stop there. He strips away the photographer as well.

Liar I picture Heubler steadily deflating throughout the short stories, until by the end he's reduced to just a whimper, a last whimper from a poor shrunken creature.

Reader Poor man. I can't help feeling sorry for poor Heubler. His only mistake was believing in art and photography . . .

Liar . . . and reality. He started out with a belief that the eye of the observer can authentically represent reality. Pretty naive.

Reader I suppose so, but it's pretty common. A lot of people believe it. I used to believe it myself. In fact I seem to be cast as Heubler.

Liar That's the risk you take. *Caveat emptor*. Herbert Badgery's not the only one selling lies. He's not the only salesman. How about Zoellner? Look what he's selling . . . definitions for sale. And he's in partnership with Roy Biv. Biv with maps and space, Zoellner with words. What a business proposition! A partnership of words and maps, recording and fixing the existence of things.

Reader All the equipment for surveying the world. Surveyors mapping out a new cartography of reality. Words as compasses, definitions as maps. Talking about compasses and lines of intersection, that reminds me. Have you read Calvino's *The Castle of Crossed Destinies*, with the Tarot cards? The geometry of characters there? All the intersecting lines and correlations. All the stories interlocking, so that they become destinies placed in the paths of other travellers. Sliding identities and overlapping paths.

Liar You can also read the pattern of stories not only horizontally and vertically, but also diagonally. In fact there are hundreds of geometric patterns possible, squares and rhomboids and polyhedrons. Wait a minute . . . I'm looking for something. All this equipment here in my desk. But where is it?

Reader What are you looking for? What is all that stuff?

Liar I've got everything here. I keep it all to hand. There's a lot more to my work than paper and pen and typewriter, you know.

Reader What's that? What's causing the refractions?

Liar That's my Perspex prism. And look here's my butterbox to put all the pages in, when I'm ready to send them to someone. Matters handles it sometimes. Here's my heap of words, the ladder I use if I've been down in the wortarium. And there are some old sloughed off snake skins. And here's some frames, ready to get into the picture. Look that's been slashed. Some vandal has cut the centre out of it. Barbarian!

Reader Where's the smoke coming from?

Liar Don't panic. It's only my alchemical furnace. I was using it earlier. Still smouldering. Look, here's a lens. The eye of the camera. Ah here it is. This is what I was looking for.

Reader What's that?

Liar My theodolite. For the survey work. And here's my compass, my protractor, my set square. For the geometry.

THE GEOMETRY OF THE LIE *MURRAY BAIL*

If Truth is measurable, the work we do here is untainted. Our lines never lie. They trace concrete facts. Geometry – and topography is a branch of geometry – follows the behaviour of real objects. Always remember that. Your pencil is outlining reality. Where a line stops there's an intersection.

'Cul-de-sac (uncompleted)'

But appearances, of events and things seen around, are deceptive. What can we believe any more? What is real? Appearances are not necessarily exact. The appearance of things is generally a lie. That has become a problem of life, wouldn't you say? . . . Where is the truth, the real existence of things? Increasingly the edges are blurred.

Homesickness

ZOELLNER & ROY G. BIV
* Definitions, Maps *

'This is the place,' said Gerald.

A tiny brass bell shivering on a spring shaped like a comma sprang into action when they entered, at odds with the sedentary calm of the shop, and remained shaking there long afterwards, like a salmon dying on a line. Undoubtedly it indicated the turbulence beneath the marmoreal calm of both Zoellner, the dying bibliophile, and his junior partner, the repressed Biv (one given to daydreaming). Still waters, so it is said, can run very deep: even these scholarly backwaters . . . Roy Biv out the back, handling the maps, glanced up. Not old Zoellner. Behind the desk where books tilted like laminations of slate he kept his head down, annotating a pamphlet on Swahili phonemes. An electric waistcoat (for warmth) restricted his movements to a tight circle: a badly frayed maroon cord fell from the light socket, into his collar. In Clarendon Bold on the wall a small sign announced: NO BAD LANGUAGE. 'This is the place,' Gerald rubbed his hands. He was evidently pleased with his find.

Words had been collected from all corners of the globe and stored in bound volumes, singly or in sets. The air was grey, teeming in effect with phosphenes – an appearance of rings of light produced by pressure on the eyeball, due to irritation of the retina. Zoellner and Biv retailed every dictionary and word-binge imaginable . . . glossologies, language maps, semantic atlases on Gleek, Anglish, Jappish, East Indian, Ptydepe and Jarman, Double Deutsch, and an indispensable phrase book on Swiss; all kinds of cocky argot, Strine and Partridges: a low shelf of Dirty Words or 'rudery' made browsers bend down or squat. (*Wowser. n.* (Aust.) Fanatical puritan; spoilsport, killjoy; teetotaler.)

The varnished steps placed to reach the higher shelves – Astronomical Definitions, Scientific Terms – were opened like the letter A, the rope stays forming a taut X. There were words and articles lying on the floor. They stumbled over certain words. Zoellner and Biv had one of the finest collections of Collective Nouns to be seen anywhere. A regular Scriptorum; polyglot's trove . . .

'We just don't have this back home,' Gerald complained. 'It's a part of the infrastructure missing. A major lacuna.'

Zoellner at his desk cleared his throat.

The storage of words, like the lines on a map, records and fixes the existence of things. Inside the shop, the repository, a feeling of serenity pervaded, as if the four walls contained the entire world and even what lay beyond, each part isolated, identified and filed. It was based upon facts, upon known quantities. Exactitude reigned. It contrasted casually with the chaos of forest impressions suffered by the travellers. It was a haven.

Homesickness[1]

•

BAIL'S LIE IS GEOMETRIC, plotted along the lines of space and time, in a vast pattern of linked planes and surfaces. All his work is a Lie of the relation between inner and outer geometry, the two modes of convex and concave, which the literary optics of the Liar insist are one. It is Godelian fiction, a Tangled Hierarchy of levels and layers of reality, of intersecting forces of dynamic larrikin energy and rectilinear grids. His work has subtlety and swift intelligence and, for all its complexity, it exudes energy and comic vitality, its pace unflagging, the shifting kaleidoscopic patterns constantly flickering. A conglomerate of events and intersecting lines of energy, reality is constantly flickering too, like the mouse at the start of *Contemporary Portraits*.

Suppose a mouse were to run across a stone. Just count each step it takes. Only forget the word 'each'; only forget the word 'step'. Then each step will seem a new movement...A flickering will begin. The mouse will start to flicker. Look about you: the world is flickering (like a mouse).[2]

Only forget the word 'stone' too, because in Bail's work even the surface on which it runs is flickering.

In the London shop where Zoellner sells words and definitions and his junior partner, Biv, sells maps, Gerald complains, 'We just don't have this back home . . . . It's a part of the infrastructure missing. A major lacuna.' The lacuna which interests Murray Bail is the sense of our own topography. In the Australian consciousness, definition is missing too, things blurred and out of focus. The major lacuna is the interior of Australia – a place existing in the consciousness largely as a blank. Murray Bail is inside the infrastructure surveying it, calculating it and reporting his measurements in the geometry of the Lie. Bail is a geometer, surveying reality, tracing trajectories of time and space and examining angles, calculating the lines of chance and the points of intersection. With his Liar's theodolite, he explores the topography of things, the horizontal and vertical angles, the lines and surfaces, curves and planes. As he covers vast distances around the world and around Australia, he maps out new co-ordinates of space and time, but the space is the Liar's space; both inner and outer, both convex and concave. Using the Liar's calculations, which are precise and absurd, comic and disturbing, Bail meditates on a geometry of chance and design, randomness and energy, place and consciousness.

Bail is not a genial Liar murmuring reassuring Lies and pandering to our image. In *Homesickness*, Australians are tourists in unfamiliar places of the mind, sightseers looking at exhibitions of the shape and definition of things, but homesick for simple Australian reality. In *Holden's Performance*, Australia is a traveller through time, on a trip through history. Like *Illywhacker*, *Moonlite*, *Trap* and *The Wort Papers*, it is a Liar's history. It is the history of Holden Shadbolt, Australia's own Holden, the vehicle of Australia's own consciousness. It is about the mode of Australian consciousness as it travels through the twentieth century, seeing a lot, remembering a lot, but thinking little, not interested in itself, no clear ideas about anything. Not many people in Australia are granted histories, observes Bail. This is history keeping pace with time but going nowhere, constantly running, constantly accelerating away from momentous events. It is an epic, but an epic of fragments, a proliferation of images of newsprint and newsreel, images seen through a windscreen. The mechanical eye of Holden Shadbolt sees all, his photographic memory files all. He is young and strong and reliable, but he is also without direction and without focus, open to any definition because he himself is blank, has no clear shape. Holden is a mechanical consciousness, the mode of Australian travel through space and time, a spectator in its own history, a sightseer in its own existence.

Amid the intersecting lines of time and space and motion, there are intersecting notions of vision and the observing eye, often the eye of the camera. Bail says he is 'morbidly – pessimistically – fascinated by photography'.[3] and much of his work is about angles of vision, the eye of the observer, the eye of the camera. Photography is part of his preoccupation with the relation between art and reality, which emerged first in the short stories of *Contemporary Portraits*. In the opening story, Bail introduces Heubler the photographer, who is, in a sense, a constant presence throughout the collection. All the stories are addressed to Heubler and to his belief that it is possible to authentically represent reality in art. Underneath the stories there is a continuing dialogue between Bail and Heubler on the nature of contemporary portraiture and the nature of art and reality, in which Bail, sometimes playful, sometimes more aloof, examines a series of propositions which arise from Heubler's conception of art and reality. The narrator of the story offers to help Heubler in his project of assembling 'the most authentic representation of the human species' by photographing *everybody*. His 'help' consists of fictions about art and reality which are also explanations to Heubler of the futility of his project, all demonstrating the absurdity of trying to represent reality authentically through the eye of the camera. The narrator demonstrates this through words, exploiting the paradoxical gap between words and photographs, and extending into an aburdist image of the problems of trying to represent anything at all in art. The addressee of all the stories, Heubler is the reader and the reader Heubler. The whole collection is an exhibition of contemporary portraits, presented to the photographer Heubler – and it becomes a dialogue between writer and photographer, between writer and reader, between art and reality.

In the dialogue on art and reality running through all Bail's work, there is much trafficking in words and definitions. He talks about reality and naming.

Early on I was influenced by reading certain philosophers, some of whose ideas demonstrated that words became a proof of reality. Hence the connection between lists of things and what we do and see...Often I am concerned with texture, with maintaining the appropriate state of mind in the work. In the case of naming, of definitions and so forth, it may be nothing less than a spirit of enquiry.[4]

In *Holden's Performance*, Bail parodies this investigative spirit and the quest for proof in the delightful figure of Vern, who is a familial spirit of Zoellner. With Vern is Gordon Wheelwright, who collects not facts but artefacts, calculating their flotsam movements in order to establish shifts in the centre of gravity. In the geometry of Bail's work, this play on fact and artefact holds throughout. Vern and Wheelwright in the rectilinear city of Adelaide and Zoellner and Biv in their London shop are partners in the quest for the things which define. The third member of the Adelaide triumvirate is Les Flies, who is not driven, who understands angles of intersection and is the bemused, mild-mannered companion to those who seek fact and artefact. The marvellous trio are all comic components of the Liar in his enterprise of definition – the geometry of the Lie.

Now living in Sydney, Murray Bail was born in Adelaide in 1941, where he attended art school for a while before moving to Melbourne and began writing short stories in the Menzies era – a time when 'Writing became inevitable . . . that time of boredom and emptiness – of almost deafening emptiness'.[3] After leaving Melbourne, he lived in Bombay for two years and in London in the early 1970s. *Contemporary Portraits* was first published in 1975 (and re-issued as *The Drover's Wife and other Stories* in 1980). *Homesickness*, his first novel, won the 1980 National Book Council award and the 1980 *Age* Book of the Year Award (shared with Ireland's *A Woman of the Future*). His second novel, *Holden's Performance*, first published in 1987, instantly proclaimed itself as a major Australian novel.

Bail has long been interested in art and was a member of the council of the Australian National Gallery for a period until December 1981. He is the author of a major study of the Australian artist Ian Fairweather, published in 1981. On his return to Australia in 1975, dismayed by the neglect of Fairweather's work, and concerned at the imbalance of attention to his bohemian activities rather than his paintings, Bail began research on Fairweather. One of the main aims of the book was to redress that imbalance, 'to set down all the facts and myths as absolutely as possible, and then reveal the course of his art'. Although art is a secondary interest, Bail points out that

the division between art and writing in certain areas of conceptual art has been crossed. Not so much here, but in Europe and America you can look at an exhibition and afterwards the only proof of its existence is the catalogue, which itself can in some cases read like a rarified form of advanced fiction.[4]

Bail regards the realist tradition as 'the great curse of Australian Literature. It's part of that Anglo-Saxon pragmatic, prosaic, empirical heritage we got from England'.[5] Bail tells a Liar's joke about being a realist in so far as his work is multi-layered, like reality. But he recalls that

In the early Sixties, Australian literature was so dry and dusty and flat, it was just like the Nullarbor Plain. The place was boring, at least to me, and so was the literature. When I read Kafka's *Metamorphosis*, it was terribly impressive because he showed what could be done.[4]

The writers Bail holds in high regard are Kafka, Marquez, Pynchon, Tournier, Raymond Roussel, the Russian realists and, above all, Proust. He delights in Patrick White's continuing to take

alarming risks for which we should all be grateful – his emotional, intellectual, even stylistic risks . . . . The artist should not hesitate to exceed the norm', someone wrote a hundred years ago: a Frenchman, not a cautious Anglo-Saxon. I agree . . . . For myself I find it natural to dwell more on situations, propositions, speculations than traditional character analysis . . . Objects already existing or invented can suggest an attitude, a personality, a system. There is room here for me, natural interest, with risks and losses, not the least of which might be the extra tolerance and imagination demanded of the reader.[6]

For the artist who does not hesitate to exceed the norm, there are rich pickings at the start of *Contemporary Portraits* in Heubler's project:

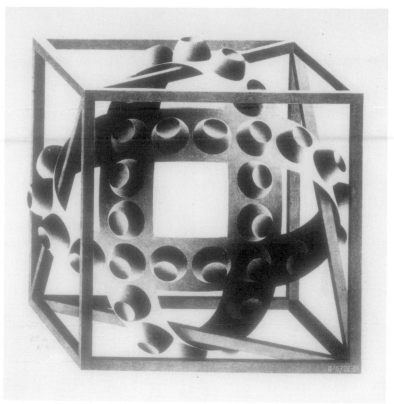

Cube with Magic Ribbons (1957)

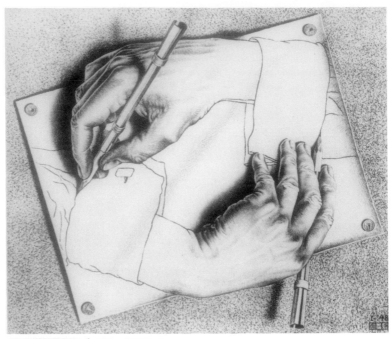

Drawing Hands (1948)

Waterfall (1961)

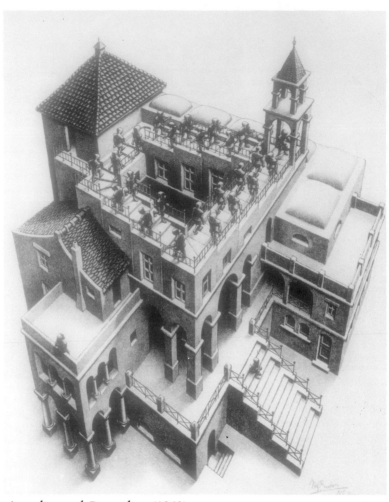

Ascending and Descending (1960)

Print Gallery (1956)

Convex and Concave (1955)

Hand with Reflecting Sphere (1935)

Still Life with Street (1937)

to 'photographically document . . . the existence of everyone alive' and so 'produce the most authentic representation of the human species that may be assembled' (p.3). Tilting his camera at the world, his eye to the lens, Heubler will encompass it all. Even an all-encompassing project has to start somewhere and Heubler's starts with a subjective list of selected types. The 'types' are clichés, like the clichés of art on which his project is based. As Heubler pits his subjectivity against the objective world, the narrator pits characters against Heubler's notion of portraiture. By the end of *Contemporary Portraits*, Heubler is surely a pitiable figure, stripped of his hubris and his wistful notions of art and reality.

Through a very deliberate structure Bail presents an apparently arbitrary choice of persons who, in the broad sweep of 'types', might illustrate one aspect of Heubler's list. The 23 people are distinguished not by visual characteristics but by value and attitude inaccessible to the eye of the camera. Among the people he proposes, there are extraordinary correlations, degrees of 'overlap' which further subvert the whole enterprise. They are 23 people through whom we peer into an impossibly complex and irreducible universe which can never be captured, not in words, not in the visual image of the photograph, not in art.

The first person is Aldridge who always has the last word and, with a word ('zynopic', 'zythm' or 'zyvatiate') proposes to defeat mortality. Next is Rivera, who would rather be almost any one else, and is disturbed by the reflection of himself in the face of his son – who is, in a sense, his defeat of mortality, the continuation of himself through time. The third one is Roberts, who is not afraid of life, but we learn only contingent details about him, so, without explanation, we depend upon the narrator's judgements, which of course we are doing all the time. Already the absurdities are starting to mount up and already there is a sense of a wondrous intelligence at work in these stories, an intelligence that delights in paradox and play. But that is just the start. After the reminder that this is all subjective and can therefore never encompass any objective reality, in the fourth, we have Schultz, who may outlive art, and we are back to art and mortality. Schultz is preserving himself in art, literally, starting with his fingers in formalin, ending in his suicide and the spectacle of his stubble continuing to grow for five or six hours after his death – which is STILL LIFE. By his death, he may

THE GEOMETRY OF THE LIE

outlive art 'and when there is no art his body, or our shocked memories of it, will remain'. (p.11). When there is no art, there will be memory. Art too is finite, mortal.

The fifth person is Miss White, who is pathologically modest, so much so she has subsumed her self into her image as Old Recluse. Only photographers are admitted into her solitude. So Heubler will be limited to a photograph of her image. What of Marilyn Duncan, who is beautiful but dumb and so probably 'has no knowledge of comparisons'? Here the narrator points out that 'Part of our brain is connected to the central nervous system to which examples of beauty are offered. Either they "fit" or are rejected.' (p.13) How is Heubler to succeed when aesthetic images will be sorted out, accepted or rejected by his central nervous system? What of Zoellner, who thinks words are as concrete as objects? He sees the shape of the self as the shape of his name. How is Heubler to see past the shapes of the names of things? Zoellner is described in precise, authenticating detail, with definitions:

Zoellner sees his name, his shape approaching along an avenue of objects, his body consisting of parts which operate also as words. To some critics, this line of thinking – Zoellner's Definition, as it has come to be called – shows a belief in nothing. Glaring nihilism, in short. The critics of course are wrong. They should read again the carefully gathered evidence, all of it published. (15-16)

Zoellner is a recurring figure, who reappears in his own story and also in *Homesickness* and even makes a brief appearance at the funeral of Holden Shadbolt's father. Here he exists beside Mrs Snell, who feels trapped by marriage, but the trap is the shape of her married name – which Heubler wants to capture in photographic form.

There are more problems ahead. What of Hume whose existence is normally uneventful, but is punctuated by two dramatic events which take him to the uneventfulness of prison? The second event is both a re-enactment and a consequence to the first and the two together constitute an absurd and arbitrary fate. What of Carpenter, who is not afraid of death, with a cross reference back to Roberts (3) and a further reference: 'See also persons (6), (7), (8). Surprising, Heubler, the number of people not afraid of death'. (p.22). Carpenter is forever standing at the point where the lines of chance intersect, forever about to place his foot fatally forward. How to photograph the life determined by contingency and hold it up as an example of anything? The kinds of problems with which Heubler must contend continue to proliferate. While Rivera (in 2) is disturbed by the image of his son, Mrs Cartwright is engrossed in a painting of herself and Ellis is disturbed by the image of his dead wife, the image of the past still haunting him as posterity haunts Rivera. What of the new Mona Lisa in a Verona market through whom art imitates reality, life imitates art? How can they be separated? What principle of selection can be valid for 'at least one person who is convinced his or her experience would make an interesting novel'? A category into which most of us fall, this entry is blank.

The whole sequence of 23 mocks the enterprise of capturing the real in art. The last person is Heubler himself, 'for whom reality is richer than the artist's fantasies'. Reality is also infinite:

Wood grain! I don't suppose you've had a chance to study it lately. Wood grain on this desk is infinite, Heubler, eddying flatly under the pad – I'm lifting the pad – like giant thumb prints, harmless isobars even. (p.39)

So who is this man who pits himself against reality? What does such a man look like? The narrator speculates on his appearance – his shape, size, his appearance in time and space. He wonders if Heubler is American, circumcised, married, healthy, bow-legged, has pimples on his back. He ponders on the energy level of an ambitious visionary who has fantasies of documenting reality, of capturing reality in art, in image, in word, in perception. The ironic correlations within 'Heubler' continue throughout the whole collection of stories, with Heubler a peripheral presence, the addressee of the stories that follow, each one shifting the perspective on the others.

In 'Heubler', Knudsen (11) is always the life of the party but we receive only random details about him, without explanation. The second story, 'Life of the Party', through a different character, becomes the explanation. Bail presents an attempt to stand outside reality and see it objectively, without the self as spectator. The protagonist climbs a tree, there to observe his unattended guests at a Sunday barbecue – as an unmediated objective reality. When the guests leave and the narrator climbs down, he is left wondering who sounded the horn at him. However cunningly concealed the observer, his presence has been identified and the spectator is also a protagonist. (Who *was* the one aware of his presence? The question subtly alters the whole spectacle of the afternoon.) Try seeing reality when it's not looking, when it's unaware of your scrutiny! It can't be done, Heubler.

The title story in a later edition of *Contemporary Portraits*, 'The Drover's Wife' is probably Bail's best known story.[7] It radically changes our perception of the Drysdale painting and the original Lawson story. As the husband summons up the memories of the past, so Bail summons up our literary heritage – the literary tradition of the bush, isolation in a hostile and barren landscape – and substitutes a contemporary urban and domestic reality. The husband, an Adelaide dentist, insists that there is a mistake in the title of the painting, which is not the drover's wife, but his wife, Hazel, who left him some thirty years before. As he contemplates an Australian work of art, he transforms it into a meaning for himself, a narrative about his own life and a subjective reality. The husband studies the face carefully:

How much can you tell by a face? That a woman has left a husband and two children? Here, I think the artist has fallen down (though how was he to know?). He has Hazel with a resigned helpless expression – as if it was all my fault. Or, as if she had been a country woman all her ruddy life. (p.56)

(How much can *you* tell from a face, Heubler? How is the artist to know?) The husband speculates and decides,

Hazel looks unhappy. I can see she is having second thoughts. Alright, it was soon after she left me; but she is standing away, in the foreground, as though they're not speaking. See that? Distance = doubts. They've had an argument. (p.57)

(See that, Heubler? See, Heubler, how the eye creates its own subjective reality?) The husband recalls their lives together, the night she left him and, with a ludic literary twist, the time she killed the snake at the beach shack one Christmas. He also remembers the drover they met on a camping trip to the bush in which Hazel was at ease and which he found desolate, lacking in sympathy and defying logic.

In the painting 'it is Hazel and the rotten landscape that dominate eveything'. He objects that there are no flies in the painting which is 'altering truth for the sake of a pretty picture, or "composition"'. (p.60). As the husband questions the truth of the painting, Bail questions the composition of art and the activity of the person who looks at art and reconstructs it into a subjective reality. (Take that, Heubler!)

'Zoellner's Definition' arises directly out of 'Heubler', where Zoellner believes words are as concrete as objects. It opens with two definitions, of 'definition' and of 'name', setting up the disparate notions of the essential nature of a thing and an individual designation with a particular vocal sound. Whenever Zoellner thinks of the shape of himself, he sees the word *Zoellner* and sees his shape walking towards him. Bail examines the components of that shape, through a series of definitions – male, face, countenance, skin, eyes, mouth, voice, clothes, height, ear, nose, arm, leg. The individual is measured against the definition, in parody of the attempt to reach through the components to the essential self. But time impinges on the shape of the self too, because 'words are proof of the present, however temporary' (p.69), but not the past and not the future. Where is Zoellner in his own curving circle of time? The last three definitions – of reality, language and words – insist the self cannot be contained in words and definitions, (nor out of an assembly of photographic images, Heubler).

But, Heubler, if you still believe it is possible to assemble the real out of its components, read 'Portrait of Electricity'. In the manner developed in *Homesickness*, Bail parodies the belief of both the exhibitors and the tourists (last year 142 870 of them) that reality can be broken down into its components. The exhibition is designed to capture and enshrine all that remains of the life of a man of 'personal magnetism' – to show the force of his existence. Bail has already offered Heubler Ellison (19), the human dummy, as a man who is 'totally without charisma'. How then do you portray charisma? How do you portray electricity? Or magnetism, an 'ability to attract loyalty', which is defined through the effect on others? The exhibits are suitably absurd: his chair, with the flattened contour of the seat; the carpet from under his desk; a sock; the shape of his shadow; traces of his last meal; a crumpled bus ticket; a photograph of the sky taken from his bedroom window; a mirror which registered his image. The guide insists that 'So much is unknown about great men

. . . that every scrap of evidence plays its part . . . piecing together the whole'. (p.84). There is even a doorway where 'his shape would have been framed' (p.80). Against the delightful absurdity of the exhibits are the incongruously realistic reactions of the tour group. When they see part of a fingernail under the glass of a coffee-table, there are sceptical murmurs, some women questioning the worth of such an exhibit. The narrator suggests it is only a problem of presentation, but the guide is reproachful ('Why should you expect everything to be clearly revealed?' p.88) and insists the great man should be studied through his influence, the electrical force of his existence. Through the guide, the tour group begins to feel close to the great man and the guide himself becomes one of the exhibits. In the exhibition in 'Dog Show', however, the owners and their dogs change roles, the exhibitors supplanting the exhibits and become themselves the exhibits. (How do you demarcate the exhibitor and the exhibited, Heubler? Any ideas? How do you keep the photographer out of the photograph, Heubler?)

Heubler must be tiring by now, probably regretting the whole venture, surely planning to keep his ideas to himself in future. But Bail has not finished yet. In 'Paradise', he returns to the problems of words and their shapes, the nexus between the name and the idea. (Have you considered the problem of trying to isolate people from things, Heubler? The way the self and the material world merge?) In 'Dog Show' and in 'Ore' (and later in 'Home Ownership'[8]), Bail suggests an interchange of characteristics. In 'Ore', Wes Williams' obsession with mining becomes an operation to drill out ore from his teeth, the inner and outer worlds connected. In 'Home Ownership', Parker and the house grow old together, drooping, wrinkled, deteriorating together, so that it becomes difficult to distinguish which one is being described. The white ant eating at the inside brings sudden collapse – and now there's only the house. Persons cannot be disconnected from the reality around them. (There is no objective reality for you to photograph, Heubler.) Space, place, substance, the terrain on which we walk, the houses in which we live, the dogs we exhibit – none of these has a fixed existence, none of these can be represented authentically, because they slide and change identity. Besides, Heubler, you are only a man with a camera, as Bail, in the last story, is only a man with the letters of the alphabet. Bail is free to choose any combination out of all of the endless permutations.

He can create worlds as exotic as Karachi, where he has never been, construct the story of Kathy's love affair in Karachi with Syed Masood, the painter, and take her back to London to weep. But he interrupts from time to time, includes an incident from his own 'real life', reminds us this is a story, just letters of the alphabet selected by a man at a typewriter. (You are only a man with a camera, Heubler.)

Some of the stories in *Contemporary Portraits* anticipate aspects of *Holden's Performance*. In 'Cul-de-Sac (uncompleted)', Bail examines spatial connections, the planes, angles and lines of reality. The Chief explains to Biv:

If Truth is measurable, the work we do here is untainted. Our lines never lie. They trace concrete facts. Geometry – and topography is a branch of geometry – follows the behaviour of real objects. Always remember that. Your pencil is outlining reality. Where a line stops there's an intersection. (p.144)

All these spatial notions are set within a story apparently linear but actually circular, and actually moving from one plane to another, to and fro, throughout the whole. Biv at the drawing board is Biv on a quest, the lines he draws there are the lines which measure reality. He is sent to the cul-de-sac where the engravers are waiting. It is close ('you can get there and back in two minutes') but elusive, ('Pencil lines converged towards it and stopped'). Its landscape inner, the story is in numbered fragments, beginning without explanation at 78, moving with detours and miscellaneous fragments to 108, and bringing Biv back to his starting point, at his drawing board in the office – where the whole movement takes place.

Carrying a standard cartographer's compass, Biv the hero moves through a labyrinth, which is both external and internal. The engravers are waiting, ready to engrave the results of his quest. His quest has its own topography and landmarks: the bridge over an industrial conveyor belt, carrying material refuse (newspapers, wine bottles, an unwanted child, a fur coat) and the refuse of broken promises; an intersection of streets where prams roll down and attack him; also a square, where the bitumen cracks and four small rainbows seep out and clutch at his ankles. The gardener explains to

Biv that 'the feeling of space or the intuition of space is the most basic force of mind' (p.142). Bail complicates space with the shapes Biv sees as his neighbour's daughter undresses; the Inspector checking the angles of intersections (and the public pressures to increase the right angle from 90 degrees); the optician connecting shape with optics, with the optical chart on high above Biv, displaying the words 'cul-de-sac'; the precision instruments which embed themselves in the mind, with the optician commenting on the beauty of machinery. Biv is also accompanied for a time by a statue stepped down from his plinth, a forerunner of Colonel Light in *Holden's Performance*, here an eminent citizen who discovered some of the Laws of Perspective.

Biv is on a quest through the Laws of Perspective, but few of Bail's characters are questers, not even Australia is on a quest. In *Homesickness*, Australians are travellers but as tourists and sightseers not questers. In *Holden's Performance*, the Australian mode of travel is more like the run along the surface in 'The Partitions', a daily mechanical run. There, the world is 'inter-reacting particles, the ever-changing pattern a cause of much bafflement. Occasionally concern.' (p.159), but the run is all, the runners concentrating on the running. To slip is to lose position, to fall is the end, to advance requires a number of victims, one explodes. Cubicles within cubicles, partitions interlocking to form new cubicles, dead-ends, they run above a labyrinth, their shadows spectral patterns on the wall. Rapid recovery and resilience are all, speed essential before the light in the last cubicle is switched off, at the end of each day. These are mechanical runners, a team of Holdens running along the surface. And this is Australia, because, as the Chief explained to Biv,

There is no 'country' as such . . . 'Country', or crust, is nothing more than an undulating base into which are screwed factories and other artificial protuberances . . . We place and arrange things on the surface, including ourselves. Have you got that? (p.151)

The protuberances, the things placed and arranged on the surface, including ourselves, are the country. In *Homesickness*, his tourists are our protuberances, dislocated beings who are sightseers looking at the exhibitions of reality.

For *Homesickness*, Bail preferred the title, 'Migration', 'suggesting both the emotional and intellectual disruptions involved in relocating oneself'.[9] The dislocation and relocation undergone by tourists on their travels is also the dislocation undergone by the readers on their travels through the literary themes of the novel. Bail has pointed out that

Homesickness operates through a kind of linear time, horizontal and already beginning (as in the story 'Cul-de- Sac'), and sliced off, with irregular confusions in the middle. A slice of time, a journey of the mind.[3]

Time and space are disrupted, requiring new bearings in this journey of the mind. The world is chaotic, not orderly nor contained in neat categories and Bail parodies the instinct to define and contain it in exhibitions and museums. All over the world, the group finds the same principle at work – man believing he can contrive a definitive collection and exhibition of aspects of the human condition. With a Borgesian precision and the logic of the Liar, Bail examines the absurdity of the exhibitions and the absurdity of the attempt to contrive definitions of the human condition.

This is not a novel in which the reader can play the observer and emerge untouched. We too have landed in a foreign country, there to become tourists, see exhibitions and be changed. It is a novel about fiction, about the foreign travel that is literature, about our expectations as readers and the nature of the homeland for which we too may be homesick. At the start, like the tourists, the reader is probably grateful for a few gum trees, hoping to hear the cry of the crow, comforted by the Australian graffiti that becomes a landmark in an alien and unpredictable world. Like the tourists we too find that nothing is as we expect, nothing is as it seems. The journey becomes a bizarre picaresque of bewildering episodes, baffling exhibitions and museums. We too will find the journey full of strange twists and reversals, sudden jaunts into the absurd and surreal. We too will return from the day's strange and baffling experiences, grateful for the comfortable familiarity of the hotel, the swimming pool, the dinners, the time to write postcards. We too will find our expectations undermined and our sense of what is real – and what is realistic – subverted.

That Bail has a literary itinerary for us is clear in the opening pages.

In Africa, 'Out there lay the beginnings of the foreign country known through hearsay (*heresy*) and photography, its name and persistent shape on the map'. (p.7) Already themes of shape, name, photography, and the word begin to emerge, summoning up the spirit of Heubler, Zoellner, Roy Biv. And hearsay (heresy), is a Liar's joke about orthodox truth. The first character to be introduced is the blind photographer, Kaddok, for whom images are constructed out of words, the words of his wife and other tourists, 'coloured and jagged with their exclamations' (p.10). Kaddok is a priestly figure, clad in clerical black, bearing the 'magic eye' of the camera, which is hooded like his eyes, as he moves down the aisle of the plane, 'blessing each seat with his hand and occasionally someone's startled head' (p.8). Kaddok is an absurd Tiresias become photographer, seeing nothing and seeing all through words, the high priest of orthodox tourists.

From the air, the land is drawn, the tracks across its surface 'hypnotic doodles', its fissures and outcrops 'old, old statements' (p.8). When they land at the airport in Africa,

It's a clear day. Yet the fragments, static and commonplace, are stationed far apart. It's a mosaic – slabs broken, separated. Soon it would become a slowly moving fresco, clarifying, but with certain parts vague or completely missing; always be missing. (pp.7-8)

This is the landscape of the novel. Throughout, fragments and images will change, move into new patterns, new conformations, but with gaps that will always be missing. When the group moves across the tarmac, their shape is 'more or less duplicating the fuselage shape of their seat positions, even maintaining the aisle' (p.9). This first shape of the group will change too, as it breaks up, fragments, reforms into new patterns and shapes.

When they leave the airport, they drive into an image, 'like a curtain pulled back on a foreign-produced film and they were driving into the scenery. It offered no resistance'. (p.9) As they drive towards the city from the airport, they discover gumtrees along the roadside.

It could almost have been their own country: those sections with the gums briefly framed like a traditional oil painting by the slowly passing window. The colours were as brown and parched; that chaff-coloured grass.

Ah, this dun-coloured realism. Any minute now the cry of a crow or a cockatoo; but no. (p.10)

But no, this is an old and tangled land, more complex than they know. This is a new and tangled novel, more complex than we know. No dun-coloured realism here, no cry of the crow here. Before the irony of the hotel scene around the pool, all insulated against the foreignness outside, before the characters are introduced individually, we must get our bearings. The image, the word, perspective and shape – all these will become part of the topography of the novel, the topography of the imagination. Into it will be subsumed literary and artistic themes, notions of vision and reality, of man as a tourist through the real.

Bail introduces the rest of the tourists, thirteen in all, around the swimming pool, with the parody scene of the French camera crew already asking their impressions of Africa. The day offers only the comfort of Australian graffiti, an Australian mark on the world, and the first of a series celebrating Australian sporting prowess. Later at dinner, there are allusions to art: woman 'steps out of skirt', how a woman's knees touch, as underlined in Life Classes (p.18), and, the work of a well-known local surrealist, a mural 'showing ("depicting")' (p.19) a tribe of wrestlers entwined in the sky above a city, the whole reproduced across the menu cover 'so that the menu or dining room seemed to vibrate from the falls of the heavy men' (p.19). Outside the city and the continent seem dark, empty, menacing. The solace of the familiar when they are huddled together as a group will be lost the next day, when they attend the first exhibition, in the Museum of Handicrafts, there to be baffled, confused and annoyed.

By contrast with the absurd and surrealistic collective experience, the tourists are realistic and conventional: North (the lonely widower), Shiela (the wealthy spinster), the Hofmanns (the unhappy wife, the dominating husband, dentist and collector of American striped art), Garry Atlas (the crass ocker), the Kaddoks (the priest-photographer and his acolyte wife), Sasha and Violet (the two single women), the Cathcarts (the couple who notch up the places they have seen, collecting them to talk about back home), the single men, Gerald and Borelli (who becomes a kind of assistant guide, a commentator raising ideas for Bail). The characters are established at the outset, become familiar but change little, subject only to shifting degrees of alarm, anger and bafflement. Skilfully catching the cadences of tourists, their language, attitudes and behaviour, Bail sets against this the absurdity of the exhibitions and the attempt to define reality through one aspect of it. While Frank Hammersly moves purposefully through the world, on a business trip (stopping only to leave his graffiti-mark on the world), the tourists are essentially aimless, wanting only to see. The whole enterprise of the tourist becomes absurd.

In the first exhibition, the Museum of Handicrafts, instead of colourful ethnic textures and shapes, they find an assemblage of cubicles of Western garbage, and a play on shapes which, like the Museum itself, are out of harmony with their environment. The Pygmy Collection similarly subverts their expectations of dimension and, instead of exhibiting themselves, the pygmies are bizarre refractions of Western political figures in attitudes towering, hectoring, oratorical. Instead of the exotic and foreign, both museums are reflections of the political and cultural nature of the tourists' own world.

In Africa, they enter the frame of a European film. This theme of entering refractions of their own world is continued in London, where they enter into a newspaper. (Later, Quito is a stage set, which collapses and disintegrates behind them.) Losing themselves 'among the columns and grey type of a vast newspaper', they trudge across London: 'A grey sludge underfoot felt like pulped newsprint and words, discarded sentences, shades of opinion and history' (pp.55–6). Shiela heads for Wimbledon, the first to reach the Sports Pages in the newspaper that is London, 'one vast montage' (p.64). Collections abound – the tennis display at Wimbledon, the curios in Christie's house, the collection by North's friend of railway stations, and the collection of Found Objects at the lost property office. Here at least the items can be touched:

Each object appeared to be close, indeed intimately entwined, in the daily lives of ordinary people. So here the recent wide distance between artist and bewildered spectator was dramatically narrowed, if not entirely bridged. These objects were strange, yet compellingly 'real'. (p.73)

Touch briefly narrows the gap between artist and spectator.

But Heubler lives and, above all, London becomes the centre of photography. In this, the 156th anniversary of the invention of the camera, the great museums are taken up with celebratory exhibitions. There are oil paintings of pioneer photographers, photographs of settings of famous paintings, and a series of boxing matches between artists and photographers. At the Imperial War Museum, there are photos of camouflage, with press photos of the art of propaganda. At Australia House, Cathcart sees photos of fencing posts and gates. X-ray photos of Renaissance paintings show

the struggling artists' 'real' intentions, ghost-like here, and their appalling errors in composition and perspective. Nothing is as it appears. Photography's efficiency had stripped away illusion. (p.61)

Bail questions the nature and status of the photographic image. In examining the relation of art and reality, the image and the real, where does the photograph stand? In what sense is a photograph an image of the real? North reflects.

Was time composed of broken fragments, some lost, some occasionally coming close, before drifting into dots? Perhaps with age the fragments become widely spaced: arms and feet plunge through and grab trying to hold onto things. (p.74)

Tourism, reflects Borelli, compresses time and events, but time is a composition of broken fragments, dots. In the midst of constant change, what is the meaning of the photographic still, the arrest of time and change? In what sense can it capture and contain the real? The photograph is an absurdist attempt to define a moment in time, capture and contain it, hold it fixed. What is the relationship between the real and the image (seen through the lens) when the image is extracted from the whole context of space, time, senses and the self? Bail is fascinated by these paradoxes of the photograph.

Each sequence has a prevailing image which Bail extends and complicates into critical notions of reality and the eye of the beholder. In Africa, space and shape and the whole construct of the tourists' expectations. In London, the photograph, the very status of the image and its representation, outside time and space. In Ecuador, perspective. In Quito, the equator scene is crucial because it is built on spatial paradoxes, the essential point of one's bearings, the point at which objects have a double reality. With a delightful absurdity and a sense of play, Bail offers a mirror image of the self across the equator, the face in two hemispheres at once: plus Kaddok tripping over the equator, the paradoxes of bath-water and the movement of natural forces. Here, empiricists, sceptics and vorticists come in droves, to contemplate spatial paradoxes and the nature of perspective. At the Museum of Legs, with History of Footwear, where their guide is one-legged, himself an exhibit, they confront the notion that movement, 'that glorious moment when *homo sapiens* first straightened his legs' (p.166) is the key to evolution. Motion and movement, the leg, human locomotion, equated with progress, man's surging ahead through time. The tourist confronted by the *a priori* principle of tourism. When they leave Quito, it collapses, disintegrates behind them. Objects, place and space exist only while the tourist eye beholds them.

From Ecuador, to the Greater Hemisphere and here Bail reminds us of the itinerary. Before we enter New York, Bail picks up again the double image crucial to the equator scenes, with a series of antitheses and correlatives, both of world and of self.

There are two hemispheres, a Greater and a Lesser. The one above of tall rectangles and glass, andromeda dazzle and the landmass; the other with its oceans, of heat and tangle, raw materials.

One is congested, the other sparse.

All things imaginable spread or screech to the south in a curve filling the emptiness, for better or for worse. The heads of antipodeans glance upwards (shielding their eyes): multicoloured wires, tightly bound, possess magnetic powers. Moths to flames? With its museums and plethora of laws and words the Centre of Gravity lies in the Northern or Upper Hemisphere. It preserves.

There are two hemispheres, Left and a Right. One has words and equations stored like insects, hemisphere of engines and Armstrongs, one step at a time. Its partner is a map of manias, of blurred phrases, rhythms, shapes, praise the Lord. The line dividing is properly blurred. The left hemisphere constructed the right-angle; the other knows the Golden Rectangle. There are three sides to every story. (p.185)

Focusing on shape and image, word and map, and the blurred dividing line between them, Bail articulates the notion of the third perspective with which he has already played. Home and foreign, north and south, art and reality, time and the stillness of a fixed image, word and reality. But there are 'three sides' to every story, three perspectives. So the real, the photograph and the photographer; the place, the self and the consciousness, blurring the lines between them; the fiction, the writer and the reader, all in geometric configurations which are constantly changing, kaleidoscopic, beyond definition. The whole journey is both across the world and across an inner landscape of space and perspective, and the topography of the imagination.

New York is geometry, a city of towering rectangles and jackhammers, constantly changing, forever New, forever being reconstructed. It is also the centre of things – you can see everything from the telescope at the hotel window, same view, different angles. Deserted, it is

Shadow slabs, tall silence, that stretch of distant avenue blocked by a slow hump. Violet Hopper mused, as if on stage: the city made a person aware of time, of its slow white volume, and how they were loose particles briefly within it. (p.224)

Here in the city of geometry and constant change, they visit the Institution of Marriage. Of the estimated 100 billion photographs in existence, a great proportion are records of married life; a selection is on display and 'We have the rest on microfilm. We believe we have just about every marriage in the world after 1950' (p.222). (Heubler territory.) Included are the marriages of the some of the tourists and Bail anticipates here the final image of the novel, where they are the exhibits and see themselves. New York is also the centre of things, where tourists can be spectators, seeing reality as it happens – at the very moment it takes place. In Central Park, on a safari tour, they witness a rape. This is reality, now, happening before their eyes, a spectacle in which the spectators are also guilty protagonists.

Bail returns to London again: home of Biv and Zoellner, purveyors of word and map, of definitions. This sequence is crucial as a turning point in the novel, reinforcing the central theme of definitions, before the two versions of the journey to Russia. A visit to the hairdresser becomes an exhibition of hair.

'Everywhere's a museum,' Sasha now complained.

213

'The whole world is a museum,' Gerald agreed.

North, and others, nodded. An interested glaze entered their eyes: reflexion and extension. The spectator is forced back onto himself.
The world itself is a museum; and within its circumference the many small museums, the natural and the man-built, represent the whole. The rocks of Sicily, the Uffizi, the corner of a garden, each are miniatures of the world at large. Look, the sky at night: the most brilliantly displayed and ever-changing museum of harmonic mathematics and insects, of gods and mythological figures, agricultural machinery. The catalogue is endless. (p.247)

The tourists ponder. If all the world is a museum, is there reason to travel? If you can see Ayer's Rock in one man's nose, is there any need to see the real Rock? We've all seen pictures. Perhaps the nose-exhibition is better than the real thing? Perhaps there's no need to see anything then?

Borelli takes Louise to meet his uncle, who

sees himself as a specimen in a glass case. He examines himself minutely. He told me last time it accounted for his stooped back; I believe him. He said his room is almost the precise geographical centre of London. It is like a small museum. The angles and lines from elsewhere press in on him, as does the entire population. It forces him further into himself. In any case, we are all specimens, he says. (p.256)

We are specimens examining ourselves, but while we describe and classify, nothing is changed: 'the normality . . . or the actuality of things goes on without our descriptions' (p.256). His uncle has vanished, without trace of his existence, and his museum room has vanished too. Perhaps he has ceased to contemplate himself. Perhaps, as North remarks, 'We destroy the very things we go to see' (p.250). So how to hold on to the nature of things? Enter Zoellner.

Purveyor of definitions and maps, Zoellner, is in partnership with Biv, the cartographer who searches for the cul-de-sac. This is the place of words, words collected, exhibited, words galore. It is also the place of Beckett, Nabokov, Conrad, Mann, Joyce, Woolf. It is the place for a detour into the history of the airletter, the use of the word 'kangaroo' in literature. This is the place of definitions, a storage of words, which, 'like the lines on a map, records and fixes the existence of things' (p.260). It is a repository of words, where exactitude reigns: a haven from the outer chaos. Not just words, but shapes too, the maps which 'make visible verifiable truths' (p.261). But the map-maker is on the surface: what about the underground world where, a mile below London, the miners inhabit a place with its own space and proximity, a colony with its own momentum, its own laws, its own rules of time, of which the sleeping tourists are totally unaware. (How to photograph that, Kaddok?)

Now, when the reader has found his bearings in Bail's new landscape, Bail enters his own fiction. He reminds us it is fiction and shows us the origin of the novel – one more illustration of crossing the line between the image and the real. He enters into his fiction and recounts his own recollections of the tour group in Russia and of being a tourist, with the 'constant state of heightened awareness' that is incumbent on the tourist. Bail offers us this inner geography of his own remembrance, his own image of his own travel, which has become the fiction we read. Pierce has called this section 'a gesture of alienation and of complicity: the fiction is arbitrarily suspended, but the author stands forth as another tourist'.[10] Anderson suggested it is 'a sort of Mannerist distancing device, in which the author disturbs the complacencies' of the reader.[11] It is a crucial sequence in the novel, where Bail is both fellow-traveller and writer apart from the tourists, contemplating them as fictive beings. Every story has three sides.

Bail has suggested the two Russian chapters, the personal narrative and the fiction, are the key to the novel, with the Russians acting as 'correctioners'.[4] The Centre of Gravity becomes the focus for the ideas already raised in the novel: gravity and perspective, gravity and coincidence, gravity and rainbows, gravity and time. Bail plays with the word gravity, testing and toying with it playfully in different contexts: ideas of 'beating gravity', repealing the law of gravity, improving on gravity, principles of least action, least resistance, grave situations, Specific Gravity. In *Holden's Performance*, Gordon Wheelwright is convinced the centre of gravity is constantly shifting, its movements indicated by the passage of flotsam around the world – which can be calculated. Gravity is history, with grave situations strung together like beads on a necklace, and it is also the pressure of reality.

'Our present theory,' the Russian rasped, 'is that we dream in order to

break away from gravity. In every dream, gravity is defied. Without such
relief the pressure would be intolerable. I' – he added a queer personal
note – 'sleep badly.' (p.291).

At Lenin's Tomb, they are warned that appearances are deceptive.

'Your eye has sharpened. As in war, travel has heightened your senses.
That is good; very good. Perhaps you are less naive?' He looked at each
one of them, taking his time. 'But appearances, of events and things seen
around, are deceptive. What can we believe any more? What is real? Appearances are not necessarily exact. The appearance of things is generally a lie.
That has become a problem of life, wouldn't you say?…Where is the truth,
the real existence of things? Increasingly the edges are blurred.' (p.301)

In an absurdist scene which culminates in drinking a toast with the
guards, the test is carried out. Lenin's body – real or fake? As in
the lost property office in London, the gap between the image and
the spectator, the image and the eye, is temporarily closed – all under
the eye of the artist. All are satisfied that the body is real.

In the last exhibition, gradually, in the words found along the
wall ('possibly a work abandoned by a muralist') they begin to fill
in the details and begin to see themselves. Possibilities include the
past and the near future and 'it was possible to consider a sense of
place, of their shape and long time.' (p.317). The last exhibition of
the novel, in which the characters, ever on display before us, finally
see themselves, is also the exhibition in which the reader sees himself. The reader is left studying a word photograph, an image, words.
We aim our cameras at the scenes of the novel, stumble and fall like
Kaddok, some strange distorted image fixed in the camera. This is
the final parody with which Bail leaves us. The parody, not only
of the traveller, but of the reader, in a darkened room, holding slide
nights, showing images to Heubler.

Bail takes the conventions of perception and sets against them a
world in constant change, breaking down our perceptions until we
become aware of their limitations, self-conscious, able to re-examine
the ways in which we define our world. He examines the relationship between language, real objects and our perception of them, in
terms of ourselves as dislocated and homeless consciousnesses in the
world. He plays with language and with the conventions of lan-

guage and the novel abounds in puns and quips, in verbal paradoxes and contradictions, as well as in literary allusions. Behind the ludic fun of the novel, there is a serious literary and epistemological purpose, couched in absurd narrative manoeuvres. Reality is untouched by our descriptions of it or attempts to represent it. We tire and grow homesick and the world is still intractable. The world never conforms with our expectations, continues to baffle and disturb. We are displaced people in the world which is constantly changing in spite of our best efforts to fix it and hold it still. Time and change means we are constantly relocating ourselves, but we resist this by clutching at part of the world, one aspect of it which we hold to be definitive of it.

Holden's Performance has a power that is often awesome, at once comic, absurdist, intelligent and disturbing. It is a poignant meditation on an Australian geometry of place and consciousness, of time and space, chance and design, randomness and energy, being and becoming. The salients of the novel are geometric: notions of symmetry and an aesthetics of symmetry; and notions of identity, a kind of psychogeometry of Holden which is also a measuring of an Australian identity, 'This problem of emptiness in vast space . . .'[12] The novel is built on a vast network of notions of time and space and motion, intersecting with an equally vast network of notions of seeing: optics, images and the representation of them by the eye and the word. Holden is the eye of the camera, the mechanical eye, registering the vast conglomerate of the epic events around him.

The most extraordinary aspect of this novel is the nature of the main character, who is essentially blank, expressionless, silent. Holden Shadbolt has a mechanical mind, a photographic memory and a lack of interest in his own identity; people hover at the edge of his attention. He functions marginally, reliable, solid, predictable, matter-of-fact, a register of the people and events around him. He has a stubbornly convincing presence as a character, in the midst of his absence. He is at once the novel's centre and yet always marginal, always out of focus. He is impassive, blank, essentially untouched by events and by people. 'Shadbolt always seemed to be focused on something a hundred yards away. It gave him an unusual expression of . . . impassive alertness' (p.268). His memory is photographic, but his identity is too. It is based on registering the shapes and images of the physical world outside him, so that he becomes the eye of the camera.

Holden is a horizontal creature, who follows the trajectory of men of energy and purpose, those like McBee, Alex Screech and Sid Hoadley, who have theories, purposes, ideas, plans – and so have clear shapes. An onlooker, he is a screen, blurred, out of focus, an ancillary of other vertical lives. He is a lens, one with memory but one which is itself blank, never turned inward to examine the construct and contours of his own inner world, nor the optics of self-awareness, nor the trajectory of his own existence. He moves horizontally, with a mechanical motion, through the circumstances and events that he encounters. He accelerates through the novel, from his first motion on bicycle around Adelaide, through to motorized speed as the Senator's chauffeur, then on foot, an absurd runner pounding along the streets as bodyguard to the prime minister, always on the run through time and space. He is a perspiring escort going nowhere, as if escorting a disintegrating statue.

In Adelaide, Holden is on the periphery of the comic triumvirate, made up of Vern, with his perpetual quest for facts and verification, Les Flies and Gordon Wheelwright, collecting the flotsam that reveals shifts in the city's centre of gravity. These three in the cul-de-sac up in the hills become one shape of Holden's adolescent years, while the rectilinear lines of the city spread out below are crossed and recrossed by McBee's larrikin motion, his 'tradition-free, larrikin energy'. (p.52) . Holden's consciousness is triangular too, three lobed: people and events come before his eye as fleshly reality, or as photographic images rising up out of his memory or as stippled proof images, blurred points on the paper in front of him, chewed up in his absurdist diet of newsprint, of solid-fact particles. He is taught local empiricism and becomes as random as the roughage newsprint he digests daily. Through the pages of *The Advertiser* pulverised into his cereal, he absorbs 'the internal laws of coincidence and charisma' (p.85), developing a fragmented view of the world. With a myriad images of news entering his consciousness daily, he has an exaggerated sense of instability, and a certain innocence derived from the juxtaposition of local trivia with news of world disasters and cataclysms. He has difficulty distinguishing between the screened image and the real face, so that faces come to him stippled. People appear and disappear before his eyes, awakening only mild curiosity, the flicker of a consciousness which saw reality flicker in front of it.

The novel opens with the geometry of Adelaide, a Mondrian city, small and rectilinear, its tram-lines connoting the straight lines of its thinking: 'Subtleties, complications and deviations were seen as unnecessary obstructions.' (p.3). It is the city of symmetry, surveyed by Colonel Light, who later, in a bold literary artifice, steps down from his plinth to become Holden's boss in Canberra, and finally is struck dead by lightning while surveying Adelaide again in preparation for a prime ministerial visit. From the straight lines and plain thinking of Adelaide, the novel moves to the sprawl of Sydney, then to the centrifugal form of Canberra. Geometric patterns and shapes overlap and interlock, all intersecting with the trajectories of chance. The whole novel becomes a vast spatial continuum, in which shapes loom up, define themselves, then fade and blur as new shapes press forward and clarify. It keeps up its horizontal run through time, from 1933 to 1967, along the surface of stillness. It generates a sense of extraordinary energy and striving, has a narrative dynamism, but at the same time is running on the spot, an engine roaring but idling, not moving, the brakes on. Behind the whole novel is a meditative image: if the brakes were off, if Australia took off into the future, all its latent power and energy unleashed, what speeds it could reach, what destinations . . .

There is a multitude of images of motion in the novel – the trams, the bicycle on which Holden rides to Vern's house in the cul-de-sac, McBee's motor-bike and his commercial zeal with dismantled aeroplanes and jeeps, cars and the Holden car, Holden's job as chauffeur of Hoadley's limousine, and later the marvellously absurdist notion of Holden as runner-bodyguard of the Prime Minister, running on foot throughout the streets of Canberra and Sydney – protecting the vertical man, the statuesque man of energy and clear shape inside the car. Behind the plethora of images of mechanical motion is Holden's immobility, his motionlessness.

At the same time, the mechanical theme extends to photography, the reproduction of the image of the real. From his diet of newsprint with Vern in Adelaide, Holden moves to Manly and the continuous newsreels of the Epic Theatre; from there to driving from event to event around the country with the Minister for Commerce, Home Affairs and the Interior; and from there to running alongside the

Prime Ministerial car. Throughout his life, Holden is marginal, at the edge of the news. The novel abounds with optical notions, of focus, shapes blurring, screen images, and Holden himself feels 'A lumpen clumsiness spread from his limbs, blurring his vision and all distinctions, a moral condition – a know-nothingness'. (p.13)

Against this Bail sets the precision of Vern, the proof-reader, with the 'pneumatic force of his perpetual questioning' (p.13) and his fastidious regard for fact and eschewing of error. Vern is part of the triumvirate, with Les Flies and Gordon Wheelwright, who become wondrous images of investigation; Vern's vast collection of fact set against Wheelwright's flotsam of artefact and his calculations of patterns of fact, and contrasting with the complaisance of Flies, his willingness to go along with his friends' obsessive drives. The monumental statues in Vern's garden, mute and motionless figures which cast their long shadows over Holden's compressed energies, include McAdam (roads and motion), Colonel Light (symmetry), Daguerre (photography). Vern considers electing Roger Bacon, Epicurus and Einstein to the godly ranks, but there are no Leichardts, no Rasputins, no dreamers, no visionaries.

One of the most endearing scenes of the marvellous trio is the Friday night in darkness, where, with Holden, they watch the usherette next door undressing, while Vern gives a factual account of the functions of the sexual features, tapping with his pointer at the window to indicate the most interesting, as they appear. But the most splendidly comic scene of the three is the journey to the beach, where they find, in accord with Wheelwright's calculations, a treasure trove of flotsam. As the trio caper naked in the water to Holden's discomfort, his naked Uncle explains the mysteries of life, the mysteries of 'mechanical reproduction' of photographic images: 'The secret is in the screen'. (p.103). By the end of the novel, Vern is a sad, stumbling figure, no longer able to match the images with the swirling knowledge-particles, his world stippled into a visual blur, become mostly mirage.

The novel abounds in colourful and eccentric characters, both minor like Holden's tea-leaf reading mother, and major like Alex Screech. Screech's addresses as master-of-ceremonies, as well as his plaintive optimism, are set against the newsreel epic events swirling in the background. 'News is nothing but the relationship of man to accidental events . . . Right now each of us is performing in many different epics at once.' (p.148). His own Epic theatre, later with its vomit map of Australia under glass in the foyer, becomes the setting of the Miss Australia contest. As he prepares for this, Screech becomes 'bogged down in more and more words, many loose particles, loose ends, a compression of words, which corresponded with the mounting pressure of events.' (p.180). Into the already vast patterning of the novel, Bail ushers in notions of aesthetics, an aesthetic of symmetry like Holden's sister Karen, or an aesthetic of twisted shape like Harriet's crippled body. Drawn to Harriet for reasons he does not investigate, Holden is disconcerted and perplexed by her expectations of response, her accusations that his presence is also a disturbing absence.

The events of the novel are epic in the midst of stasis. Like the newsreel interrupted only by night and by Alex's addresses on the theme of EPIC, events run on, complicating and multiplying without changing. In ludic self-commentary Bail uses the fragment headings of the epic form at the start of each of its four sections, Epic denotes change, the grand sweep and swirl of event across time, but here there is stasis, passivity, immobility, a parody of epic, no change, no progress, no clarity of shape.

Screech, Hoadley, and McBee, all rise up, scaling the rungs up through time, without changing, without motion. Screech is the most endearing of these, his pathetic optimism transparent, doomed. McBee's trajectory curves up throughout the novel, from the moment of his first appearance, blurred by the fly-wire door at the Shadbolt house in Adelaide, through to his rivalry and victory over Hoadley – whose trajectory began outside the time and the space of the novel. They intersect in Canberra, and Hoadley plummets. In the Minister's commerce with the female constituents, a seemingly endless round of sexual encounters going nowhere, his circumstances become complicated and implode. His neat schedule of sexual ministering breaks down and all the fragments of it become chaotic, until ultimately they conspire to his downfall.

I'm a nuts and bolts man. I believe in concrete, the smooth path, the joining together of people; I'm a modern man. It's through strength and geometry we'll go forward. (p.231)

But in Bail's geometry, Hoadley's unflagging energy turns in on itself and pushes to his downfall, until he makes way for the next rise of energy, McBee in his upward trajectory.

Throughout the novel, there are intersections: Lance with his bullet in Egypt, Reg Shadbolt intersecting with the pole, Hoadley becoming Ambassador to Egypt, accompanied by Holden's landlady, Mrs Younghusband. Human purposes intersect in comic and bizarre ways with contingency and coincidence, casually encountering the superior forces of chance. Bail plays with many similar intersections: Les Flies, driver of the tram the night of Reg's death, Colonel Light having his tea-leaves read by Holden's mother, Karen the Miss South Australia entrant at the beauty quest in the Epic Theatre. Bail plays freely with chance and coincidence inside the whole geometric structure of the novel, in a proposition of the Liar's literary probability.

Time is horizontal too. With his photographic memory, Holden summons up images from the past in the midst of the present, so that time for him becomes not movement and change, but essentially the same, horizontal, stippled continuum. Yet Bail establishes clearly, with the resonances of eras, the chronology of the novel – from 1915 in Egypt to Hoadley's death in the late '60s, from the 1930s in Adelaide to the death of Harold Holt in 1967, taking into its sweep the 1940s in Adelaide, the '50s in Manly and Canberra in the '60s. There is an unchanging solidness and predictability in Holden, which forms an ironic trajectory through the sweep of event. As he thuds along the streets as bodyguard, he becomes a contrary image of immobility, of running on the spot, a blurred image to himself, going nowhere. Through to his 35th year, when Holden, in a marvellous ludic move, is sent as foreign aid to the U.S.A., the years of Holden himself are always established through others, through the energies and power of the vertical men. The last of these is Colonel Light, through whom Bail takes us in a beautiful loop back to the city where it all began.

Adelaide is straight lines, Sydney a chaotic sprawl on the coast, Canberra a city of circles and columns. Colonel Light, surveyor of Adelaide, is the central character in Canberra, surveying its streets and circles for terrorists, organizing a tight schedule of runners through its streets ever watchful for the violence waiting to erupt and disturb the symmetry of Australian political order. Colonel Light is a man of action, leader of a bodyguard team, a planner, an agent, but also a contemplative man who on Black Mountain, with Jimmy the tracker, can sit in silence, a surveyor who measures (his religion –

theodolite), but who meditates too. A man of two sides, double image, but ironically one eye (the other lost in a day/night doubleness of twin sisters). But he remains a statue image, forever linked with the symmetry of the rectilinear city of Adelaide. A statue stepped down from his Adelaide plinth, pulling us in a contrary movement back to the rectilinear beginnings of the novel.

Throughout the novel, images of energy, change, vertical rise, purpose, are set against fundamental stasis and blankness, through the interplay of reality, photography and memory, which overlap and blur together. Vern continues sending proofs to Holden, wherever he is, and Holden's sense of the outer world becomes an amalgam of all three, reality, photograph and memory, as he shifts from one to the other across the blurred boundaries between them. But his engagement with time and place and person does not move beyond the surface, even with Harriet. He is fond of her angles and curves, her softness, baffled by her taunts and reproaches. His photographic memory is of detail of appearance, face and distinguishing feature, without perception, value, critical assessment, without moral component. He is a register of the visual, the eye of the lens, a camera eye which sees and records, but cannot interpret. Holden is Australia, living on the edges of himself. Absorbing all the news of the world, but untouched by it, unchanged by it, without a reflexive capacity to interpret it, to critically examine it, to establish congruences of any kind other than the visual. At his centre, there is emptiness. A vast and hulking figure, he is blank inside, out of his own focus, blurred in his own angle of vision. And silent, unable to find words, unable to give expression.

By the end, Holden's multitudinous images inside his photographic memory have begun to cross the boundaries of time – he spots characters from his own past in the crowds lining the streets where he thuds along. His past spills into the present, is its accompaniment, keeping pace beside him as he beside the limousine of VIPS. The faces of history crowd round him, more numerous and more clamorous, but without pattern discernible to him, without any meaning he can recognize. History becomes a host of blurred impressions, glimpses, stippled images, photographs, in constantly changing configurations. His strength, his endurance, as he pushes himself to complete the run that is his function, is a final image of waste, senseless absurd exhaustion. In this last part of the novel – the fourth component of its mechanics and its geometry – the meaningless motion of Holden's existence Bail renders as more and more absurd, a runner through the vast streets of Australia, pushed to the limit, without thought, without perception, without self-awareness, without awareness of meaning. A runner whose run is repeated time after time, a runner who grows more and more spent, but who, in the 'aesthetics of exhaustion', has not the beauty of self-awareness, has not the beauty of identity behind the stippled image. He is Holden, Australia's own car, a mechanical consciousness, his epic performance following the cycle of the four–stroke combustion: intake, compression, power, exhaust. The novel ends with his specifications, but his performance we have to assess, decide whether or not that is the way we want to travel. Behind the novel Bail is a geometer, tracing trajectories and triangles, examining the ratios between things, calculating the lines of chance and the points of intersection. The novel is a geometric spider constructing the web of a geometric pattern, in which we ourselves are caught, Australia in its web. When we affix our eye to the lens, we see ourselves . . . running and sweating, going nowhere . . . It's a Lie, a geometer's Lie.

SEVENTH DIALOGUE

Reader: You seem very preoccupied, worlds away. What are you thinking about?

Liar I was thinking about events in the good old days, when the galaxies were being formed. Do you remember in that Calvino story in *Cosmicomics* about cosmic bets through time, when the Dean is remembering the old days when they first started betting on events in the future? No? Let me read it to you. He's waving pages of newspaper around,

And I think how beautiful it was then, through that void, to draw lines and parabolas, pick out the precise point, the intersection between space and time where the event would spring forth, undeniable in the prominence of its glow ...

Reader That's atavistic thinking. That's eons ago.

Liar Of course. It's ancient geometry. The Dean goes on,

whereas now events come flowing down without interruption, like cement being poured, one column next to the other, one within the other, separated by black and incongruous headlines, legible in many ways but intrinsically illegible, a doughy mass of events without form or direction, which surrounds, submerges, crushes all reasoning.[1]

That's geometry these days and it's Holden's diet, his intake. The flow of events a doughy mass that he feeds on.

Reader Australia's own Holden, on a diet that crushes all reasoning ... that's his intake, then compression, then power and finally exhaust.

225

Liar Yes, and so much for eye-witnesses. The witness is part of what he's seeing. Holden Shadbolt *is* what he sees and remembers. He is the events he witnesses, the news he engorges. That's Australia for you.

Reader That's what Bail says. But is it true?

Liar True? What do you mean true? A theodolite does not lie.

Reader But you're assuming that truth is measurable.

Liar No, I'm not. It's the other way round. Truth is not measurable but Lies are. That's what the geometry's all about.

Reader You know one of the big problems about reading Lies. Everything is plural, everything is complicated, the random and the contingent keeps cutting across events. Reality is not to be trusted any more, reality plays tricks. Everything that blurs and deceives is right in there.

Liar But that's the way things are. It's all true.

Reader But it's the same point I made a long time ago. It's not supposed to be like that in art. People have enough chaos and confusion in the real world without finding it in literature too.

Liar This is atavistic thinking, going right back to where we started. I suppose you were bound to regress at some point, but it's a terrible blow nonetheless.

Reader Is it? It shouldn't be. What I'm saying can't just be wiped out. Lots of people want to get away from the chaos. People *do* have needs when they read. There has to be more to it than telling them their needs are wrong.

Liar That's not what I'm saying. I'm saying there is a multitude of ways of meeting their needs. One of them is the way of the Lie. Surely we don't have to go back over all of that again. This is so depressing.

Reader But there is a real problem for people when they're trying to cope with a bewildering world that's constantly changing, where nothing is fixed and stable. Where the centre of gravity has shifted and is still shifting. Where there's no truth.

Liar But that's what the Lie is all about.

Reader Look this is the age of computers and data processing. Reality's so complex we need machines to handle all the data, all the information. Can you blame readers who want a single narrator, who tells them a plausible story in a straightforward way, so they know exactly where they are? Where events make sense and go from start to finish, with all the links and connections clearly explained? People don't get that in real life.

Liar I don't *blame* readers who want plausibility. It's a perfectly valid need. And look how the realist writers in this country are flourishing. I think the truth of the way things are is the Lie. But people don't have to choose. We're not enemies, at war. It's not an either/or situation, where people have to declare their allegiances and line up like opposing armies. Some people, critics and reviewers, see it like that. But I don't. There's room for all of us.

Reader But why should people contend with Lies? Why should they put up with all your subterfuge and scheming?

Liar It's just a different way of reaching the truth. And the whole point is the truth is slippery, constantly elusive, so that we end up clutching at spectres of it. That's the truth. I give you my word.

Reader Your word! Your word's the Lie.

Liar Think about the Dean's doughy mass of events, that crushes all reasoning. Look at Hasluck's novels. Reality is like a plot, random chaos, a plot without any deliberate purpose, just a flow of circumstance with nimble fingers that periodically selects a victim. Then flows on to the next one. That *is* how reality seems to many people. So what *is* plausible?

Reader Lies? Lies are plausible?

Liar The whole point of Hasluck's work is how to interpret events in the midst of chaos, how to survive with it, how to *know* anything. You say this is the computer age. Hasluck writes about data processing: how to assemble and order our knowledge of things, knowledge that comes to us in a myriad of tiny fragments, like a kaleidoscope broken open.

Reader And we have to keep trying to put it all together into a pattern again. Then the next moment it has fallen apart.

Liar Reality *is* just splinters of information we receive without any pattern or logic behind them. So the logic is the Liar's logic: it's all true at once, all the contradictions and absurdities, all the paradoxes and ambiguities, they're all true.

Reader Shades of Ar Wat's Tlute! Ar Wat becomes a detective, a private eye tracking down Tlute.

Liar Why not? Reality is a mystery, with all the clues coming to us at random. Except that the Liar sets up limits and manipulates the disclosure of information, in a way that makes us process the data.

The suspense is the mystery – the mystery of how we know anything.

Reader Liars like mystery and doubles. Look at Borges, Fowles, Robbe-Grillet. Hasluck. And I'm the dupe.

Liar Of course. Everything is doubled. The whole convention of the mystery thriller and suspense is a doubling technique. Pitting different constructions of events against each other. Someone's got to be the dupe. It wouldn't be plausible otherwise.

Reader What about the good old days, of truth, the whole truth, and nothing but the truth? The old days of word of honour. Look at your word now.

Liar But there is no whole truth. Truth is a matter of advocacy. Not just the measured inflection and the advocate's gesture. It's a matter of plea and testimony, cross-examination.

Reader Except it's not quite so safe as that. It's more violent, like Hasluck's story, 'The Case Against the Past'. Do you know it? Mafia style gangs of historians, including Knuckles and Scarface and hit men with grubby spats, reach a showdown in the struggle to take over the Past and run it their way.

Liar Gang war. Historians in spats. How delightfully absurd!

Reader Yes it is, but it's dangerous too, if you get caught in the cross-fire. There's a lot more of the showdown in Hasluck's work than the discreet tones of lawyers. And it's not just the Past that's at issue. It's the truth. Mafia-style gangs of truth-tellers, in the struggle to take over the truth and run it their way.

Liar The battle of truth. The thriller and whodunnit.

Reader There's even a hit man with a contract on me! And Hasluck's the hit man.

Liar But you survived it. It's only fiction.

Reader Is it? How do you draw the line between fiction and truth. Look at what Hasluck says in *The Bellarmine Jug*. Fiction is a disguise, a convoluted undercover operation. A lie accepted as true. So how do you draw the line?

Liar There isn't one. Look, I'm a Liar and I know all about undercover operations. I only tell the truth.

Reader It might be true but is it art?

Liar Oh no, not again. That's where you started. Saying art is supposed to be order, make sense of it all. After all we've talked about, you go right back to the start again, with the same statement.

Reader To tell the truth, I'm lying.

Liar You're lying? It was a lie?

Reader Why are you so shocked? I was just presenting a case – playing advocate and making out a case against truth.

Liar I can't believe you'd lie to me. I thought readers could be trusted. I used to be able to trust them. I could always predict their reactions, knew exactly where they'd be. I thought we were supposed to be working together, collaborating? How can I work with you if you're going to tell lies and deceive me?

Reader You want me to stay the dupe always?

Liar Liars need dupes. Self-deceivers, people hungry for half-truths. But actually there is no truth. The evidence is truth doesn't exist.

Reader Can I have that in writing? I'm interested in truth. The case against truth.

THE CASE AGAINST TRUTH
NICHOLAS HASLUCK

But so often, the minds of men being invisible, we have to make do with what we can get, half-truths, dissembling utterances; for the most part, preferring to forget that the world of appearances, which seems so tangible, is, in reality, a world of shadows.

'The Whole Truth' [1]

Islands which have
never existed
have made their way
on to maps nonetheless.

And having done so
have held their place,
quite respectably
sometimes for centuries.

Voyages of undiscovery, deep
into the charted wastes,
were then required
to move them off.

'Islands'[2]

'You've heard about the inquiry, then?'

Niesmann nodded. 'Most of it. Not the details. How can I be sure what people are saying to each other outside the inquiry?'

Leon was aghast. 'But that's fantastic. Do I take it from everything you say . . . ' He waved his hand at the desk. 'From all that material, that the Pelsaert text *is* genuine? The jug? That Aveling's allegations are true?'

Niesmann laughed. 'What is the truth when you have a melting pot of cross purposes? When people are acting strangely, disguising their motives, there is probably one of the old unmentionables at the bottom of it all. Greed, perhaps. Sex. Lust for power. Whichever one it is will be skilfully tucked out of sight, buried beneath an avalanche of noble phrases. What should we believe – the rationalization or the glint in the eye, the plausible words or the perplexing act, the surface or the hidden truth? Perhaps you have the answer?'

'Don't play games,' Leon warned. He was angry. 'I'm sick of sophistry. We should start with whatever facts we can get hold of and go further if we have to. I repeat my question. Is Aveling telling the truth?'

'My dear young friend,' Niesmann cautioned. 'Because you view the world in a straightforward way doesn't mean that I am obliged to do the same. Truth will always be conditioned by the context. There is the lawyer's truth – a painstaking attention in the courtroom to what exactly happened and in what order. But against that must be weighed the truth of the situation as a whole. What made things happen? What is the root cause, the emotion behind it all? The questions lawyers never seem to bother with. Indeed, bound by their technical rules, the questions they congratulate themselves on never asking. They like to skate about on the surface. Let them. But for some of us there is another world; a world we can't help wishing to explore, a world of fables and misconceptions. Why should we proceed as if the world of reason annihilates the other? Come, come. I don't have to say such things out loud. You know it for yourself by now. Illusions linger in some minds longer than a formal verdict. The imagination wanders off on its own path. The state of a man's mind is as much a fact as the state of his bank balance. Decide for yourself what kind of truth you want. I am entitled to see the matter through my own eyes, and according to my own standards.'

The Bellarmine Jug[3]

·

HASLUCK'S NOVELS ARE 'voyages of undiscovery/deep into the charted wastes', in search of the islands which have never existed but have somehow made their way on to maps. Among all the untruths, his characters blunder around the charted wastes, in constant hope that the true islands will appear before them, solid truths rising up from the waters, definitions to be marked on the map of things. Amid the mystery and intrigue of crowded charts, islands dissemble, blur and deceive, prove intangible and vanish. Each new twist of circumstance drives the Hasluck character deeper into the charted wastes, his moral bearings lost. Hasluck navigates the passage of the Lie easily, charting events in plots which are taut and intricate, rich in the suspense and intrigue of the thriller mode. While events work to obscure vision and deceive his eye, the Hasluck character keeps searching for landmarks that point the way to the talismanic truth. But there is no island of truth, only shadows holding their place quite respectably, mirage truths dancing across the charts, beckoning. Hasluck's is a Liar's voyage of undiscovery, a cartography of untruth.

In Hasluck's novels, truth is a matter of advocacy too. It is a matter of litigation and appeal, of eloquent pleading and measured inflection. In Hasluck's short story, 'The Case Against the Past', Mafia style gangs of historians, including Knuckles and Scarface and hit men with grubby spats, reach a showdown in the struggle to take over the Past and run it their way.[4] This delightfully absurd story shows the kind of contest in all Hasluck's work, a battle of advocates, with conflicting testimonies and contradictory evidence. The characters play double roles; at once plaintiffs demanding truth, and defendants pleading extenuating circumstances. Insisting they were mere spectators, they are forced under cross-examination to admit their complicity, the furtive moments of choice which made them guilty accomplices of chance. Pitted against the whole sordid prosecution of reality, they are witnesses on the stand, forced to admit their own collusion in events.

In Hasluck's work, existence is the *faszad* of *Quarantine*.

It denotes a sordid intrigue. An intrigue so complicated by the variety of motives and false testimony required to bring it to fruition, that it might almost be described as a conspiracy without a cause; a chain of events bearing all the hallmarks of a calculated plot – that is to say, a process which closes in on a victim, which seizes some unfortunate being against his will and breaks him, leaving him enmeshed in the ganglions of perjury and greed which brought about his downfall – but nonetheless, a process which in fact has no clearly defined purpose; as if the intention was simply to trigger off some iniquitous proceeding in the expectation that pickings of one kind or another would be there for nimble fingers in the end.[5]

Casual event and random circumstance combine into a *faszad* which closes in on its victim, and tightens round him until he is enmeshed in it, butterfly-pinned. In the midst of this, Hasluck's character searches for some moral construct by which to steady himself until the whole conglomerate of random intrigue flows on to engulf the next victim. In *Quarantine*, the *faszad* is in a desert quarantine station, isolated in some anonymous land somewhere in the Middle East, where unknown authorities hold a group of travellers in Kafkaesque detention. In *The Blue Guitar*, the nimble fingers of the *faszad* find pickings in the commercial deals of Dyson Garrick and pluck the strings of his blue-guitar ideals. In *The Hand That Feeds You*, the fingers reach into an absurdist future, a nightmarish Australian society. In *The Bellarmine Jug*, the hand of the *faszad* grips tight, clenching around events both recent and remote, then unclenching only to tighten again; the pickings rich as Leon Davies blunders through the twentieth century seeking an untrammelled truth. Leon Davies wants logic, not the Liar's logic, where reality perplexes, dissembles, becomes chameleon and counterfeit, but an either/or logic, where truth is fixed and self-contained. He wants explanations that hold, a truth that is his to keep.

With historical intrigue reaching back to the wreck of the *Batavia* off the coast of Western Australia in 1629 and using a construction of political and philosophical intrigue, *The Bellarmine Jug* is composed of small and large mysteries which shift and turn throughout the novel. It is a compelling mystery thriller wherein Leon constructs theories only to have them demolished by the disclosure of new data and new configurations of truth. Like Leon, the reader too is constantly constructing theories which break down with the disclosure of new information. What comes out of this is more than an intellectual mystery thriller, as the writer, in the convention of the mode, challenges the reader to compose events into a construction which can contain the whole conglomerate of circumstance and event. More than that, it is a novel about how we determine anything in the midst of twentieth century chaos, the *faszad* of indeterminacy. It is a novel about trying to make determinations in an indeterminate existence. The Liar plays master of ceremonies, conjuring up a talismanic truth by sleight of hand, but it is a truth that is never still, never fixed, a chameleon truth that shimmers on the horizon, an island which has made its way on to the maps but has never existed.

The investigative mode sets up an intellectual suspense, like the contest between writer and reader in John Fowles' novel, *A Maggot*. When the five travellers disappear in the Devon wilderness on Mayday, 1736, different versions of events emerge from the testimonies of witnesses, out of which the investigating lawyer, Ayscough, tries to construct a logical pattern. As Fowles discloses the 'secret pattern' and the casual conspiracy of random factors, like Ayscough, the reader constructs hypotheses, pitting these against the truth as it is gradually disclosed – until it suddenly becomes not a matter of believing a structure of facts so much as having a capacity for belief and thus a capacity for dissent. Hasluck too, in *Quarantine* and *The Bellarmine Jug*, uses this investigative mode to examine the reader's capacity for belief and dissent. This dialectic runs through all his work, in a running battle of dissent and assent conducted through the suspense of the mystery mode.

Like Borges' 'secret plot', Hasluck's novels are convoluted undercover operations, on the surface mysteries both moral and political, but built on man's capacity for self-deception and his willingness to be duped, the delicate ambiguity of man's hungering more for half-truth than truth. Hasluck traffics in truth and spectral images of it, through layers of meaning until the moment when the Lie turns back on the reader and, in its mirror, shows the reader his own image, his own yearning for self-deception – the image of the Liar's dupe. The Borgesian theme of man caught in his own unwitting trap is central to Hasluck's work. In Borges' 'Death and the Compass', Lonnrot's calculations of the determined pattern of the three murders lead only to his own murder, at the hands of his enemy, Scharlach, who has constructed the pattern for the purpose of trapping him. In Hasluck's novels, the reader, like Lonnrot, uncovers a scheme and is trapped inside the pattern constructed by the Liar. In *Quarantine*, the narrative is a manuscript novel written by the narrator, in which the reader, quarantined in the Lie, is trapped and charged with complicity in the horrors of the world, the Escher hand of the Liar pointing an accusing finger. In *Truant State*, Hasluck's narrator plays Scharlach to the Lonnrot reader. Like Borges, Hasluck takes out a contract on the one who has been calculating and discovering the secret pattern behind events – the reader. Hasluck's narrator turns murderer in the absurdist end – the murder of the reader. Behind the novel is a notion of the Lie as a contract with and *on* the reader. The reader's own quest for the solution to the mystery, the quest for truth, lures him to the scene of the crime, where he himself becomes the victim and is murdered. At the end of *Truant State*, Hasluck mocks the reader's quest for truth, the quest for the island that never existed, a quest that in the Lie proves fatal.

Nicholas Hasluck was born in Canberra in 1942, the son of Sir Paul Hasluck, the former Governor-General, politician, historian and writer, and Dame Alexandra Hasluck, the author and historian. He studied law at the University of Western Australia and at Oxford, before working as an editorial assistant on a London newspaper. He returned to Australia in 1967 and began a career as a lawyer as well as a writer. In 1976 he studied at the Hague Academy of International Law, which yielded some material for *The Bellarmine Jug*. Hasluck is a former deputy chairman of the Australia Council, and has an interest in the small publishing company, Freshwater Bay Press.

A lawyer, Hasluck lives in Perth with his wife, Sally-Anne, curator of the Claremont Historical Museum, and two children.

Apart from short stories and poems published in literary journals, Hasluck's first work was *Anchor and Other Poems*, published in 1976. Hasluck's remarkable first novel, *Quarantine* (1978) received considerable acclaim both in Australia and overseas and excited comparisons with Kafka, Golding, Camus and Conrad, but it was difficult to obtain until Penguin Books re-issued it in 1986. His collection of short stories, *The Hat on The Letter O*, also 1978, was followed in 1980 by the poetry collection, *On The Edge* (with William Grono), and by two novels, *The Blue Guitar* (1980) and *The Hand That Feeds You* (1982). His major novel to date, *The Bellarmine Jug*, was published in 1984 and won *The Age* Book of the Year Award. In 1985 Hasluck and C.J. Koch combined to produce the travel memoir, *Chinese Journey*. His latest novel is *Truant State*, published in 1987.

The Hat on The Letter O includes comic stories like 'Orlick', an amusing account of two young lawyers starting work on the same day, but one is bored and amuses himself by creating the subversive fiction of Orlick, the diligent lawyer toiling in the basement, dealing with all matters proceeding. Most of these stories are minor, of interest as tangents to the novels. In 'The Whole Truth', there are shades of *The Bellarmine Jug*, with a narrator staying in a bungalow on the coast to write a manuscript on a political scandal and speculating on the processes of arriving at the truth and the boundaries of discretion. 'Flowstone' is a brooding story, with the measured, meditative tone of *Truant State*. The narrator recalls a room that haunts him: he examines it with curious detachment, then focuses on the flowstone ashtray with which he strikes the girl in the room, before resuming his dispassionate examination. 'Keeping It Clean' contrasts the private lives of four passengers on a ship delayed in port by a union dispute, a story which runs at a tangent to *Quarantine*.

In *Quarantine*, rather than exploring the chance encounter of different characters, Hasluck is examining the mechanisms and workings of the closed society in the seedy hotel in the desert. In a Kafkaesque predicament, the passengers are stopped suddenly in the night, without explanation, and the nature of the putative disease is never specified. The passengers are held in ignorance, subject to unknown forces with which they must try to negotiate. In the absence of authorities other than the cynical Doctor Magro and the sly, slippery figure of Shewfik Arud, this society has to construct its own definitions and sanctions – while caught up in the workings of the *faszad*.

Forty years after the events at the quarantine station, the narrator is compelled to re-examine all that happened, ostensibly to finally acknowledge his guilt. He sets out to recover the past, that 'kaleidoscope of unreality'(p.9), still seeking an answer, still seeking some moral antidote.

As always, although many years have passed, the memory of the affair sets up an itch in my mind which wants scratching. The anomalies, the gaps in my understanding of what happened, the half truths – the memory begins to fester; it begins to trouble like some blemish of the skin, some residual disaffection which comes and goes but never heals. (p.3)

Even though he has dressed it up through the years into amusing anecdotes to be paraded with port before his academic friends, he suffers still from the memory. As the narrator writes now, Hasluck stands at a dissociative distance from him, exposing the continuing evasions of the narrator, the moral side-stepping by which he still dodges his own complicity in events. What the narrator writes now to his friend is not a confession but a defence case, a plea of extenuating circumstance in hope of acquittal. The reader becomes juror. But in the Loop of the novel, the reader is the defendant too, quarantined in the Lie.

The narrative shifts back and forth through time, anticipating, retracing, encircling, breaking up our sense of chronological sequence and our sense of easy causal connection. The narrator plays with time, admitting to his own premonitions; the narrative pace slows as the narrator's anxieties quicken, so that it seems both impatient and evasive. The narrator plays around the actual events, insisting on their complexity and thereby initiating his own defence. And Hasluck creates a style befitting his narrator, mildly posturing in an academic way, discursive, witty and urbane. In the Loop of the novel, which draws reader and narrator into alliance, this becomes a comic image of the reader too – until the charges against the reader are pronounced.

Within the conglomerate of intrigue are numerous contingent factors, including the schemes of Arud and his negotiations with his purchaser; Burgess' pettifogging faith in discipline and committees;

David Shears' relations with Isobel and her mother's disapproval; the thick, simian brutality of Bricky and his mates; the narrator's experiences in the brothel and, with his passion for Isobel, his rivalry with David. The idiosyncrasies of the minor characters become caught up in the *faszad* too – the scrapbook man's Sisyphean labours, or the elderly floor-thumping sister, or Mr Harwood, grand master of boredom, or Bricky and his mates blurting out obscene, thick encouragement to Burgess. The novel has a subdued comic element, with Dickensian minor characters and a lighter comedy of errors (such as the bedroom scene with David and the narrator). There is also more sinister black comedy, much of which lies in the absurdity of being caught up in the all-encompassing flow of the *faszad* whereby small contingencies take on new menacing significance. Shewfik Arud is a masterly comic figure, with his forlorn optimism, his crestfallen pandering to his guests, his unwavering support for the League of Nations and his courteous twisting of the truth into more agreeable shapes. To him, truth is a form of hospitality, organized to suit the needs of guests. But he has a more bizarre quality too, which, coupled with the *faszad*, suddenly becomes horrifying. As the *faszad* flows on with all the appearance of calculated plot, Hasluck maintains the mystery and suspense with a fine tension.

The passengers gladly surrender responsibility to Burgess and the committee. Determined to preserve the status quo, Burgess insists on communal codes, which become a stand against individual action. He becomes the voice of the closed society as it searches for an explanation of its predicament, the voice of a society held in captivity by anonymous gods, who might be appeased by obedience. Assent becomes their code. Like the 'beast' in Golding's *Lord of the Flies*, created by the boys to give shape and form to their own fears, David Shears becomes the 'beast' of the quarantine society, the scapegoat identified by his individual action, his dissent, as the threat to the safety of the society and the eventual release. As the *faszad* closes in on David and the narrator, all the moral possibilities are confused and blurred, so that even the critical moment of choice is obscured. This is the narrator's defence plea. But this plea has never satisfied nor convinced the narrator himself. He is still trying to identify the 'beast' years later when he meets Burgess again and privately nominates him as scapegoat, offering him up to atone for his own guilt.

Within his narrative, the narrator has included camouflage passages: the witty passage on 'Surbiton' after the encounter with Burgess years later, to cover up Burgess' implied accusation (pp.56–8); and the speculative passage on boredom, to cloak an evasion on his part (pp.102–6). Such ploys are at once the posturing of the young law student and the evasions of the professor observing his own past. He is both observer and participant in the events at the quarantine station, struggling to preserve the role of innocent bystander, as he retraces his own role. The narrator is witty, urbane, amusing, but he is also guilty, still mumbling his excuses to the past, still pleading extenuating circumstances. He has transformed the memory of his moral failure and his complicity in David's fate into an academic platform on which he struts, proclaiming the need for individual responsibility. Only now can he admit to the morass below the surface of his life, like Doctor Magro at Lake No.

I always knew that, despite my gesture of affirmation, my fracturing of the lake's smothering silence, nonetheless, at some stage of my visit, I was bound to find myself dragged down knee-deep into glutinous mudflats . . . dragged down and saturated by that foul water, that swamp where every foothold is treacherous, until, saturated, I would begin to feel its water seeping into my bloodstream. (p.50)

Only now, after forty years, can he confront the truth which has seeped through his life.

The novel is a dialogue between past and present, with the narrative discrete and fragmented, according to the pattern of the narrator's evasions of the truth it contains. As he relates the events, he is inside his own narrative dodging its meaning and import. He offers his version of events, designed to establish his own innocence, against Hasluck's stubbornly contestant version of his guilt. But the narrator is writing the draft of a manuscript, a fiction, and the whole novel becomes an extraordinary dialogue between writer and narrator, and between Liar and reader. When he reaches the crucial point of his story, where he denied David Shears, the narrator asks the friend he now addresses,

Can you imagine how it has been for me – the memory of that Quarantine Station, that final meeting, being always in my mind? The spectre of it always in my mind? On sleepless nights, those bailiff shadows of the old transaction rifling through my mind with wallet fingers saying: 'We are reality.' (p.177)

This is his spectre: when the community chose David as its scapegoat, the narrator was no mere spectator, no mere observer of the horrors perpetrated by others. He was a guilty participant and, by his silent assent, an accomplice. The narrator is urban man, who

sits, bleary-eyed, in front of an aggressive screen: a spectator and, simultaneously, because of his own apathy in a darkened room, his inability to resist events, a barbarian at the gate, a horror-stricken protagonist in all that happens anywhere on the earth. (p.130)

The novel is set between the aggressive screen which demands action and the passive spectator who sits bleary-eyed, watching. Hasluck's narrator, the spectator, is also a protagonist and a barbarian at the gate. The whole weight of the novel comes to this point: the spectator who assents is also the protagonist. This truth the narrator evaded, blaming the circumstances, exonerating himself, as we all do when we sit bleary-eyed in a darkened room, passive spectators, watching the horrors of the real world. But then he is writing the draft of a novel, and the real charge is directed at the reader, who is quarantined in the novel.

Quarantine is set on the eve of World War 11 and, like Camus' *The Plague*, the novel is a fable of our times and the disease of moral inertia spreading unchecked. When the passengers leave, they are still carriers of an insidious disease. Passive assent is active guilt, the guilt of collusion and collaboration. Behind it is a case against the reader who is quarantined in the novel, no longer a passive spectator who can shrug off moral responsibility or try pleading extenuating circumstances. The reader is marked out as guilty too, collaborator and carrier of disease – one of the barbarians at the gate.

Hasluck's world is a place of moral commerce, moral negotiations and deals by which we traffick for survival. As his characters blunder through the *faszad* chaos, the deals become complicated, the old ideals blur and fade, and the real negotiations start. In *The Blue Guitar*, commerce is both a metaphor and the literal context of Dyson

Garrick's deals; the guitar both a commercial enterprise and a metaphor for his own ideals. Speculator, promoter and developer, cavalier go-getter, Dyson Garrick sallies forth into the commercial arena, brandishing his blue guitar. He launches it grandly, offering it as a panacea to the ills of the contemporary world.

All the moral issues clear and untrammelled, Garrick sets out with a simple commitment to Hermann, the inventor of the blue guitar, to negotiate the optimum deal. Garrick too is enmeshed in a *faszad*, which leaves him blundering through the city's

jumble of dark configurations. A haphazard geometry of lines and spaces. Office buildings with lights glimmering, cranes towering above a building site – reinforcements quietly taking up their accustomed positions, etching themselves into the sepia sky.[6]

Against this, Garrick pits his own moral geometry, trusting the world will remould itself to the shape of his design.

At the start, Garrick is confident, elated at the prospect of a new deal. He sets out sure-footed, moving easily between his own world of shiny new enterprises soaring high above the city and Hermann's world of ramshackle buildings and dilapidated hopes. There is a clear line at the start between Garrick's world of energy, change, construction and enterprise, and Hermann's stillness in a desolate environment, a patch of waste ground dwindling as the city moves towards it. Hermann is 'a scarecrow in cast-offs', 'a scarecrow stepped down from his wooden post for a moment' (p.47). He inhabits a wasteland, in a city which is

a ghost pattern. A reflection of disorder. An ominous X-ray image of the streets . . . Tom Tiddler's ground, a geometric maze of undergrowth and useless tracks, eroded by indifference. (p.141)

As his commitment to Hermann becomes ever more tangled and the *faszad* gathers speed and momentum, Garrick's energy changes into frenzy and panic in a world of discord and disorder. Gradually Hermann's wasteland becomes an emblem of Garrick's moral wasteland, with its ramshackle principles and debris integrity scattered across the arid, sullen surface of his own Tom Tiddler's ground.

Through Garrick, we enter a world of chameleon businessmen,

lurking in their offices and negotiating shifty deals and counter-deals, hatching schemes and contracts, concocting clauses that trap and riders that trip. Here dealers fly high for dizzying moments before they plummet. The bank, calling up the guarantee, is the first of a series of pursuers hounding Dyson Garrick deeper into the *faszad*. Hasluck writes with biting humour of the most bloodthirsty pursuit by Hollins, the fraud investigator, who is offended by the flimsiness of his case against Garrick and so begins dogging relentlessly. Creyke pursues Dyson Garrick more deviously with a lure, a bait, tempting him to the quick and easy escape from his predicament. Athol Garrick contributes a kind of moral hounding by expounding noble principles (which he later recants with a quick expediency). Pursued by the consequences of his own ignorance of the development schemes for Hermann's land, Garrick becomes a fugitive, on the run with his blue guitar. His predicament extends beyond his financial plight into a sense of personal dissolution. He is driven to end his affair with Karen, he loses his alter ego, Pascoe, and whittles himself down to a subsistence self. After the elation of flying high, he becomes another entrepreneurial casualty, 'a body in a field of mud, the parachute trailed out, flapping and struggling' (p.175). He can do anything – except go back up. He can only swing a few protesting kicks as he plummets. Amid the chaos of his affairs, Garrick has to create his own definitions. In court he contemplates wistfully the clearcut simplicity of the law's definitions, while outside 'there was a world of untidiness and confusion. Intricate relationships. Ambiguity.' (p.96). Outside are the smudged definitions of the *faszad*, with no indelible answers.

Resourceful, enterprising and brash, Garrick possesses an integrity which might prove stalwart – only one quick compromise and he could salvage all but his integrity. Like the narrator of *Quarantine*, Garrick chooses the moment of sly betrayal. He chooses to conform to the prevailing definitions of his society and chooses his own survival, for which he pays with Hermann's dreams. In the *faszad* tangle of circumstance, the moment of choice rises up to the surface, then vanishes, leaving behind only its ineradicable consequences. In the *faszad* of contemporary existence, where every contingency acts in collusion, it is easier to submit. It is easier to move freely through the city without the encumbrance of the blue guitar.

He broke into a jog again, finding the going easier without the guitar, panting as he worked his elbows, the jumbled barricades of motley junk rising up on either side of him and ahead of him to where the track was disappearing between two further mounds . . . all of it pushed up bleakly into crude, serrated skylines, the air within the labyrinthine canyons dank and lifeless; the feeling of it, stifling, suffocating, oppressive. (p.206)

This is Garrick's world now; the wasteland with its labyrinthine canyons becomes his own. *The Blue Guitar* is a minor Hasluck novel of moral suspense and intrigue, touched with sharp ironies and sometimes absurdity. It is one of the few Australian novels about commerce, and Garrick himself is an intriguing figure, observing his own moral side-stepping as he picks his way through events which obscure and tangle his path, events which scarcely reveal their pattern to him until it is too late.

Republican Australia, brave new society of conformity, greed, inertia and a parasitic feeding on the governmental hand: this is the futuristic vision in Hasluck's third novel, *The Hand That Feeds You*, sub-titled 'A Satiric Nightmare'. Into this moral chaos stumbles Dee, an expatriate writer and an innocent-eye observer marvelling at the absurdities of this society. The future is also an absurdist version of the present, which Hasluck elaborates until he suddenly shifts the angle of our vision on the whole structure and form of the novel. It becomes a novel within a novel and at the same time, a novel about fiction, complete with a kit of reviews for the critic. By the end, through the layers of literary parodies, it emerges as an amalgam of narratives by the Liar and his character, edited by another character, in a parody of its own strategies and artifice.

Hasluck develops his vision through a kind of comic accretion, beginning as a comic sniper taking witty potshots at passing targets, then building up into a comic bombardment. Equality and free enterprise are the catchcries of the new order: free and equal manipulation of the system of welfare, grants and subsidies; free and equal biting of the hand that feeds. The public interest is equal to the sum of all self-interests. His targets are many, his aim sure. He brings down unionists and bureaucrats, tax-dodgers and politicians; he fells welfare workers, lawyers and academics; and he wings passing intellectuals and film-makers. He fires off rounds at schools, where kids study 'applications' for grants and subsidies; at universities where, in the interests of equality, all forms of assessment have been abolished; at employers dependent on the Incompetent Staff Subsidy; at miscellaneous committees which, amoeba-like, split and multiply; at citizens plotting their 'deductions' and subsidy coups against the government. He takes in the whole system of bureaucratic minutiae, loopholes, dodges, lurks, schemes, the whole conundrum of machinations by which Republican Australia functions.

At the outset, Dee gazes in comic bewilderment at these elaborate social antics. As his bewilderment changes first into disbelief, then into comic horror, he finds himself stumbling through the characteristic Hasluck maze, all his moral bearings lost. Around him, everything is distorted, misshapen, and 'the helping hand was scabrous'.[7] Like the narrator of *Quarantine* and like Dyson Garrick, Dee is driven deeper into the tangled undergrowth of the system, until he too is confronted by the moment of moral choice which looms up suddenly in the Republican *faszad*. Manipulated into standing for Parliament, a risk taken only by the eccentric or foolhardy in hope of tax deductions, Dee is aghast to find himself elected. A political innocent trapped in the new order, he finds himself hounded by the media because of his indictments of the system. Clutching obsolete and aberrant notions of independence and self-reliance, Dee searches Sydney for a way out. He goes underground in search of Meynard, the politician who ushered in the Republican era and then disappeared. The search for Meynard, which provides the structure for Dee's tumultuous passage through this society, is a search for explanations. When he finally finds Meynard, Meynard points at him and murmurs about the Connacht king. In this climax of his mock quest Dee is denied explanations, flees and breaks his leg. Thus comes the moment of climactic illumination in this pastiche of the picaresque novel.

Hasluck satirises his own and others' fictions as he explores the function of writers in this society. At the very start of the novel, as the plane is about to land in Sydney, Dee encounters the Interrupted Man, who complains, 'Interruption is inevitable. Pre- ordained'. (p.9). Later the Interrupted Man protests,

'Fragmentation: the only thing this country understands . . . The test of a mind is the ability to hold two contradictory thoughts in counterpoise at once. Even as I start to speak I fear the worst. Even as I begin to make my point, to get the message over, to describe the anguish of constant interruptions, discontinuous narratives, fractured silences, spasmodic prayers, yes, even as I start, some vandal with a scant regard for discourse comes breaking in. (p.26)

As well as jokes about fragmentation, discontinuous narratives and vandals 'with a scant regard for discourse', there are jokes about the comic risks of writing original fiction and the financial drawbacks of being 'a promising talent'. Writers must be licensed and must write safe, plagiarised novels ('factual fiction' p.55) to keep their grants. Dee resolves to maintain the purity of his writing and resist the temptation to facile denunciation,

to preserve the purity of the language. That was the primary commitment of the writer; the only way in which integrity could be preserved. He had to probe, observe, record. Search for the truth. (p.62)

Hasluck links the theme of fiction with the nightmare reality of the outer world, where charade-elections are run by private companies in seedy backrooms and 'The trappings of democracy have become empty forms, meaningless fictions . . .' (p.114). When Dee submits a sample of his writing, an impressionistic account of Meynard's life, he is told that satire is outmoded and 'Kafka imitations' are all the rage. As Dee's predicament becomes more Kafkaesque, Hasluck debunks his own fiction, playing an elaborate literary game. Dee speculates about his role as a character.

If this was an avant garde novel, Dee reflected, bitterly, the whole thing would be sprawling everywhere. Fantasy. Farce. Pastiche . . . The critics would be ecstatic.

But instead, here he was, slogging away in the realist tradition with a dash of gothic, digging his own grave. Plot? Very thin – three out of ten. Style? Pretentious codswallop – no marks. Characters? Didn't notice any. Nil. (pp.163–4)

The satiric game develops into a new fiction and a new literary framework for the whole novel. Finally submissive and reconciled to the new order, Dee becomes a licensed writer and writes an approved 'factual fiction' entitled 'The Hand That Feeds You', including three alternative reviews (wildly inaccurate, cerebral/posturing, waspish/stinging). The novel within the novel ends, not with the traditional sombre 'cry of the crow', but with the mocking quardling of the magpie. In a final note, in which he plays editor (the Interrupted Man in disguise), Hasluck outlines the history of the manuscript, harking back to the era when novels were written by individuals instead of the current committees. He suggests the novel is a comic amalgam of his and Dee's narratives, in overlapping fictions, a collaboration of writer and character. This is a clever novel, witty and inventive in its comic play on jargon and idiom, parodying the ties between ideas and language. As well as teasing notions of the writer blundering through a literary maze, which is also the characteristic Hasluck *faszad*, there is rivalry between writer and characters and the lines between fiction and reality are blurred, in intellectual games which are crucial to the elaborate structure of the novel. Hasluck is inside this novel, parodying his own enterprise.

The Blue Guitar and *The Hand That Feeds You* are both good novels, but neither has the power of Hasluck's three major novels. With its subtly shifting perspectives on the events of forty years before, *Quarantine* anticipated some of the suspense and complexity of *The Bellarmine Jug*, which is Hasluck's best novel to date and a major novel of the 1980s. It has an extraordinary range and depth of concerns – historical, political, espionage and philosophical. In interview, Hasluck has talked about the fascination of intrigue and the shifting balances of power at the centre of government and, in jurisprudence,

the notion of the grundnorm, the kind of central premise upon which society is founded. If you can erode or subvert that premise then you are left with no valid law, the entire legal system falls in a heap . . .[8]

The *grundnorm* is the cluster of premises and assumptions, arising out of the political and historical consciousness of the society in question: the hotch-potch of geography, race, religion, social customs, communal myths, political habits. The *grundnorm* becomes the real measure of things, the grounds for communal self-measure. In *Quaran-*

tine, the community has to construct its own definitions and establish a *grundnorm* that might hold for the quarantine predicament: it settled for assent and obedience. *The Bellarmine Jug* in a sense is a series of meditations on the *grundnorm*, the role of morality and justice, the importance of the myths and the collective consciousness of the community, the boundary between dissent and subversion, and an examination of the nature of truth.

Sustaining throughout a high pitch of suspense and intrigue, Hasluck controls skilfully the multiple layers of the novel, the plotting and the pace beautifully taut. There are many powerful sequences, some bizarre, some hauntingly speculative, and some with the appeal of subtle intellectual strategies. The whole is a Tangled Hierarchy of levels, both inside and outside the Grotius Institute, an institute based on a belief central to Hasluck's work, that human affairs are too complex to be governed by a single set of principles. Underneath all the conflicting versions of truth, up and down the hierarchy of conflicting truths, the novel is a celebration of the Lie. *The Bellarmine Jug* is written by a Liar to honour a teacher of subversive truth, a Lie pitted against the hunger for self-deception. In the loop of the novel, Leon Davies is both character and writer, observing his own wistful quest with a mockery that is only revealed at the last – and is then turned on the reader.

At the start of the novel, there is an apparently trivial incident, in which Aveling hands notes to Leon Davies just before entering a preliminary examination at the highly esteemed Grotius Institute in Holland in 1948. From that moment, the narrative extends and grows complicated into a series of related mysteries and Leon is a characteristic Hasluck figure blundering through a labyrinth and searching for a simple and uncluttered moral truth by which to act. He searches for landmarks, but

The terrain he was passing through had seemed to bear no relation to the tangle of his thoughts . . . he couldn't help feeling that he had overlooked something, a landmark which would point him to some underlying truth. He couldn't put the feeling into words. It was as though nothing which had been said to him so far quite added up; as though he had been using the wrong map; or looking at it upside down; or staring out the wrong window . . . It was as though some other game was going on beneath the surface. (p.133)

Leon tries to determine a principle that will hold in the midst of circumstances which conspire to obscure and confound the moral issues. Each time he thinks he has hold of the truth, he confronts the Warden with it, only to learn he is holding one tiny sliver of truth, a jagged refraction of truth. As Humphrey McQueen suggests, the novel is 'a study in evidence' and 'an infinity of mirrors'.[9] Each level opens into another and another, each one refracting a jagged image in the maze of possibilities. As the perspective shifts, Leon is confronted by conflicting testimonies and versions of events, by different guises and disguises of truth. These constantly challenge his moral definitions and force him to contrive new moral stances, always in the hope of one that might be capable of withstanding all the chaos and contingency of reality.

With large and small mysteries coiling and uncoiling throughout, *The Bellarmine Jug* is a gripping thriller. Tangled together in the hierarchy of layers are the student unrest and the tumultuous enquiry into the expulsion of Aveling from the Institute; the political upheaval in Indonesia's struggle for independence; Rosicrucian involvement in the mutiny and the Abrolhos atrocities following the wreck of the *Batavia* off the coast of Western Australia; the seventeenth century struggle for power in the East Indies; marine archaeology in Australia; Australian links with the Sukarno independence movement; and an espionage mystery relating to the Cambridge spy circle, which includes negotiations for the British atomic test sites in the late 1940s and the Petrov affair. Thirty years later, the connections are under investigation, the past being cross-examined amid the mystery of the purpose of Grantham's investigation in the present.

From the outset, Hasluck portrays Leon's uneasiness and fear of being trapped by Grantham, whom he already regards as 'my examiner' (p.5). As Grantham begins questioning Leon and constructing his version of events, Leon ponders, 'Perhaps it wasn't over as far as he was concerned. Perhaps it never would be.' (p.11) Through all the elaborate movement of the narrative, Leon's fears and perplexity in the present, in London in the 1970s, are an attendant mystery, which holds past and present in dialogue. A man of stubborn integrity, Leon looks back for a beginning and a sequence, asking, 'At what point did one thing start leading to another?' (p.14). The answer to that lies in Leon's confrontation with the fugitive and stealthy truths that lay beneath the surface of events in Den Haag in 1948. He seeks a direct causal sequence and a stable truth that, once perceived, becomes his to keep. Instead the Liar reveals the indeterminacy of things, the kaleidoscope of truth, with events and motives and strategies ever changing, each one glimpsed in the continuum, but never at rest, never a final, absolute truth.

As the novel develops, all the layers are so tightly bound together that extrapolating them is like recognizing different faces of the whole, faces which appear and recede, sharpen and darken, as Hasluck shifts the angle of vision or plays with the narrative light. Each new disclosure sets new possibilities in motion: 'Twist the kaleidoscope and things fall into a new and startling pattern. Gradually, he begins to see a shape emerging, a refractory figure'. (p.213). Reading becomes investigative, a search for explanations, constructing theories, discovering new pieces in the kaleidoscope, rearranging, reconstructing, all while Hasluck continues to disclose new information making these processes continuous. One reviewer suggested Hasluck's novels are 'epics of plausibility' and in this novel there are 'a number of increasingly cogent explanations, which fragment and regroup at a nudge'.[10] The novel is about plausibility, about the processes of constructing plausible interpretations, and it is also about fiction, the plausibility of the Lie and the Liar's subversive activities in contest with the reader's wish for explanations. Underlying the narrative is a constant battle of structures, with the Liar constantly withholding the single all-encompassing truth the reader is seeking – the island that does not exist.

Truth, in Hasluck's work, is mutinous, rising up against our conception of it, against the established order. One pattern in the kaleidoscope of *The Bellarmine Jug* is the historical theme of mutiny, part of the wider philosophical theme of mutinous truth. Part of this is the mutiny on the *Batavia*, and the attempt to establish a new constitution and a new order which culminates in the Abrolhos atrocities and the consequent trials. The student upheaval at the Grotius Institute is mutinous too, their demands for an enquiry into Aveling's dismissal becoming a rebellious stand against the authorities of the Institute. Of course Leon Davies is mutinous too, determined to rise up and claim the truth from the Warden, but the real mutiny is the one against him, the one where truth turns on him and will not proceed in the orderly way he demands. Truth runs riot, rebellious.

Shake the kaleidoscope again and another pattern appears. Now the novel seems like a Socratic dialogue on justice/power/morality. Grantham, the British investigator, plays Socrates to Leon's Glaucon, as he leads Leon again through the events at the Institute thirty years before. So too, the Warden, Van Riebeck, the enigmatic and bland voice of authority, plays Socrates each time Leon presents his version of events:

'I can see the pattern. Repression. Retribution. Self-serving, unctuous lies. I've had enough. An inquiry was instituted; a fair hearing promised. The Arbitrator can sort out what's right and wrong. All you want to do is defend yourself.'

Smoothly, Van Riebeck insists that Leon's analysis is too easy and proposes a different version of justice:

'Is not a body politic entitled to defend itself? Your conception of justice is a narrow one. A fair hearing. The vindication of an individual's right. Such a notion presumes stability. A legal system. Defined procedures. Nice, indeed, to have it if you can. But here on the Continent we have just seen constitutions uprooted and legal systems swept away. Subversion has a meaning to us . . . Justice is not merely fine points of evidence in a court of law. There is economic justice. Distribution. Welfare. Continuity. Keeping things intact. Those things depend on order. Strength.' (pp.183-4)

In each sequence of their Socratic dialogue, Van Riebeck attempts to examine the concept of justice in terms of contemporary political realities and so extend Leon's simplistic notion of it. Yet the Warden is one of the 'Muederherren', who are both 'officers of mud' (p.104) and those 'appointed to keep the water-ways free from obstruction'(p.73). This ambivalent concept of authority plays over the whole moral and political structure of the novel as well as historically, through the conflicting image of Grotius, codifier of international law and accomplice to a historical cover-up. The Grotius Institute and the Warden are delicately ambiguous, carrying the menace of a sinister expediency.

Shake the kaleidoscope again and the novel becomes an espionage thriller. Grantham's determination to identify the spy working behind the scenes in the Institute is another facet. The gradual exposure of an agency at work behind the apparent *faszad* in 1948 leads, through a circuitous route that takes in Burgess, Petrov and the British atomic tests in the Monte Bello islands, to the identification of an ex-Cambridge spy, an Anthony Blunt figure entrenched for thirty years within British security circles. Who is the spy, the agency behind events? Hasluck teases with the notion of Leon as the spy, as Grantham relentlessly tracks down the fugitive detail, the giveaway splinter that identifies the spy in the novel. Through the espionage mystery runs the philosophical notion of an undercover truth, hidden deep below the surface of events but working to its own ends, the mole truth which lies waiting to act.

The extraordinary achievement of *The Bellarmine Jug* is that it offers such chameleon images of truth, explores such complex moral and philosophical ideas, while sustaining the historical and political mysteries with a constant suspense. Historically the major mystery is the aftermath of the wreck of the *Batavia* and the role of adherents of the Rosicrucian cult which then reached the Dutch East Indies. The Rosicrucian theme also connects with the twentieth century political mystery of the purposes of Sanwar in the struggle for Indonesian independence and of the role of messianic cults in political unity. The possibility of a centuries-old cover-up emerges, which includes the falsification of maps designed to further the interests of the Dutch East India Company. The cover-up was also designed to prevent the discrediting of Grotius, by concealing the role of his son in the atrocities. Hasluck plays with the bizarre possibility that the first white settlers in Australia were three mutineers with Rosicrucian beliefs and, through Aveling, he examines the possibility of traces of the Rosicrucian cult near Geraldton.

Hasluck's original title for the novel was 'Examination', and this is the most stubborn pattern in the kaleidoscope: Pelsaert's examination of the mutineers; the hearing enquiring into Aveling's dismissal; Grantham's examination of Leon in the present; Aveling's evidence in the Petrov enquiry in Australia; Sukarno's examination in the 1920s; all these are part of the structure of examination in the novel. Leon's development is measured in part through the three formal examinations, each time on the same topic: 'Justice is the interest of the stronger party. Discuss.' (p.6) His responses to the question shift from brash and cocksure to vitriolic, and finally to a measure of understanding. In a sense, all the circumstances of events in Den Haag, all Leon's experiences there, were his actual examination. The Institute's examination system is 'subtle; complicated; unconventional' (p.117) and the nature of the Grotius Institute is the pivot of the novel:

Previous generations were taught to read. This generation must learn to read between the lines . . . Here, at the Grotius Institute, the process of education is speeded up. We examine our students at a deeper level. We articulate what every politician instinctively knows to be the case: that human affairs are too complicated to be governed by a single set of principles . . . The successful student will be one who attempts to see things as a whole; and then inclines towards compassion: a man or woman who seeks to encompass all. (p.127)

Niesmann suggests the real examination Leon is undergoing, 'the central question which every academy worth the name should be concerned with – the relationship between knowledge and virtue'. (p.149). This relationship is the mode and the content of the novel, each sequence in the narrative offering new knowledge which demands the construction of a new moral and intellectual position. Niesmann explains to Leon:

My friend, this world has been crisscrossed by journeys and migrations that you and I can hardly dream of. Ideas float on timeless currents, they travel through subterranean channels and on overgrown tracks. They are taken up, embraced, discarded, and taken up again. They never cease to exist. The scholar hears the ceaseless hum of pollination. We are one world. We are part of a mighty whole. (p.145)

Instead of a truth fixed in his grip, Leon finds ideas and versions of truth in constant change, constant motion, a traffic in which nothing is finally knowable.

In a novel about subversion Hasluck uses the form of espionage thriller and mystery in a subversive way. Through his discourses with Grantham, Leon engages in a Socratic dialogue with his own past, interrogating his conduct and convictions in the past. Under questioning, Leon's past self confesses its limitations, its contradictions and ambivalences. Through it emerges Hasluck's fable of a mind coming to grips with the political and moral mysteries of the twentieth century. There are no fixed truths. Truth slips away, is glimpsed from time to time, but is stealthy, ever in motion, never contained in a single conformation.

The last pattern is the Liar's. In the Epilogue, when Hasluck shakes the kaleidoscope for the last time, the last Lie appears. The novel is a *Festschrift*, a work composed in honour of a respected teacher, Mondrian, the creative historian. Mondrian regards legal fictions as a kind of conjuring trick and suggests fiction is

Something false accepted as true. By a sleight of hand, the adopted child is treated as the natural child. Abracadabra . . . A form of disguise, a means of suggesting stability in the course of effecting change. A convoluted under-cover operation which some people would say is typical of the legal mind.' (p.219)

The whole novel is a Lie, a 'convoluted undercover operation' and a 'form of disguise', full of chameleon images of moral and philosophical truth. It is an offering to Mondrian, one who regards everything as 'infinitely malleable' (p.81). History, learning, truth, morality, reality: nothing is finally knowable, all is speculative, tentative, changing, chameleon, the Lie.

Grantham suggests that 'The skilful examiner merely encourages the subject to look into himself and draw the answers out.' (p.214). As Grantham draws forth Leon's intuitive knowledge of Walter Chapman's complicity, so too the Liar draws forth the reader's intuitive sense of historical and philosophical complexity. Leon and the reader undergo the processes of discovering that untrammelled definitions and clear-cut categories will not hold. Hasluck plays skilfully with every tiny sliver in the kaleidoscope, negotiating his way with nimble fingers, with rich pickings for the Liar. As Leon blunders on, trying to disentangle his moral choices, still yearning for a simple truth and a simple reality, one where the moral signposts are clearly emblazoned, Hasluck examines and disrupts this yearning by subjecting Leon to chaotic, contingent reality. The Liar, like the Institute, seeks to introduce us to 'the real world, the world of complicated motives and hidden depths' (p.129). But like *Quarantine*, where the reader is in the end the guilty party and the Liar the accuser, the reader in *The Bellarmine Jug* is the real examinee and the Liar the examiner.

In the prologue to *Truant State*, the past is waiting: 'First it was real; now it's a story . . . It's there. Waiting to run through a mind like yours again. Biding its time.'[11] The Lie is waiting to run through the mind of the reader, the Liar ready to shake the kaleidoscope into new patterns and configurations. The Liar is waiting too, biding his time, moving more slowly and meditatively in this novel, but implacably, setting in motion a calculated, pre-meditated plot against the reader. Hasluck's narrator is Scharlach setting the trap to catch the Lonnrot reader, while Borges and Hasluck watch.

Truant State is a meditation on history and morality, and on a truancy which moves outside the confines of reality into the realm of vision and dreamscapes. It is the Liar's truancy, his freedom to move outside the boundaries of routine reality, a truancy the novel celebrates as an ambiguous freedom, the freedom of the dreamer whose dreams can be creative but also damaging, destructive. The novel is also a dialectic between Jack Traverne and history, a man who applauds a visionary but discovers he is the guilty accomplice of the damage wrought by the vision. As he contemplates the jagged pieces of history and tries to construct them into a pattern, he becomes both player and observer, both a register and a guilty participant. The moral measure of Jack's own role in the time and place of history is Romney Guy, a man of imagination and dream, volatile, an agent of change, but at the same time a corrupt and ruthless figure, willing to subsume all into his own overriding purposes, determined to remould the world to his own design.

Like *Quarantine* and *The Bellarmine Jug*, *Truant State* is an examination of history and human complicity. History is a conundrum, a *faszad*, and, for Jack, history is the image on the ancient Roman tombstone at Bath, the horses' hooves of the passing Roman legion trampling the flailing human form. History is a vast mosaic, a multitude of circumstances in which man is flailing about but which nonetheless will test and measure his moral quotient. Like the narrator of *Quarantine*, Jack attempts to play observer but he too is 'a barbarian at the gate', forced to confront his own complicity in history. Unlike Leon Davies, who, though constantly thwarted, is seeking a simple, uncluttered truth, Jack Traverne is not at first a seeker. Apart from having vague misgivings, a sometime queasiness, he is content with the way things are, content with the ambiguous gestures of Romney Guy, and content to be the observer – until these stances are no longer tenable. After the fiasco of Jack's concert, Romney Guy is the man of the celebratory gesture and, although Jack questions the significance of the gesture, the applause of an iconoclast, he is generally content to accept Romney Guy's version of himself. In the course of the novel, Jack is forced to look behind the gestures, gestures in time and place and history, and he discovers a moral truancy he ultimately cannot endorse. Jack's own role is tied to Romney Guy's and the multitude of forces of which Guy is somehow the ambiguous core, and Jack is forced to measure the visionary against the moral consequences.

The novel is also about Western Australian history: the political turmoil that accompanied the secession movement in Western Australia, the New Guard movement, the dockside disputes in Fremantle with the Premier and his volunteers trying to break through the picket lines. It moves through the Western Australian goldfields, the upheaval of the Depression, the new settlement schemes and the de Groot episode at the opening of Sydney Harbour Bridge. It is history played from the inside, first in 1919, then in 1932, so that in the continuum of history, strands of the past reach through time, already sending out runners into the future, already coiling and uncoiling its premises and its consequences around the observer.

Throughout the novel Hasluck plays with the notion of a beginning, with the Traverne family coming to Australia to begin again. The central image of a new start is Butler's Swamp, which is also an image of the quagmire below the surface of events. It is an eerie, stricken place, weed-infested, where men wallow. Yet it is a place to be reclaimed and rehabilitated, a new start – not only for the land, but a site of political reclamation too. The workers there are a strange assembly of itinerants, fugitives and exiles who will save the land and prepare for a new community which will grow around the dehydration plant, part of the new order. This is Romney Guy's utopian vision, but beneath it is decay, rot, corruption, a wasteland. When Jack works at Butler's Swamp, he sees the workers as mud-stained dentists extracting molars from a rotten jaw, probing cavities of decay. He also thinks of it in terms of a war zone, like photographs of the battlefields at Flanders, landscapes dotted with ruined trees. Yet at the same time Jack is also an innocent, contemplating the age-old mesh of history with a young man's trust that somewhere there is a pattern, a vast mosaic which will one day be pieced together. His wistful vision of a pattern is built on the chaos of event and agency which is history, just as the syndicate is built on fraud and the vision of the new community is built on the rotting land of Butler's Swamp and, (at least until Lacey's death forces a separation of the two), on the start of the sinister West Guard movement.

At the end of Part 1, when the syndicate has crashed, Jack ponders on Romney Guy's attitude to Henry Traverne's flight into exile in Northcliffe. The counterpart of Peter the Painter, the subversive force and anarchist underneath history, Romney Guy is also a man of vitality, ingenuity and flair, charm his shield, rhetoric his sword, and ambiguity attaches to everything he touches. But amidst all his schemes and ploys and strategies, it is the derring-do that is remembered, not the worthy deeds, the myth not the reality. Jack marvels at the cold pomposity of Godfrey Mayne, the sinister ease with which he and Agar dismiss vision, dream and inspiration, all that Romney Guy represents. Hasluck suggests that man has a hunger for truth, but a greater hunger for self-deception, for the glorious half truths that nourish and sustain, enrich him with infinite hope. For most of the novel, Jack himself hungers for half truths, prefers the myth to the reality, the derring-do to moral truth.

Secession is both Guy's private dream and a communal dream. Through the secession theme, Hasluck is exploring the *Grundnorm*, the myths and collective consciousness that gives a community a sense of itself. In Jack's story of Moo Cow Mitchell and the Great Emu War, Moo Cow Mitchell blames the eastern states for W.A.'s problems. Emus invade from the east and soldiers are sent to fight them off. The war ends finally when the people vote for secession and a petition is sent to Westminster. These attitudes to T'othersiders run through Hasluck's account of the secession movement as an attempt to deflect the community from the real issues and problems, and substitute Romney's kind of utopian dream, his political gesturing. The novel becomes a drama played out between the spectator and the agent of change – careless, destructive change, change without moral impulse, yet the kind of change that gains a foothold in community consciousness, becomes a collective myth.

Jack considers the muffled voices of history.

Attics caves, old cathedrals: things rose and fell. But up there in the planet's rafters, you could well imagine, night by night, there would be a kind of murmuring, an echo of ancestral undertones – voices gossiping, pleading, lying, praying, trafficking, testifying, or merely entertaining, voices which wouldn't be silenced. If only you could listen in. (p. 145)

The voices he strains to hear are lost amid the partisan babble of the present. After the climactic scene of the storming of the Treasury Building, Jack recognizes that he is Romney's lickspittle, dredging up facts, not to describe things as they really are but to concoct a partisan truth, one which will serve the interests of the man who pays him – a dupe's truth. He sees himself as merely a cipher, a creature of empty gestures without substance, the dupe of a man who believes only in gestures. The dream of secession is truancy too, a kind of collective utopian gesture – a dream of political release from the tyranny of reality. The whole notion of secession becomes an image of truancy, played by a whole state when the state votes for secession and the petition is sent to Westminster. Behind the truancy is a visionary ideal of the future, founding an ideal world, which is a political truancy, a dalliance with possibility.

Truancy is a delicately ambiguous notion – a time of truth, a time of epiphany, but also a time of dreams and visions which are a temporary respite, a secession from reality. It is this ambiguity which is the very core of the novel – the point at which the dream and the reality meet, the private vision and the public reality, the public dream and the private morality. Jack ponders on the intricate pattern of an individual life, and conceives its running to

a landscape containing, also, overgrown but crucially important tracks, lines of secret strength, seldom used, perhaps, but avenues upon which we often feel we are most ourselves: a tunnel running through the silent foliage to a distance crystal point of brightness, a place in which our hard won lessons seem to meet, a place in which we feel the tremor of the past and of the future, a truant place. (p.259–60)

This is the place of the self's most intransigent yearnings, a place outside the day-to-day reality where we traffick with what we must do. Truancy is a mischievous truth, free-wheeling, playful, time out. But it is also secession from reality and so self-deception, a dupe truth.

The Lie is truancy too. *Truant State* negotiates between history and morality, between moral substance and the gestures behind history, between reality and truant dreams of reality. But it is also a meditation on the point where reality and the Lie meet and on the reader as the Liar's dupe. As Jack's expectations of history are measured out, so too the reader's expectations of fiction are measured in a way which ultimately is a haunting twist in the mystery thriller form.

The novel becomes a double-edged murder mystery, the murder of Lacey becoming the trap for the murder of the reader. In the Prologue, Hasluck suggests the loop: 'First, it was real, now it's a story . . . It's there. Waiting to run through a mind like yours again. Biding its time'. (p.3) Jack follows the tramtracks secretly, a truant, free and majestic. So too, history is there, biding its time, history become a story. And when it has run through the mind again, it is still there, like heirlooms in the attic, biding its time. And the story is waiting for the reader, biding its time. Among the heirlooms, curios, letters, the flotsam of history, stories appear, in flurried patterns of conjecture, motifs appear, stories are taking root, as they did in the past, when rock carvers and diary keepers and song makers and story tellers began to create, manufacturing local meanings. What each newcomer made of the landfall, of the *terra incognita*, was the beginning that the present embellishes and the future remembers and refines, making legends.

At the beginning of Part 2, Hasluck returns to the spectre of heirlooms and ponders on the reader's impatience, reflecting on the nature of this story:

I learnt my writing on the goldfields with Ollie Dent where every bar was chock a block with cynics, stoics, versifiers, company promoters, bullshit artists and bush lawyers and where the critics, then as now, came at you in the alleyways with boots and jagged bottle ends. So don't ask me to budge. (pp.196–7)

He plays defiantly with the reader's expectations of the whodunnit, stubbornly insisting on his own purposes, and insisting the critics, then and now, are killers in alleyways with boots and jagged bottle ends. It is the Liar's assertion of the freedom of his Lie, his to create, his to use as he chooses, even to lure and entrap.

The lingering mystery of Lacey's death, renewed by Mena Tom-

NICHOLAS HASLUCK

kins' evidence in London and Lynton's theory of the gun in the cistern, becomes the trap for the reader. In London, Lynton talks of landscapes and dreamscapes and insists that the only revolution that matters is the age-old protest, the struggle with the pain of existence. Ultimately, in a serpentine movement, the reader is lured into the fiction, into the moment of plunging his hand into the cistern. The lure is the promise of truth, of finally knowing, but it is a trap, Scharlach's trap, with the reader duped into playing Lacey in the murder scene, re-enacting Lacey's movements on the night of his death. Step by step, the reader is crunching across the gravel, hearing footsteps, with a pained foreknowledge and wonderment at their meaning.

Must it happen this way? Must it be like this? So soon?
Something is beside you now . . . something aged and incontinent and with a sour breath, some shadow which has heard a million stories, thousands of entreaties, something which has come to take you to another country and will not listen to you, and will not be denied . . . (p.312)

Implacable, relentless, this is the end of ends, the reader's exit: inevitable, complete, with the serenity of finality. The reader is the accomplice in the Lie but becomes the victim of the Liar, as Lacey to his killer. It is a strange and haunting ending, which both reasserts and subverts the fiction in a single, beautiful narrative movement. Hasluck the creator, Hasluck the killer – a superb Godelian Loop. 'First, it was real; now it's a story.' In the Prologue, Jack feels the majestic freedom of truancy, as he traces the hidden tramtracks across the landscape. Later it becomes a story, called *Truant State* by Nicholas Hasluck, the Lie, biding its time, waiting to run through a mind like the reader's.

The Lie is truancy too. An ambiguous world that is free-wheeling and celebrating its own freedom, it is also a secession of a world which can become a trap. It is outside the real world of complicated motives and hidden truths, but is itself a convoluted undercover operation that confronts the reader with his own capacity for self-deception, his own hunger for half-truths. The Lie conjures up half-truths in a world where there is no truth. The Liar is the skilful examiner encouraging the reader, his dupe, to look into his own deceptions and his own lies.

EIGHTH DIALOGUE

Liar Have you ever thought of *The Bellarmine Jug* as really a novel about epistemology? How we know, how we assemble what we know, how we take it apart again when we acquire a new piece of information, how we construct theories?

Reader Of course. I told you before. I'm interested in the case against truth. Leon's frantically trying to construct an interpretation that will encompass it all, but the truth is not finally knowable. I must say it's much more exciting and suspenseful than I expect epistemology to be!

Liar Yes of course it is, but don't forget it's a philosophical thriller about knowledge and truth – written by a Liar.

Reader A Liar's epistemology.

Liar Yes, and it's true. It's an honest epistemology, outside the simple laws of honesty that most of us accept without much demur. It is honest within the laws of the Lie.

Reader Liars are honest?

Liar Of course. Liars are the most honest writers of all. I am a Liar and I'm honest. I'm a Liar and that means I tell the real. I tell things as they are. We all do. Could you look Elizabeth Jolley in the eye and tell her she's dishonest? But *she*'s a Liar.

Reader Even though she does keep writing Lies, it seems rude or indelicate or something to call Jolley a Liar, let alone going as far as dishonest.

Liar See how you are now making a distinction between dishonesty and Lying! There *is* a difference, but you haven't always accepted

that.... Anyway, why is it more 'indelicate' as you put it to call Jolley a Liar than any of my other colleagues? Sounds sexist to me.
Reader Perhaps it is, but do you realise that Jolley is the only female Liar in this book? It seems extraordinary to me that when there are so many major women writers in this country there's only one among your colleagues. I mean, look at the major women writers there are at the moment – Jessica Anderson, Helen Garner, Thea Astley, Beverley Farmer, Barbara Hanrahan, Jean Bedford, Blanche d'Alpuget, and new writers, like Kate Grenville, Margaret Barbalet, Georgia Savage. Lots of others writing – and only one Liar.
Liar Do you think any of those are Liars? Can you think of any major women writers who write Lies – apart from Jolley?
Reader No, I suppose not. At least, not major writers. I suppose there isn't any other major female Liar in this country.
Liar It's not just in this country. There are very few anywhere in the world. I mean look at all the Liars in South America for example, dozens of them. Look at this – 41 South American writers collected in *The Eye Of The Heart*, short stories from Latin America edited – that means chosen and arranged – by a woman. Of the 41, 5 are women: Mistral, Bombal, Queiroz, Somers and Lispector.
Reader That's about the same ratio as here. We've got 1 in 8 What percentage is that? 12.5%.
Liar This is becoming very precise and mathematical.
Reader That's not even a very good example, because then there's the question of translation. Probably all the translators are male or the publishers or something. Too many imponderables there. What about the question of reviews and factionalism and the critical push towards women writers?
Liar Depends where you are standing at the time. Perhaps this is some kind of balance to that. I don't know. I think there *are* too many imponderables to tackle here, but you're probably right about the translation problem. There was a recent anthology of short fiction by Latin American women, called *Other Fires*,[1] selected by a man this time. Some of the women in that are prominent in their own countries but their work has only been translated sporadically and so for most English readers, that anthology is the first chance to read them.
Reader Are they Liars?
Liar Well there are fables, science fiction, surrealist tales, magical

realism, tales of role reversal. Armonia Somers is in it, Lydia Cabrera and Angelica Gorodischer. But they're mainly realist stories, many of them about power in relation to men, and mainly by older women writers from Brazil, Argentina and Mexico. But then what about the selection? Perhaps significant younger writers are left out. Young Liars, like the Argentinian, Vlady Kocianich.

Reader So there are women Liars just not getting exposure?

Liar Undoubtedly. I'm just trying to point out that there are few major women Liars. Apart from Jolley, the only one I know of who has been acclaimed is Isabel Allende. *The House of the Spirits*[2] is a Lie, a brilliant one, luminous in its play on truth and fiction. But there are so few female Liars. The point is Jolley is the only major female Liar in this country.

Reader Why? Why are there so few anywhere? . . . Don't just shrug. It's a serious question.

Liar Of course it is, but I think there is no all-encompassing answer. No single truth that will explain it all.

Reader Probably, but we can at least speculate.

Liar Well it depends where you're standing. Someone suggested to me that after all the changes in women's status, it is still true that women are still burdened by reality, in ways that men are not, still forced by all sorts of factors to concentrate on the real world, and have not yet been able to free themselves in the way men have been free as writers.

Reader Balderdash. That's like saying Liars, whether men or women, have more freedom than realist writers. As though realist writers are still chained and restricted, but might one day be free. That's rubbish.

Liar Yes I think Lying is just a different way of going about things, not necessarily any more free.

Reader That argument makes it sound like that story of Hasluck's we were talking about before. The one with the Mafia gangs of historians having a showdown, except this time it's Liars and realists. In a showdown, with Scarface and hit-men.

Liar Yes, and hit-women. It's not like that. It's really a matter of invention and whether your mind runs sideways or inside out or something . . .

Reader Whose mind?

Liar Yours and mine. Both. We've got something in common after all. Even though you found it hard at first.

Reader Which way do you think Jolley's mind runs?

Liar It certainly doesn't run straight. There are no straight lines in Jolley's work. Ellipses, overlaps, intersections, up and down Tangled Hierarchies of levels, criss-crossing. And inside out. It's all in the eye. You blink and what was absurd has become poignant. Look closely and it's absurd, stand back a bit and it's plaintive. All of it in splendid conjunction, congruence.

Reader All in the eye? Or the ear? It seems to me her novels are made up of voices, which supplant each other in turn. One voice enters, murmurs, the next breaks in, cacophonous. The murmuring shifts to a muttering, then a guffaw, the raucous laughter drowning out the distant thrum of entreaty. Voices spring out of the depths and pitch up high to splendid absurdity, then suddenly plummet back to where we started. Much more to do with voices, I think, not the eye.

Liar We're both right. Which is of course the kind of contradiction Jolley presents in all honesty. The Lie of contradiction. On the one hand, reality, on the other, illusion.

Reader . . . and on the third hand, the one outside the frame, the one that does the drawing?

Liar You know, people think E. Jolley means Elizabeth Jolley. Actually it's Escher–Jolley. Look at *Foxybaby* and *Milk and Honey*: it's like Escher's *Ascending and Descending*, with the monks in an endless loop, or *Waterfall* with the dropping down at the waterfall and yet all flowing on the same level in an endless loop.

Reader That conjures up marvellous images of Miss Peabody tagging along with the monks and happily chattering away to them as they climb endlessly up and down!

Liar Or the waterfall. Think of the water in Escher's *Waterfall* flowing impossibly up and down in *The Well*.

Reader I still maintain it's more to do with voices. Bach-Jolley, offering a fugal Lie instead of Bach's fugues and canons. It's a wondrous fugue of voices, voices which guffaw and moan, splutter and mutter, while Jolley's own voice sings its own unending descant. Like Bach's *A Musical Offering*, it's also an acrostic fugue. A Liar's fugue.

Liar A Liar's Fugue, 'A Literary Offering' by E. Jolley.

A LITERARY OFFERING   *ELIZABETH JOLLEY*

'Looking over my own work I have been surprised to find how important is the theme of exile . . . Perhaps for me, encountering and accepting strange territory is a necessary part of learning to be a writer.'

'A Child Went Forth'

'Play with it,' she said.

'I beg your pardon!' Miss Porch stared at Miss Peycroft.

'What I say,' Miss Peycroft said, 'play with the whole place. You are absolutely free! You have *carte blanche* to go where you like. Arrange things as you wish them to be. Simply roam whither thou willest, or words to that effect.'

Foxybaby

'I'll have to be getting off home now,' Mr Privett said. 'Good afternoon to you,' he said and, hitching up the overlong pyjamas, he slipped from his place on the bed and out into the passage.

Mr Scobie, having, temporarily, the small room to himself, groped under his bed and brought out his cassette player and his Bible. He selected some music, choosing because of strangeness in his new surroundings the first cassette he put his hand on.

'Lord, make me to know mine end, and the measure of my days, what it is: that I may know how frail I am.'

The sustained bass voice and the music swelled in the narrow room overflowing along the passage. Miss Hailey, walking carelessly to the bathroom, paused in the doorway.

'Normally,' she said, 'I don't have intercourse with men. I mean,' she said, 'I mean, in parenthesis you understand, I am adding a footnote – I mean not with any men here. Of course, you understand, I am using intercourse in its older and more dignified meaning.'

Mr Scobie immediately, out of politeness, turned down the volume. He was shocked to see a lady in her dressing gown and carrying intimate things like a towel and a sponge bag. His shock was increased as Miss Hailey had made no attempt to fold over and tie up her dressing gown. He was embarrassed too because the music had caused tears to fill his eyes, and his cheeks were wet with them.

'Oh! Don't turn it off!' Miss Hailey said. 'I haven't had any spiritual refreshment for years.' She paused. 'I know that, in spite of my feelings about men, we shall be firm friends.' Her chin, bristling, squared on the words 'firm friends'. She leaned over Mr Scobie with a terrifying earnestness.

'I've brought you my ms,' she said gazing into his eyes, 'my manuscript. I'm a writer, a poet and a novelist. I concentrate on "la petite phrase",' she said. 'Here, take it before the Muse insists that I make an alteration. Ah! the re-writing, the re-writing!' She dropped a floppy cardboard book into his unprepared lap.

'Everything's there,' she said. 'Birth, marriage, separation, bigamy, divorce, death – several deaths, all kinds of human effort, memories, joy, pain, excitement, transfiguration, love and acceptance.' Without waiting for a reply, she walked on down the passage with an admirable nonchalance.

Mr Scobie placed the untidy loosely bound papers on the chair. The whole thing was held together with bits of ribbon, some pages were not attached. The title, in green and purple ink was 'Self Stoked Fires'. There was also an illustration on the cover, a healthy but languid naked woman. Carefully Mr Scobie turned the whole thing over so that the title and the drawing did not show.

The Brahms was upsetting him. He tried Chopin instead but that was not any better. He began to think of Lina.

Mr Scobie's Riddle[1]

•

BACH'S FUGUE, *A MUSICAL*

Offering is a large delicate internal configuration of constant and varying parts, comprised of three-part and six-part fugues, ten canons and a trio sonata. As each new 'voice' supplants the previous one, the inner movement constantly changes the distribution of patterns, so that, as Hofstadter suggests, the whole, with a graceful totality, becomes an agent slowly transforming itself. As voices cross from one level to another, the mode of listening changes from following a single voice to listening to the whole, so that we flip from one to the other involuntarily. One part, the endlessly rising canon, leads us through successive modulations to remote provinces of tonality, but unexpectedly returns us to the original key, in a Strange Loop. Like Bach's *Offering* composed for Frederick the Great, Elizabeth Jolley's literary offering composed for the reader is one large fugue, made up of component literary fugues and canons, each one a fiction in itself, and the whole a graceful totality. Conflicting and analogous voices enter, each new voice supplanting the previous one and changing the coherency, triggering changes through the delicate distribution of the whole. A volition emerges, an intricate configuration of constant and varying parts, the whole a strange shimmering structure, an agent slowly transforming itself.

Throughout Jolley's work there are musical themes and variations, within the fugal whole. 'Voices' or strands combine to state and develop the theme contrapuntally, each voice attracting others in compositions which reflect different configurations of her world. Her novels work through congruence and points of contiguity rather than consequence. Some are a vast assemblage of component voices and some have the profound inconsequence of dream or reverie, with events happening more or less independently of time in a continuum. Some, like *Foxybaby* and *Milk and Honey*, take us to remote provinces of imagining, then, in the Strange Loop, return us unexpectedly to the original key. Each fugue in the whole literary offering is a new, rival voice in the configuration of her world. Her world is fluid and shifting, full of splendid incongruities and strange territories. Her characters stand at intersections, contemplating rival worlds of which the edges are blurred. Place contends with displacement, the pressures and strains of place striving with the remembered past, until the lines between them break open. Time scales slip and break open, the lines between real and imagined blur, viewpoints shift and the narrative takes sudden twists and turns until it opens out in new territory or breaks through into clear, precise images of truth. In the spaces between the novels and short stories, characters, themes, places, images all intersect, changing from one work to another, voices chasing others away. Identities slide, real and fantastic worlds contend for the claims of consciousness and the narratives take unexpected twists and turns, crossing to new levels of possibility.

Jolley's characters are displaced persons, who construct their own worlds in hostile circumstances, configuring their own realities and dreams. Their inner worlds are in transition, a composite of real and prospective selves, as she explores the negotiations between their private and public worlds. She disrupts the narrative line and interweaves rival fictions to draw forth the possibilities of time and place and consciousness that intersect within a given moment. The continuum of her work is extraordinary, each component of it setting up reverberations of others and revealing its dynamic character, such that a later work may cause us to see an earlier one in a new light. Her characters slip in and out of her work, disappearing and re-appearing, their circumstances changing, the planes of time and space shifting, as characters slip into remembrance or across into some contiguous world of illusion or into another prospective self.

The novels work through the double vision of Escher's convex and concave. We flip to and fro between reality and illusion, place and displacement, pain and absurdity, from the frighteningly banal to the hilariously bizarre, from exile to lodging, from truth to Lie, all within a circular movement of time and sliding space. The narratives shift constantly between figure and ground, the observer spilling into the observed. In Escher's *Print Gallery*, we can 'collapse' the whole into sections, the gallery is 'in' the town, the town 'in' the picture, the picture 'in' the mind of the person, the crossings 'in' the mind of the observer. In the same way, we can 'collapse' a Jolley novel into its component levels, but we flip from one to the other constantly across the boundaries between them, always circling around the eye of the Loop, the vortex where all levels cross, which is the Lie of Elizabeth Jolley. Jolley's Lie makes claims on reality and illusion, but it is a mode of its own beyond these, an Escher Lie with its own congruence and its own shimmering volition.

In her self-portrait, 'A Child Went Forth', Jolley writes of her childhood in the coal-mining English Midlands, the Black Country, where she was born in 1923, into a household she describes as 'half-English and three-quarters Viennese'. Her father, a pacifist and idealist jailed as a conscientious objector in World War 1, met her Viennese mother, the daughter of an Austrian general, when engaged, as a Quaker, on famine relief in Vienna after World War 1. Her mother was always homesick and had a difficult time in the English Midlands. In the 1930s into their home came refugees from Europe. Jolley suggests, 'Perhaps my vicarious experience of homesickness and exile starts, without any knowledge or understanding, from the early memories of incomprehensible unhappiness.'[2]

In her childhood, she and her family were exiles in their own street, marked out because they were 'foreigners'. Jolley was further isolated by being educated at home, and later at a Quaker boarding school. In 1940 Jolley began training as a nurse and met her husband, also a Quaker, when he was a patient at her first hospital.

(Their relationship and the struggle for his divorce, difficult for a Quaker, Jolley discusses candidly in an interview in *Meanjin*.³) Later she worked with wounded soldiers in Birmingham and in 1959, came to Western Australia with her husband and three children. After working as a door-to-door saleswoman and as a nurse in a nursing home, Jolley became a part-time tutor at the Western Australian Institute of Technology and at the Fremantle Arts Centre, as well as conducting writing workshops in prisons and country centres. She and her husband (now retired from his position as The Librarian of the University of Western Australia) have a small orchard and goose-farm.

The first story, written in Western Australia, was 'A Hedge of Rosemary', about 1960, which Jolley describes as 'a re-enactment of the reality of transplantation and chosen exile experienced vicariously during childhood'.⁴ Her first novel, though published much later, was *Milk and Honey*, also about exile and displacement. Her stories began appearing in journals in the 1960s and 1970s, and her first published works were short stories, collected in *Five Acre Virgin* (1976) and *The Travelling Entertainer* (1979). These were followed by her first published novel, *Palomino* (1980) and a short novel, *The Newspaper of Claremont Street* (1981). Then appeared, in quick succession, two major novels, *Mr Scobie's Riddle*, winner of *The Age* Book of the Year Award (1983) and in the same year, *Miss Peabody's Inheritance*, as well as another collection of stories, *Woman in a Lampshade*. In 1985, Jolley published two more major novels, *Milk and Honey* (winner of the NSW Premier's Award for 1985) and *Foxybaby* and, in 1986, *The Well* (winner of the Miles Franklin Award). In 1988, *The Sugar Mother* was first published.

Jolley regards the morality of her work as 'the morality of the single person against the crowd' and has written,

Moments in the lives of the apparently commonplace men and women, some kinds of criminals I have come to know in prison, the sexually unconventional and those for whom there is no place in our society form a vehicle for my picture of life.⁵

In her short stories, there are 'apparently commonplace', displaced people negotiating with the world and devising strategies for survival, sometimes incongruous, sometimes cruel, often plaintive. Her outsiders are inmates of nursing homes and boarding houses, dispossessed refugees and migrants from Holland and the Black Country, travelling salesmen, matrons, cleaning ladies, lesbian couples, characters dreaming of or fiercely clinging to the talismanic five acres, characters constructing alternative dream worlds to dislodge a harsh reality.

Lines of connection and continuance run through her short stories, intersecting with later stories and novels and criss-crossing in such a way that it is difficult to isolate any single story. The first six stories in *Five Acre Virgin* are from a collection of twelve, called 'The Discarders'. In her introduction to *Stories* (which includes a later edition of *Five Acre Virgin*), Jolley suggests that in these twelve stories she has 'tried to present the human being overcoming the perplexities and difficulties of living . . . The characters appear to inhabit a crazy world. I think it is our world.' These six are about the Morgan family, with Mother, the cleaning woman, Donald (the Doll) and Maise (Mary) the daughter-narrator (who is later extended to Weekly and who also becomes Jolley's Night Sister). These include the delightful story 'A Gentleman's Agreement', with the planting of the jarrah trees as the one crop allowed to mature before the new owner takes possession of the land. The Morgan family reappears in stories in *Woman in a Lampshade* and Mother is closely allied to Weekly, in *The Newspaper of Claremont Street*. Weekly reappears in 'Pear Tree Dance' celebrating her land as the sun shines through the jarrahs. 'Pear Tree Dance' is 'the idyll' of the novel, *The Newspaper of Claremont Street* – 'the rustic picturesque scene and the ambition realised without the sinister aspect that is in the novel'.[6] Donald, about to marry Pearl Page in 'The Wedding of the Painted Doll', reappears in 'It's About Your Daughter, Mrs Page'.[7] Thus do the serpentine lines of continuance run on and through.

Other stories explore the redolence of land and the five acre dream, often allied to memories of the Black Country in England. In 'Pear Tree Dance', Weekly's dream of owning land seems an 'impertinence', but her childhood memories are of smouldering slag heaps and hot cinders on the paths. She dreams of pear blossom and fecundity, until her bridal celebratory dance. In 'Adam's Bride', Adam marries a retarded woman in order to gain possession of her shack and few acres and, in a sober courtroom sequence, pleads in her defence. In 'Bill Sprockett's Land', the fiction of land ownership is maintained and embroidered by correspondence although the money to buy it is lost.

The five acre dream is at the heart of *The Newspaper of Claremont Street*, a novella of the dream of Weekly, provider of a cleaning and news service to the households of Claremont Street, and kin to Mrs Morgan from the short stories. Weekly is a sad and moving figure, toiling in drudgery with cheerful and patient spirit, generously offering her people 'treats' and promises of order she will confer upon their homes, their shower curtains and their lives the next week. In the corner shop daily she provides news for the street, issuing bulletins of their collective life, while preserving the precious privacy of her own. Alone at night, she rests her aching body and reverently contemplates her shining mountain of money, an exquisite coneshaped mountain, with a silver scree of coins on its steep sides, glowing in the darkness. Sometimes she ponders on the past in the Black Country of England or the later period toiling in other people's houses and subsidizing her brother Victor, whom she now regards with guilty reverence (in a manner similar to the way The Doll is regarded in the Morgan family). Sometimes she puzzles over the contradictions in her people, marvelling at their hypocrisy and treachery, pitying their empty loneliness. Weekly is a woman of simple dignity, courage and endurance, sustained by her dream of the future, the Jolley dream of land.

With a kind of innocent cunning, Weekly plays on the rivalry of the people of Claremont Street and their shared concern for their reputations, thereby acquiring for free, a car, expensive repairs to it and driving lessons. With her shining mountain of money, she finds her dream land, a place of enchantment though menaced by the alien presence of Nastasya Torben, a refugee from the old world clinging to Weekly to escape loneliness and exile. Unable to extricate herself from Nastasya's demands, Weekly enters her own dream, accompanied by Nastasya's relentless complaints. Weekly's apparently innocent betrayal of Victor to his enemies becomes more sinister as the novel reaches the culminating dark irony of Nastasya's fate. As Weekly performs her celebratory dance around the pear tree, there is a sinister face to her joy, a ruthlessness in pursuit of her dream.

It is possible to see now in *Palomino* some of Jolley's later concerns and characters but it is melodramatic and lacks humour, pathos, and precision, all the hallmarks of Jolley's later work, where the incisive and often elliptical style heightens the comic pathos. *Palomino* anticipates Jolley's later use of the musical motif, and the later fugal structure. It works through alternating narratives, from Laura to Andrea, diary extracts and letters, and a fragmented chronological line. It plays with comic confusion between correspondents in the story of Laura's love for her distant colleague, Esme, only to be appalled by the reality when they meet. *Palomino* is often ridiculous rather than absurd, with much bathos and wordy earnestness and it suffers from a terrible plot: a de-registered doctor, once imprisoned for murder, has an affair with an ex-lover's daughter, who is pregnant from an incestuous affair with her brother.

The lesbian theme emerged early in Jolley's work, as a sense of displacement, even exile: Laura writes in her diary about her loneliness and her rigid, self-imposed discipline, 'I am my own wardress',[8] and is always aware that the idyllic period with Andrea is a brief interlude in her painful isolation. The novel contains melodramatic scenes of Andrea's riding her horse, Dove, while Laura rides Charger manfully around her property, as well as numerous scenes of Andrea's erotically unbuckling Laura's belt. In the later novels, the lesbian theme is both more absurd and more celebratory. The Murphy family is more interesting, the whole family scornful of Laura's kindness but immovably lodged on her farm. Murphy himself is feckless but has a quiet, perplexed dignity in moments with Laura. Wheedling, intrusive and drearily persistent, the awful Mrs Murphy undermines Laura with her shrill whine and leaves her feeling smeared and trapped.

The story, 'The Libation', has close ties to *Palomino* to which it is virtually a sequel. In her room in Vienna, the narrator discovers part of a letter written in reply to a publisher's cruel letter of rejection of the writer's novel. The narrator (Laura) realizes the novel is about her own lesbian affair with the writer (Andrea) years before and decides she must offer a libation to her former lover, who died in that room the week before. The narrator is accompanied on her trip to Vienna by Miss Ainsley, a poor creature who regards her as a goddess (anticipating the way the hapless Miss Edgely regards Miss Thorne in *Miss Peabody's Inheritance*). The story is part of the Jolley continuum and also offers another slant on the nature of the writer who is often a distrait creature for whom reality is fuzzy.

Entrapment and enclosure are recurring themes, together with sinister figures, spectral and real, but the sinister is usually in collusion with the absurd, that exquisitely mordant humour which is Jolley's. This meeting of sinister and absurd very often occurs in hospitals, notably in *Mr Scobie's Riddle*, of which some of the short stories are embryonic. In 'Surprise! Surprise! from Matron', the Doll and his mate Fingertips have won the Ferns Hospital for the Aged, in the nocturnal poker games with Matron Shroud's brother. 'Night Report'[7] is another version of the start of *Mr Scobie's Riddle*, the whole story an exchange of notes between Night Sister Shady and Matron Shroud. Other stories set in hospital include 'The Performance', 'Winter Nelis' and 'A New World', where an old man, No. 14, gives his food to No. 12, the only comfort he has to offer, a plaintive but dignified oblation. 'The Bathroom Dance',[9] about Jolley's early nursing days during the war, is a story with the characteristic blend of pain and absurdity, and includes a scene of watery delights in the bathroom, like the scene Miss Alma Porch overhears in *Foxybaby*. One of the best short stories with a hospital setting is 'Hilda's Wedding' (in *Woman in a Lampshade*), where the narrator, a night shift nurse, decides the unlovely maid, Hilda, should be married. The night staff create her wedding, in a story that is painful, absurd and strangely haunting. The narrator decides the time is right for the ceremony, because the wafting Night Sister Bean, generally regarded as a witch, is safely out of the way after a transfusion for varicose veins. The wedding guests include the wondrous Feegan, who dances through the hospital all night checking the fire-fighting equipment, as well as Smallhouse and Gordonpole, the cleaners with fantasies of 'farmyard stress'. Dressed in her X-ray gown with a veil of surgical gauze, with a 1851 cricketers Manual as a Prayer Book, Hilda is married just before she goes into labour in the lift, and just before the dawn brings back the order of day. The whole story has a sinister atmosphere, in spite of the hilarity and nocturnal craziness of the ceremony, a succinct black comedy.

Mr Scobie's Riddle is Jolley's first major novel, a black comedy about the public conundrum of a nursing home for the aged and the private riddle of mortality. It has a driving energy and comic agility, its style sharp and precise, moving easily from the plangent to the comic grotesque. Composed of fragments which move in and out of public and private lives, to and fro between past and present, up and down the scales of absurdity, its voices rise and fall in contrapuntal movements, chasing each other through the chaos of institutional life. Like *Foxybaby*, it is a fugal novel with constant shifts in mood and mode, a shimmering of voices and comic incidents. In the corridors of the St Christopher and St Jude Nursing Home, voices shriek and squabble – the raucous obscenity of Frankie and Robyn, the strident complaints of Matron Hyacinth Price, the derisive squawks of the cook. In the rooms, voices whisper and tease, seducing the aged and the dying back to the remembered past. There where the aged are huddled together without dignity, memories accrete, luring the inmates back to a gentler past. The narrative shifts in and out of private pain and perplexity, in and out of the absurd chaos of the nursing home where the inmates are trapped, yearning for the past, for freedom, for dignity.

In the prelude to the novel, the hilarious exchange of notes between Matron Price and Night Sister Shady (unregistered) sets up an absurdist image of the reality of the nursing home, through elliptical understatement. 'Nothing abnormal to report' writes the night sister, while nocturnal chaos erupts. The prelude of notes is followed by a three-ambulance accident at the gates of the hospital, which leaves Mr Scobie and his two roommates the stunned captives of the institution. Over all reigns Matron Price, a splendidly absurd tyrant scheming to swindle Mr Scobie's money and so keep the nursing home solvent, while her brother gambles their money away with the nocturnal poker players, all relatives of Night Sister Shady. Their drunken carousings on medicinal brandy, supervised by Night Sister Shady (unregistered), are the nocturnal voices punctuating the sleep of Mr Scobie and the other perplexed octogenarians. Mr Scobie and Mr Privett make periodic journeys into the outer world, wandering off in search of the past, but are recaptured and can only meander off into remembrance. As the outer chaos batters at them, Jolley sustains the fragile patterns of remembrance of each of the three men, which are brief vivid images of freedom and dignity. There is a poignancy in their yearning and loss which deepens as the outer chaos engulfs them, dislocating their dreams and hopes and edging them closer to death, while in the corridors still the lewd and raucous voices continue their shrill accompaniment.

In the midst of Mr Scobie's anguish and perplexity, while he wards off Matron Price's financial schemes and pleads with his sleazy nephew to rescue him, he contends with the cultural attentions of Miss Hailey who recognizes in him a kindred spirit and proffers 'la petite phrase', quickly, before 'the Muse insists that I make an alteration', the manuscript entitled 'Self Stoked Fires', with a languid naked woman on the cover. Miss Hailey is a noble and pathetic figure, who totters brightly on the edge of absurdity, but maintains a contrary dignity, even when her manuscript is rejected for the forty-second time, even when she goes out into the night to recite poetry or sing Wagner, or submits her manuscript to the Health Inspector. Like Mr Scobie, who once was shamed in an incident with one of his music students, Miss Hailey committed an indiscretion with a student on a trip to Bayreuth, which left her stranded in the clutches of Matron Price. At the end of the novel is the coda when Robyn and Frankie invite Miss Hailey to live in the commune in Mr Scobie's house as a god-mother to the child. Jolley comments,

In a sense that was Hailey's golden mount . . . she dances her wonderfully expressive dance on the verandah. She is so full of joy at being invited by Robyn and Frankie that she throws her sponge-bag and her whisky into the bushes. Later she searches for it with Matron. They talk in the dark on the lawn and Hailey realises once again that she can never leave St. Christopher and St. Jude.[6]

Complete with pith helmet and manuscripts, Miss Hailey is a splendid creation, a cadenza character who pursues the hapless Scobie with cultural oblations and proclamations of their intellectual kinship. Unable to recognize his kinship with this bizarre figure making obscure demands on him, Mr Scobie sees her as a voice speaking in riddles within the whole conundrum of his predicament.

Mr Scobie's Riddle is a fugue of voices, voices which knell, entreat, shriek or murmur of pain and indignity, voices in inner dialogue with the past and voices in outer cacophony. Yet, as the novel explores the indignities of old age and of entrapment, the pain of the dislocated and the dispossessed, the voices which prevail finally are those of a paradoxical dignity. Even the predatory Matron Price is allowed a curious dignity when she becomes victim, after the nocturnal poker players finally win the hospital. Like all Jolley's work, the novel is set at the crossing-points of public and private, of past and present, of pain and absurdity, a longing for order and an entrapment in comic disorder. There the plaintive inmates stand, looking back with yearning at the remembered past, perplexed and displaced in the present and contemplating the riddle of mortality.

Characters slide and change shape through Jolley's novels. In a way which is both comic and sombre, Miss Hailey anticipates Miss Arabella Thorne in *Miss Peabody's Inheritance*, yet her grateful, drunken consolation with Matron Price anticipates the role of the abject Miss Edgely. Miss Hailey is related also to Miss Moles, from one of Jolley's most powerful stories, 'Grasshoppers', in *Stories*. This story slides between absurdity and pain, drawing them into fearful liaison. An old woman minds two children who trample across her world and besmirch it. In characteristic Jolley fashion, the story moves suddenly from the grandmother's horrified entrapment to the comic portrayal of Miss Moles. Subject to frequent visits from the Muse, Miss Moles suffers from unavoidable literary effusions mingled with typical comic haughtiness and is 'herself an eternal school girl', who 'had the kids in the East End absolutely bonkers over Keats' (p.264). Then Jolley makes a quick shift to Peg and Bettina, the mothers in India in a lesbian affair which moves quickly from the delicately happy into the sinister and menacing. With Peg's daughter dead and the grandmother lying terribly wounded, the ending is haunting. 'Grasshoppers' is written with beautiful control and poise, as Jolley plays with the ambivalences of her characters to expose the predatory and ruthless, behind the apparently innocent.

Miss Moles and Miss Hailey are comic and poignant faces of the writer, whose absurd predicament in the scheme of things is explored more fully in Miss Alma Porch, in *Foxybaby*. Like *Mr Scobie's Riddle*, *Foxybaby* is a fugue of voices in an institution, with all the play of tumultuous incident this entails, and with its main character a stunned captive yearning for escape and home. The miserable inmates of St Christopher and St Jude become the equally helpless College captives, whom Angela Carter described in her excellent review of the novel, as 'lonely, loony, unhappy, existentially deranged'.[10] Talking of the 'high pitch of the fastidiously bizarre', Carter suggests Jolley 'takes occasional recourse in a distracted winsomeness that camouflages an acute emotional insight that might otherwise seem too cruel' and blends 'profound feeling with low farce, high camp with agonized lyricism'. A wondrous blend of the ludicrous and the poignant, absurd and painfully real, *Foxybaby* is a nightmare of voices, that drum and pound through Miss Porch's consciousness. But like *Miss Peabody's Inheritance, Foxybaby* is composed of rival fictions which begin to merge, the boundaries between them ever more blurred, until Miss Porch, as Miss Peabody will later do, makes the saving crossing between them.

Like *Mr Scobie's Riddle, Foxybaby* has a prelude exchange of letters which are a comic measure of the distance between the correspondents and gently anticipate some of the comic horror which awaits Miss Alma Porch at Trinity College. There, as a visiting Summer School tutor and a novelist giving readings from her work-in-progress, Miss Porch is trapped in the absurd chaos of the College. It becomes a writer's nightmare as her own gentle and compassionate voice murmurs helplessly against the voices of the College, voices which shriek high or drop plangent, which mutter of pain and loneliness or guffaw raucously all around her, day and night, together a hilarious cacophony of all the College voices. Set in an isolated and barren landscape, the College is run by the trinity of Miss Peycroft (reputed to be an ex-prioress) and her paramour-secretary Miss Paisley, and Miles, the ubiquitous racketeer with a monopoly on the food. Like Mr Scobie, Miss Porch arrives bruised and shaken from a car accident organized by Miles and his colleagues in the Smash Repair business. It is the first of a succession of entrapments and ambushes which hold Miss Porch a stunned captive. She is captive too because of her own compassion for students, like the babbling Jonquil Castle, who jostle her, hemming her into herself but constantly dragging her back out. Dislocated and bewildered, she must expose not only herself but, worse, her novel, to the relentless absurdity of the College. Her comic bafflement at the outset shifts rapidly through wistful dreams of escape, alarm, wry and desperate imaginings, and ultimately into fears of the total dissolution of the self and/or death. It is at once dislocation and entrapment in a nightmarish perplexity, an absurd exile in which her novel is the battleground of Jolley's novel, the intersection of assault and defence.

A kind of creeping comic horror circles around her, reaching out to clutch at her and the reader. The residential summer courses have a culturo-dietary nature: artistic activities, such as sculpturing with chicken mesh or Scrap metal Pop Art or Multi-Racial Tolerance Through Fasting, all aim to nurture mind and soul and so reduce weight. Opening Day includes a talk by Miss Peycroft with 352 slides and a bush ramble. Weakened by a diet of raw carrot and lettuce leaf, by misery and exhaustion, the students are all lonely and displaced people and as much car-less captives of the College as Miss Porch. Only the wealthier students can afford the midnight meals sold by the enterprising Miles to the starving. While Miles holds the College to ransom or cavorts with the lusty Mrs Finch, Miss Peycroft disports herself in 'nude rehearsals' with Miss Paisley, ponders on the notion of a 'musical hermaphrodite' playing cello and double bass at the same time, entertains sadistic images of Miss Paisley in a burning cauldron and utters largely undifferentiated cultural exhortations. Miss Peycroft offers herself alarmingly to a shrinking Miss Porch:

'Take me!' she said suddenly holding out her arms.

'I beg your pardon.' Miss Porch was immediately ashamed of uttering such banal words . . . the language of a bourgeois housewife, a commonplace remark . . . Just when she wanted to impress.

'Use me!' Miss Peycroft had not noticed the lame phrase.

'What d'you mean?' Miss Porch was aware painfully of her poor quality accent. She forgot to raise one eyebrow.

'Use me!' Miss Peycroft cried in ringing tones. 'I am absolutely ready. Pure, so to speak, and unsullied, ready and waiting to be the heroine of your next novel.'

'Oh I see,' Miss Porch said. 'Thank you. Thank you very much.'[11]

Foxybaby is an absurdist version of the displacement of the writer, the whole experience a writer's nightmare, with Miss Porch submitting her fiction to an absurd world and helplessly watching its fate. She begins with some inkling of the dangers:

It might be better, before suggesting discussion of any kind, to see what sort of people turned up in the classes. For some people, she realized from experience, the term 'discussion' might suggest an animated exchange of recipes or anecdotes about operations or intestinal troubles while travelling. There were too the ever present dangers of politics and religion. (p.45)

The reality is even more absurd: in a series of Tableaux Vivants, daily readings and dramatizations of the Foxybaby manuscript are accompanied by Miss Peycroft on cello and Miss Paisley on Tapping

Sticks, ludicrous miming gyrations from the students and the sexual frolickings of Anders and Xerxes in the agapanthus – the whole debacle recorded on video for the evening literary symposia, which tend to consist of barrackings for favourite characters amid the exchange of recipes and odd shots of pubic hair on video.

Like all Jolley's work, *Foxybaby* shifts easily from comic exuberance to the truly plaintive and back to mordant or whimsical humour. Bizarre happenings constantly erupt and irrupt into Miss Porch's life: Anna, who plays the role of Sandy in the Foxybaby fiction, giving birth after the midwife falls from an upstairs window; Miss Harrow plunging into the pool in a blue movie shot and promising Miss Porch sexual delights in the attic with Anders and Xerxes; various assignations and watery squawkings in the bathroom; the splendid Mrs Viggars entertaining the impoverished starving at midnight or shyly offering a poem ('Porch old man . . . Is it a poem d'ye think?' p.190). Beneath the rich satire on such colleges and courses, there is a sad realism and disturbing truth. Amid all the swift and tumultuous passage of incident in *Foxybaby*, all the assignations and eruptions of college life, all the contestant voices in quick, hilarious cadences, Miss Porch is a wonderful creation, aghast, contemplating with misery the absurd chaos around her, with only occasional plans to hit Miles on the head and escape in his bus. But while Miss Porch is plagued by the voices of the College, she is sustained by the dignity of her own Lie inside Jolley's Lie. The novel is finally an extraordinary battleground, in which Jolley fights fiction with fiction, absurdity with the saving power of the Lie.

Foxybaby is also about the ground where characters and readers meet. Like the movement of *Miss Peabody's Inheritance*, the inner and outer fictions of *Foxybaby* begin to merge. The inner fiction in the manuscript is narrated resolutely in spite of all the tumult and the shouting. It is incongruously sequential, a linear plot whose shape runs oddly counter to the shape of Miss Porch's nightmare. The sequences, with a more sober and brooding style, present the plight of Dr Steadman, an eminent academic, who struggles to save his pregnant daughter, Sandy, from drug addiction and despair when she is released from prison into his care. He yearns to recapture the idyllic period of her childhood but, in a dark and subtle way, Jolley suggests through the Foxybaby game and the foxfur image, an incestuous passion which slinks across the dark perimeters of memory.

Full of secrets, the glassy eyes of Miss Porch's own foxfur in her College room suggest her own dark knowledge of the past. As the students play out the Foxybaby sequences, the inner and outer fictions of the novel are drawn together very gently, until the line of demarcation between them is blurred, the College players spilling over into the Steadman narrative.

The main players in *Foxybaby*, Mrs Viggars and the vulpine Anna, take on roles in reality which emulate the fiction and complicate the connections between the rival fictions. From this Jolley reaches towards the fantastic notion of Miss Porch, nudged foward by Mrs Viggars, entering into her own fiction, joining her characters inside it:

'See for yourself,' Mrs Viggars said. 'He's carrying a baby,' she said. 'Go on!' she urged. 'They belong to you. They are yours. Don't let them go now. Go on! Go!'

. . . Mrs Viggars seemed now to be falling behind. She was no longer keeping up . . . 'They are still coming towards you. Don't, whatever you do, turn away from them now. They are coming towards you. Make the most of it. Till Easter, then.'

Like the waves, the two figures, the man and the girl, were coming closer. Carefully the man held against his chest a baby.

Miss Porch, pulling her feet steadily out of the wind-blown drifting sand, kept on slowly walking towards them. (pp.259-60)

The image of Viggars thrusting Miss Porch into her own fiction is marvellous. We are so far into the conundrum of the novel it seems that the inner fiction has its own volition and its own substance. After the delicate absurdity of this ending, the sudden jolt of the ultimate ending seemed to me at first a disappointing cliché. It seems that, as Miss Porch regains consciousness in her car after the accident with which the novel began, we are asked to regard the novel as the concussed delirium of an accident victim. But it is not so simple as that. On the contrary, Jolley is suddenly returning us to the original key, in an extraordinary Strange Loop, which leaves us with a strange intimation of the possibilities inherent in a single moment, the infinity of the Lie contained in a finite moment. The Lie is inside the fugue which ends as it began, on the other side of a single moment.

Like *Foxybaby*, *Miss Peabody's Inheritance* is a novel of battle between rival worlds, where fiction contends with a reality that is narrow and oppressive. But here the battle opens up another possibility, that of the constant transit between rival characters and situations, the notion of unity. It becomes a novel of initiation, of admission into undiscovered and exotic possibilities of existence, through entrance into the Lie. With absurdist scenes which slip suddenly across the edge into pathos, it is constructed out of rival fictions, the subject and countersubject of fugue, with Miss Dorothy Peabody at their intersection. Through fiction, Miss Peabody can meditate on all that has been outside the boundaries of her real world. At first diametrically opposed such that Miss Peabody is fully aware of the transit from one to the other, the two worlds begin to merge until she can no longer be entirely sure of the boundaries. Miss Peabody becomes an absurdist visionary, who sees beyond the conflict of the two worlds to their unity. An absurdist Escher figure, she sees that convex and concave are not mutually exclusive modes of vision, but paradoxically one.

Miss Peabody's days are static reality, the dreary routine of the office where she has worked for 35 years and the evenings with her mother's querulous voice calling petulantly down the stairs. But the nights open up strange new territories, 'a world of magic and enchantment',[12] dynamic and mobile, shifting through space and time freely. 'The nights belonged to the novelist', to the letters from Diana Hopewell offering the fiction of the splendid Miss Arabella Thorne (Prickles), the travelling headmistress and her entourage. Day and night are two distinct worlds at the start, two modes of existence with crossing points she passes through confidently, the landmarks clearly etched. Through Diana, Jolley points the way to the Lie, the third mode, the reader's mode in which day and night, convex and concave, will become one.

Diana writes, 'It is a tremendous pleasure to initiate a person whom one believes innocent. To be the initiator.' (p.34). The fiction is the initiation and, apart from comic gestures like colour-coding characters and underlining clichés, she provides gentle reminders of the status of the fiction and a gentle warning:

I do not always write everything in the order in which things appear in a finished book. There is too thin a line between truth and fiction and there are moments in the writing of fantasy and imagination where truth is suddenly revealed. (p.15)

As mentor, she offers comfort and reassurance to Miss Peabody during the disturbing changes of initiation and urges her to further discoveries of freedom and passion. Through Diana, Miss Peabody discovers sensuality. Diana initiates her too into the possibilities of another land. From the outset, Miss Peabody recognizes that the 'loneliness and the harshness of the Australian countryside fitted so exactly with my own feelings' (p.5). Trapped in empty urban routine, she discovers the Australian landscape and the exotic – from the images of schoolgirls galloping by 'on their strange, erotic, nocturnal adventures'(p.46) in Diana's novel 'Angels on Horseback', and in Miss Thorne's engaging in bra-burning rites and toffee apples with the gels ('absooty scrumptious') or guiding her entourage around Europe with lusty vitality.

The variations on the theme of initiation are played out in the rival fiction, with Diana's role counterpointed by Miss Thorne's cultural and erotic initiation of Gwendaline. The journey is 'a kind of short pilgrimage to bring out in the gel a true appreciation of beauty in all its forms' (p.27). Miss Thorne 'enjoys exciting hitherto unknown, as she thinks, passions in the breasts of young girls while remaining calm and dignified herself, in charge, as it were, of their passions.' (p.35). This is the stance of the mentor and of the novelist – Diana and Jolley – watching the impact of the fiction on the reader. These two patterns of initiation follow inverse curves: while Gwendaline abandons Miss Thorne for Mr Frome and reveals marked resistance to the joys of Wagner, Miss Peabody is ever more responsive to the changes she is offered. While Miss Thorne eventually yearns for the security of her 'fortress' school, Miss Peabody's journey is away from Fortress Enterprises where she has long been confined.

The lesbian theme is a comic commentary on the possibilities of freedom. There are some marvellously comic scenes between Miss Thorne and her lovers, such as the 'exquisite naughty' (p.11) with Miss Snowdon. These culminate in the comic and plaintive night of consolation with Miss Edgely, 'Come away to bed swee-sweedle . . . I'm absooty bonkers over you Edge deah' (p.139). When Gwenda unexpectedly discovers the lovers, the public exposure temporarily forces a different perspective. Miss Thorne then regards it as a 'ridiculous and shameful scene', a 'horrible sight', even referring to 'perversion' (pp.140 and 143). This moment recalls the plight of Laura in *Palomino*, yet, the lesbian scenes are more often comic and poignant. The lesbian theme becomes another voice in the whole absurdist vision of the novel, the vision of another mode of existence, outside the simple oppositions of gender and sexuality, or of night and day.

All that Diana offers Miss Peabody is an inverse image of the constituents of her own real existence: without freedom, without power to initiate, without sexuality, without movement, without the exotic, all the elements of her life are turned round to offer their own antitheses. As Miss Peabody encounters the opponent images of her own real life, she stands at the edge of the real, and as she prepares for the crossing, tries to see the world as Diana would, searching for the shapes of the sky among the buildings of London. She draws Diana's landscape into her own, even searching for Miss Thorne and her companions in the London streets, as though searching for her own prospective selves. Miss Edgely is a comic-pathetic figure, who embodies one aspect of Miss Peabody herself. To Miss Peabody, Diana is the Goddess of the Hunt. 'Daughter of Zeus. Diana. The lord of Free Nature. She goes hunting on the mountains with her maidens.' (p.136). Above all, she is an image of freedom, forever pictured dismounting from her horse at sunset or galloping over the Australian landscape. In counterpoint, the hapless Miss Edgely regards Miss Thorne as a Goddess, Goddess Ella, 'able to hunt for whatever you want and take it' (p.137) while she herself is tossed around on the edges of Miss Thorne's overriding passions, occasionally their object when consolation is needed. In her polyester tartan trouser suit, Miss Edgely is forever landing in ignominious situations, even being found bound and gagged in the pantry, as absurd a scene as that of Miss Peabody's clambering through the bathroom window.

Amid all the splendid absurdity of *Miss Peabody's Inheritance*, there is a contrapuntally serious movement, in which Jolley is examining the complex bond between writer and reader. Miss Peabody is the reader actively involved in the fiction and undergoing change through fiction. Ultimately she makes the transition into the new world, into the landscape of Diana's fiction, wherein she herself inherits the role of the novelist. There day and night, time and space, all the contestant possibilities, belong to the novelist, with new energies of thought and sensibility. Behind Miss Peabody's transition into a new unity of vision, Jolley is meditating on the paradox of the Lie and drawing an extraordinary literary counterpart of Escher's visual Lies.

In the story 'Paper Children' Jolley blurs reality and fantasy gracefully, offering a series of versions of the reunion of the Viennese mother and her daughter Lisa, in Australia. It is a story written with poise and poignancy, each sequence a projection of Clara's fears, a proposition she puts to herself, giving it substance, exploring it until it reaches the dead end of displacement. Through them all, Clara fills the dread of her own approaching death with dream and fantasy. The remoteness between her and Lisa is filled with transit, a kind of wandering between reality and dream and an inner dialogue on possibility. In the story, 'Two Men Running', there is a similar sense of perpetual inner dialogue, with rival worlds of past and present, of motion and stasis, memory and dream. One man running on the spot in the exercise yard, in urgent converse with his own past, both narrator and audience, each day travelling along the passages of memory and illusion.

This sense of passage and transit, of urgent converse between reality and dream, is the substance of *Milk and Honey* and of *The Well*. In both, she plays with possibility, with putative states of mind and marginal selves making claims on the real self. The structure of *Milk and Honey* is the most delicate of all Jolley's work, its interplay between reality and illusion the most intricate, such that, in an entrancing way, it becomes ever more difficult to determine the substance of the real world of the main character, Jacob. The psychological aspects are indeterminate, the action in the plot seems problematic, even milky, with intimations of presence and events not wholly explicated. Jolley plays with time, adopting a forward movement with the competing backward- and cross-movement of fugue. Plot appears in the guise of a continual present and events form a conundrum which cannot be read univocally. The novel has a timelessness – crucial events seem without time, sometimes even without space. It creates the illusion of giving us access to an unmediated reality but also gives grounds for seeing the same moment in different ways concurrently. Jolley offers contradictory possibilities as though they were conjoined, clenching and unclenching the tension with superb control. It becomes more a pondering on themes and their variations, than a wholly determinate plot, in which full information is given. The narrative moves forward by omission, by ellipses and by shifting relations among the parts, moving along a set of gaps in the 'explanation'. *Milk and Honey* is at once a novel of exile, of dislocation and relocation, and also a meditation on enclosure. Jolley sees it as 'closed-in . . . as though I'm hunched up inside it'.[13] It is a work where Jolley holds the Lie poised, the Lie which makes claims on reality and on dream, which stands at the crossing points between them – but which has its own shimmering volition.

The world of the household and its inhabitants, especially the Tantes, is substantial yet sometimes the whole household seems to be a single collective figure with different faces and voices. Jacob's marriage to Louise, which happens to him 'without any effort on my part',[14] without his full awareness or consent, seems to be a marriage to the household as though Louise is but one creature of the whole. He is rarely alone with her, seems scarcely to engage with her except as part of the household. Through this, Jolley extends and elaborates the notion that Jacob too contains many selves, some of whom are the members of the household. Behind this is the constant notion that Jacob is all the selves of the novel and is confined within himself, exploring the possibilities of his own selves.

Waldemar seems an ugly spectre conjured up by the household to hold Jacob, binding him to them with invisible cords, imprisoning him first with kindness, later with guilt (as 'murderer' of Waldemar and later as father of the baby). Yet Waldemar seems also a spectre of Jacob himself, some monstrous creature flung up from his darkest imaginings or from 'the shuddering, muttering, mocking nightmare which belongs with childhood' (p.106). For much of the novel, it is unclear and also curiously unimportant, whether Waldemar is Jacob's creature or the creation of the household or even exists. After Waldemar's 'death', Jacob ceases going to school and accepts that he is to have no more contact with the outer world. He regards himself as a murderer and accepts his imprisonment, yet the narrative continues to explore his excursions into the outer world. Briefly Jolley eases the tension when it is confirmed that Waldemar is still alive, only to tighten it again through the question of the fatherhood of the baby. The tension becomes tighter, more complex, as she plays with contrary possibilities.

Throughout the novel, Jacob is isolated, even when he is most entrapped and suffocated by the household, even when he is closest to Madge. Madge has a brash, earthy vitality, which is alien to the household and draws it into tight, defensive unity. She becomes the focus of both change and stasis which is part of the curious stillness of the novel, its sense of being outside time and space. Jacob is accustomed to being apart, searching the house for explanations, but his life becomes 'a series of contrivances to see Madge', elaborate schemes and propositions that will enable him to traffick freely between the two worlds. He struggles to integrate his two worlds, concocting the fantastic notion of the riverside house where Madge will be sequestered in the black curtained room and the rest of the family unaware of her presence, one world a secret inhabitant of the other. In a similar struggle to reconcile his two worlds, he takes Louise and the others to the cottage in a scene that seems fantastic because it seems that Louise could not have any substance outside the boundaries of the house.

After the scene of Jacob with Madge at the cemetery, with images of flames, rot, death and decay, the discovery of Madge's body is a coda heralding the climactic movement of the novel. From Jacob's fear of his own distorted reflection, Jolley moves swiftly to the fire in which Tante Rose is burned to death and begins the dissolution of the component selves. The whole narrative becomes an agent slowly transforming itself. The component selves reform into one and Jolley returns us suddenly to Jacob, the travelling salesman waking screaming from a nightmare in a motel. Through a Strange Loop, the narrative returns from remote tonalities to the original key, the finite moment in which the whole meditation was contained.

As well as fugal shifts throughout the graceful totality of the whole, *Milk and Honey* has its own musical commentary with lieder and requiem motifs. Music is part of the ligatures binding Jacob to the household as well as another means of exploring his urge to extricate himself through Madge. Jacob addresses Madge through Boccherini, but plays for Leopold as though his music is enclosed still within him, and he plays in an ugly, discordant fashion when he is separated from Madge. As in the short stories, here too the variations on the music theme hark back to Vienna and the constructs of the old world at the same time as they suggest exile in the new world. With great delicacy, Jolley uses the language of music as a register of the deeper fugal movements of the novel.

Milk and Honey had a mixed, even confused, reception. Jolley talked about this in an interview:

Some reviewers didn't care for the book. It was as if I had touched something in them which disgusted them. Jacob, the main character, is shown to be warped by over-devotion. I wanted to show what could happen to individuals when they become refugees and try to survive on each other. How people can mean well but are unable to see what they are in fact causing. It is one of the first novels I wrote.

I suppose *Milk and Honey* is dealing with certain unpleasant aspects of life and I've tried to show in fiction what happens when people are turned in on themselves, and it isn't very pretty. On the other hand, by the end of the book, Jacob, who has been thwarted and warped, has found a structure, a way of conducting his life. After all, we are all in a structure.[15]

When asked about Madge's death, Jolley answered that she was not concerned how Madge died and was shocked when someone thought the book was a who-dunnit. 'I'm not sure I even know who killed Madge, although I've got my suspicions . . .'

Like *Milk and Honey*, *The Well* is a novel of profound reverie, of dark and brooding enclosure. Jolley is meditating, 'hunched up' in this novel too. The beginning of *The Well* seems slow and meandering, as if circling uncertainly round its own potential themes, hinting at possibilities while maintaining a curious stasis. Yet midway it gathers sudden momentum and tension which then remains tightly clenched through to the very end. Like *Milk and Honey*, with its extraordinary meditation on illusion and reality, *The Well* becomes a remarkable blend of dark mythic possibility and enclosed domestic reality, so that each is a refraction of the other, with dark subterranean fantasy breaking through the surface of reality. It becomes a perpetual inner dialogue, urgent converse between the two women, conducted through the dead man in the well, the ugly spectre that is the creature of their imaginings and, at the same time, their Waldemar. Called Jacob, the dead man is the shape of the dark imaginings of Hester and Katherine, their Waldemar, who speaks to them in the shuddering, muttering voices of themselves.

The Well opens with a car accident, a chance collision which sets in motion not contingent events but the infernal truth that was always

there, biding its time. The narrative then retraces the previous three
years of the two women in the car, Hester and Katherine, from the
time of Hester's bringing Katherine home from Mrs Grossman's store,
reminiscent of acquiring a doll.

'What have you brought me then?' her father, holding his whisky towards
the setting sun, said as if asking for chocolate biscuits or sweets . . .
    'I've brought Katherine, father,' Miss Harper said, indicating with a toss
of her head where Katherine should put the sack of sugar she was dragging across the boards. 'But she's for me,' she added.[16]

Hester's adoption of the fourteen-year-old Katherine begins a period
of education and initiation. Unlike Miss Thorne with Gwendaline
or Diana Hopewell with Miss Peabody, the initiation is not into
new and exotic worlds but rather into a close domestic world. The
women evolve their own domestic ceremonies, their own rituals of
continuance.

a little ceremony during which libations of fresh milk or wine would be
poured into valuable cut glass and afterwards they would wash each other's
hair with home-made infusions of rosemary. (p.13)

They enjoy a girlish happiness of shared activities, trying on clothes,
cooking, and indulging in shopping expeditions. Hester, deformed,
elderly, repressed and repressive, nurtures Katherine according to her
memory of the idyllic friendship with her governess, Hilde, when
she herself was fourteen. Some of the curious stillness of the novel
comes from Hester's attempt to retrieve and reconstruct the past,
while Katherine conjures up adolescent fantasies of the future. Taking on a contrary, undercover agency, the present is tenuous and
fragile.
    As Hester tries to fortify the present, her financial affairs begin
to decline bringing the move to the shepherd's cottage, but forces
of change are mustering outside: an impending visit of Joanna, Katherine's friend who might supplant Hester; outsiders such as Mr Bird,
warning of Katherine's sly motives; or the hints of captivity, by outsiders, such as Rosalie Burden, who regards Katherine as trapped
in an adolescent role. The strongest sense of menace however comes
from Hester's own fears that Katherine will leave her. While Hester

tries to ward off change and barricade them in a magical timeless world, the real threat is not outside, but inside, already resident. After the car accident with which the novel opened, the threat appears, in the form of truth and in the shape of the dead body in the well.

To this point, Jolley seems still to be playing with contrary possibilities, echoing the story 'Grasshoppers' through the possibility of intruders (such as Joanna with Katherine in collaboration) who might cruelly dominate the household and trample over Hester herself. Jolley also hints at the possibility that the initiation of Katherine may develop along the lines of *Miss Peabody's Inheritance* and so take us to Europe in the manner of the small Grand Tour Hester supposedly made with Hilde years before. While these possibilities hover, the narrative moves in a slow and circular fashion until the sudden shift in the middle of the novel into a contestant vision, in a tense and intense narrative. The accident and its aftermath combine to expose dark possibilities which have lurked deep below the surface domestic happiness of the two women.

The well itself has already loomed on the borders of the narrative, with Hester at the beginning remembering from her childhood the song, 'Unter die Erde', which she associated with secret pictures of water flowing deep below the ground. The well has also been a source of light speculation and fantasy for Katherine, with imaginings of a troll who lives in its depths.

To amuse themselves they pretended that someone lived in the well. A troll with horrible anti-social habits had his home down in the depths. They invented too an imprisoned princess, the possession and plaything of the troll. (p.32)

Fairy-tale myth and reality have already brushed lightly together, but, in the stillness of the first part of the novel, time and change seemed not to impinge, as though all evil were safely kept at bay beyond the peripheries of their world. The body becomes their real troll under the surface of their fairy-tale lives. From the moment Hester returns from the township where she has purchased the rope in preparation for Katherine's climb down into the dank darkness of the well to recover the money – from that moment, Jolley sustains beautifully a series of contrary possibilities, making the reader position himself at different points along the narrative simultaneously and entertain opponent ideas of truth and illusion. Katherine's account of his changes of mood, his demands, his pleading, threatening, begging, his bitterness, ring strangely true. Katherine embellishes the story of her relationship with the man, her Waldemar, called Jacob, in fantastic ways, such as the claim that he has proposed marriage. However fantastic, Jolley plays with the reader's doubt, forcing us to entertain the possibility that the man is alive. Hester herself is seduced into believing in the possibility that he is alive and even determines to restrain Katherine from spreading the story:

She tried to think of ways of detaining her so that, so that, she stumbled in her thoughts, so that he might, if left unattended for long enough, die – again. (p.127)

Hester also resents Katherine's revealing personal details to him:

It was one thing to read of these things in magazines and then, with common sense, discuss them with Kathy, say after dinner, when they were sitting with their sewing; to have such private matters discussed with a strange man was something very different. (p.128)

Hester speculates on the experience of being down the well on an underground bank of earth and crumbled rock, trying to imagine Jacob's feelings and trying to reconcile the horror with her previous notion of the enchantment of the well.

In ordinary circumstances there was a fairy-tale enchantment about the idea of secret streams and caves beneath the ordinary world of wheat paddocks, roads and towns . . . . In the rocks themselves there would be faces of dwarfs and other fairyland creatures, there would be battlements and turrets of silent castles and little steps and slides leading from one cavern to another. Some caves might be lined with jewels. (pp.131-2)

When Jolley relaxes the tension and the man's survival seems least credible, it is suddenly tightened again with the $100 bank note Katherine produces. Like Jacob in *Milk and Honey* searching for explanations through the house, Hester tries to construct explanations, suspecting Katherine has stolen the money.

This whole sequence has a terrible suspense and a bewildering conjunction of mutually exclusive possibilities, which lie alongside each other as if harmonious. Illusion and fantasy and reality all blur into a nightmare for Hester, out of which she is driven into the truth of her relationship with Hilde. While Jolley holds us fixed inside the present, the novel seems to move outside space and time, the dead man a spectre from Hester's past, stubbornly mocking her fairy-tale dream of the future, and blocking time. At the same time the dead man connotes Katherine's subterranean yearnings which now break through in grotesque images of marriage. Hester links the revulsion she once felt for Hilde's relationship to her father with the disgust she now feels at the image of Katherine in a sexual relationship. Forced to confront the truth of the past with Hilde, she realizes they had been playing 'surprisingly childish games', and recognizes the link with her life with Katherine. She realizes

The fantasy created over the years contained in its invention all that was romantic and beautiful; the fairy-tale lovers and the safe dangers of cosily imagined evil lodged in some distant place. There was the idea of a world of caverns lined with jewels and perhaps the possibilities of magic practices which made wishes come true. There were the sounds too of the rushing wind, the dripping of precious water and the unintelligible murmurings of voices, which could be human, in the depths of the well. (p.144)

The dead man is indeed their troll living deep below the surface of their lives, bringing up from the depths the repressed fears and imaginings of both women. The movement to and fro between the reality and the fantasy, the fairy-tale and the horror, is constant, an opening and closing of contestant worlds.

Until the arrival of Borden at dawn two days later, Hester continues to oscillate between the two worlds, reality succeeding fantasy which then swings back to another glimpse of truth. The whole sequence from Katherine's first announcement of her conversation with the dead man to the arrival of Borden is painfully intense. Then suddenly Jolley eases this high pitch of tension, and with the release, after Borden's men have re-sealed the well, comes a kind of dazed post-nightmare pondering on what has happened. There is a period then of cleaning in preparation for the coming of Joanna and in celebration of the closing of the well. Katherine is still entertaining adolescent notions of American culture and the glamour of Hollywood which will make her vulnerable to Joanna's new evangelical/American urge. But, after the horror of the dead man's irruption into their lives and all the flood of dark imaginings and dark memories of the past, the coming of Joanna holds only subdued menace. The fairy-tale has already broken open and admitted the intruder, the troll truth, that always lurked at the bottom of the well.

Gently at the end Jolley introduces a different level of meditation on truth and fantasy, moving up from the dark depths to a lighter notion of fiction. Back at Mrs Grossman's store, Jolley re-introduces the writer-character who is looking for a narrator and in need of 'an intruder to distort a relationship' (p.157), already anticipating *The Sugar Mother*. She offers Hester the framework of the ultimate fiction: the novel ends with Hester narrating to Rosalie Borden and her children the story of the smashed light on the roo bar, composed as a bizarre fiction about an intruder, which she, as the one who has experienced it in truth, is best suited to narrate. The novel loops back to its beginning, becomes a story of the crash with which it began, and the grim truth it contains is left circling round endlessly in the dark and dank depths underneath the narrative surface.

Not all of Jolley's readers liked *Milk and Honey*, some preferring the novels of absurdity and comic pathos, the ones where hilarity cuts across the disturbing plaint. I think the brooding meditations of *Milk and Honey* and *The Well* are part of the one absurdist vision in all Jolley's work. Shift the angle of vision slightly and the troll truth seizes its chance and breaks through. It is the same plaintive voice, whether the surface is a cacophony of voices that guffaw and shriek and titter or contrapuntal voices that shudder and mutter and will not be silenced. It is the same voice, the one that always sings its own contradictions and becomes its own descant.

Dancing behind *The Sugar Mother* is the notion of the surrogacy of the Lie. In this novel about a surrogate mother, the Liar explores the surrogacy of fiction, working out the pressing claims of the intangible world, here, the intangible world of Dr Edwin Page, nearly fifty-four years old, an academic specializing in the literature of the Renaissance. For him, the surrogacy of the imagination allows love of fifteen-year-old Leila and the birth of their son. There is a cost! One wonders what the cost is to Elizabeth Jolley. Do intruders take over her house, her marriage, her life? Do intruders manipulate her into paying them her deepest attention and denying the claims of all else? Do the intruders have, for a time, her guilty assent, her complicity? Until the book is born? The Lie is Jolley's sugar mother, as surely as Leila is Edwin's.

Like *Miss Peabody's Inheritance*, the novel is Edwin's playing out the components of his innermost self, negotiation between his real and putative lives. The novel takes place in Edwin's 'notebook of the intangible', one of his three notebooks wherein he records manifestations of his existence. Throughout the novel, there are gentle intimations of the blurred status of its events, which take place in 'a world of disorderly notions, picked out of his books, crowded his imagination'.[17] This is a novel about the intruding forces Edwin admits into his home, the forces which, with his collusion, inveigle their way into his life, forces that are at once external and internal, presences which are given body but spring from his own intangible world.

At the start, Edwin turns away from a film on television about a middle-aged man having an affair with a fifteen-year-old girl and moves to his desk where he draws out his notebook of the intangible. Consoled by the thought of his own affinity to the Renaissance period, he soon hears the first soft tapping at his window, the sounds he hears again at the end of the novel. After several patterns of sound, he opens the window to Leila and admits into his life the surrogate beings of his innermost self. Sinister, sly, superbly awful, Leila's mother quickly establishes her claims, quickly belongs, as though she had always belonged. Like Leila, she does belong in Edwin's home. Both are true residents in his own intangible world.

In *The Sugar Mother*, there are no absolute lines, no final line between fantasy and truth, which in the end participate in each other. Jolley proposes at the start the notion that 'perhaps happiness was in reality simply the state of being not unhappy' (Ch. 2). Perhaps Edwin is free to create his own state of being. The thought snakes across his anguish. Out of this Jolley constructs an elaborate fiction beautifully sustained to the end, a world that exists in the deepest recesses of Edwin. While he continues his daily life, remembering episodes from the past with Cecilia, preparing lectures, attending university, coping with the antics of the friendly couples, walking with Daphne in the pine plantation, he also explores his surrogate life, his trembling joy in Leila and his assent to the mother's ministrations.

A sinister presence, Leila's mother recalls other sinister figures in Jolley's work, some distant kin of the family in *Palomino*, perhaps the children in 'Grasshoppers'. But in the end, in *The Sugar Mother*, the most sinister aspect of the novel is not the manipulations of Leila and her mother but the anguish and the disappointment in Edwin's life, a pain so urgent he must disinherit his outer self and give possession of his life, for a time, to creatures of his own design.

Against the sinister menace associated with Leila's mother is set the wondrously comic dignity of Daphne. With her hunting-horn voice, her bright hockey spirit, Daphne is privy to Edwin's dreams, a kindly and plaintive presence willing to care. Daphne is at once gruffly warm and clumsily comic, with her own gawky dignity. The scene of her playing decoy-lover pitches up to the sound of the resonant braying issuing from the bathroom; Daphne's Indian Love Call, designed to drive away the interlopers and to express some of her hidden and plangent love for Teddy.

There is a moment where Edwin recalls a passage from a Mozart piano concerto with 'both lots of notes sometimes going in opposite directions but complementing and supporting and emphasizing each other' (Ch. 7). Such is the movement of the novel, with Edwin his own composer inside the Jolley composition. Sitting in the car outside the market, waiting for Leila and her mother, Edwin realizes he is inside a design, that there is a drawing hand.

He could have made this place in one of his games long ago. Perhaps every place made in childhood games persisted . . . Perhaps every person walking along the street had been drawn, created by some child somewhere . . . It was an idea of the ancient Greeks, he thought, that an idea, a vision, if written about, could be brought into existence. He wondered, as he saw them coming, who it was had created Leila's mother, and Leila . . . he did not pursue the question as to who was, at this moment perhaps, just drawing and decorating with paints or crayons their unborn baby.
(Ch. 11)

He shuns the moment of recognizing his own hand, drawing his own design across the painful design of his real life.

Cecilia's voice is impossibly distant during the jagged phone conversations from overseas, reaching Edwin not only from another hemisphere but from another world. At the same time, with a delicious inconsequence the phone calls conjure up the wonderfully absurd situations of Cecilia and the brawny Ilse Vorwickl, with or without 'the Strudel'. Just behind the image of this trio at Niagara, almost visible, is Miss Arabella Thorne with her entourage and the hapless Miss Edgely.

For Edwin, Cecilia connotes endurance, named after St. Cecilia, who someone tried to kill by steaming her to death in a bathroom, but who endured and did not die. She is truly a Jolley saint, a bathroom saint. Cecilia's laughter is often mocking, sometimes with the intonation of Edwin's university colleagues, Tranby and Busby-or-is-it-Burton. Not so the creatures of his own design, whom he pits against the mockery and the sad figure of a disappointed man. There is no mockery either in Leila's mother, who tends and fosters his needs farthest reaches and deepest plumbings of her own intangible world, at least for a time, pays him quiet homage.

Later, after the joy and the insouciance, comes the awakening to some of the awful consequences, not only the cost, not only the prospect of Cecilia's return, but more urgently, Edwin's own doubt about his claims on the child, an intimation that the substance of his claim does not exist. Edwin struggles to reconcile the two contestant worlds of Leila and Cecilia, of alluring fantastic possibility and sad estranging reality. With Edwin pondering on the years of preparation which precede war, the sad press of years behind this most painful conflict, the ending is beautifully still. It is delicately motionless, the novel resting finally with Leila and her mother and the child returned to residence in the dark house adjacent, the house beside the place where Edwin writes in his notebook. Each world has its own constant claims, the truth and the Lie adjacent.

In Jolley's Lie, it is as though each novel is one aperture into that crowded absurd and suffering world that is constantly there, the constant companion of each novel, as though all her characters were pressing forward begging to be admitted to each one. There is finally that sense of a still figure at a desk, the Liar in her own workroom, writing in her own 'notebook of the intangible', while, perhaps, at one window, the creatures and the disorderly notions of her imagining, tap at the window, scraping at it, as if stirred by the breath of her inspiration, demanding admission. Once in, they play out the farthest reaches and deepest plumbings of her own intangible world, her Lie.

All Jolley's novels are wonderfully visual, with a collage of short sharp scenes, both hilarious and plaintive, and a fugue of voices and voice-overs. Each novel is kin to the others in her family of fiction and a family photograph would surely centre on Matron Price and Mr Scobie, surrounded by Miss Hailey in her pith helmet, Miss Peycroft wielding her cello and double bass as a musical hermaphrodite, Miss Peabody opening a letter from Diana Hopewell while Weekly is propped on a chair in the corner easing her aching bones, Jacob searching the house for explanations, Hester and Katherine parading round in new clothes, and Miss Thorne cuddling up with Miss Edgely for comfort.

The novels would lend themselves to film and would need soundtracks – voices shrieking and guffawing and murmuring quietly of pain and loneliness; somewhere someone sobbing in the night, amid obscene squawks of delight from unseen frolickers, or the querulous voice of Mrs Peabody amid the murmurs of the octogenarian lost, while snatches of lieder are heard distantly and Wagner and Beethoven engage in titanic musical struggles off camera.

It would need motion, with Miles pursuing the inestimable Mrs Finch, a couple rolling in the agapanthus, a poker game going on in the background, some students gyrating absurdly in mime, perhaps a midwife tumbling from an upper storey window or an octogenarian wandering dimly in search of home, in which case this section of the film really needs to be a distance shot, and so could encompass various refugees and travellers on the roadway, certainly miscellaneous car accidents at crossroads, and in between could be the vast expanse of five acre holdings, (Weekly dancing round the pear tree in celebration of hers, Laura striding manfully round hers) or a dark figure struggling over a well in a storm.

And over the film would lie the shadow of the writer, pondering on her relationship with the assemblage, constantly shifting the oblique angle of the lens, or drawing out the voices with the movements of her baton. Or perhaps, like Miss Arabella Thorne, exciting hitherto passions in the breasts of readers, 'while remaining calm and dignified herself, in charge, as it were, of their passions'. At the end, the Loop back to the stillness of the single moment, which is the beginning and the end of Jolley's Lie, the crevice moment from which the whole fugue poured forth. This is Jolley's Literary Offering.

NINTH DIALOGUE

Liar I wonder what happens when Cecilia comes home? Perhaps they can all continue their separate lives. I suppose Leila and her mother and the baby can all go on living in the house next door.
Reader Of course. Just neighbours. The only difference is that the next-door neighbours are inhabitants of the Lie. What did you expect? Mortal combat? With Jolley as umpire?
Liar I was thinking back to *The Well*. We seemed to be back with dead bodies there. And Madge dead. I still think there's a lot of dying and murdering in the Lie. Shades of Scharlach and Lonnrot.
Reader Not so much in Jolley, though. It's more spectral there, more a haunting possibility, more indeterminate. I like the idea of Jolley's saying in interview that she has her suspicions of who killed Madge! It's like keeping the Lie going. If you think about that statement, she's still blurring fiction and reality, still Lying, even in an interview!
Liar Yes, that's delightful. The Lie looping round the interview too!
Reader Do you know the Julio Cortazar story called 'Continuity of Parks'? A man reading a murder mystery and he himself, the reader, becomes the actual murder victim. It's very brief, only about three pages, but a beautiful loop from the murder in the book to his death.
Liar A 'beautiful' loop? So the loop is beautiful now, is it? That story's like the murder mystery in *Truant State*, that ends with the murder of the reader. You objected to that when we first met. Now you say it's beautiful!
Reader Well it can be beautiful. It's not always comfortable, but it takes you right across the boundaries between fiction and reality. I've changed. I've come to appreciate the beauty of that movement.

301

Liar It *is* a movement. You're right. Never still, never fixed. The aesthetics of the Lie come through movement. The key to it is the hierarchy, the Tangled Hierarchy of a continuum of opposites.

Reader Like moving in and out of reflections. Like moving into dream, a dream with its own shimmering volition, transforming itself to truth.

Liar What's that other Cortazar story, the one about dreaming? What's it called? I can't think of the name of it. I always connect it with Miss Peabody for some reason. Something to do with the nights.

Reader Oh yes, I know, 'The Night Face Up', where a motor bike rider is in an accident and in hospital he dreams he is the victim in an Aztec sacrificial ritual.

Liar That's it. But then he realizes that it is true and the motor bike accident was the dream. It twists around to 'the infinite lie of the dream'. I like that phrase – 'the infinite lie of dream'.[1]

Reader The 'night face'. That's why you think of Miss Peabody. 'The nights belonged to the novelist.' But what about Miss Porch in her car accident at the start of *Foxybaby*? She's not exactly the victim of an Aztec sacrificial ritual, but almost! Images of Miss Peycroft with the sword and Miss Porch tied down to the altar rock, while the students gyrate round her in loin cloths chanting ritually!

Liar Or worse still, her novel tied to the altar rock while she watches its fate helplessly ... But seriously, the 'night face up' and the 'infinite lie of dream'. This is what the Lie's all about. The dreamer turns out to be the dreamed one. The narrator is a figure in someone else's dream. The dream inside the dream. That's how it seems on reflection.

Reader On reflection ... You know, 'on reflection' takes on new meaning now. Not just thought, but thought that is a mirror of possibility, a mirror that throws back a distorted image, as mirrors do. Inverting the image. Throwing back a distorted double. It's Borgesian ...

Liar Like Tlon, where no book is complete unless it contains its opposite.

Reader Exactly. It's Tlonian, opposites hand in hand.

Liar Drawing each other, hand in hand ... I like that! Very Escher ... What's the word? Escheresque? Sounds balletic doesn't it, the *pas de deux*, the whorling, pirouetting vision?

Reader Perhaps it should be Escherite. Sounds write.

Liar Very baroque.

Reader That's how Borges described his own style, as baroque . . . How did he define 'baroque'? As 'that which deliberately exhausts (or tries to exhaust) all its own possibilities and borders on its own parody'.

Liar It is baroque. Baroque Music and the baroque Lie. Borges and Jolley's fugues and Bach . . . what a combination. Three baroque writers.

Reader And Murnane. The exhaustive examination of all possibilities, the border of self-parody . . .

Liar We're up to a quartet already. We could work up a fugue of our own . . . You're not listening.

Reader No, I was remembering a short story I once read, by Brigid Brophy. It was about Borges and the nineteenth-century writer, Ambrose Bierce. It was called 'A Literary History' and I think it was in *The Adventures of God in His Search for the Black Girl*. It's a strange story.

Liar I remember it vaguely. Something about Bierce disappearing in Mexico? He wrote short fiction, didn't he?

Reader That's right. Brophy suggests that when Bierce disappeared he found the secret of longevity, changed his name and went to South America, where he reappeared as Borges. What I'm wondering is, what happened after Brophy revealed the story? Perhaps Bierce-Borges moved on again after Brophy exposed them/him. What if Borges came to Australia?

Liar That's absurd! Fantastic! It's a Lie.

Reader Yes, a Lie, but think about it. So many Australian Lies are Borgesian. Take Murnane, for example. Borges loves libraries and doubles and labyrinths and infinite regression, and circular time. Think of the men in 'The Library of Babel' who spend their lives in constant search for meaning. If you were Borges and you did decide to go undercover and change continents and names, you might write something about a library out on the plains.

Liar Yes, but this is just fantasy. You're not serious?

Reader Are you suggesting that fantasy and being serious are contradictory? That I can't tell a fiction in all seriousness?

Liar No, but you don't really believe Borges came to Australia? You don't honestly mean it?

Reader No, not honestly.

Liar It is true that Borges always delights in mysteries and doubles and secret passages in his fictions. Crevices of unreason . . .

Reader . . . and dreams and dream landscapes, the idea that we are all figures in someone else's dream. Like the fiction in that circular amphitheatre where the magician is about to be consumed by flames, then discovers he's a character in someone else's dream. Like the protagonist that dreams a son, only to find that he himself has been dreamed by somebody else. I was thinking of Murnane's 'The Battle of Acosta Nu', where he dreams he is Paraguayan and dreams the death of his son. In fact, it's so in all his work.

Liar But it's not just Murnane. It's all of my colleagues. I don't wish to be immodest but I think we're all pretty Borgesian. Jolley, Bail, Carey and the others . . . all of us.

Reader I do too. I'm just testing it out with Murnane. The connection of the Lie and the dream. Each one a reflection of the other, in an infinity of mirrors.

Liar Escheresque like *Hand with Reflecting Sphere*. The hand holding the sphere is inside the reflection and outside at the same time. It distorts but reflects the face of the observer and the room behind him. The Lie is the double, just as the Lie is the dream.

Reader Yes but think of Murnane: if he held up an Escherite reflecting sphere, you'd probably see a tiny figure disappearing like a flaw in the mirror-glass over the edge of the haze of the horizon.

Liar And another one and another one in an endless stretch to the furthest horizon of all.

Reader But all the horizons are inside. The reflection would probably show a lone warrior, dancing across the plains, brandishing his Lie at reality, daring it to try and break through the sphere.

Liar Or sitting in the library on the plains, inside and outside at the same time. Convex and concave. Or better still with Murnane – like Escher's *Print Gallery*. Change the scenery to Melbourne and the gallery to a Harp Gully exhibition of artists' landscapes. Then take the eye of the loop, the whorl right at the centre, where Escher has signed it. That's it. That's Murnane's spot. The signature written across the horizon.

Reader Or what about *Still Life and Street*. Where the books on the desk and even the desk surface itself are part of the street. I think Murnane would like that. The desk where he writes is also the head

of the advancing landscape. I wonder if he knows Escher's work?
Liar Murnane at the head of the advancing landscape. The landscape
of the Lie.

THE LANDSCAPE OF THE LIE
GERALD MURNANE

I looked for anything in the landscape that seemed to hint at some elaborate meaning behind appearances . . . I recall clearly a succession of days when the flat land around me seemed more and more a place that only I could interpret.

I'm trying to piece together a plain where nothing exists but what artists claim to have seen. And when I've fitted those landscapes together into one great painted plain, then I'll step outside one morning and begin to look for a new country. I'll go in search of the places that lay just beyond the painted horizons; the places that the artists knew they were only able to hint at.

The Plains[1]

No one talking or drinking with me in a particular town could guess which other town it was where I became myself at last. I enjoyed imagining a road junction, like many I had passed carelessly through in the late afternoon, where two approximations of myself happened to meet for a moment (not driving cars but striding through the straw-coloured roadside grass like parodies of some English poet out for his daily stroll). They met, and barely paused before they went their different ways. But their passing at a place marked by no township, under a fading sky, and with no word and not even an understanding glance between them – the image of their passing like that and then going their ways towards even lonelier junctions where they might meet up with and pass still other men resembling themselves was an image that saved me from straining to imagine the one man I should have become. My skin and soul and nerves had long since stopped bothering me. If I needed to think of my ruling faculty I thought of my imagination – not as something with any colour or shape but as a space wide enough for a system of roads to intersect in it and then diverge and then perhaps meet up again by way of strange branchings and detours.

The only writers I know are those whose photos I see each week in the book review pages of *Time*. I envy most the men who pose against trunks or branches of trees, patches of unkempt grass, or corners of old buildings. I assume that these photos are the same ones that appear on the dust-jackets of the men's books . . . I see the author standing easily in the foreground of the landscape he has chosen to define himself. I postulate the existence somewhere in the depths of that landscape of a horizon too fine for my eyes to make out, the horizon between the end of that landscape and the beginning of the landscape which is the equivalent of the contents of the book. Last of all, I speculate about the subtlest of all horizons.

This quite imperceptible boundary would mark, if any one saw it, the beginning of the furthest of all landscapes, the place that the writer once looked at before he composed his book.

Landscape With Landscape[2]

•

GERALD MURNANE IS ONE of Australia's most inventive and Borgesian Liars, who insists that the Lie of fiction is the only reality. His work is pervaded by a haunting and often poignant sense of exile and displacement, a consciousness in quest of its most cherished landscape, its own inner topography. At the same time, usually in the same dichotomous breath, Murnane is a wittily morose voice, standing outside himself and marvelling at his own most gauche and comic stumbling. His is a voice almost painfully candid, at one remove contemplating his own most absurd gestures and misadventures. All Murnane's work is about the Lie of fiction, where he, embattled, stubbornly insists that it is the only truth, the only reality. In a sense all his work is one central proposition that the Lie of fiction is the truth. Whether he is alone out there on the vast plains defending his country even after he has been deserted by the plainsmen who are his creatures and his allies, or whether he is the founder of his own city of words, defending it against all the invading reality, stopping up its gaps and buttressing its ramparts – he is always the fierce and indomitable guard of his own landscape, which is his own Lie. His work is among the most solitary and the most beleaguered in Australian fiction – besieged by the reality outside, by the impossibility of his own enterprise and by his own self-parody.

Any proposition in his fiction is utlimately the one proposition of the Lie as the truth. Behind it there is a series of related propositions, accompanied by doubts, contingencies, tangled implications, challenges from within. Every proposition carries a host of counter-propositions, sometimes growing out of a small crevice, one small gap which nags at him, until he locates it, only to find another one. Behind his novels there is not only a battleground but a kind of mystery and suspense, as he detects and investigates, checking out his own proposition painstakingly, with an almost obsessive distrust, hunting down its flaws and weaknesses. It is as though his cherished landscape might escape, vanish, and leave him destitute, empty. It is a constant territorial battle, with Murnane warding off all threats and challenges to his own regime. Apart from the flicker of momentary doubts as though the sharp edges of his landscape are blunting or blurring, Murnane never considers surrender, never even ponders on truce, but remains a fanatic committed to victory. He accepts nothing on trust, never picks up the nearest metaphor, the one lying close at hand. He examines the possibilities closely, selects one meticulously, then teases out its meaning suspiciously, watching for the loopholes, through which the meaning he plans to entrust to it might escape and be lost. An image, a word, a metaphor, they are all risks, dangerous allies which might betray him and leave him bereft of meaning. He studies them suspiciously, sometimes spotting intellectually bizarre dangers, a gathering mob which, berserk, might wrest meaning from him and run off with it. He contrives contingency plans, back-up reserves, constructing a fortress stronghold in which to stow his private landscape. He is ever vigilant, watching for the first stirrings of the reality lurking outside, waiting for him to weaken, fall asleep, and leave the borders of his private landscape unguarded.

Murnane is a writer who generates myths, a mythopoeic writer who has wrought transmutations. As O'Hearn suggests in his review of *The Plains*, 'We have fallen into the hands of a thaumaturge',[3] a worker of miracles in the endless quest of the artist for the magic and poetry of life, for the inexpressible and the ineffable. Penny Hueston talks of 'a process of contemplative and interpretative alchemy',[4] as Murnane works at transmutations, seeking the 'essence' across the vast landscapes of his own reality. He explores the interior world and conjures up a mythic landscape, working through an implosive effect, where the impact of the tensions and reverberations drives inward to expand the parameters of space and time of the interior world. The narrative folds in on itself, outwardly static but underneath a perennial struggle. The voice is laconic and allusive, vestigial and pared down, yet intricate and convoluted. Out there in the ranges of fiction, Murnane is the lone ranger, sending back to the reader the despatches which testify to the victory.

Murnane's Lie too is an Escher Lie, a mirror in which inner and outer are one, convex and concave one. The inversion is large, macroscopic, with a vast and grand sweep to the most distant horizon, yet at the same time microscopic, a microworld of the fine grasses on the plains of his landscape. Landscape stretches interminably far out of reach of the most dedicated and indefatigable explorer, away to the elusive blue-green haze of the horizon, which lures Murnane on with its magic and awe – a numinous film on the edge of landscape. In *The Plains*, the film-maker ponders on the old quarrel between the Horizonites and the Haremen, between the 'art of the horizon', the lure of 'the scant layer of haze where land and sky merged in the farthest distance' (p.26), and the art of the promise and mystery of the plains, of the plains hare, the mythic creature which persisted in 'seeing the shallow grass of the plains as a fortress against intruders' (p.28). One creature of Murnane's is the plains hare:

Observers had remarked on the animal's attempts to hide by flattening itself in the grass. The early settlers had walked boldly up and clubbed hundreds of the creatures to death for their barely usable hides. Rather than flee, the animal seemed to trust to the last in its colouring . . . It might have used its powerful claws for digging the spacious, well-concealed tunnels that kept other species safe. But it was obliged to cling for safety to its barren surroundings; to persist in seeing the shallow grass of the plains as a fortress against intruders. (p.28)

This is a small and vulnerable creature, trusting always in its own colour and shape, pitiably vulnerable were it not for its stubborn courage and the strength of its conviction. Murnane's other creature is the figure disappearing into the landscape, moving across vast spaces in quest of the horizon, towards the blue-green veil which urges him to dream of a different plain. He moves towards

the blue-green haze as though it was itself a land – a plain of the future, perhaps, where one might live a life that existed only in potentiality on the plains where poets and painters could do no more than write or paint . . . the zone of haze was as much a part of the plains as any configuration of soil or clouds. (p.27)

In Murnane's work, there is a trafficking between these opponent images, a continuing process of severance and conjunction, of transience and possession. Murnane himself is both Hareman and Horizonite. This dichotomy in the culture of the plains is also in Murnane's own inner dialogue, a tension between the immanent and microscopic and the lure of the haze, the vast macroscopic world running ineffably far to the horizon, which is forever elusive, forever drawing him on towards it, a magnetic haze.

Gerald Murnane was born in a northern suburb of Melbourne in 1939. He spent part of his childhood in country districts in Victoria, notably Bendigo, where he made his first journeys into the inner landscape which is the setting of all his fiction. On Saturday afternoons in the Lyric Theatre in Bendigo, he began the search for his landscape, his pure scenery.

The films I watched made me discontented. Scene after scene disappeared from the screen before I had properly appreciated it; the characters moved and spoke much too fast . . . I thought of pure scenery as the places safely behind the action: the places where nothing seemed to happen. Occasionally I glimpsed the kind of scenery I wanted. Behind the men on horses or the encampment of wagons was a broad tract of tall grass leading back to a line of hills . . . I wanted to feel that waving grass and that line of hills somewhere inside me. I wanted grass and hills fixed inside the space that began, as I thought, behind my eyes.

I had first been attracted to my scenery because nothing seemed to happen there; my grasses and hills were never the site of the frantic action that took place in the foreground of films. But when I was tired of waiting to understand my empty places, I allowed certain things to happen there.[5]

Having discovered that 'the best vantage point for studying a brightly lit landscape was a dark place within the landscape', he conceived the Man from Idaho who, behind the drawn blinds of his spacious house, understood the hidden hollow of land in the pure scenery all around him. The Man from Idaho later became the estate owner and the film-maker of *The Plains* and led also to the dream-prairie in the town of Ideal in *Inland*. The Man from Idaho built racecourses where races like those in Murnane's first novel, *Tamarisk Row*, were run. Later Murnane discovered that Kerouac too, the man who crossed prairie-landscapes, ran races of marbles over racecourses.

The chief difference between Jack's races and mine was that he had always rolled: his races were brief and hectic . . . Apparently Jack had never thought of slow-motion races around a rug, of studying the patterns of gradual change, of prolonging his pleasure.[5]

In Murnane's marbles races in *Tamarisk Row*, with the prismatic play of his private colours, complex patterns unfold, through an exquisite slow motion meditation. His planned Kerouac-style journeys across Australia became journeys across his own plains. Murnane moved back to Melbourne in 1949, and has never left since. He is married and has three sons, and lives in a northern suburb of Melbourne. In *Landscape with Landscape*, the narrator points out

I unfold my favourite map (Broadbents Number 222: *Melbourne's North-East Country*) and I point to the line I have plotted from the inner northern suburb where I now live. I explain that the line shows me to have been moving all my life in a north-east direction at an average velocity of 0.75 kilometres per year. I move my finger slowly across the map to show where the line will have taken me by the age of fifty. (p.217)

In terms of outer geography, he has had a largely stationary life, its ambit small, but in his own landscape his journeys have been long and many, in criss-crossing patterns, with battlegrounds among the grassy plains that stretch interminably far to the haze of the horizon that dips down to another and another.

Murnane's first novel, *Tamarisk Row*, was published in 1974 and was a finalist in *The Age* Book of the Year Award. It was followed by *A Lifetime on Clouds* in 1976 and, after a long interval, his brilliant short novel, *The Plains*, published by Norstrilia Press in 1982, also a finalist for *The Age* Book of the Year Award. Before *Inland*, *Landscape with Landscape* was published in 1985, also by Norstrilia, a small press which publishes much science fiction. An article by Bruce Gillespie about *Tamarisk Row* appeared in *Science Fiction Commentary*[6] with the transcript of an address by Murnane to science fiction writers, the substance of which is that novels such as Vonnegut's *Slaughterhouse Five*, Canetti's *Auto da Fe*, Musil's *The*

Man Without Qualities, Mervyn Peake's *Gormenghast*, and, of course, Borges' fictions, are more truly inventive than science fiction. Murnane does not mind the connection with science fiction although he doubts the 'science' part.

Murnane's Lie is often Borgesian, an art of exploration of the reaches of the interior and the transmutation of time and space into the essence of inner existence. In his short fiction, 'Land Deal',[7] he plays with the conjecture that Australia was not colonized at all, that white settlement is just a white fantasy, a white dream. With wry, delicate logic, he manipulates the notion of Aboriginal Dreaming, twisting it around through the 1835 Batman Land Deal, with Aboriginal voices deciding they must be characters in the white man's absurd dream that it is possible to *possess* the land. The movement into the interior of dream in this story, in a historical paradox of dreaming, is the kind of Borgesian passage that runs throughout Murnane's work. But more often he himself is both dreamer and dreamed at the same shimmering moment.

Murnane's inward movement began in *Tamarisk Row*. The author's note points to its intricate mosaic structure.

If you could fill each square on a calendar with a picture instead of a number, and if each picture could show clearly some event or landscape or recollection or dream that made each day memorable, then after a long time and from a great distance the hundreds of pictures might rearrange themselves to form surprising patterns.
Tamarisk Row is one such pattern.

The patterning of the novel is very succinctly expressed in this image of a calendar of pictures. Picture is foremost, picture composing itself into a fragment of a pattern, hundreds of pictures which, as if on planes of their own, supplant the idea of lines of causal sequence, of event giving rise to another, of days in collocation touching each other. Picture prevails, with the fragmented refractions of a mirror glass mosaic. There are sharp shards of incident, slivers and splinters out of the whole pattern, but passages too where the prose drives towards a distant horizon, with an almost mesmeric quality. Long and intricate sentences take us inside the whorl of consciousness as if its colours and configurations could be contained in a single sentence – if words could only break up into new patterns at

turn. The prose moves through long questing sentences, then back
again to the sharp slivers of incident, in which a solemn and earnest
child refracts through Murnane's laconic humour the consciousness
of a nine year old in a country town in the 1940s.

While proposing the notion of a calendar of childhood and locating his narrative solidly and convincingly in the 1940s in Basset,
Murnane nevertheless supplants the very notion of consecutive time
and establishes through the mock picaresque structure a chequered
time, fractured into component moments of experience, as elusive
and yet stubbornly real as the Tamarisk Row landscape. The pictures in the days of Murnane's calendar rearrange themselves to form
a surprising pattern of event, landscape, recollection and dream, and
these conjoin, touch and blur, transmuting each other and always
crossing the boundaries between real and imagined. In a sense, the
narrative forms a cubist grid, a geometry of intersecting planes, the
constituent planes touching and tilting at each other, but opening
out into a spatial continuum which recedes to a culminating point
on the horizon or dips down beyond it. Colour is iridescent, prismatic.

While space and distance lure him, Clem has an intimation of an
essence of things and he considers the perplexities of colour inside
a marble, trying

to explore all the wine- or flame- or honey- or blood- or ocean- or lake- or
stained-glass-coloured skies or plains where winds or clouds or ranges of hills
or curls of smoke are trapped forever and to decide what secret tunnels or
caves or valleys or walled cities or thickets or abandoned laneways might
never be explored because they lie deep inside it close to its very essence where
its truest colours would envelop any traveller who reached there trying to
discover what has lain for so many years in the heart of the glass . . .[8]

Like the narrator of *Landscape with Landscape*, Clem suspects for a
while that secrets are hidden in small dark places, like girls' pants,
or Therese Riordan's Foxy Glen, or dark corners of the house where
the Brothers live, or in the heart of the Wallaces' aviary. But Clem
is increasingly aware that the real secrets are in space and distance,
the space inside the whorls of colour in the marbles, or inside the
greenish-gold glass of the front door, where creatures seek a land
of plains and cities. Clement watches as

big slow plains are creeping sadly away from the house. A haze of dust from the north makes a sign in the sky and tries to reach Bassett, but the blinds are pulled down all over the city and no one sees the silent empty places where they may all be going. (pp.33–4)

These silent empty places endure, while the colours which give access to them shimmer and change, prisms of possibility. Colour connotes a dynamic and protean world of possibility, but it also connotes the fateful and the ineluctable, the given and a priori of existence. When Augustus wins at the races, Clement ponders on the single, evanescent pattern of colour.

Colours too variable to fix in the memory have gathered at the edge of the northern plains, have run together into a thousand patterns that melted again as soon as they were formed, have assumed for an instant one fateful formation with his own device outstanding at its front, have massed themselves into a desperate gesture as if a finger pointed down from the north, and have scattered and will never again be assembled in that place. (p.66)

Colour becomes the child's meditation on the pattern of his own existence, his measuring of the fixed and unfathomable against the vast open spaces and the prismatic configurations in his life. The patterns of his consciousness are subsumed into the flying and shifting colours of the jockeys in his Gold Cup race.

To protect Tamarisk Row from his parents' disapproval, from casual observers and from the dreaded and brutish Barry Launder, Clement shrinks its physical existence and extends its inner substance until it stretches towards the haze on the horizon of his consciousness. In the macrocosmic world inside him, he is the Hareboy crouched low in the plains of his own landscape. He gazes more often at the landscape that is always there, making the crossing whenever he chooses with a wondrous celebratory freedom as long as it is kept secret and private. He thinks about the boy who lived in the house before him, as if the Silverstone boy were another self, a projection or spectre of himself. Each component of himself becomes a colour and a shape in the Gold Cup Race, through which he reaches back in time and ahead across the vast plains to the future, and he plays with the mysteries of planes and angles of vision. As Clement listens attentively for explanations of things and then puzzles in his quiet earnest way, chaffing at them for meanings, Murnane too is chaffing at each image in the mirror mosaic, seeking the meanings in the changing patterns, as the whole calendar of images becomes more and more prismatic and intricate. And as Clement runs the Gold Cup race, so Murnane runs the narrative, the flashing and shifting colours of incident and image in the life of a nine year old boy running to the realization of his own landscape. Before he leaves Bassett, Clement seeks again the creatures in the stained glass whose country is a translucent plain lying at an absurd angle to the sun. He can find no traces of them except wavering indefinable outlines, but as the last of the sunset reaches across Bassett, he conceives of some huge watchful figure, yearning for the creatures to begin the most perilous, far-reaching journeys and waiting to welcome them into a country like his own. Murnane is the watchful figure delighting again in the interwoven journeys and shapes and images of Clement's creatures and welcoming them into his landscape.

Tamarisk Row is a major novel in itself as well as the first topography of the landscape of all Murnane's work. Clement Killeaton becomes the film-maker in *The Plains*, the voices in *Landscape with Landscape* and the narrative voice of *Inland*. There is a remarkable integrity and consistency of vision in Murnane's work, each fiction a voice of the others and each one of them a face of his own landscape, first discovered and entered in *Tamarisk Row*. Clement knows – seems always to have known – of the existence of an imponderable expanse of treeless grasses, 'a country deep inside what people who live near its borders call the country' (p.30). As he half-closes his eyes and strains with his tongue to force the juice from the milkstone, he sees 'a boy who has already reached a city across a hot difficult landscape' (p.107). The Hareboy who has fled from his home in an inland town and crouches low in the grasses of Tamarisk Row becomes the Hareman of *The Plains*. The boy protecting his Tamarisk Row becomes the lone plainsman, still stubbornly defending the plains when even the great and powerful landowners have surrendered.

Clement also becomes Adrian Sherd, in *A Lifetime on Clouds*. Like some spectral being Sherd slides in and out of the crevices of his own world when he pleases without ever leaving behind him any unattended aperture through which the encircling reality might break into his stronghold. But this novel is lighter, with fantastic sexual imaginings, and the mood is primarily comic. Behind it is what John Tittensor calls a 'fevered search for a religio-sexual syncretism',[9] and behind the dry ironies and sharper absurdities, there is the theological rigidity and sexual bafflement of Catholic adolescence in the 1950s. Adrian's theology is dogmatic and mechanistic, derived from rigid 'Catholic Truth' sources, but coloured by his wry imaginings and comic earnestness.

A Lifetime on Clouds has sustained comic sequences such as the map of his masturbating peers with colour codes and the history of the world through masturbation, from the Garden of Eden through ancient Rome to the Dark Ages and the Reformation, and the present, all narrated with a dead-pan theological humour. Adrian also travels across America, in search of film stars in his year of masturbation, and licence, the licence of Mormons practising polygamy somewhere far out beyond the prairies. At the same time, he conceives the lost kingdoms of Australia, where joyful fellows are surrounded by bare-breasted women. His journeys to America and his journeys through history stop when he meets Denise and begins his marriage and life-time with her. His theological explications are designed to prove to Denise the spiritual riches she will amass by satisfying him sexu-ally. His marriage to Denise and their life in the Catholic community, Our Lady of the Ranges, is so elaborately developed and maintained, that we forget he has not yet addressed a word to her in 'reality' – on the outside, so to speak. But inside, he is in deep and close com-munion with her, attendant to her every spiritual need, solicitous and tender, though troubled by his own rapid acceleration of their marriage such that it begins to pall. He is untroubled by the gap between inside and outside, gliding easily back and forth between the two worlds.

The Plains is a short, singularly close and densely textured fiction, its prose laconic but meditative, a novel which never settles into defini-tive completed meanings, but continues to suggest putative, contiguous ideas at each turn. The contiguity becomes part of the novel's geography – 'real, that is spiritual, geography' (p.37) – with Murnane's anonymous narrator the explorer and the mapmaker. *The Plains* is first a narrative of the discovery, exploration, settlement and growth of the narrator's private reality. It is also the story of its siege and its defence, an extraordinary battle story, a novel about the central battle of the Lie. Like any war story, it is about fear and courage, about victory and defeat, about territorial claims, about transience and possession, severance and conjunction, about sides, allies and enemies, and it is also about history – the transitions of time, the past, the present and the future which turns upon the present. Murnane's narrator becomes the lone warrior dancing across his plains, embattled, courageous, indomitable, and ultimately victorious in the struggle to withstand the siege of reality and maintain his own private construct. The novel is sometimes painfully moving and poignant, but always Murnane draws on extraordinary reserves of strength and courage to defend the landscape of his own private reality against all the besieging forces that lie in wait outside its borders.

Like the moment in Ireland's *City of Women* when Billie Shockley has to defend the City, the fiction, against the onslaughts of reality at its gates, in *The Plains* too, the narrator reaches the critical moment where an outer reality is menacing his and he defends the vast expanses of the plains. Like Billie Shockley, he is victorious. Where Billie Shockley constructs a City, and populates it with the creatures of her self, Murnane's narrator constructs Inner Australia, with the plainsmen, the town and the hotel where the landowners meet with their petitioners, amid the vast spaces of the plains. In one sense a series of related explorations which deliberately subvert our sense of time and spatial movement, the novel is also a battle story in which Murnane's narrator is the lone defendant of his own reality. Even when the plainsmen themselves are prepared to surrender the plains Murnane's narrator fights on, stubborn and immovable, a moving, poignant figure, defending the ineffable.

The central paradox on which the whole novel turns is the project of representing visually the inner landscape. In *Landscape with Landscape*, Murnane sets his own activity against that of the landscape painter, examining his own purposes and strategies in relation to him. But here in *The Plains*, the parallel medium is film. While the narrator prepares his notes for the filmscript of 'The Interior', in counterpoint Murnane is presenting his words in *The Plains*. Throughout the novel, meditations on the nature of fiction run parallel to meditations on the visual. Both the film maker and the novelist are engaged in a battle, the struggle to represent an inner landscape in art.

At the start of *The Plains*, Murnane recounts the narrator's jour-

ney to his own private landscape 20 years before, after he first heard
of the existence of the plains. In the first few days at the hotel in
the town, Murnane recalls that first crossing of the novel, from Other
Australia into the interior, across a succession of days and a land with
valleys and roads rising to hills. When he reached the town, he
immediately felt a sense of belonging. He is content with the
knowledge that he had reached the plains, that there are more plains
ahead, that this is the beginning. It is a moment of recognition and
affirmation that becomes the stubborn and ineradicable premise of
the novel, at the same time as it connotes, by its very simplicity,
a poignant history of exile and displacement. He enjoys the climate
of the plains, glad there is no snow because he wants to see 'the
true configuration of the earth itself and not the false hillocks and
hollows of some other element' (p.11). The 'false hillocks and hollows' are part of the world he has left behind, but he will glimpse
them again towards the end of the novel.

In the opening pages, the narrator cherishes his anonymity, and
the privacy of his destination. He is anxious to be accepted by the
plainsmen and prepared for any test, determined to prove he is no
mere tourist or sightseer, but one who seeks residence, a petitioner.
After a few days in the hotel, he has devised a story, almost devoid
of events or achievements, such as the plainsmen prefer. It is the
kind of story that appeals to their own writers – not the kind of
story that belongs in the foreshortened landscapes of Other Australia. In these first few pages, Murnane has already established the
topography of the novel, through a series of rival notions which
introduce the central battle of the novel. But even as we begin to
find our bearings from the new co-ordinates of space and time, they
are already shifting and changing. They continue to shift throughout the novel, into new intuitions of meaning and new configurations
of time and space, as the narrator continues his journey inside the
plains.

The contestant notions include plainsmen and outsiders, landowners
and petitioners, the labyrinthine bars and lounges of the hotel and
the vast expanse of the plains, past and present, interior and exterior.
There is also the polarity of word and film, of fiction and film. Behind
all of these is the central opposition of the narrator and the plainsmen. Although the film-maker seeks admission to their ranks, a patron
among the great aristocratic landowners – all explorers of the cul-

ture of the plains and all projectors of possibility – yet the film-maker is always marked out from the plainsmen. They prefer single, subjective visions, each one liking to appear as a solitary inhabitant of a region only he might explain, each one laying private claim to the meaning of the plains. But there is also a history of polarity, 'the colours' of Blue-Greens and Old-Golds. The narrator is another pole, not one of them, set aside by the film he will make, in which he will show the plains. He is of them but apart from them, moving among them, but marked out by his own all-encompassing purpose. Among the petitioners seeking positions on the estates of the landowners, his project is unique. Where the other petitioners propose schemes which are variations and counterpoints of existing projects, the narrator proposes to visually represent the plains, in film. Not for him the heraldic arts, the history of decorative arts, not formulae for standards of elegance, and not the collation of private diaries and letters of the great families. Not for him the plotting of family graphs along the co-ordinates of culture and not the founding of a religion. For him, nothing less than the visual representation of the plains.

The narrator has considered proposing the project of reconciling all the conflicts from the old quarrel between the Horizonites and the Haremen, the Blue-greens and the Old Golds. The dichotomy within the culture of the plains is also Murnane's, and he transmutes this into the history of 'the colours' conflict, weaving intricate threads of artistic manifestos, sporting conflicts of polo teams, local government parties, secret societies with opposing political platforms for the status of the plains. Murnane plays freely with notions of The Brotherhood of the Endless Plain and The League of Heartlanders, teasing political paradoxes out of the plains of Inner Australia, and summoning up notions of Australian pastoral history. While the polarities are being extended through history, giving the plains another stubborn dimension of reality, the narrator is working towards the notion of reconciliation. He notes, 'I, a film-maker, am admirably equipped to explore this landscape and reveal it to others.' (p.38).

When he is summoned before the landowners, the fragments of a Socratic dialogue articulate parallel motifs of the novel, of exploration, of surfaces, freckles and skin colouring, map-making, and journeys, including some anecdotes which are delightfully Borgesian, like the story of the man who spent his life exploring one small square of his property (p.54). Among plainsmen, their 'lifelong task the shaping from uneventful days in a flat landscape the substance of myth' (p.19), the narrator wants to shape the greatest myth of all, the reconciliation of inner and outer worlds, the reconciliation of art with an internal landscape. Only film, he insists, can satisfy the contradictory impulses of the plainsmen. As Director of Film Projects, he will produce a film of one man's search for the Eternal Plain. His landscape is not the landscape of dreams. The first part of The Plains ends with a disclaimer of the notion of a landscape of dreams – like those of the painter which resemble the ordinary landscapes of Outer Australia. It is an inner landscape of the real: this is the substance of the film-maker's scheme and of Murnane's Lie of fiction which he will defend to the last.

In the second part of The Plains, ten years later, Murnane again shifts the parameters of the novel, this time away from the spatial and into a meditation on Time. The film-maker looks back at depictions of illusory and spurious plains, 'the false notions, the absurd distortions, that I once took for descriptions of plains' (p.80). These illusory plains become part of a literary argument about time and the real self, beginning with the contrast of what are called novels in Outer Australia and philosophy on the plains. Murnane plays with literary theory here, within the construct of his own landscape, rejecting wholly the notion that the real life of a person can be told through a linear biographical sequence, 'bound by the vicissitudes of his flesh' (p.80). He plays with literary paradoxes of novels about childhood, memoirs and fictional versions of the 'tenuous links and faint reverberations' of the self and he repudiates these. In an aside he toys with another way of exploring the self.

(I must one day satisfy my curiosity, though, about their theory of the Interstitial Plain: the subject of an eccentric branch of geography; a plain that by definition can never be visited but adjoins and offers access to every possible plain.) (p.86)

This Godelian intuition of the Interstitial Plain, which is behind all his work, later becomes both the form and the content of Landscape with Landscape. Here in The Plains, his patron's preferred theory is Time, the Opposite Plain, but the narrator suspects this is a decoy theory, while he privately investigates his own theory, having become 'one of those doctrinal solitaires aware of a Time whose true configurations only they perceive' (p.88). Murnane engages in some literary self-parody, as he talks of the impatience of critics and readers with those who 'have made their private labyrinths of Time the settings for their poetry and prose' (p.88).

Again the fiction shifts ground suddenly, moving into a self-enclosed sequence of speculation about the patron's wife who, each afternoon, comes to the library to the section where the books on Time are housed, a section he himself was once tempted to visit. He considers the relationship of husband and wife, the loneliness of the wife living with a man 'who still had not explained himself' (p.92). She reads what Other Australia calls novels, but here on the plains are works of philosophy written by 'vindicators of the evanescent' (p.93), who are also 'philosophers of the lost' (p.94). With the kind of superb elliptical reasoning that is characteristic of Murnane, the narrator begins to speculate on how to make contact with the wife. Months pass as he muses on how to break the silence between them, and considers writing a short book which could be lodged on the shelves she visits. Contingent problems nag at this plan, but he decides that if all between them existed only as a set of possibilities, his aim should be to broaden the scope of her speculations about him. He wants their relationship to be unrestricted by common notions of time and space. He imagines her discovering catalogue references to his book, but he finally abandons the whole project because he is too troubled by the possibility of her writing a book to explain herself to him. He realizes that his meditating on the possibilities between them has itself disturbed the poise of the worlds around them and betrayed both their putative selves. From then he avoids the section where the books on Time are housed, because of 'a fear, perhaps unreasonable, of finding myself beguiled by images of what almost came to pass.' (p.101). Prefering an ascetic abnegation from ideas of Time, the film-maker has echoes of his patron, both 'doctrinal solitaires' eschewing accepted theories of Time. But this tentative conjunction of the film-maker and his patron is a prelude to the conflict between them.

After the almost hypnotic rhythms of the narrator's speculation about the wife and the dangers of Time there is a sudden climactic sequence as the narrator describes the monthly 'dusks'. To these meetings in the main drawing room, the patron invites celebrated guests, some of the famous recluses of the plains. The narrator senses in these men

GERALD MURNANE

a quiet dedication to proving that the plains are not what many plainsmen take them for. They are not, that is, a vast theatre that adds significance to the events enacted within it. Nor are they an immense field for explorers of every kind. They are simply a convenient source of metaphors for those who know that men invent their own meanings. (p.104)

This is an extraordinary moment, a sudden denial of all that the plains have come to represent to us. It is a shock, a moment of tension and suspense, that Murnane springs on the unsuspecting reader. But what then is the effect on the narrator, as even the plainsmen deny the reality of the plains and assert that the plains are only a convenient source of metaphor? It is a measure of how deeply we are entangled in Murnane's vision at this point, that this sequence is so disturbing. If the reader is shocked, how does the film-maker cope? Surely the film-maker will not accept that? Some critics have accepted this scene as the point of surrender – the moment of conceding the plains are only metaphor. Neither the film-maker nor Murnane makes any such concession.

The film-maker suggests that this is a viewpoint to which he is regularly subjected in these monthly meetings. Sitting among the celebrated plainsmen in the twilight, he understands their silence to assert that the world is something other than a landscape. He wonders morosely whether anything he has seen is a fit subject for art. And he suspects the truly perceptive plainsmen are those who turn their faces away from the plains. This runs counter to everything the film-maker believes: surely he will not surrender so easily. In his own stubborn way, with all the intransigence of his vision of the plains, the narrator continues

yet the next morning's sunrise dispels these doubts, and at the moment when I can no longer look at the dazzling horizon I decide that the invisible is only what is too brightly lit. (p.104)

His momentary doubts in the twilight are quickly discounted and the reality of the plains is defiantly re-asserted: 'the invisible is only what is too brightly lit'. The film-maker resumes his project, insisting that his only significant difficulty is the daughter's understanding of the role she must play in his project.

In the delicate movement of this novel, the sequence of twilight

325

doubt becomes itself a coda, heralding the climactic movement of
the novel. It jolts us into the process of extricating us from the plains
and shifting our perspective on them. At the start of the third part,
the narrator concedes that the library is not always a secure refuge
and that he is now more aware of the hills than he was in earlier
years, outside his window the hills where the five creeks rise, the
'false hillocks and hollows' he left behind in other Australia. He puzzles over the hills and is reminded that he is now in a district where
people often lose sight of intervening features in their concern for
the larger plains. The books in the library confuse him too, because
the categories follow a different system of classification from the conventions of the plains. He begins to wonder whether all his
investigations have been mere glances at the deceptive surfaces of plains.

Here starts the real siege of the plains, with the narrator the lone
defender, deserted even by his patron. The defence of the plains is
rendered in a superb counterpoint, which takes us back to the central proposition of the novel – that it is possible to represent the inner
landscape in art. The film-maker's chosen medium is visual, the film
of 'The Interior'. To reach this, Murnane takes us out of the library
and the house into the open spaces. We go on a 'scene', a family
picnic, where the patron spends much of the afternoon taking photographs. His photographs are designed to show up an absurd
error – the disregarding of change such that all they see in the photograph has already ebbed away into darkness. If the visible world
was anywhere it was somewhere in that darkness. Even the plains
can be blotted out by darkness, he tells the narrator: 'We're disappearing through the dark hole of an eye that we're not even aware
of'(p.113) and, in apparent self-mockery, he takes some more photos,
with his camera 'that renders things invisible' (p.113). He warns the
narrator he has always credited the plainsmen with too much subtlety and assumed they are privy to sights he himself is searching
for, but even the most perceptive of them has never asked precisely
what the plains *are*. He warns him not to be deceived and insists
that nothing they say that day exists apart from the darkness.

This is the great siege. How can the narrator contend with this
challenge to his beloved plains? A challenge from his own patron,
a direct and personal challenge to the strength of his own belief in
the plains. The answer is beautifully rendered as Murnane shifts us
round from the visible of film to the visible of fiction, to the Lie

of fiction. None of the photographs seem to represent what was real at the time and the narrator feels no connection with them. Instead he explores the word. At the annual revelations, where he is expected to present the best of his recent projects, he presents an empty projector and a blank screen – and words. Later he discards the screen. He considers changing his profession to become a novelist or landscaper, but his audiences are untroubled by such distinctions, trusting that

the more I strove to depict even one distinctive landscape – one arrangement of light and surfaces to suggest a moment on some plain I was sure of – the more I would lose myself in the manifold ways of words with no known plains behind them. (p.125)

He is last seen taking his awkward grip on an antiquated camera and staring obligingly at some empty zone ahead of him:

No one afterwards could point to a single feature of whatever place I stared at. It was still a place out of sight in a scene arranged by someone who was himself out of sight. But anyone might have decided that I recognised the meaning of what I saw. (p.126)

This last sight of the film-maker is inside a photograph taken by his patron, a photograph of the moment

when I lifted the camera to my face and stood with my eye pressed against the lens and my finger poised as if to expose to the film in its dark chamber the darkness that was the only visible sign of whatever I saw beyond myself. (p.126)

The last vision of the novel is of the film-maker poised to expose his inner landscape, his beloved plains, to the film, while his patron is filming him. This is not the work of a man who surrendered the plains on the word of a few celebrated plainsmen in drawing room twilight. They might concede that the plains are 'simply a convenient source of metaphors for those who know that men invent their own meanings'. We might, but Murnane does not. Nor does the film-maker, who is still the solitary defender of the plains, warding off the besieging outer reality.

The Plains has no end and it loops inside itself up and down levels of meaning and visions which are never fixed and closed. It establishes its own parameters of time and space, its own co-ordinates and its own 'real, that is spiritual, geography'. In the paradox of the Lie of fiction, the film-maker is under the hand of Murnane, inside the dimensions of his interior landscape, moving freely through the house of his patron and through the years of his work. At the same time, the plains are an objective correlative of the centre of Australia, the grand vast sweep of its centre, with the ordinary world clinging to its edges. Like Thomas Livingstone Mitchell on his expeditions into the interior of eastern Australia, quoted at the start of the novel, 'We had at length discovered a country ready for the immediate reception of civilised men'. All of us, readers and other explorers, can journey across its plains and, as we travel, pass by the house of the film-maker's patron and perhaps glimpse Gerald Murnane at the window, making notes, perhaps under the heading, *Landscape with Landscape*.

Behind *Landscape with Landscape* is a contest between the painter's landscape and the writer's landscape – a talismanic landscape shimmering beyond the horizon of the real, with Murnane in constant trek across the spaces stretching towards it. Here the battle in *The Plains* is turned around. Instead of the film-maker searching for a visual image of the plains and resorting to words, here the narrator is a writer struggling with words and marvelling at the apparent ease of the visual image. Except that the landscape of the artist, the one who paints the real landscape he sees outside him, is just the surface – and not the real landscape at all. The real landscape is the one which is contained in the Interstitial Plain of vision, which adjoins and gives access to all the others. The Interstitial Plain intimated in *The Plains* becomes both the form and the content of *Landscape with Landscape* – a Godelian hierarchy, where levels normally conceived as hierarchical intersect, each crossing to the next. Each story opens out of its predecessor, each one implanted in a crevice in the previous one, in a strange Loop which is never ending. Like Escher's *Waterfall* or the monks endlessly ascending and descending, the six 'stories' of *Landscape with Landscape* never end but continually open into the next one, and the last into the first.

In her excellent article on *Landscape with Landscape*, Penny Hueston talks about this narrative loop and the 'literary optical illusion' suggested by the title

a book about a writer writing a book in which an artist paints a landscape in which we see a writer . . . But then, in his despairingly cerebral way, our nameless anchorite-like narrator constantly confounds himself, and us, by seeing himself in some 'blank middle distance' of his own landscape.[4]

The six stories are set in interstices of each other, offering access to each other and together creating a shape to match the contours and topography of his private landscape. Together they make up a novel – that is, if we conceive the form as a Tangled Hierarchy, wherein each face is a refraction of the whole, each one set in an aperture of another. Each 'story' or level of the novel has the same distinctive voice, immediate, poignant, close, a voice which is private but has also the cadences of the writer's perennial quest for the elusive world behind his eyes, the vast and foreign country of his own landscape, which is made up of all the hierarchical levels of the novel.

One level is Melbourne, its real places and suburbs, Fitzroy, Brunswick, Sorrento, Carlton, Harp Gully, from the period of the 18 year old clutching his Housmanesque solitude inside the Public Service through the next twenty years of searching for the beginning of his own landscape. But lying across the face of Melbourne from the 1950s to the 1980s is another city and another level, the 'whole continent spread out inside me'. Through the flickering landscapes of the stories, Murnane creates a prismatic image of Melbourne, with his own landscape lying in the hollows and suburbs of the city. The city is also his city, a city of words. The two cities, Melbourne and his city of words, are built on the paradox of seeing landscape clearly while standing inside it. Another level is journeys, real and putative. He contemplates his restless quest around Melbourne in the 1950s and 1960s, his planned Kerouac-style pilgrimage to Queensland, his trips to and from Harp Gully and the artists' community there, there to ponder on their visual landscape and marvel at the ease of their rendering it. There are numerous journeys and crossings in and out of his private landscape, mapping out a private city with suburbs and districts spaced according to his own private co-ordinates, a Melbourne of his own in the crevices and interstices of the real city.

A third level is his continuing quest for the woman who will become his reader and understand his writing, and see his landscape. Thus love and fiction are the joint romantic quests of his existence, somehow comically confused and confusing. His yearning to see a woman's landscape becomes a sexually mysterious program. A fourth level is now, the vantage point on the past where moments jut out inconsolably, rising up stubbornly to become a reciprocal vantage point on the present. Murnane crouches low and peers back at the space and the time he has traversed, the past criss-crossed with his journeys and his treks. The writing is spare, pared down, strong and allusive, at times almost painfully candid, yet wryly ironic, self-deprecating and self-parodying. The narrator has the dignity of an almost brutal candour as he regards himself over a twenty-year period, seeing again with the exquisite pain of remembrance, his own bumbling, awkward self, warding off the real world to meet the larger claims of his private landscape. Yet another level is the overtly fictive one, in which Murnane creates an obvious fiction of the most extraordinary journey in a work criss-crossed with journeys. In the centre piece, 'The Battle of Acosta Nu' Murnane sets up a private landscape through a refraction of the historical quest of the Paraguayan settlers in search of an ideal world. With a quick flick of the Lie, as deft as the one in the short story, 'Land Deal', Murnane turns this round to a dream of Australia and Australians, exiles amid the alien Paraguayan culture. This sequence is a powerful vision of exile and the dream of finding true compatriots of his own sacred land, amid the alien and foreign world of the real. There is a haunting loneliness and isolation in this story, refracted through its fantastic fiction.

But the most stubborn and talismanic level is the horizon in front of him, the one he is journeying towards but which constantly shifts, opening up more and more horizons. The movement of the narrative enacts this, with the Loop taking us back through all its levels, opening up more and more inner horizons. At his most vulnerable moments, the narrator insists that he is speaking of a character in a work of fiction and thus he is also the author of the fiction – and his statement of this is fiction too. This is the Liar's elaborate artifice, a strategy designed to protect himself with a cladding of fiction. It is also the paradox of vision which is the setting of the whole novel – at the edge of the furthest of all landscapes, the place the writer once

looked at before he composed his book, the beginning of the landscape inside the fiction.

The crossings from one level to another within the six stories are
extraordinarily complex, with an inner spiralling that becomes a literary whorl. Out of the first, the second opens, 'Sipping the Essence',
a kind of self-parodic variation on the dialogue with the Freckled
Woman. His dialogue with Carolyn remains putative in a sense, hidden behind the literary statements by which he couches his feeling
for her. The last story is in close bond with the first too – as the
narrator dances around behind the stained glass of the Artist's landscape, dappled like the freckles on the woman's skin in the first story.

Freckles are 'the landmarks of a particular skin' (p.4), which grow
inevitably from the depths beneath the skin like the unique mottled
and freckled surface of the real world. In 'Landscape with Freckled
Woman', the narrator is at a committee meeting with nine women
and, in an imagined discourse, is representing his private landscape
to one of them. Anticipated in the landowners' dialogue in *The Plains*,
this is incisive and pared down, a story which sets up the space and
time co-ordinates of the whole novel and ensnares the reader. He
imagines creating for the woman who will be his reader the story
of his past and his 'genestran' mood, struggling to construct a fiction on the blank page before him which is the foreground of a
remarkable tract of country, with its own landmarks and strange
contours. Behind the surface places of Fitzroy and St Kilda, Murnane begins to map out the co-ordinates of his own city, its suburbs
and districts sized and spaced according to the intensity of his feeling, driving to its margins the shrivelled remains of places where
feeling failed him.

For a few days, with his back to the window and the chocolate factory,
he felt that he himself might have had the shape of a far-reaching city.
What had once seemed the vaguest part of him – his dreams and imaginings – were the hub of its intricate network, and he had only to shrug
his shoulders or wag his fingers to upset the tiny mountains or to stop
the trickle of sea at its edges. (p.13)

While he gropes for the words to found his city, he conceives a notion
of landscape lying within some broad but invisible zone of himself
and he holds on to this notion of his own city inside the narrative

of the discovery of landscape. When his first novel is published, it is 'not itself a landscape, but it marked out the space around him where a landscape could have been' (p.20). The narrator conceives of himself reaching out to touch the horizon between the present and the past's pre-figuring of the present, but it vanishes as he reaches for it. He is left in the interstices, groping for the point at which the real world and his landscape intersect. Towards the end of the committee meeting, he sees the absurdity of talking to the freckled woman about the real world, because the notion of fiction intervenes and he realizes

There was only one situation in which such a woman could be taken as speaking truthfully. If I were to write a work of fiction with a freckled woman as a character in it, then I, in the person of the narrator, might insert in the fiction such words as 'she answered truthfully, at last . . .' (p.24).

Thus Murnane begins *Landscape with Landscape* with the insistence that the Lie, the Liar's paradox, is the only truth. His city too becomes the only real Melbourne, his landscape the only reality.

Some stories are more personal and biographical than others and Murnane provides the contours of an autobiography through fragments and glimpses on the surface of the whole novel. Beneath that is the creation of the real landscape, to which the biographical details are a surface counterpoint – a dappled surface with the details not always entirely consistent, so that the boundaries of fiction and reality are blurred, the crossing-point obscured. Some are more self-mocking than others. In 'Sipping the Essence', there is a cruel humour about the narrator's wooing of Carolyn, a courtship which seems to consist mainly of his delivering to her a series of prepared talks on literary giants, until his friend Kevin Durkin wins her. Inside the self-deprecating humour of his wooing of Carolyn and his marvelling at sexual mysteries, there is a tight stumbling pain, both in the past and in the present as he regards himself again. In 'Charlie Alcock's Cock', the narrator contemplates the pattern of his life and that of his priest-cousin as rival landscapes pitted against each other. From the afternoon under the dark screen of trees, they are rivals, both are interested in the dark spaces and the sacred mysteries of life. For the narrator, the dark spaces are 'a huge projection of some intricate pattern behind my eyes' (p.214), which he will spend his life exploring and interpreting – a pattern as sacred as any religious calling, with its rites and rituals, he the sole sacerdotal celebrant of his own numinous landscape. The sacredness of his calling, the vocation of landscape, is flipped over to its contrary in 'A Quieter Place Than Clun', where the narrator is 18 and torn between 'soul-silver' and 'skin-gold', between a Cistercian monastic possibility and the call of the flesh. Much of this story is set in Cheshires Bookshop in Melbourne in 1957, as he searches through Thomas Hardy, Housman, Jungian mandalas, peering through literary foliage at the real world, until the moment of epiphany: he murmurs the words 'literary landscape' 'as though I was naming my lost homeland, announcing a destination that I was about to make for, and explaining the oddness that others seemed to see about me' (p.133). It is the first glimpse of his homeland.

'The Battle of Acosta Nu' is the crucial sequence of the whole, where Murnane composes a fiction to set against his compositions of the real. It is a remarkable sequence because it is presented as a fiction, in a novel which alleges everything else in it is not fiction but the real. Here the narrator is an exile, searching through Paraguay for his compatriots, those who share his country of dreams. The quest for his Australian compatriots is a truly Borgesian paradox and dilemma because of the danger of comparing a continent almost wholly conjectured with someone else's conjecture about a place of the same name. He sees the routes of his journey to his sacred land as 'a pattern like those graphs of equations that tend towards but never reach a certain axis' (p.97). He is alone and besieged in the alien culture of Paraguay, 'a man with a vast and foreign land behind my face' and 'a whole continent was spread out inside me' (p.82). His hopes are vested in his son, whom he prepares for the revelation that he is an Australian, but the narrator fears punishment too for his years of spurning Paraguayans. When his son dies, he sees himself on the battlefield of Acosta Nu searching among the bodies of the dead children, searching for the mutilated corpse of his son. He realises finally that he is a Paraguayan, of the land for which his son died. Then he identifies the people around him as Australians.

They were the exiles: the people whose ancestors had travelled in search of an illusion, the people who still dreamed of a vague land they believed themselves shut out of. They were the exiles and I was the man who had come to his senses after all and stood, sure at last of his whereabouts, in his native land – in Paraguay. (p.122)

In this way the narrator turns the image of exile full circle. No longer the exile, he perceives that the people around him are exiles from the land he understands is his native land – the land of Paraguay, the land of the plains, his own landscape. It is a beautiful rendition of the siege of a consciousness which converts his loss into a triumphant and invincible assertion of his own native land.

As in all the stories, the next is anticipated but, in the spiral form of *Landscape with Landscape*, Murnane could have started at any point in the circular loop. In 'Charlie Alcock's Cock', the narrator refers to his first published piece of fiction, 'a story about a man who had travelled backwards and forwards over his territory whereas I had circled around my own' (p.214). As he continues to circle, the final story has the internal structure of the whole, with shifts of time and space and perception which refract the movement of the whole. In 'Landscape with Artist', there are echoes from the earlier stories, inside his continuing struggle to set down clusters of words from his private collection and so bridge the gap between himself and the real. He seeks still the horizon between the external landscape and the beginning of the landscape inside the writing. Here he is in the midst of the artists of Harp Gully, secretly despising them but envying their ability to find their subjects in the real world they inhabit – while he writes by stepping inside a painting and walking back to the furthest detail to see still further landscapes rising to view. There is a brilliant scene here of him dancing drunkenly on the verandah, to the song, 'Poetry in Motion', outside a stained glass window with a landscape. As he dances about, he hopes the Artist inside the room might glimpse the movement and at least for a moment wonder about the writer's landscape – the one set on the other side of the visual. It is a marvellous moment in Murnane's work, partly because it shifts the angle of vision around to show him 'at the head of an advancing landscape'. He sees

the landscapes of Harp Gully advancing over the hills to engulf the house where the arrogant artists have gathered. I station myself at the head of the advancing landscape, I, the only man on the hilltop who has tried to see twenty years of his life as a kind of landscape. (p.248)

At the end, there is this wondrous image of the narrator, the lone warrior out there defending his landscape, actually turning himself round to lead the forces against the narrow and arrogant vision of the Artists, the narrow landscape of the merely real. There is Murnane, triumphant and glorious, 'at the head of the advancing landscape'.

Before the novel continues its circle back to the beginning and 'Landscape of Freckled Woman', there is a disclaimer of fiction as there was in that 'first' piece. The narrator imagines himself writing a piece of self-conscious fiction but rejects the notion.

Yet I have read enough to know that such fiction would seem nowadays merely modish, that my self-conscious narrator would seem only a figure of artifice and not a means of telling the truth. And so I decide never to write such a story. And I keep to my decision. (p.267)

So the fiction will not be written. There will be no fiction, only the reality, only truth. The final paradox of vision is the Liar's paradox, a reassertion of the Lie of fiction. No lines here, no linear sequence. Instead, in a marvellous conundrum of shape – the shape of the vision, the shape of the Lie – in circles and loops and a spectral figure lightly brushing across the shimmering planes.

In a recent short story, 'Stone Quarry', Murnane writes about the Waldo school of fiction, with writers attending a Waldo workshop, where all communication is exclusively through prose fiction, the whole in monastic retreat and silence. Not a single apostasy has ever been recorded. Of all the schools he might have have joined, the narrator is drawn by

this earnest undertaking by Waldo writers to shape their sentences not according to habits of thinking in their own day but as though each writer is writing from a separate island just short of the notional beginning of the mainland.[10]

This workshop is in Melbourne, but the Waldo school originated in America and Murnane toys with the talismanic image, America, as a mirror of itself, as a page in a dream-atlas, America as a literary continent.

But of all the thousands of embellishments and verbal puzzles and aimless or fragmented roads and trails now added to America, what most appealed to the writers in the stone house was the simple notion of a Beautiful Plain as the primordial setting for fiction and the Handsome Plainsman as the original of all fictional characters, if not of all writers of fiction. (p.508)

Murnane's new novel, *Inland*,[11] has this primordial setting of the Beautiful Plain with the Plainsman as the original of all characters – and perhaps writers. But here he glides from Plain to Prairie, from Melbourne to the dream-prairies of the vast inland regions of the globe. The notional beginning of *Inland* is Borgesian: none of us is any more than a figure in someone else's dream, ghost figures in a ghost of world. Ghost-images in the Lie, character becomes author and narrator becomes character, in a fiction with an extraordinary current of menace and intrigue, of forgery and truth.

In the opening pages of *Inland*, like the film-maker in his patron's house in *The Plains*, the narrator is on a vast estate, contemplating the plains from the library window, but this is his own manor house, where he lives with his wife, daughter, servants and farmhands. Here, in Hungary, in Szolnok County, he ponders on the letter he has received from his editor, Anne Kristaly Gunnarsen, who lives in America, in the South Dakota town of Ideal, where she is employed in the Calvin O. Dahlberg Institute of Prairie Studies.

The image of a dream-America has danced across Murnane's earlier work, but here, a new topography is appearing, in that vast and foreign place where characters live, receiving letters in the Magyar language from their editors. The new territorial expansion, takes in all the steppes and sveldts and prairies and grasslands of the world, a vast universal hinterland, from Transdanubia to America and its prairies, the South Dakota Institute and further on, to Buenos Aires, the steppes of Central Asia and the hinterland of the narrator's own Szolnok County. Beneath the establishing of new places and co-ordinates, the narrator is motionless, sitting in his library in Szolnok County, his a quietly murmuring voice which has no accent, no cadence of time, no urgency. He is critical of his own words, already turning back to re-examine them, troubled by them. From every view in every window in every manor house in Szolnok County can be seen a well-pole pointing at the sky from the sweep-arm well. He meditates on whether he remembers the well-pole or dreams it, and promises us he will try to distinguish between seeing and dreaming, and between dreaming of seeing and remembering. The promise of demarcation lures and intrigues. The Liar's promise. The Liar gives his word.

In his library on the Great Plain of Hungary the narrator reflects on his letter, comforted by finding on his table a few pages like these, in which his editor seeks his help in her candidature for the position of editor of 'Hinterland', the journal of the Institute of Prairie Studies. Pages from the prairies of America. Pages from a dreamer, written to the character of her dream, who is the narrator of the fiction written to us, in a delicately meditative narrative. But the Liar insists the pages we are reading are not 'the drifting pages of books', but real pages, written to a living woman.

This is a new configuration of Murnane's dream of the woman who will one day see his landscape. Born in Transdanubia, Anne is his editor and his translator, his correspondent from the Great Plain of America, working at the desk to which all the admirers of steppes and sveldts and prairies, all Plainsmen, are trying to find their way. Later, in a luminous sequence, the narrator becomes a spectral presence in the Institute, a sky-scraper with windows looking at prairies, true and false, on the Great Plain of America, a place of white marble and black glass and carpets of geranium-red. Into its carpets have been crushed all the pages in the parcels sent by the men of the grass-lands. The Institute has an enemy presence, the scientists of the prairies, who are not dreamers, who, like Anne's husband, Gunnar T. Gunnarsen, have no prairie dream.

Murnane suddenly subverts the measured movement by introducing menace and subterfuge – and a murder plot – when the narrator realizes the signature is forged, 'the penstrokes of someone who dreams hardly ever of grasslands'. He realizes the letter is the husband's plot on his life, that Gunnarsen, the Swede scientist, has always resented his existence and always wanted him dead, has always hated him because 'I see him and he cannot see me'. When Gunnar has learnt about Anne's past with the narrator, there will be no more letters from America. Anne would read the letter announcing the narrator's death, then write his epitaph to appear in the rear pages of 'Hinterland' among the reviews, the advertisements, requests for penfriends, all the notices about plains (definitely no mountains or sea-coasts).

An exquisite dilemma, the narrator who is the character confronts the possibility of his editor's being duped into believing him dead, by the machinations of a figure from the other side of reality. Outside the frame, Murnane the Liar, drawing the image of his own death by lies. But is it so? The only evidence of the murder plot is 'the penstrokes', the first strokes in a maze of suspicion. What to do? Perhaps move deeper and deeper into his own landscape, closer to the horizon beyond the horizon, the one with the numinous haze which is where he celebrates his Lie? Or perhaps accept his death? Assenting to his 'death', he writes his own obituary notice for the pages of 'Hinterland' and sends Anne a photograph of the family graveyard. He reflects on his death.

It is not easy to think of myself as a man who is thought of as dead. And perhaps this is what some writers do before they begin to write. They think of themselves as dead. Or they think of themselves as thought of as dead . . . . They died, or they thought of themselves as having died, or they thought of themselves as thought of as dead – and then they wrote. (p.24 MS)

A writer of books visits him at his manor and, in flick of vision, the two figures merge, diaphanous shades of each other. The narrator pretends to be a writer of books, and the writer pretends to be a man who looks out the windows of his library in a manor house in Szolnok County. Identities slide between the dreamer and the other, already writing, already dead. In this fiction about the life of fiction, Murnane proposes writers as ghosts exploring ghost-images, writing in the language of ghosts, seeing ghosts of images of pages, drifting over ghosts of plains in a ghost of a world.

But the pages the narrator is writing now are not ghost–images but true, addressed to the enemy presence, the forger.

I have been writing about myself dreaming. I have been writing only to confuse you, Gunnarsen. I have confessed nothing. Read on, Gunnarsen, and learn what kind of man I am in fact. Read the true story, forger. (p.32 MS)

What is the true story? In the first part of the novel, Murnane explores putative and marginal selves, so that it seems the whole novel will be an elaborate kaleidoscope, a dazzling image of the composite self. Reaching out for notions of enemy interference, he examines each self in turn: first his editor; then her husband, the visiting writer of books; then the woman from Nebraska who will pretend to be his editor; then the man from the Institute archives, who may be the enemy-forger after all. The self is as multi-foliate as the flora patterned through the novel, a self set in the vast prairies of the world, but bearing a haunting sense of loss. The gang of scientists works to restore the virgin prairie and the narrator's editor contemplates her virgin prairie, each one, in a series of locations, playing out possibilities of loss and recovery of the narrator's innermost self.

At the same time, Murnane suggests the reader is shifting and turning too. Sometimes the reader is directly addressed, sometimes a hostile presence, sometimes critical, sometimes a third person presence. The reader also becomes another face of the composite self of the narrator, so that he is his own interlocutor in a beautiful play of dialogue. Meanings shift and turn throughout, like the motif running through the rest of the novel, 'no thing in the world is one thing'. (p.52 MS) Every person is more than one person, every place more than one,

the chief pleasure of my life, which is to see two places I had thought far apart lying in fact in one place—not simply adjoining one another but each appearing to enclose or even to embody the other. (p.113 MS)

Each word is more than one word, with elusive, contestant meanings lying underneath the surfaces of words.

In this part of the novel, the narrator seems the still point of a turning world, his marginal selves swirling around him, making claims of consciousness on him, while he, the sentinel self, stares out of the library window. Amid all the geographical patterns and shifts of the novel, vast journeys of space and time, the narrator is motionless in the hinterland of himself, pining for his reader but afraid of imposters in the glass-walled Institute, of enemy readers intruding on his territory for their own inimical purposes.

Murnane moves closer to Gunnar momentarily, shifting the notion of scientists by considering himself as a scientist, first of grasslands, then or words, language and patterns, then a scientist of his own writing. The novel is both mapping out a physical journey and exploring new territories of his own self. Behind the narrative there is siege.

I am not sorry for you, reader, if you think the worst. I can hardly forget the trick that you played on me. You caused me to believe for a long time that I was writing to a young woman I called my editor. Safe in the depths of your glass-walled Institute, you even had me addressing you as reader and friend. Now, you still read and I still write but neither of us will trust the other. (pp.48-9 MS)

Still distrustful but defiant, the narrator leads the reader on a journey, beyond Climax, beyond the Great Divide, to the other side of the watershed, to a district at the edge of the land. This is the turning point of *Inland* and from here, Murnane sheds most of the Institute material, sloughing off that framework like a territory left behind, on the other side of the watershed. The narrative now moves into the autobiographical mode, the narrator's adolescent years, opening with his grandmother's house, the caravan park and the girl from Bassett. It is an uneasy transition, in spite of Murnane's more urgent addresses to the reader. There is a sense of extricating himself from a complex but exciting narrative, shrinking back from the most urgent drive of the opening material. He retains the pattern of reader address, which quickens the sense of internal dialogue, but, with an almost audible, writerly sigh of relief, reverts to the kind of autobiographical material he has written in earlier novels. Once again, he writes such material well, with poignancy and wry, warm humour, but he has lost something there too, and although parts of the narrative remain densely textured, the rest of the novel is disappointing.

Clinging to the novel is a haunting sense of death, as though Murnane were enquiring into the Magyar heaviness of his own mortality. Driven right back into the recesses of himself—the furthermost reaches of his own inland zone—he conducts a dialogue about death and about survival with a series of selves, the ultimate of which is the reader. At the end, there is a lingering sense of grief, with the narrator weeping over a grave in the place where 'all my lives, actual or conjectured, will end' (p.180 MS). He weeps as he does for the end of a man or a woman in a book he has just read to its end, hearing the silence of death. But in the coda before this scene, before the last solemn themes toss themselves against the storm, the narrator has learnt that a reader need not be alive, that he is his own reader. His grief finally is for the closure of the other world, the one mirrored in the pages of a book,

a place that can only be seen or dreamed of by those people known to us as narrators of books or characters within books. If you or I, reader, happen to glimpse part of that world drifting past, as it were, it is because we have seen or dreamed of ourselves seeing for a moment as a narrator or a character in a book sees or dreams of seeing. (pp.112–3 MS)

But the novel carries finally the irony that Murnane seems to accept the enemy-archivist as the narrator's most substantial self. The second part of the novel is archival, retracing old journeys. Although the novel is a mapping of the self, in which the narrator plays cartographer and scientist of grasslands, explorer of the flora and of the silence that falls in the prairies of the self, it is finally a map in which Murnane has drawn back from the new uncharted territories with which he began *Inland*. He becomes instead a cartographer retracing his passage through areas already mapped.

Inland begins as a delicate play of Lie and truth, flickering from character to writer to editor to reader, ghost-images in a ghost of a world. Refracting their images across the vision of the narrator, the two worlds coincide, but are in impossible rivalry, each ready to supplant the other if Murnane relaxes his vigilance. In the contest of the Lie, Murnane is the lone contestant engaged in the battle of all his fiction, in urgent converse with the reality waiting to break through his Lie and destroy it. All Murnane's Lies are subtle and delicate, as if we are looking into a spiral of mirrors, from which the Liar plucks the most distant and elusive image and, by some sleight of hand, holds it close and sings through it. The Liar at the head of his own advancing landscape, dancing his own celebration and singing his own Lie inside the numinous haze which is the only reality, the only truth.

TENTH DIALOGUE

Reader So the whole of *Inland* proceeds in an atmosphere of mutual distrust. Beware impostors. Beware enemy-readers. All those who dwell in the glass-walled Institute, behind the sheen of black glass.

Liar I find it moving, particularly in the first part, because of this plangent fear of you.

Reader He is very suspicious, as though I might wrest the meaning from his words.

Liar Or use his writings for your own false purposes. He has to be wary. He's searching through the Institute in the hope of finding a true reader. Perhaps you're not a true reader.

Reaer Yes but he's also negotiating with himself as reader.

Liar Safer that way. He's fearful of enemies within, who might crush his words into the carpet and announce his death in the pages of its journal. Less risk if he plays his own reader.

Reader You and I are almost one here, both conjectured selves, inside a maze of suppositions and conjectures.

Liar All the marginal selves in crevices. Don't forget: 'no thing in the world is one thing'. No person, no place. Each place, each time, each person, encloses another. All on congruent planes.

Reader A Tangled Hierarchy. A new map of time and place.

Liar Yes! Exactly, and not just with Murnane. A new map of the Lie. We can redraw the map of Australia. A Liars' Map! Look, in the centre you'd have Murnane on the plains or in his library, while outside his window Alethea the leopard runs past in savage full-pelt freedom. Trap would be here, look, heading for the mission and bumping into William Wort over here, see, at Orebul Downs. Then here we'd have

Carey's soldier guarding the border between east and west. And over there the *Batavia* wreck.

Reader What about the cities? It'll need to be very detailed. The Pet Shop in Sydney, Holden Shadbolt in Manly, Adelaide, Canberra, Trap down here in Fitzroy, the Puroil refinery in Sydney, the man with the blue guitar, Billie Shockley in her flat . . . How are you going to show her City?

Liar It'll have to be an Escher map of course. And out in the countryside, D'Arcy D'Oliveres in Dog Rock, Herbert Badgery in the Western district, Moonlite on the goldfields with Sunbeam, Miss Peabody writing in a convalescent home, Leon searching for the Bellarmine Jug on the west coast, Harry Joy in a commune, Percy Wort careering around on the Norton, Holden driving the Minister all over the Interior, Miss Porch looking across the grasslands near the College. I can see it all. What a map!

Reader What about overseas? Bail's tourists in Africa, Ecuador, London, Christian Rosy Cross in Rhodes and Damascus, the Plumbum rock band in India, Hasluck's travellers in quarantine in the Middle East. Miss Peabody in London searching for Miss Arabella Thorne. Then other Jolley people in Vienna. Foster's twins in Venice. Murnane's editor in Ideal. Leon in Holland . . .

Liar You'd have to work out some way of showing planes of time. Time's a problem.

Reader A problem! How are you going to show the time differences? It can't be done.

Liar I'll think of something. Some underlying plane perhaps, and crossing points. I don't have to worry about time. Or space for that matter. I can just Lie. I can borrow Bail's theodolite or Ireland's Perspex prism. Anyway, as long as I've got the base matter, I can use Foster's furnace.

Reader But the map would have to show itself. I mean, if it's a real map, it would have to be detailed enough to show itself. You'd have to have a map showing the map showing the map . . . and so on. To infinity. It's not easy.

Liar Maybe we can work out a circular map, one that keeps going back to the starting point. Some kind of Loop.

Reader But you need an accompaniment of voices too. A contrapuntal form. A fugue, perhaps?

Liar Maybe that's it! Do you remember in *Trap*, when David David is pondering on Effect X – Trap produces Effect X, so Adamov becomes X and he himself becomes David David Adamov X?

Reader Yes I do. What are you getting at?

Liar If you kept that going, imagine Fugue X . . . A fugue of Liars! An eight part fugue, beginning with Mathers, then Foster, then Ireland (still keeping the Mathers and Foster voices going), then Carey (now keeping Mathers, Foster, and Ireland going), then add Jolley (now keeping Mathers . . .) and so on. Building up a fugue of Lying voices . . .

Reader So, by the end of Murnane, you're carrying seven other voices already, and he returns us to the first.

Liar And he can take us back to back to back to Mathers, back to the start. Each writer is a level, a stratum, a voice in a Tangled Hierarchy of 'authors', through which each level mirrors its metalevel . . . The Liars' Fugue. Fugue X.

Reader Fugue X? That's not Fugue X. Effect X is you and me together, but you've left out the readers. And that makes it impossible, mathematically impossible. It can't be done.

Liar Why not?

Reader Writing a six-part fugue is like playing sixty games of chess simultaneously and blindfold, winning them all. An eight-part fugue is beyond human capability. If you draw readers into it too, it's impossible.

Liar I don't see why. If I can conceive the idea of Fugue X, I don't accept that it is beyond human capability.

Reader Of course not. You're a Liar. You're not confined by reality.

Liar Are you suggesting I'm not a realist? That's like you were saying before, that Liars are not honest . . .

Reader What do you mean you're a realist?

Liar Of course I'm a realist. I write real. All Liars are realists, but of course not all realists are Liars. The point is, this is what reality is all about. The problem of illusion. I'm a realist. Existence is a Lie. The Lie is the New Realism.

Reader I was right. Borges did come to Australia.

Liar Look the Lie's been going on here for more than twenty-one years. You said yourself it all started in 1966, with *Trap*. Effect X is already more than 21 years old, mature, with its own independent existence, its own power and authority.

Reader Ready to take its place in world literature.

Liar No, more than ready. It has already taken its place in the world, made its mark. And we worked out independently that existence is a Lie. Even though Borges certainly got there before us. What did he say?

We have dreamt the world. We have dreamt it as firm, mysterious, visible, ubiquitous in space and durable in time; but in all its architecture we have allowed tenuous and eternal crevices of unreason which tell us it is false.

Reader We are all figures in someone else's dream.

HD Excuse me, sorry to disturb you. May I join for a few moments?

Liar Certainly not, this is a private conversation. I'm sorry. You'll have to wait. No interlopers. Who are you anyway?

Reader You're not a critic, are you? We don't want critics here.

HD No, certainly not. I'm just a reader. An interested reader, but I have played a part in all this. Just wanted to introduce myself. My name's Helen, Helen Daniel. This is my manuscript.

Liar What do you mean, *your* manuscript? It's ours. We've been hand in hand throughout it.

HD I'm the one behind all this. The third hand, the one outside the frame.

Reader The Pig Tyrant Daniel.

HD No, not at all. I don't think that's fair. I haven't subjected you to any of the horrors Echion suffered. Just a little dialogue.

Liar But you're going to do something to us ... What is it? Stop us talking? Silence us?

HD No, that's not so. In fact, I'm rather disappointed that you have such an idea. Do you think this is all linear? After all we've been through together, do you really think it can stop, that there's an end? I can't silence you and I certainly don't want to. No, I simply want to reassure you. There's no need for you to stop. In fact, you haven't much choice. You're bound to continue.

Reader Because *you* say so?

HD Of course not. It's up to you. As long as you continue to write.

Reader This is ridiculous. You've got us mixed up! That's the Liar there. I'm the Reader. This is absurd. If, as you say, this is your manuscript, how could you possibly get us mixed up? Unless you're an impostor ... Or a liar.

HD I'm no impostor, I'm just a writer like you. Surely by now you realize every reader rewrites what he reads? You've heard of Pierre

346

Menard ... the author of *Don Quixote*. Don't you remember Borges saying that the book by Cervantes and the book by Menard are verbally identical, but the second is almost infinitely richer? Of course you're a writer. Call it Effect X ... if you prefer. I heard you talking about it a moment ago.

Reader All right, if I'm the writer, who's that?

HD Depends how you look at things. Liar, character in the Lie, character in my reading, partner in your dialogue, another writer, your collaborator ... It's all tangled together in a hierarchy of levels. A Loop.

Reader After all we've been through, you mean this is a Loop?

HD Of course, there is no end. There is no way out. Baroque, isn't it? Just a moment, while I switch on the record-player. Hear this? It's part of Bach's *A Musical Offering*. You know, Bach used to remind his pupils, that the separate parts in their compositions should behave like 'persons who conversed together in a select company'. Hear the voices? And look, I just happen to have a few jottings on Godel's theorem here too ...

And see that print on the wall, the Escher one, *Drawing Hands* ... ? By the way, I'd like you to meet a friend of mine. He's waiting to join us. Is it O.K. if I bring him in? ... Good, this is Mr. Epimenides. He's from Crete. When we were talking earlier, he mentioned to me that all Cretans are liars. Does that seem paradoxical to you?

NOTES

NOTE TO INTRODUCTION: *THE LIAR'S PARADOX*

1. The material here on 'The Liar's paradox' and on the work of Escher is based on the start of Douglas Hofstadter's book, *Godel, Escher, Bach: An Eternal Golden Braid*, Vintage Books, New York 1980.

NOTES TO PRELUDE: *THE LOGIC OF THE LIAR*

1. See 'Schrodinger's Cat', in Heinz R. Pagels: *The Cosmic Code: Quantum Physics as the Language of Nature*, Pelican, 1984.
2. For example, Walker Percy: 'The Diagnostic Novel: On the Uses of Modern Fiction', in *Harper's Magazine*, June 1986, p.41.
3. John Berger, *Ways of Seeing*, B.B.C. & Penguin 1983, pp.16–17.
4. Sarraute, *Tropisms and The Age of Suspicion*, trans. Maria Jolas, John Calder, London, 1963, pp.84, 93–4.
5. Jean Franco, *An Introduction to Spanish American Literature*, Cambridge University Press, 1969, p.361.
6. Introduction to Don Anderson (ed.) *Transgressions*, Penguin 1986, p.ix.
7. quoted Martin Stabb, *Jorge Luis Borges*, Griffin Author Series, St. Martin's Press, New York, 1970, p.87.
8. *Godel, Escher, Bach: An Eternal Golden Braid, op.cit*, p.706.
9. *Illywhacker*, University of Queensland Press, 1985, p.549.

NOTES TO PETER MATHERS: *ALARUMS AND EXCURSIONS*

1. *The Wort Papers*, all references to Penguin edition, 1973, pp.14, 17.

2. From the interview by Laurie Clancy, in *Australian Literary Studies*, Vol.8, No.2, October 1977.
3. 'How It Is' Owen Webster (ed.), *Disenchantment*, Goldstar, Melbourne, 1972.
4. Owen Webster, in review of *The Wort Papers*, *Overland*, No.57, Winter 1973.
5. D.J.O'Hearn: 'Re-Reading Peter Mathers', *Overland*, No.85, October 1981, pp.47, 49–50.
6. From the interview by Ken Linnett, 'The Reluctant Mathers Comes Out to Play', *The Melbourne Times*, 31 July, 1985.
7. Teresa Dovey: 'A Late Entry in the Uppersass Reporting Prize: Another "Writing" of Peter Mathers' *Trap* and *The Wort Papers*', *Southern Review*, Vol.17, No.2, July 1984, pp.200, 196.
8. Vincent Buckley: 'Peter Mathers' *Trap*', *Ariel*, Vol.5, No.3, July 1974,, pp.127, 118.
9. *Trap*, all references to the 1970 Sphere Books edition, pp.9–10.
10. Michael Wilding: 'Worts' World: The Great Australian Dream', *The National Times*, 15–20 January, 1973, p.18.
11. Gerard Windsor: Review of *A Change For The Better*, *Overland*, No.96, September 1984, p.67.
12. *A Change For The Better*, all references to the Words and Visions edition, Adelaide, 1984.

NOTES TO THIRD DIALOGUE

1. 'A Path for the Future Novel', in Alain Robbe-Grillet, *Snapshots and Towards a New Novel*, Barbara Wright (trans.) Calder and Boyars, London, 1965, pp.56–7.
2. 'The Physicist's Conception of Nature', quoted Matson, *The Broken Image: Man, Science and Society*, Doubleday Anchor, New York, 1966, pp.128–9.

NOTES TO DAVID FOSTER: *THE ALCHEMY OF THE LIE*

1. *The Adventures of Christian Rosy Cross*, all references to the King Penguin edition, 1986, pp.59–60.
2. Interview with Candida Baker, in *Yacker: Australian Writers Talk About Their Work*, Picador, 1986, pp.113, 119, 120ff.
3. Foster's 'Statement', in Frank Moorhouse, 'What happened to the

Short Story?', in *Australian Literary Studies*, Vol.8, No.2, October 1977, pp.196–7.

4. *The Pure Land*, all references to the Macmillan edition, 1974, p.3.

5. From an interview with Janet Hawley: 'Plumbing Rock Culture', *The Age*, 10 December, 1983.

6. *Moonlite*, all references to the Macmillan edition, 1981, p.47.

7. Michael Cotter's review of *Moonlite*, in *Overland*, No.88, July 1982, p.64.

8. Quoted in Harrison-Ford, 'The Applause Begins', in *The National Times on Sunday*, 7 September, 1986, p.38.

9. *Dog Rock*, all references to the Penguin edition, 1985, p.55.

NOTES TO FOURTH DIALOGUE

1. *The Life and Opinions of Tristram Shandy*, Penguin, 1967, p.127.

NOTES TO DAVID IRELAND: *DOUBLE AGENCIES*

1. *The Unknown Industrial Prisoner*, all references to the Angus and Robertson Classics edition, Sydney, 1973, pp.361–3.

2. Machado de Assis, 'The Psychiatrist', in Barbara Howes (ed.), *The Eye of The Heart: Short Stories from Latin America*, Avon, New York, 1973.

3. See Colin Roderick's review of *A Woman of the Future*, in *Townsville Daily Bulletin*, 4 June, 1980, and report in *The Courier Mail*, 'Winning Book "Sewage" – Judge', 6 June, 1980, p.2.

4. Details in *Double Agent*, Penguin, p.162, Note 17.

5. Published stories are 'The Bronze Overcoat', in *The Bulletin*, Centenary issue, 29 January, 1980, pp.180–7; 'The Wild Colonial Boy', in the *National Times*, 25–31 January, 1981, pp.25–7; 'Injections', in *The Bulletin*, Literary Supplement, 22–29 December, 1981, pp.172–7.

6. *The Chantic Bird*, all references to Angus and Robertson Classics edition, Sydney 1973, p.27.

7. David Porush, *The Soft Machine: Cybernetic Fiction*, Methuen, New York and London, 1985.

8. *A Woman Of The Future*, all references to Penguin edition, 1980, p.25.

9. *City of Women*, all references to Allen Lane edition, Penguin 1981, p.2.

10. *Bloodfather*, Penguin, 1987.

NOTES TO FIFTH DIALOGUE

1. Kurt Vonnegut, *Slaughterhouse Five*, Triad Panther, 1979, p.62–3.

NOTES TO PETER CAREY: *LIES FOR SALE*

1. In 'Peter Carey Speaking', Interview by Giulia Giuffre, 'Literary Magazine', *The Weekend Australian*, 6–7 July, 1985, p.3.
2. *Illywhacker*, all references to University of Queensland Press edition, 1985, p.11.
3. 'Concerning the Greek Tyrant', in *The Tabloid Story Pocket Book*, Michael Wilding (ed.), Wild and Woolley, Sydney, 1978, pp.191–205.
4. In 'How an Ad Man Found Bliss', Interview by Janet Hawley, *The Age*, September 26, 1981, p.26.
5. *The Fat Man in History*, all references to University of Queensland Press edition, 1974, p.114.
6. In 'Candid Carey', Interview by Carey's wife, Alison Summers, *The National Times*, 1–7 November, 1985, pp.32–3.
7. Interview with Candida Baker, in *Yacker: Australian Writers Talk About Their Work*, Picador, Sydney, 1986, pp.70, 71.
8. Interview by Frank Moorhouse, in 'What Happened to the Short Story?', *Australian Literary Studies*, Vol.8, No.2, October 1977, pp.182–7.
9. 'Bizarre Realities: An Interview with Peter Carey', by John Maddocks, *Southerly*, Vol.41, No.1, March 1981, pp. 27–40.
10. *War Crimes*, all references to University of Queensland Press edition, 1981, p.280.
11. *Bliss*, all references to the Picador edition, 1982, p.8.
12. Adrian Mitchell, 'Weaving a Tangled Web of Lovely Lies', review of *Illywhacker*, *The Weekend Australian*, 6 July, 1985.
13. See above review by Adrian Mitchell; and see reviews by Laurie Clancy (*Australian Book Review*, August 1985, pp.14–15); and John Hanrahan (*The Age*, 6 July, 1985).
14. *Oscar and Lucinda*, all references to MS, kindly lent to me by the author in September 1987.

NOTES TO SIXTH DIALOGUE

1. M. Escher 'Approaches to Infinity', in *The World of M. C. Escher*, J. C. Locher (ed.), Abrams, New York, 1971,

NOTES TO MURRAY BAIL: *THE GEOMETRY OF THE LIE*

1. *Homesickness*, all references to Macmillan edition, 1980, pp.258–60.
2. Quoted from the notebooks of A.I. Vvedensky (1904–1941), at the start of *Contemporary Portraits and Other Stories*, all references to U.Q.P. edition, St. Lucia, 1975.
3. From a written interview with the editors of *Going Down Swinging*, No.2, 1980, pp.38–45.
4. From an interview with Jim Davidson, in *Meanjin*, June 1982, pp.264–276.
5. From an interview with Stuart Sayers, *The Age*, 9 August, 1980.
6. Murray Bail's 'Statement', in Frank Moorhouse, 'What Happened to the Short Story?', in *Australian Literary Studies*, Vol.8, No.2, October, 1977, p.188.
7. There is an interesting comparison by Jim Legasse of 'The Drover's Wife' with Barthelme's story 'See the Moon?', in 'The Voice of the Form and the Form of the Voice', *Westerly*, Vol.25, No.1, March, 1980, pp.92–101.
8. 'Home Ownership', in Edward Leeson (ed.) *Winter's Tales 27*, Macmillan, London, 1981, pp.120–7.
9. From an interview with Michelle Field, in 'Bail's Grand Tour of the Ocker Quixotes', *The National Times*, 12–18 October, 1980, p.62.
10. Peter Pierce's review, 'Conventions of Presence', *Meanjin*, Vol.40, No.1, April, 1981, pp.107, 108.
11. Don Anderson's review of *Homesickness*, *Westerly*, Vol.25, No.4, December 1980, p.94.
12. All references to *Holden's Performance* from the Viking Penguin edition, 1987, p.268.

NOTES TO SEVENTH DIALOGUE

1. Italo Calvino, *Cosmicomics*, Abacus, 1982, pp.92–3.

NOTES TO NICHOLAS HASLUCK: *THE CASE AGAINST TRUTH*

1. 'The Whole Truth', in *The Hat on The Letter O*, all references to the Fremantle Arts Centre Press edition, 1978, p.127.

2. *On The Edge*, Freshwater Bay Press, Perth, 1980, p.37.
3. *The Bellarmine Jug*, all references to the Penguin edition, 1984, pp.140–1.
4. In 'Literary Magazine' *The Weekend Australian*, 6–7 July, 1985, p.8.
5. *Quarantine*, all references to the Macmillan edition, 1978, p.3.
6. *The Blue Guitar*, all references to the Macmillan edition, 1980, p.26.
7. *The Hand That Feeds You*, all references to the Fremantle Arts Centre Press edition, 1982, p.113.
8. Interview with Candida Baker in *Yacker*, Picador 1986, p.168. Other comments on the *grundnorm* arise from the transcript Hasluck kindly lent me, of 'Watergate Revisited', an address he gave at Latrobe University, 15 May, 1986.
9. In his review of *The Bellarmine Jug*, 'Even if you know the story, it's only half the story', *Sydney Morning Herald*, 11 August, 1984.
10. Jim Crace, 'In the Melting Pot', review of *The Bellarmine Jug*, *Times Literary Supplement*, 8 March, 1985.
11. From *Truant State*, all references to the Penguin edition, 1987, p.3.

NOTES TO EIGHTH DIALOGUE

1. Review of Alberto Manguel (ed.), *Other Fires*, Clarkson N. Potter, New York, 1986, in *The New York Times Review of Books*, 4 May, 1986, pp.35–6.
2. Isabel Allende, *The House of the Spirits*, Magda Bogin (trans.) Black Swan, U.S.A 1986.

NOTE TO ELIZABETH JOLLEY: *A LITERARY OFFERING*

1. *Mr Scobie's Riddle*, all references to Penguin edition, 1983, pp.22–3.
2. 'A Child Went Forth', in *Stories*, all references to the Fremantle Arts Centre Press edition, 1984, p.303.
3. Jolley discusses her childhood and the influence of her Quaker background in the interview with David Headon, *Meanjin*, Vol.44, No.1, March, 1985, pp.39–46.
4. In Author's Note, at the start of *Stories*.
5. 'Statement', *Australian Literary Studies*, Vol.10, No.2, October 1981, p.214.
6. Interview with Candida Baker, *Yacker*, Picador, 1986, pp.220, 223–4.

7. In *Frictions: An Anthology of Fiction by Women*, Anna Gibbs & Alison Tilson (eds), Sybylla, 1983.

8. *Palomino*, all references to 1980 Outback Press edition, p.136.

9. This story is in *Overland*, No.92, 1983 and in Don Anderson (ed.) *Transgressions*, Penguin, 1986.

10. Angela Carter's review of *Foxybaby*, in *The New York Review of Books*, 24 November, 1985, pp.1, 36.

11. *Foxybaby*, all references to the 1985 University of Queensland Press edition, pp.43–4.

12. *Miss Peabody's Inheritance*. All references to the 1983 University of Queensland Press edition, p.98.

13. Interview with Stephanie Trigg in *Scripsi*, July 1986, Vol.4, No.1, p.250.

14. *Milk and Honey*. All references to the 1984 Fremantle Arts Centre Press edition, p.57.

15. *Yacker*, *op. cit.* pp.222, 232.

16. *The Well*, all references to Viking Penguin edition, 1986, pp.9–10.

17. All references to MS of *The Sugar Mother*, kindly lent to me by the author in September 1987.

NOTES TO NINTH DIALOGUE

1. 'The Night Face Up' and 'Continuity of Parks' are in *End of The Game and Other Stories*, Collins and Harvill Press, London 1968, p.76.

NOTES TO GERALD MURNANE: *THE LANDSCAPE OF THE LIE*

1. *The Plains*, all references to Penguin edition, 1984, pp.1, 56.

2. *Landscape with Landscape*, all references to Norstrilia Press edition, 1985.

3. D. J. O'Hearn's review, 'In the Landscapes of the Mind', *The Age*, 21 August, 1982, pp. 165, 223.

4. Penny Hueston, 'Gerald Murnane: Landscape with Author', in *Scripsi*, Vol.3, Nos.2 & 3, August 1985, pp.64, 68.

5. Murnane, 'On the Road to Bendigo: Kerouac's Australian Life', *The Age Monthly Review*, Vol.6, No.1, May 1986, pp.3, 5.

6. Bruce Gillespie: 'Something Marvellous That No One Else Had Discovered: An Appreciation of *Tamarisk Row*' pp.31–46; and Gerald

Murnane, 'Other Eyes, Other Universes', pp.47–54, both in *Science Fiction Commentary*, Nos. 41 & 42, February 1975.

7. 'Land Deal', in Don Anderson (ed.) *Transgressions*, Penguin, Australia, 1986.

8. *Tamarisk Row*, all references to Heinemann edition, 1974, p.101.

9. John Tittensor, review of *A Lifetime on Clouds*, 'Looking Back on a Strange Breed of the Early Fifties', *The Age*, 4 December, 1976.

10. 'Stone Quarry', in *Meanjin*, Vol.45, No.4, December 1986, p.506.

11. Comments here are based on the MS of *Inland*, kindly lent to me by the author in September 1987.

SELECT BIBLIOGRAPHY

GENERAL: NON-AUSTRALIAN

ALTER, ROBERT. 'The Self-Conscious Moment: Reflections on the Aftermath of Modernism'. *Tri-Quarterly*, No.33, Spring 1975.

BERSANI, LEO. *A Future for Astyanax: Character and Desire in Literature*. Marion Boyars, London, 1978.

DAVIES, PAUL. *Other Worlds: Space, Superspace and the Quantum Universe*. Abacus, London, 1982.

FRANCO, JEAN. *An Introduction to Spanish American Literature*. Cambridge University Press, London, 1969.

GALLAGHER, D.P. *Modern Latin American Literature*. Oxford University Press, London, 1973.

GEDULD, HARRY M. (ed.). *Film Makers on Film Making*. Penguin, U.K. 1967.

GUERARD, ALBERT J. 'Notes on the Rhetoric of Anti-Realist Fiction', *Tri-Quarterly*. No.30, Spring 1974.

HOFSTADTER, DOUGLAS R. *Godel, Escher, Bach: An Eternal Golden Braid*. Vintage Books, New York, 1980.

———. 'Prelude . . . Ant Fugue', in *The Mind's I: Fantasies and Reflections on Self and Soul*. Composed and arranged by Hofstadter and Daniel C. Dennett, Penguin, U.K., 1982.

HUTCHEON, LINDA. *Narcissistic Narrative: The Metafictional Paradox*. Methuen, New York and London 1984.

LOCHER, J.C. (ed.). *The World of M.C. Escher*. Harry N. Abrams, New York, 1971.

MATSON, FLOYD W. *The Broken Image: Man, Science and Society*, Doubleday Anchor, 1966.

PAGELS, HEINZ R. *The Cosmic Code: Quantum Physics as the Language of Nature*, Penguin, 1984.
PERCY, WALKER. 'The Diagnostic Novel: On the Uses of Modern Fiction'. *Harper's Magazine*. June 1986, pp.39–45.
PORUSH, DAVID. *The Soft Machine: Cybernetic Fiction*. Methuen, New York and London, 1985.
ROBBE-GRILLET, ALAIN. *Snapshots and Towards A New Novel*. Calder and Boyars, London, 1965.
SARRAUTE, NATHALIE. *Tropisms and The Age of Suspicion*. John Calder, London, 1973.
SCHOLES, ROBERT, KELLOGG, ROBERT. *The Nature of Narrative*. Oxford University Press, London, 1968.
SONTAG, SUSAN. *Styles of Radical Will*. Delta, New York, 1970.
STABB, MARTIN S. *Jorge Luis Borges*. The Griffin Author Series, St. Martin's Press, New York, 1970.

GENERAL: AUSTRALIAN

ANDERSON, DON, Introduction to *Transgressions*, Penguin, 1986.
—— *Hot Copy*, Penguin, 1986.
BAKER, CANDIDA. *Yacker: Australian Writers Talk About Their Work*. Vol. 1. Picador, Sydney, 1986. Vol. 2, Picador, Sydney, 1987.
BENNETT, BRUCE. 'Australian Experiments in Short Fiction'. *World Literature Written in English*. Vol.15, No.2, November 1976.
MACAINSH, NOEL. 'The Collage-Principle in Recent Australian Writing'. *Westerly*. Vol.23, No.2, June 1978.
MOORHOUSE, FRANK. 'What Happened to the Short Story?'. *Australian Literary Studies*, Vol.8, No.2, October 1977.
PIERCE, PETER. 'Finding Their Range: Some Recent Australian Novels'. *Meanjin*, Vol. 40, No.4, December 1981.
WEBBY, ELIZABETH. 'Australian Short Fiction from *While the Billy Boils* to *The Everlasting Secret Family*'. *Australian Literary Studies*. Vol.10, No.2, October 1981.

INDIVIDUAL LIARS:

MURRAY BAIL:

Contemporary Portraits and Other Stories, also published as *The*

Drover's Wife and Other Stories, University of Queensland Press, St. Lucia, 1975.

Homesickness, Macmillan, Australia, 1980.

Holden's Performance, Viking Penguin, Melbourne, 1987.

'I Spend My Days Slowly', short story in Under Twenty-Five, A.O'Donovan, J.Sanderson, S.Porteous (eds.), Jacaranda Press, Australia, 1966.

'Home Ownership', short story in Winter's Tales, Edward Leeson (ed.), Macmillan, London, 1981.

'Past Memories Renewed', review of Remembrance of Things Past, The Age, 29 August, 1981.

'Statement', in Frank Moorhouse: 'What Happened to the Short Story?', Australian Literary Studies, Vol.8, No.2, October 1977,

AHEARNE, KATE. 'Games Murray Bail Plays' and Interview with Bail, Going Down Swinging. No.2, 1980.

ANDERSON, DON. Review of Homesickness. Westerly, Vol.25, No.4, December 1980.

DAVIDSON, JIM. Interview with Murray Bail, Meanjin, Vol.41, No.2, June 1982, pp.264-76; also published in Sideways from the Page: The Meanjin Interviews. Fontana-Collins, 1983.

FIELD, MICHELE. 'Bail's Grand Tour of the Ocker Quixotes', review of Homesickness. The National Times. 12-18 October, 1980, p.62.

GREEN, W. Review of Contemporary Portraits and Other Stories. Westerly, No.4, December 1975.

LEGASSE, JIM. 'The Voice of the Form and the Form of the Voice', Westerly. Vol.25, No.1, March 1980, pp.92-101.

PERKINS, ELIZABETH. 'Australian Anatomy of Civilisation', Review of Homesickness. Quadrant, Vol.XXV, No.4, April 1981, pp.66-8.

PIERCE, PETER, Review of Homesickness, Meanjin, April, 1981, Vol. 40, No. 1.

PETER CAREY:

The Fat Man In History, University of Queensland Press, Australia, 1974.

War Crimes, University of Queensland Press, Australia, 1981.

Bliss, Picador, Australia, 1982.

Illywhacker, University of Queensland Press, Australia, 1985.

'Concerning the Greek Tyrant', in *The Tabloid Story Pocket Book*, Michael Wilding (ed.), Wild and Woolley, Sydney, 1978, pp. 191–205.

MS of *Oscar and Lucinda* (to be published by University of Queensland Press, 1988.)

AHEARNE, KATE. 'Peter Carey and Short Fiction in Australia'. Interview with Carey, *Going Down Swinging*. No.1, 1980.

CLANCY, LAURIE. 'Some Beautiful Lies: Our History Mythologized', Review of *Illywhacker*, *Australian Book Review*. No. 73, August 1985.

DOVEY, TERESA. 'An Infinite Onion: Narrative Structure in Peter Carey's Fiction'. *Australian Literary Studies*. Vol.11, No.2, October 1983.

DUTTON, GEOFFREY. 'Unlocking the Showman's "beautiful lies"'. Review of *Illywhacker*. *The Bulletin*. 16 July, 1985, p.90.

GIUFFRE, GIULIA. 'Peter Carey Speaking', Interview, *The Weekend Australian*, 6–7 July, 1985.

GLOVER, RICHARD. 'Peter Carey: From Advertising to Tall Stories', Interview, *The Age*. 6 July, 1985.

GREEN, W. Review of *The Fat Man in History*. *Westerly*, No.4, December 1975.

HANRAHAN, JOHN. 'A Dealer in Dreams, Visions, Images and Lies', Review of *Illywhacker*. *The Age*. 6 July, 1985.

HAWLEY, JANET. 'How an Ad Man found Bliss', Interview, *The Age*. 26 September, 1981.

IKIN, VAN. 'Peter Carey: The Stories', *Science Fiction: A Review of Speculative Literature*. Vol.1, No.1, June 1977.

—— 'Answers to Seventeen Questions: An Interview with Peter Carey', *Science Fiction: A Review of Speculative Literature*, Vol.1, No.1, June 1977.

LEGASSE, JIM. Review of *War Crimes*. *Westerly*. Vol.25, No.2, June 1980.

MCKERNAN, SUSAN. 'Recent Fiction'. Review of *Bliss*. *Overland*. No.88, July 1982, pp.56–9.

MCSHERRY, BERNADETTE. 'Power and Subjugation: Australian Society in the Fiction of David Ireland and Peter Carey'. *Melbourne Journal of Politics*. Vol.15, 1983-4.

MADDOCKS, JOHN. 'Bizarre Realities: An Interview with Peter Carey'. *Southerly*. Vol.41, No.1, March 1981, pp.27–40.

MITCHELL, ADRIAN. 'Weaving a Tangled Web of Lovely Lies'. Review of *Illywhacker*. *The Weekend Australian*. 6 July, 1985.
PIERCE, PETER. 'I dips me lid to a glorious vagabond'. Review of *Illywhacker*. *The National Times*. 5–11 July, 1985.
SUMMERS, ALISON. Interview with Peter Carey, *The National Times*. 1–7 November, 1985.
TRANTER, JOHN. 'Hell Without Logic Loses Credibility', Review of *Bliss*. *The Age*. 3 October, 1981.
WEBBY, ELIZABETH. '*Illywhacker*: A Great Short Story Trapped in a Fat Novel'. *The Sydney Morning Herald*. 13 July, 1985.

DAVID FOSTER:

North South West, Macmillan, Australia, 1973.
The Pure Land, Macmillan, Australia, 1974.
The Fleeing Atalanta, Maximus, Australia, 1975.
Escape to Reality, Macmillan, Australia, 1977.
The Empathy Experiment, with D.K.Lyall, Wild and Woolley, Australia, 1977.
Moonlite, Macmillan, Australia, 1981.
Plumbum, Penguin, Australia, 1983.
Dog Rock: A Postal Pastoral, Penguin, Australia, 1985.
The Adventures of Christian Rosy Cross, Penguin, Australia, 1986.
Testostero, Penguin, Australia, 1987.
'Statement', in Frank Moorhouse, 'What Happened to the Short Story?', *Australian Literary Studies*, Vol.8, No.2, October, 1977, pp.196–7.

ANDERSON, DON. 'Dogged Pursuit of Rural Follies'. Review of *Dog Rock*. *The National Times*. 4–10 January, 1985.
CLANCY, LAURIE. 'Novelist Intoxicated by Language and Rock-'n'roll'. Review of *Plumbum*. *The Age*. 28 January, 1984.
CORRIS, PETER. 'Misfits and Depressives in the Raw'. Review of *Escape to Reality*. *The Australian*, 5–6 November, 1977.
COTTER, MICHAEL. 'The Experimenters'. Review of *Moonlite*. *Overland*, No.88, July 1982.
FORSHAW, THELMA. 'Penetrating Heavy Metal'. Review of *Plumbum*. *Quadrant*, June 1984.
HANRAHAN, JOHN. 'A Waltzing Heretic'. Review of *The Adven-*

tures of Christian Rosy Cross. *The National Times On Sunday*, 7 September, 1986.

HARRISON-FORD, CARL. 'The Applause Begins', ibid.

HAWLEY, JANET. 'Plumbing Rock Culture'. Interview. *The Age*. 10 December, 1983.

MITCHELL, ADRIAN. 'Disjunctive Worlds That Never Really Make a Point'. Review of *Plumbum*. *The Australian*, 24 December, 1983.

———. 'Surprise Touch of Nostalgia'. Review of *Dog Rock*. *The Australian*, 19 January, 1985.

———. 'The Alchemy of Words'. Review of *The Adventures of Christian Rosy Cross*. *The Australian*, 16 August, 1986.

PIERCE, PETER. 'Finding Their Range: Some Recent Australian Novels'. Review of *Moonlite*. *Meanjin*, Vol.40, No.4, December 1981.

NICHOLAS HASLUCK:

The Hat on the Letter O, Fremantle Arts Centre Press, Australia, 1978.

Quarantine, Macmillan, Australia, 1978.

The Blue Guitar, Macmillan, Australia, 1980.

The Hand That Feeds You, Fremantle Arts Centre Press, Australia, 1982.

The Bellarmine Jug, Penguin, Australia, 1984.

Truant State, Penguin, Australia, 1987.

'The Case Against the Past'. 'Literary Magazine', *The Weekend Australian*, 6–7 July, 1985.

BRADY, VERONICA. 'The Novel as Anti-fiction'. Review of *The Blue Guitar*, *Australian Book Review*, November 1980, p.12.

BURKE, JEFFREY. Review of *The Blue Guitar*, *The New York Times Book Review*, 29 September, 1980.

CLANCY, LAURIE. 'Mystery, and much more, on board the *Batavia*'. Review of *The Bellarmine Jug*. *The Age*, 8 September, 1984.

CLARK, TOM. 'A Wasteland of Getting, Spending'. Review of *The Blue Guitar*. *Los Angeles Times*, 9 November, 1980.

COLMER, DOROTHY. 'Comedy and Terror out of Quarantine'. Review of *Quarantine*. *The Weekend Australian*, 27 May, 1978.

CRACE, JIM. 'In the Melting Pot'. Review of *The Bellarmine Jug*.

Times Literary Supplement, 8 March, 1985.

HARRIS, MAX. 'The Haslucks: Literary Family of Distinction'. *The Weekend Australian Magazine*, 1–2 December, 1984.

KEESING, NANCY. 'Old Bones Given a New Shake'. Review of *The Bellarmine Jug*. *The Weekend Australian*, 28–29 July, 1984.

LORD, GABRIELLE. 'Complex Academic Thriller'. Review of *The Bellarmine Jug*. *The National Times*, 17 August, 1984.

MACLEOD, MARK. 'Conspiracy with No Clear Cause'. Review of *Quarantine*. *The Sydney Morning Herald*, 15 July, 1978.

MCQUEEN, HUMPHREY. 'Even if you know the story, it's only half the story'. Review of *The Bellarmine Jug*. *The Sydney Morning Herald*, 11 August, 1984.

RUDDELL, SIMON. 'Hasluck's Guitar has Market on Strings'. Review of *The Blue Guitar*. *The Weekend Australian*, 13 December, 1980.

SEYMOUR-SMITH, MARTIN. Review of *Quarantine*, *The Financial Times*, 15 June, 1978.

SHAPCOTT, THOMAS. 'This Hits the Right Chord'. Review of *The Blue Guitar*. *The Courier-Mail*, 3 January, 1981.

TUOHY, FRANK. 'Things as They Are'. Review of *The Blue Guitar*. *Times Literary Supplement*, 18 April, 1980.

DAVID IRELAND:

Image In The Clay, University of Queensland Press, Australia, 1964.

The Chantic Bird, Angus and Robertson Classics, Australia, 1973.

The Unknown Industrial Prisoner, Angus and Robertson Classics, Australia, 1973.

The Flesheaters, Angus and Robertson, Australia, 1972.

Burn, Angus and Robertson, Australia, 1974.

The Glass Canoe, Macmillan, Australia, 1976.

A Woman Of The Future, Allen Lane, Penguin, Australia, 1979.

City Of Women, Allen Lane, Penguin, 1981.

Bloodfather, Penguin, Australia, 1987.

'The Bronze Overcoat', in *The Bulletin*, Centenary Issue, 29 January, 1980, pp.180–7.

'The Wild Colonial Boy', in *The National Times*, 25–31 January, 1981. pp.25–7.

'Injections', in *The Bulletin*, Literary Supplement, 22–29 December, 1981, pp.172–7.

'Statement', *Australian Literary Studies*, Vol.8, No.2, October 1977, pp.192–3.

GUNEW, SNEJA. 'What Does Woman Mean? Reading, Writing and Reproduction'. *Hecate*, Vol.9, Nos. 1 & 2, 1983.

MCSHERRY, BERNADETTE. 'Power and Subjugation: Australian Society in the Fiction of David Ireland and Peter Carey'. *Melbourne Journal of Politics*, Vol.15, 1983–4.

PONS, XAVIER. 'Paranoia as a Way of Life'. *Quadrant*, January–February 1982.

RICHARDS, TIM. 'Treacherous Sands: Limit and Transgression in David Ireland's *A Woman of the Future*'. M.A. Thesis, University of Melbourne, 1985.

(Recent articles only are listed here: for further references, see Bibliography in DANIEL, HELEN. *Double Agent*, Penguin 1982.)

ELIZABETH JOLLEY:

Stories (containing *Five Acre Virgin* (1976) and *The Travelling Entertainer* (1979) and 'A Child Went Forth'), Fremantle Arts Centre Press, Australia, 1984.

Palomino, Outback Press, Australia, 1980.

The Newspaper of Claremont Street, (first pub. 1981), Fremantle Arts Centre Press, Australia, 1985.

Mr Scobie's Riddle, Penguin, Australia, 1983.

Woman in a Lampshade, Penguin, Australia, 1983.

Miss Peabody's Inheritance, University of Queensland Press, Australia, 1983.

Milk and Honey, Fremantle Arts Centre Press, Australia, 1984.

Foxybaby, University of Queensland Press, Australia, 1985.

The Well, Viking Penguin, Australia, 1986.

'It's About Your Daughter Mrs. Page'. 'Night Report'. 'Poppy Seeds and Sesame Rings'. in Anna Gibbs and Alison Tilson (eds.) *Frictions: An Anthology of Fiction by Women*, Sybylla, 1982.

'The Bathroom Dance', in Don Anderson (ed.), *Transgressions*, Penguin, 1986, pp.12–24.

'Statement' *Australian Literary Studies*. Vol.10, No.2, October 1981.

'Landscape and Figures'. *Westerly*. Vol.23, No.4, December 1978.

MS of *The Sugar Mother*, to be published by Fremantle Arts Centre Press, 1988.

ACKROYD, PETER. 'Two Cultures, One Transplanted'. Review of *Milk and Honey*. *The New York Times Book Review*, 15 June, 1986, p.12.

BURNS, GRAHAM. 'Chronicler of Time's Slow Attritions'. Review of *Stories*. *The Age*, 14 July, 1984.

CADZOW, JANE. 'A Compulsive Writer who sifts Shadows from another World'. *The Australian*. 9 September, 1984.

CARTER, ANGELA. 'Dreams of Reason . . . and Foxes'. Review of *Foxybaby*. *The New York Times Book Review*, 24 November, 1985, p.1, 36–7.

COLMER, JOHN. 'Romp at the Summer School'. Review of *Foxybaby*. *The Australian*, 7 September, 1985.

CLANCY, LAURIE. 'A Melancholy Novel, Darkly Disturbing'. Reviews of *Milk and Honey* and *Palomino*. *The Age*, 3 November, 1984.

DIBBLE, BRIAN. 'Dream-crowded Inferno'. Review of *Foxybaby*. *Australian Book Review*, No.77, December 1985/January 1986, pp.29–30.

DUTTON, GEOFFREY. 'Obsessed with what's down the well'. Review of *The Well*. *The Australian*, 20 September, 1986.

ELIOT, HELEN. Review of *The Newspaper of Claremont Street*. 'Australian Perspectives: Character and Situation'. *Island Magazine*, No.14, Autumn 1983.

FORSHAW, THELMA. 'The Comic Muse'. *Quadrant*. April 1984.

FROST, LUCY. 'The Grotesque and The Innocent'. Reviews of *Palomino* and *Milk and Honey*. *Overland*. No.97, December 1984.

GARNER, HELEN. 'Elizabeth Jolley: An Appreciation'. *Meanjin*. Vol.42, No.2, June 1983.

HARRISON, MARTIN. 'Passages: A Reader Loiters in a Public Place'. *The Age Monthly Review*. Vol.5, No.1, May 1985.

HEADON, DAVID. Interview with Elizabeth Jolley. *Meanjin*. Vol.44, No.1, March 1985, pp.39–46.

JONES, DOROTHY. 'The Goddess, The Artist and The Spinster'. *Westerly*. Vol.29, No.4, December 1984.

——. 'Which hend you hev?': Elizabeth Jolley's *Milk and Honey*, *Westerly*. Vol.31, No.2, June 1986.

KEESING, NANCY. 'Lampshade Reflects Great Talent'. Review of *Woman in a Lampshade*. *The Australian*. 12 March, 1983.

KIRKBY, JOAN. 'The Nights Belong to Elizabeth Jolley: Modernism and the Sappho-Erotic Imagination of *Miss Peabody's Inheritance*'. *Meanjin*. Vol.43, No.4, December 1984.

LITTLE, BRENDA. 'When Honey Becomes Gall'. Review of *Milk and Honey*. *The Australian*. 22 September, 1984.

NOONAN, WILLIAM. 'Satirical Peek at Miss Peabody'. Review of *Miss Peabody's Inheritance*. *The Australian*. 22 October, 1983.

PIERCE, PETER. 'Narrative Ambiguity'. Review of *Miss Peabody's Inheritance*. *The Age*. 19 November, 1983.

RIEMER, A.P.. 'Between Two Worlds: An Approach to Elizabeth Jolley's Fiction'. *Southerly*. Vol. 43, No.3, September 1983.

RIEMER, ANDREW. 'Displaced Persons: Some Preoccupations in Elizabeth Jolley's Fiction'. *Westerly*. Vol.31, No.2, June 1986.

TRIGG, STEPHANIE. 'Elizabeth Jolley: Something Remarkable Every Time'. *Scripsi*. Vol.4, No.1, July, 1986.

—— Interview with Jolley. *Scripsi*, Vol.4, No. 1, July, 1986.

WILLIAMS, BRUCE. 'Three Short Story Writers: Peter Cowan, Elizabeth Jolley, Justina Williams'. Review of *The Travelling Entertainer*. *Westerly*. Vol.25, No.2, June 1980.

PETER MATHERS:

Trap, Sphere Books, London, 1970.

The Wort Papers, Penguin, Australia, 1973.

A Change for the Better, Words and Visions, Adelaide, 1984.

'Pittsburgh Identity: 0000000621'. *Overland*. No.39, August, 1968, pp.12–16.

'How It Is', in Owen Webster (ed.) *Disenchantment*. Goldstar Publications, Melbourne, 1972.

BUCKLEY, VINCENT. 'Peter Mathers' *Trap*'. *Ariel*. Vol.5, No.3, July 1974.

CLANCY, LAURIE. 'Peter Mathers' Words'. *Meanjin Quarterly*. Vol.33, No.3, Spring 1974.

—— 'An Interview with Peter Mathers'. *Australian Literary Studies*, Vol.8, No.2, October 1977.

DOVEY, TERESA. 'A Late Entry in the Uppersass Reporting Prize: Another 'Writing' of Peter Mathers' *Trap* and *The Wort Papers*', *Southern Review*. Vol.17, No.2, July 1984, pp.188–202.

LINNETT, KEN. 'The Reluctant Mathers Comes out to Play'. Interview, *The Melbourne Times*. 31 July, 1985.

O'HEARN, D.J. 'Re-reading Peter Mathers', *Overland*, No.85, October 1981.

WEBSTER, OWEN. 'Comic Genius', Review of *The Wort Papers*, *Overland*. No.57, Winter 1973.

WILDING, MICHAEL. 'Worts' World: The Great Australian Dream', Review of *The Wort Papers*. *The National Times*. 15–20 January, 1973.

WINDSOR, GERARD. 'How Do You Like Your History Done?' Review of *A Change for The Better*. *Overland*. No.96, September 1984.

GERALD MURNANE:

Tamarisk Row, Heinemann, Melbourne, 1974.

A Lifetime On Clouds, Angus and Robertson, Australia, 1978.

The Plains, Penguin, Australia, 1984

Landscape with Landscape, Norstrilia Press, Australia, 1985.

'Land Deal', in Don Anderson (ed.), *Transgressions*. Penguin, 1986.

'Stone Quarry', *Meanjin*, Vol. 45, No. 4, December, 1986.

'Other Eyes, Other Universes'. *Science Fiction Commentary*. Nos. 41/2, February 1975, pp.47–54.

'Meetings with Adam Lindsay Gordon'. *The Age Monthly Review*. Vol.4, No.8, Dec. 1984/Jan. 1985, pp.19–20

'On the Road to Bendigo: Kerouac's Australian Life'. *The Age Monthly Review*. Vol.6, No.1, May 1986, pp.3–5.

MS of *Inland*, to be published by Heinemann, Australia, 1988.

ANDERSON, DON. 'A Compelling Sort of Tedium'. Review of *Landscape with Landscape*, *The National Times*. May 24–30, 1985.

CARTER, PAUL. 'Writing in the Round: Gerald Murnane and the New Fiction', *The Age Monthly Review*. Vol.2, No.9, January 1983.

GILLESPIE, BRUCE. 'Something Marvellous That No One Else Had Discovered: An Appreciation of *Tamarisk Row*', *Science Fiction Commentary*. Nos.41/2, February 1975.

HUESTON, PENNY. 'Gerald Murnane: Landscape with Author'. *Scripsi*. Vol.3, Nos.2 and 3, August 1985.

KIERNAN, BRIAN. 'The Pattern of Our Days'. Review of *Tamarisk Row*, *The Age*. 19 October, 1974.

KYNASTON, EDWARD. 'Vision Splendid of Plains Australia'. Review of *The Plains*, *The Australian*. 21–22 August, 1982.

O'HEARN, D.J. 'In the Landscapes of the Mind'. Review of *The Plains*, *The Age*. 21 August, 1982.

———. 'Murnane Captures the Local Textures', Review of *Landscape with Landscape*, *The Australian*. 15–16 June, 1985.

PRESTON, ANDREW. 'Tales with Tails: Murnane's Circular Fiction', *The Age Monthly Review*. Vol.5, No.3, July 1985.

SALUSINSKY, IMRE. 'A Word or Two about *The Plains*', *Scripsi*. Vol. 3, Nos.2 and 3, September 1985.

TITTENSOR, JOHN. 'Looking Back on a Strange Breed of the Early Fifties', Review of *A Lifetime on Clouds*. *The Age*. 4 December, 1976.

———. 'Inner Australia: The Novels of Gerald Murnane', *The Age Monthly Review*. October 1984.

———. 'Gerald Murnane's *The Plains*', *Meanjin*. Vol.41, No.4, December 1982.

WINDSOR, GERARD. 'Flawed Fiction from a Local, Modish Messiah'. Review of *Landscape with Landscape*. *The Bulletin*. 25 June, 1985.

OTHER FICTION:

ADAMSON, WALTER. *The Institution*. Sonja Delander (trans.), Outback Press, Australia, 1976.

ALLENDE, ISABEL. *The House of the Spirits*, Magda Bogin (trans.) Black Swan, 1986.

ASSIS MACHADO DE. 'The Psychiatrist', Barbara Howes (ed.), *The Eye of the Heart: Short Stories from Latin America*. Avon, New York, 1973.

BORGES, JORGE LUIS. *Labyrinths: Selected Stories and Other Writings*. Penguin, U.K., 1970.

CALVINO, ITALO. *Cosmicomics*. Abacus, U.K., 1982.

CORTAZAR, JULIO. *End of The Game and Other Stories*. Collins and Harvill Press, London, 1968.

FOWLES, JOHN. *A Maggot*. Jonathan Cape, London, 1985.

IBARGUENGOITIA, JORGE. *The Dead Girls*. Asa Zatz (trans.). Chatto and Windus, The Hogarth Press, London 1983.

LUNN, RICK. 'The Roger Mirror', 'Marco The Molasses Man', *The Divine Right of Dogs*. Randolph Press, Beecroft N.S.W., 1982. 'Mirrors', in Don Anderson (ed.). *Transgressions*, Penguin, 1986.

SELECT BIBLIOGRAPHY

MALOUF, DAVID. *Johnno*, University of Queensland Press, 1975

MANGUEL, ALBERTO (ed.). *Other Fires*, Picador, Australia, 1986.

OAKLEY, BARRY. *A Wild Ass of a Man*. Penguin, 1970.

—— *A Salute to the Great McCarthy*. Penguin, 1974.

—— *Let's Hear it for Prendergast*, Penguin, 1971.

REED, BILL. *Stigmata*. Hyland House, 1980.

——. *Ihe*, Hyland House, 1982.

—— . *Crooks*, Hyland House, 1984.

STERNE, LAURENCE. *The Life and Opinions of Tristram Shandy*, Penguin, 1967.

VONNEGUT, KURT. *Slaughterhouse Five*, Triad Panther, 1979.

INDEX

FOR THE BEST IN PAPERBACKS, LOOK FOR THE

PENGUIN

Hot Copy Don Anderson

A collection of book reviews and articles on literature from the past ten years. They have appeared in a number of newspapers and magazines and on radio. Anderson covers a range of writers and genres, mostly Australian.

The Music of Love Dorothy Green

Dorothy Green's essays tell us as much about our world as the works of novelists and poets. For more than thirty years her essays have contributed to cultural debate in Australia, illuminating not only the works under review but also the society and values from which they spring. She discusses, among others, Patrick White, Mary Gilmore, Germaine Greer, Manning Clark, Grant Watson, Martin Boyd, Frank Moorhouse, Robert Drewe, Tom Shapcott, Colleen McCullough and A.G. Stephens with an independent and fearless voice.

Books by David Foster in Penguin

The Pure Land

Three generations of a family move restlessly from the Blue Mountains of New South Wales to the east coast of the United States and back in search of spiritual fulfilment.

Moonlite

The hero, Finbar Macduffie, driven from his frigid perch on the outermost British Isle by the Clearances, makes his way to the Southern Hemisphere and the grog-soaked goldfields of the New West Highlands.

'the most wonderfully individualistic, broad-ranging satire on Australian life ever written' Susan McKernan, *Bulletin*

Plumbum

Australia and New Zealand proudly present the world's most notorious rock band! Featuring the unbelievably beautiful and confused Sharon Scott on vocals and the unbelievably fat and materialistic Roland Rocca on keyboards – the ultimate heavy metal experience.

Dog Rock

Dog Rock, a small New South Wales country town, harbours a dangerous killer. Assistant Postal Officer and Night Exchange Attendant D'Arcy D'Oliveres becomes inextricably tangled in the mystery – and even he is not all he seems . . . A marvellous, hilarious murder-mystery spoof, portraying a small Australian town with love, accuracy and much poetic humour.

FOR THE BEST IN PAPERBACKS, LOOK FOR THE

PENGUIN

Books by David Foster in Penguin

The Pale Blue Crochet Coathanger Cover

The irrepressibly snoopy postman, D'Arcy D'Oliveres, gets mixed up in another string of mysterious deaths in the sleepy town of Dog Rock. Pitched out of the shift work at the telephone exchange by modern technology, D'Arcy now has more time for investigation than before, and makes the most of his dry observations on life in general as the corpses pile up.

The Adventures of Christian Rosy Cross

A comic retelling of the Rosicrucian Myth which draws its inspiration from the occult epigrams of Michael Maier, the seventeenth century alchemist and chief apologist for the Rosicrucian Movement. Foster's iconoclastic account of his hero's travels in the East is a scholarly and hilarious contribution to the history of spiritual alchemy.

Testostero

Set in Sydney, London and Venice this is Foster's funniest and most ingenious novel. The plot turns and twists with incredible speed; it revolves around identical twins separated at birth as part of an experiment. One grows up in Sydney's Western suburbs, the other in a British aristocratic environment. The book begins when they are thrown together as adults in the most complicated of circumstances.

Books by David Ireland in Penguin

The Glass Canoe

Meat Man is a regular at The Southern Cross, an old, battered and experienced pub somewhere in the centre of Sydney. He views his world – the world of the pub and its clientele – through his beer glass, his glass canoe, which transports them all to other worlds.

Winner of the Miles Franklin Award, 1976.

The Flesheaters

A novelist who lives up in a tree; a child who likes to paint dead bodies; a granny who lives in a kennel and bites ... these are some of the characters of this extraordinary novel set in a dilapidated stone mansion in Sydney. Bizarre, bitingly satirical, richly ambiguous, it is an image of the modern world which the author sees as a 'madhouse without walls'.

FOR THE BEST IN PAPERBACKS, LOOK FOR THE

PENGUIN

Books by David Ireland in Penguin

A Woman of the Future
The time of this remarkable novel is the near future. The place is Australia. *A Woman of the Future* is the diary of Alethea Hunt and her personal odyssey in a harsh society and world of tomorrow.
Winner of the Miles Franklin Award, 1979 and co-winner of *The Age* Book of the Year Award, 1980.
'a novel of immense originality, wit and gritty wisdom ... David Ireland has reached the top' Patrick White.

The City of Women
The city of women is love, Billie Shockley says. But in the city of women that is her world, love takes strange forms. Arresting, provocative, shocking, yet pierced with a sublime tenderness, David Ireland's bizarre symbolism compels the imagination.

Archimedes and the Seagle
'I have to listen to all sorts of crackpot remarks from humans with little knowledge and be thought to agree.' So says Archimedes, from his dog's-eye view of the world. As he marvels at the soaring, solitary flight of the seagle, he recognises how much of his own joy and energy are social. And that even the earthbound can dream of the sky.

Bloodfather
The novel traces the development of a young artist – from birth to the age of seventeen. Davis Blood is a precocious child. He asks questions and looks for answers to the mysteries of the world. He falls down stairs, he runs, he draws, he plays cricket. And he has verbal volleys with his aunts – the obsessively punning Aunt Mira and Aunt Ursula who, although confined to a wheelchair, opens up many corners of the world for young Davis. David Ireland plumbs the depths of the obsessions of a young artist and sheds light on the well-springs of creativity.

FOR THE BEST IN PAPERBACKS, LOOK FOR THE

PENGUIN

Books by Murray Bail in Penguin

Homesickness

A group of Australian tourists visits countries and museums like all tourists, yet nothing is as it seems. Subjected to the differences of history and culture, and the 'museums of their own obsessions', they are unavoidably changed.

Winner of the National Book Council Award for Australian Literature, 1980 and co-winner of *The Age* Book of the Year Award, 1980.

Holden's Performance

Holden's Performance is an account of Australia's post-war history through the life story of the main character Holden Shadbolt, who registers the events happening around him with extraordinary accuracy but is unable to understand or learn from them. Bail uses a subtle permeating metaphor of mechanics and geometry to convey a parallel image of Holden's psyche and the psyche of Australia in the post-war era, developing a changing identity. At once comic, absurdist, intelligent and disturbing, the novel abounds with colourful and eccentric characters.

Books by Gerald Murnane in Penguin

A Lifetime on Clouds

The humorous story of Adrian Sherd, a teenage boy isolated in Australian suburbia of the 1950s – in the last years before television and the family car changed the suburbs forever. He dreams of orgies with film stars but later renounces these and dreams of marrying his Catholic sweetheart and having eleven children by her.

The Plains

On the Plains the landowning families on their vast estates have preserved a rich and distinctive culture. A nameless young film-maker arrives and chooses the daughter of his patron for a leading role. But nothing in this memorable work of fiction is as it seems.

FOR THE BEST IN PAPERBACKS, LOOK FOR THE

PENGUIN

Books by Murray Bail in Penguin

Landscape with Landscape
A man feels urged to give an account of himself to a room full of strange women
But before he can speak to the women he becomes trapped in his recurring dreams
of landscapes and the women in them. Another man spends twenty years
searching the hills near Melbourne for a landscape and a woman that no artist
could paint. On his last night in the hills he enacts a drunken ritual to make
himself and his landscape invisible in the eyes of the artists he despises. These two
stories and four others make up an elaborate and unforgettable pattern of dreams
and reality.

Books by Elizabeth Jolley in Penguin

Woman in a Lampshade
In this masterly collection of stories, Elizabeth Jolley has created a splendid array
of characters, all of whom fail to achieve the expected.
'Elizabeth Jolley is a major figure in recent Australian writing' Thomas Shapcott,
Westerly

Mr Scobie's Riddle
Mr Scobie stands apart from the others at the nursing home of St Christopher and
St Jude. For long-term resident and eccentric, Miss Hailey, he represents a kindred
spirit; for Matron Price – a lady of questionable practices – the latest victim. But
unwittingly Mr Scobie has some recourses – his very simple riddle . . .
Winner *The Age* Book of the Year, 1983.

The Well
One night Miss Hester Harper and Katherine are driving home from a celebration,
a party at a hotel in town, when, in the deadly still countryside, they knock
something down. It's a man, whose body they proceed to dump, with great
difficulty, in the farmyard well. The next morning cries are heard coming from the
bottom of the well . . . An extraordinary original novel with Elizabeth Jolley's
usual potent mixture of scarcely suppressed violence and eroticism.

FOR THE BEST IN PAPERBACKS, LOOK FOR THE

PENGUIN

Books by Nicholas Hasluck in Penguin

Quarantine

A tale haunted by what the teller has become. An ageing lawyer recalls the trips he took through Suez in his youth, and the intrigue which follows when he and his fellow passengers are suddenly detained in a seedy quarantine station on the edge of the canal. Witty, eloquent, but evasive, he pours out his confession, a story which starts with the apparently harmless antics of the quarantine station's proprietor, moves to the formation of the vigilante group under the leadership of the austere Burgess, and ends in betrayal and a violent death. These traumatic memories compel the narrator to face up to the truth about himself.

The Bellarmine Jug

The Bellarmine Jug is a complex tale traversing three times and three places: 1629, 1948 and the early 1980s; north-west Australia, Holland and England. The plot encompasses the wreck of the Dutch ship Batavia, the Petrov affair and international espionage.

'I finished it in a sitting . . .' Humphrey McQueen *Sydney Morning Herald*

Winner of *The Age* Book of the Year Award, 1984.

Truant State

Set in the years following the Great War, the novel examines the slippery relationship between business and politics in the developing state of Western Australia. The Traverne family, newly migrated from England are taken up by their next door neighbour, the newspaper maverick Romney Guy, and find themselves caught in a web of political and financial intrigue. The love affair between Jack Traverne and Diana Guy is manipulated at every twist and turn by Romney Guy. At last, in the midst of the mounting turmoil of the depression years and the secessionist movement, the Travernes are forced to take a stand.

Note: Rights to all books are not available in some countries.